Earth Trusteeship and the Sovereign State

This book makes an argument for the legal role and responsibility of sovereign states in the trusteeship of the Earth.

In 1972, the first photo of the Earth – Blue Marble – sparked the imagination and need to care for our planet. In the same year, the world's first UN conference on the environment adopted the Stockholm Declaration, proclaiming that the Earth's natural resources and ecosystems "must be safeguarded for the benefit of present and future generations". Today, the Earth's ecological systems deteriorate at accelerating speeds, as if Earth does not matter to law and governance. But what if it does? Earth system science and related jurisprudence provide clear guidance for effective law and governance, in particular the trusteeship responsibilities of sovereign states. This book closes the gap between the promises of international environmental agreements and the concept of state sovereignty. Maintaining that state sovereignty is not an end in itself, but rather a means to protect the autonomy and freedom of citizens, the book develops the argument that sovereignty includes fiduciary duties for matters of global concern, such as human rights and ecological sustainability. Autonomy and freedom of citizens can only prosper if states protect human rights and ecological sustainability both inside and outside national boundaries. This is the logic behind global governance. And, as this book demonstrates, at its core stands the ancient idea of trusteeship: that is, of acting on behalf and to the benefit of those who cannot act for themselves.

This book's argument that Earth trusteeship and the sovereign state mutually condition each other will appeal to scholars of environmental law, international law and environmental science and others with an interest in ecology and global governance.

Klaus Bosselmann is Professor of Law at the University of Auckland, New Zealand.

Part of the
LAW, JUSTICE AND ECOLOGY
series

series editor
Anna Grear, *Law School, Cardiff University*, UK

A GlassHouse Book

Earth Trusteeship and the Sovereign State
Transforming International Environmental Law
Klaus Bosselmann

for information about the series and details of previous and forthcoming titles, see https://www.routledge.com/Law-Justice-and-Ecology/book-series/LAWJUSTECO

Earth Trusteeship and the Sovereign State

Transforming International Environmental Law

Klaus Bosselmann

Routledge
Taylor & Francis Group
a GlassHouse Book

First published 2025
by Routledge
4 Park Square, Milton Park, Abingdon, Oxon OX14 4RN

and by Routledge
605 Third Avenue, New York, NY 10158

Routledge is an imprint of the Taylor & Francis Group, an informa business

A GlassHouse book

British Library Cataloguing-in-Publication Data
A catalogue record for this book is available from the British Library

ISBN: 9781032673998 (hbk)
ISBN: 9781032674063 (pbk)
ISBN: 9781032674049 (ebk)

DOI: 10.4324/9781032674049

Typeset in Sabon LT Pro
by Apex CoVantage, LLC

Contents

Preface

In 1972, a famous photo of the Earth ("Blue Marble") sparked the imagination and the need to care for our planet. In the same year, the world's first conference on the global environment adopted the UN Stockholm Declaration. Principle 1 proclaimed the "solemn responsibility to protect and improve the environment for present and future generations", and Principle 2 specified that the Earth's natural resources and ecosystems "must be safeguarded for the benefit of present and future generations". This marked the beginning of international environmental law. In 1992, nation states declared their commitment to protect and restore the "health and integrity of the Earth's ecosystem" (Principle 7, 1992 Rio Declaration). This commitment has been repeated in more than 25 international agreements including, for example, the 2015 Paris Agreement on Climate Change.

Meanwhile, the integrity of the climate system is deteriorating at an accelerating speed and with it, the entire Earth system. Yet despite these dramatic developments, the Earth system does not feature in the laws and policies of states. But what if it did? Earth system science and related jurisprudence provide clear guidance for more effective law and governance. At their core are trusteeship obligations with respect to the Earth.

This book aims for closing the gap between the Earth system and the world system of sovereign states. Hypothesizing that the sovereignty of states is not an end in itself but a means to protect the autonomy and freedom of citizens, it develops the argument that sovereignty includes fiduciary duties for matters of global concern, such as human rights and ecological integrity. Autonomy and freedom of citizens can only prosper if states protect human rights and the integrity of ecological systems across national boundaries. This is at the heart of global governance, which, in turn, depends on mutual respect and solidarity. In the Anthropocene, this must include trusteeship responsibilities towards the Earth. Trusteeship means acting on behalf and to the benefit of those who cannot act for themselves. It is an ancient concept, known in all legal cultures and highly suitable for protecting the community of life and the Earth, our common home.

The book owes its existence to global movements towards peace, human rights, indigenous rights, climate protection, ecological law and rights of nature. It is written in the spirit of the Earth Charter, a covenant for a peaceful, just and sustainable future. Created by global civil society, the Earth Charter regards human beings as members of the community of life and, hence, responsible for protecting its integrity. We, individually and collectively through our political institutions, must act as trustees of the Earth.

I am grateful and proud to be associated with several of these movements: in particular, the Ecological Law and Governance Association, the Global Ecological Integrity Group, the IUCN Ethics Specialist Group, the UN Harmony with Nature Network, Earth Charter International and the Earth Trusteeship Initiative.

My thanks go to my colleagues and friends, who have inspired and reassured me over the years. A number of them are actively involved in the advocacy of Earth trusteeship at national and international levels – too many to name here. For ideas and support in the writing process of this book, I am particularly grateful to Prue Taylor, Ron Engel, Kathryn Gwiazdon, Hans van Willenswaard, Paulo Magalhaes, Neshan Gunasekera, Alyn Ware, Kristen Jones, Justin Sobion, Megane Botrel, Olivia Grainger, Airu Teng and Muna Panyasong.

Klaus Bosselmann
October 2024, Waiheke Island

Introduction

Of all areas of law, environmental law is the one that most eludes its subject. Whether at international or domestic levels, the law concerned with human-nature relationships has yet to define its topic, content and scope.

What is it that environmental law is trying to protect? Humans or the environment? Or both? The answer lies in what is meant by "environment". Is it the natural environment, things like water, air, soil, forests? Or is it ecosystems, things like plants, animals, landscapes, local weather conditions and the interrelationships between them? And are humans part of ecosystems or not? Can the human sphere be separated at all from the non-human biosphere? Or should the focus be on interrelationships between all forms of life within a single ecological system called planet Earth?

For more than 50 years now, environmental activists, scientific experts, philosophers, lawyers, politicians and governments have been grappling with these questions. Some emphasize this aspect, others emphasize another, but there is little common ground between those who perceive the natural environment as separate from humans and those who don't. So far, environmental laws have followed the former: humans are not part of nature and only interested in what it has to offer them (natural resources, decent weather, enjoyment).

To be sure, there has been progress since the 1960s and 1970s when the first environmental laws were enacted. Today, virtually every country has environmental protection laws in place. Global collaboration has helped repair the ozone layer, phased out leaded fuel, increased the percentage of renewable energy and saved some endangered species from extinction.[1] And there's more. The whole world has now become alert to humanity's common destiny as we experience the triple planetary crisis (climate change, pollution, biodiversity loss) and enter the Anthropocene. In fact, many feel there is

1 UN Environment Programme 2022, *UNEP@50: success over the years*, (https://www.unep.org/news-and-stories/series/unep50-success-over-years#:~:text=For%20the%20past%20half%2Dcentury,from%20going%20extinct%20and%20more).

DOI: 10.4324/9781032674049-1

something profoundly wrong in the way our lives, societies and governments are organized. And few disagree that major transformations are needed to keep up hope for "sustainable development".

Despite 50 years of environmental protection measures, we are closer to the brink of societal collapse than ever before in human history. Environmental law must have overlooked something important.

This book aims to show what this "something" is and how it can gain more prominence in law and governance. In essence, the gap between Earth (as the whole) and the world (as the fractional) has to be narrowed. Governments and states must learn to see the big picture and act with the whole in mind. There is no escaping from the laws of nature.

1. Losing the Forest for the Trees

The present gap between Earth as an ecological system and the world as an assembly of sovereign and often competing states is glaringly obvious. The Earth, our common home, functions according to the laws of nature, while states, in charge of individual territories, function according to domestic laws. So far, domestic laws have ignored the laws of nature. While international agreements often evoke global cooperation and the need for protecting the integrity of the Earth's ecological system, this has not been recognized and implemented by states. After all, they are sovereign and not accountable to anyone outside national borders. The laws of nature, as important as they may be, do not really matter in domestic affairs that governments are focused on. The common home represents the big picture, but more important is what's going on "at home": i.e. inside national boundaries.

The phenomenon of not seeing the big picture, not noticing what's really going on, is foremost a psychological phenomenon. If someone is not able to pay attention to what is in front of them, psychologists call that "inattentional" or "perception blindness".[2] This blindness is like overlooking the elephant in the room. Or the gorilla. The "invisible gorilla test"[3] is a famous experiment in which researchers asked participants to watch a video of people tossing a basketball. The observers were told to count the number of passes or to keep track of the number of throws versus bounce passes. Afterwards, the participants were asked if they had noticed anything unusual while watching the video. Across all the tests, approximately 50% of the participants reported seeing nothing out of the ordinary.

2 Wright, TJ, Roque, NA, Boot, WR & Stothart, C 2018, 'Attention capture, processing speed, and inattentional blindness', *Acta Psychologica*, vol. 190, pp. 72–77.

3 Simons, D & Chabris, C 1999, 'Gorillas in our midst: sustained inattential blindness for dynamic events', *Perception*, vol. 28, no. 9, p. 1059.

But, in reality, something odd *had* happened. In some instances, a woman dressed in a gorilla suit strolled through the scene, turned to the camera, thumped her chest and walked away. While it may seem impossible that the participants missed such a sight, since their attention was focused elsewhere and on a demanding task, the gorilla basically became invisible.

The implication is that rather than paying attention to the whole, we tend to concentrate on things that are most important to us at any given moment. If something does not fit into our idea of what a basketball game is supposed to look like, then it gets overlooked. The gorilla is essentially ruled out as a component that could help understand what is happening before our eyes and what is needed to carry out the task at hand.

In the realm of the human species, the gorilla stands for nature. Nature may be omnipresent, but it is not seen as essential to social organization and human development. Consequently, laws pay attention only to negative impacts on the human condition, ignoring cumulative effects, dynamic interactions and tipping points: in a word, nature.

From a perspective that does, in fact, pay attention to nature and Earth, both international and domestic laws have completely failed. Overlooking 50 years of environmental law, the best we can say about it is that it has saved some trees but done nothing to protect the forest. Modern societies – and their political institutions – have designed laws that fit the basketball game (pursuit of growth and prosperity) but ignore the gorilla (Earth). This has helped with some environmental fixes but worsened the prospect of preserving the integrity of Earth's ecological system (including the atmosphere, hydrosphere, biosphere and geosphere). We are losing the forest for the trees.[4]

2. 50 Years of Failure

Yet the forest – in our context, the Earth – was always there for everyone to see. This has been true at least since 1972, when three game-changing events occurred. One was the publication of the Club of Rome's report "Limits to Growth"; another the famous photographic image of the Earth, the "Blue Marble"; and further, the world's first conference about the Earth, the United Nations Conference on the Human Environment in Stockholm. Seemingly unrelated, these three events set the scene for decades to come with no end in sight. Ever since, the central question for humanity has been whether and how the growth paradigm (of economic and population development) can be reconciled with living on a finite Earth (within planetary boundaries).

The 1972 Stockholm Declaration marked the beginning of environmental law. Its first principle proclaimed the interrelatedness between humans and

4 Bosselmann, K 2010, 'Losing the forest for the trees: environmental reductionism in the law', *Environmental Laws and Sustainability: Special Issue of Sustainability*, vol. 2, no. 8, p. 2424.

nature: "Man is both creature and moulder of his environment, which gives him physical sustenance and affords him the opportunity for intellectual, moral, social and spiritual growth". The next four principles describe various responsibilities that humans have towards the Earth.

Ten years later, the United Nations General Assembly adopted the World Charter for Nature "aware that man is part of nature" and "convinced that every form of life is unique, warranting respect regardless of its worth to man" (Preamble). The first three principles state: "Nature shall be respected and its essential processes shall not be impaired" (1), "the genetic viability of the Earth shall not be compromised" (2) and "all areas of the Earth, both land and sea, shall be subject to these principles of conservation" (3).

Fifteen years later, the Brundtland Report observed in its opening statement that the sight of our planet from space may have "a greater impact on thought than did the Copernican revolution of the 16th century" as this allowed us to "see and study the Earth as an organism whose health depends on the health of all its parts".[5]

Remarkably, these early documents of international environmental law highlighted the uniqueness and vulnerability of the Earth, the interconnectedness and intrinsic value of all life forms and a fundamental duty of caring for the Earth.

Twenty years later, at the 1992 Rio Summit, states adopted the first global environmental treaties. They declared the "Earth's climate" and "biological diversity" a "common concern of humankind" but also reaffirmed their sovereign rights to exploit their own natural resources. In this way, any global responsibilities appeared derivative and secondary to national interests. As a result, environmental treaties have focused on specific fragments of the Earth with obligations built on the lowest common denominator rather than on what the integrity of the Earth system required. This approach was further compromised by signatory states deciding completely for themselves whether and how they should be implemented. Despite the Brundtland Report's call "From One Earth to One World", states have not narrowed but widened the gap.

Fifty years after Stockholm, as has been observed at Stockholm+50 for example,[6] it is evident that international environmental law has failed. Some trees have been saved, but the forest is disappearing. States have kept their proclaimed responsibilities toward the Earth as mere promises, neither codified into law nor guiding their policies in other ways. What may be less obvious is that this carelessness is not just a lack of political will, but a

5 World Commission on Environment and Development 1987, 'Brundtland report ("Our Common Future")', UNGA A/42/427 (4 August 1987).

6 The United Nations Stockholm+50 Official Report A/CONF.238/9 (1 August 2022) recognized deficiencies and shortcomings of the current system and made "Recommendations for accelerating action for a healthy planet" (p. 25).

manifestation of weak state sovereignty. Instead of using state sovereignty as a tool for global action, it has been used as a shield against it.

The biggest stumbling block has always been the resistance of states against "new kinds of institutional arrangements and novel procedures of decision-making, on both national and international levels". The person who wrote this was Maurice Strong, initiator and Secretary-General of the 1972 Stockholm conference. A year after Stockholm, he observed that the state's "responsibility to ensure that activities within their jurisdiction or control do not cause damage to the environment of other States or of areas beyond national jurisdiction" (Principle 21 Stockholm Declaration) is "a far more revolutionary matter than has yet been generally acknowledged or comprehended".[7]

Principle 21 reappeared as Principle 2 in the Rio Declaration adopted at the 1992 Earth Summit, again under the leadership of Maurice Strong as Secretary-General. Probably the most significant provision of both declarations is the "no-harm" rule now widely recognized as a principle of customary international law whereby a State is duty bound to prevent environmental harm to other States. The crux is that the no-harm rule does not include "areas beyond national jurisdiction", the global commons or Earth as a whole. A conventional understanding of State sovereignty would not allow for this. An obligation *erga omnes* to safeguard the Earth does not exist. It may be emerging, though,[8] considering the many initiatives, declarations and agreements that have since been produced by civil society, professional bodies and international organizations.

Maurice Strong himself initiated the Earth Charter that the 1987 Brundtland Report had called for, but it was rejected by states during the 1992 Earth Summit. As a cross-cultural, cross-religions consensus of global values, the 2000 Earth Charter gained recognition among governmental agencies, several States, UNESCO, IUCN and other global organizations. Its key principles are Respect and Care for the Community of Life (Part I) and Ecological Integrity (Part II).[9]

Both principles directly address what international environmental law was and is in urgent need of: i.e. an overall objective and obligation to protect the integrity of the Earth's ecological system. Its ethical core is our belonging to the "community of life", in contrast to the Western anthropocentrism that has shaped traditional, ineffective environmental law. The Earth is not an assembly of natural resources for human consumption but a living whole

7 Strong, M 1973, 'One year after Stockholm', *Foreign Affairs Magazine*, vol. 51, no. 4, p. 690.
8 Robinson, NA 2018, 'Environmental law: is an obligation Erga Omnes emerging?', conference presentation at the panel discussion at the United Nations (4 June 2018, 1 pm–2.45 pm, Conference Room 12).
9 Earth Charter Initiative 2000, *The earth charter*, (https://earthcharter.org/).

that humans are part of and need to respect. Fundamentally, this means that humans – and their political institutions – have responsibilities towards non-human members of the community of life or Earth community.[10]

3. The Subject of Environmental Law

Underpinning the concept of environmental law are two legal constructs. One is the body of international environmental agreements as it emerged half a century ago. The other is the concept of State sovereignty as it emerged nearly a half millennium ago. The concept has never been static but evolved according to changed ambitions of the time. It has not, however, caught up with today's reality of global interrelatedness: demographic, cultural, political, economic and ecological.

There is a huge and ever-widening gap between the promise of environmental protection and ecological realities. Singular successes are vastly outdone by system failures: the world's climate is heading for a tipping point, ice caps are melting, the stabilizing functions of oceans and rainforests are weakening, fish stocks are disappearing and biodiversity is diminishing. Humanity's ecological footprint keeps getting bigger without any signs of the reverse. The integrity of the planet's ecological systems – at local, regional and global levels – is now at risk.

Measured by their own intentions and purpose descriptions, environmental policies and laws have not achieved much at all. Rather, they mitigate ecological damage inflicted by industrial economies and Western-type lifestyles. For any prospect of real success, the examination of beliefs, values and principles underpinning the law seems much more relevant than the findings of conventional legal research into the effectiveness of laws. Unless these underpinnings are addressed, no amount of environmental law will bridge the gap between promise and fulfilment.

Essentially, environmental law is hampered by a reductionist approach to its subject: i.e. environment or, more precisely, the human-nature relationship. This relationship is misconceived because of the domination of certain philosophical and cultural traditions in European history. As a consequence, modern legislation to protect the natural environment has developed in a compartmentalized, fragmented, economistic and anthropocentric manner. For environmental legislation to become effective, broader coverage and better enforcement are not enough. The inherent design flaw in these laws is the absence of a fundamental rule prohibiting harm to the integrity of ecosystems. Such a rule requires the acceptance of sustainability as an overarching ethical and legal principle.

10 Earth Trusteeship 2018, *The Hague principles for a universal declaration on responsibilities for human rights and earth trusteeship* (10 December 2018), (www.earthtrusteeship.world).

The basic problem of environmental law, whether domestic or international, has been to regulate individual activities in terms of their cumulative effects. This is best described by comparing individual entitlements with their cumulative impacts on nature or the "commons", as Garret Hardin called them in his classic essay "The Tragedy of the Commons".[11] Although Hardin's central thesis is well known, it is worth repeating some relevant passages here:

> The tragedy of the commons develops in this way. Picture a pasture open to all. It is to be expected that each herdsman will try to keep as many cattle as possible on the commons. Such an arrangement may work reasonably satisfactorily for centuries because tribal wars, poaching, and disease keep the numbers of both man and beast well below the carrying capacity of the land. Finally, however, comes the day of reckoning, that is, the day when the long-desired goal of social stability becomes a reality. At this point, the inherent logic of the commons remorselessly generates tragedy.
>
> As a rational being, each herdsman seeks to maximize his gain. Explicitly or implicitly, more or less consciously, he asks, "What is the utility to me of adding one more animal to my herd?" [T]he rational herdsman concludes that the only sensible course for him to pursue is to add another animal to his herd. And another. . . . But this is the conclusion reached by each and every rational herdsman sharing a commons. Therein is the tragedy. Each man is locked into a system that compels him to increase his herd without limit – in a world that is limited. Ruin is the destination toward which all men rush, each pursuing his own best interest in a society that believes in the freedom of the commons. Freedom in a commons brings ruin to all.[12]

At a global scale, Hardin's pasture includes such commons as the oceans, water, soils, forests, energy and, ultimately, the entire planet. No one is denied entry. Anyone may lay claim to the common resources. The tragedy occurs when any concern for the common good slips through the system of individual claims.

The most interesting aspect of Hardin's essay is the assumed inability of the individual actors to look beyond the here and now. They consider it rational to maximize individual gain and would not question such rationality even if presented with the information that the accumulation of individual pursuits is disastrous for everyone. They are locked into a system of self-destruction. The question is, of course, how rational it really is to maximize individual gain at the expense of others and everything. As a remedy against such

11 Hardin, G 1968, 'The tragedy of the commons', *Science*, vol. 162, p. 1243.
12 Hardin, 'The tragedy of the commons', p. 1244.

twisted rationality, Hardin recommends that we "legislate temperance",[13] and he calls for "mutual coercion mutually agreed upon".[14]

Following this recommendation, modern environmental law aims to regulate individuals who act in the Here and Now in order to avoid tragic consequences in the There and Then. The assumption is that human enterprise, as it is, will not change unless coerced by formal legal rules.

To be sure, influencing and changing human conduct is the objective of any set of rule – in fact, of law at large. The law's sole purpose is coercing human conduct when it does not follow socially agreed standards. For example:

- Family law is needed to prevent spouses and parents from escaping their duties, ultimately to protect the family;
- Company law, competition law and consumer law are needed to prevent companies from escaping their duties, ultimately to protect the availability of consumer goods;
- Tax laws are needed to prevent citizens from escaping their duties, ultimately to secure budget revenues;
- Human rights are needed to prevent governments and members of society from unjustified interference, ultimately to protect dignity and freedom; and
- International law is needed to prevent states from unjustified interference, ultimately to promote peace and justice.

And so on.

Each branch of law has a specific objective justified by an assumed social consensus. The same is true for environmental law. It is needed to prevent individuals from overusing the commons, ultimately to protect our living conditions. Structurally, therefore, environmental law is no different from other branches of law.

Conceptually, however, environmental law is very different. It is not a mere piece of the legal cake, like family law or tax law, but more an ingredient in all of it, adding texture and flavor to the entire legal system. In this regard, environmental law is similar to human rights and public international law in its fundamental universal validity.

Further, the target group of environmental law are all of us, not merely one segment of society. In our various roles as citizens, taxpayers, professionals, producers, consumers, house owners, car drivers and private persons, we all have environmental duties, albeit to varying degrees. Legal persons – holders of rights and responsibilities like corporations, companies or states – are

13 Hardin, 'The tragedy of the commons', p. 1245.
14 Hardin, 'The tragedy of the commons', p. 1247.

equally affected. Environmental law adds a new dimension to the entire legal system. Essentially, all human activities are, or should be, covered by environmental law.

Beyond its broad scope, the objective of environmental law is also far reaching. Its objective is to protect the natural environment that humans are part of and depend on. Ultimately, the goal is to preserve the integrity of the Earth system.

Such a broad scope and objective requires close coordination between environmental law and other legal disciplines. But something more is required. Environmental law fundamentally differs from the rest of law with its peculiar space and time dimensions.[15] The natural environment is without boundaries and strangely at odds with legal boundaries. Environmental protection laws are not consistent among and across jurisdictions, causing disruption and disorder. Moreover, unlike most other legal fields, environmental law tries to provide for long time horizons. Activities in the Here and Now are controlled to achieve something in another place and time. This makes acceptance of radical measures difficult. Yet the environmental impacts of human development can now be seen everywhere and in a new time horizon: i.e. the Anthropocene. This alone requires urgent action.

In sum, at least three unique factors bear upon the design of environmental law: its broad scope (each person), its broad objective (protecting the commons, ultimately the Earth system), its wide space (global) and complex time horizons (short term and long term). The "challenge" of environmental law is that people have a right to pursue prosperity and well-being, yet in doing so, we collectively threaten the very conditions that make life and well-being possible in the first place. The challenge is to hold planetary overshoot[16] and re-organize our lives within the limits of planetary boundaries. This is the promise of ecological integrity.

4. The Challenge for Environmental Law

In trying to meet the challenge, lawmakers must decide how much protection of the conditions of life will be required. This decision is inevitable as it affects the rights and duties of people living today. Fundamentally, only two solutions are available: either protection of our living conditions must set a benchmark against which all rights and duties are to be measured, or environmental measures will be considered merely relative to other concerns such as economic prosperity and social equity. This may be seen as the "dilemma"

15 Lazarus, R 2005, 'Human nature, the laws of nature, and the nature of environmental law', *VA Environmental Law Journal*, vol. 24, p. 231.

16 Rees, W 2023, 'The human eco-predicament: overshoot and the population conundrum', *Vienna Yearbook of Population Research*, vol. 19, p. 1.

of environmental law. A dilemma is a problem offering two solutions, of which neither seems practical or achievable.

Upon closer examination, however, it appears that the dilemma can be meliorated somewhat. Behind the concern for the commons and our living conditions really lies the concern for the characteristics that make their continued ("sustainable") existence possible. There is neither a need nor a practical possibility for absolute protection of ecological systems to ensure their "natural" state: i.e. free from any human intervention. Even though absolute protection may be the purpose of specific laws, such as those that create natural reserves or protect endangered species, ultimately, all commons and ecological systems are areas of human intervention and interaction. This is matter of how intensive (low or high impact) or extensive (local or global) human intervention should be. What really matters, therefore, is the protection of the characteristics of ecosystems. In other words, the health or integrity of ecosystems.

The book's contention is that the reductionist worldview underpinning the perception of "the environment" must be overcome. The opposite of reductionism is holism. While the reductionist approach tends to separate and isolate individual components of the whole, the holistic approach considers the context and complexity of human behaviour and existence. With respect to "nature", holism is the awareness of humans being part of nature. Applied to law and governance, holism advocates the shift from environmental law to ecological law.[17] To get there, we must first of all realize some of the main characteristics of environmental law: i.e. its flawed design, its underlying assumptions and the resulting environmental reductionism.

a) *Flawed Design*

The challenge of environmental law can be described as reconciling the environmental demands of people living today with the environmental demands of people living in the future. It asserts that lawmakers must decide "how much" environmental protection is presently required. This decision depends on an assessment of the key characteristics and functions of the natural environment (integrity of ecosystems). How the preservation of ecological integrity relates to other (social, economic) demands creates a moral dilemma. This dilemma is inevitable and can only be resolved by either prioritizing or compromising ecological integrity.

Practitioners, politicians and lawmakers are not normally confronted with the philosophical foundations of environmental law. For the most part,

17 Oslo Manifesto 2016, *From environmental law to ecological law: a call for re-framing law and governance*, Ecological Law and Governance Association (June 2016), (https://elga-world.org/oslo-manifesto).

environmental issues are seen as factual matters to be dealt with in a practical, "rational" manner. Statutes and cases may raise some deeper questions of interpretation and application, but those questions, it is felt, can and must be resolved with legal argument, not ethical reasoning.

On the other hand, students of environmental law are inevitably confronted with ethical and philosophical questions. Many of today's textbooks of environmental law contain introductory chapters on theoretical foundations. This is certainly the case in Germany and New Zealand, possibly in a number of other countries, but arguably less so in the UK, Canada and the USA. The leading New Zealand text, for example, describes the ethical debate surrounding anthropocentrism versus ecocentrism as a key subject matter of environmental law and states: "The complex and multi-faceted nature of 'the environment' and the ethical dimensions of human interaction with other elements of the ecological community, demonstrates the challenge of defining environmental law".[18]

Birnie, Boyle and Redgwell's classic text on international environmental law answers the question, "What is the environment?" by quoting Lynton Caldwell: "It is a term that everyone understands and no one is able to define". It concludes that "any definition of 'the environment' will have the Alice-in-Wonderland quality of meaning what we want it to mean".[19] An important clue perhaps! The first chapter of another classic text by Kiss and Shelton has in-depth discussions on religious roots, anthropocentrism, environmental science and economic rationality to then conclude that "policies emerge from religious and philosophical beliefs but must also be based on scientific and economic realities that require an integrated and interdisciplinary approach".[20]

These few samples indicate the importance of values and worldviews that have shaped and continue to shape environmental law. In fact, it seems reasonable to suggest that environmental law scholarship is a journey into the long history of both natural law and positivist traditions that define the relationship between humans and nature.

The question might be asked why lawyers should be concerned with the deeper dimensions of legal constructs when there are experts like sociologist, psychologists, philosophers, anthropologists and so on. Arguably, the issues

18 Grinlinton, D 2015, 'Defining the nature and boundaries of environmental law', in P Salmon & D Grinlinton (eds), *Environmental law in New Zealand*, Thomson Reuters, Wellington, p. 10.
19 Birnie, P, Boyle, A & Redgwell, C 2009, *International law and the environment*, 3rd edn, Oxford University Press, Oxford, p. 5.
20 Kiss, A & Shelton, D 2000, *International environmental law*, 2nd edn, Transnational, New York, p. 27.

involved here are still at the periphery of academic training and scholarship.[21] The very fact that there are environmental philosophers, environmental economists, environmental lawyers and other "specialists" is a manifestation of reductionism in academia. Environmental lawyers must recognize their subject as interdisciplinary. That such recognition and expertise hardly exist also explains, to some degree, the flawed design of environmental laws.

The magnitude and urgency of the global ecological crisis make it imperative to address questions such as:

- In the light of physical reality, how can the human-nature relationship be defined?
- How did we come to this state of mind and affairs, and whose interests are being served by maintaining the status quo?
- Why do most people in modern society fail to relate personally or collectively with this unfolding human tragedy and do something about it?

b) Legacy of the European Cosmology

The Western mindset that has shaped both capitalism and socialism has its roots in the project of modernity or, as German philosopher Rudolf Bahro termed it, the "European cosmology".[22] That cosmology includes a distinctive set of notions including **d**ualism, **a**nthropocentrism, **m**aterialism, **a**tomism, **g**reed, and **e**conomism (**damage** for short).

Dualism emphasizes the separate rather than the complementary nature of opposing categories. Western dualism manifests itself in many ways: for example, in such commonly drawn distinctions as Good versus Evil, Reason versus Emotion, Material versus Spiritual, Civilized versus Primitive, Humans versus Nature, Economy versus Environment, Individual versus Community or Rights versus Duties.

The idea of anthropocentrism posits human beings and human society as separate from, independent of and above the natural world. Anthropocentrism has deep cultural and historical roots encompassing the Enlightenment and going back to the dominant interpretation of the biblical Genesis.[23]

Linked with Descartes's mind-matter dichotomy, the modern concept of materialism tends to see matter as dead and inert, lacking validity on its own. This view leads to a "disenchantment of nature"[24] and to the belief that

21 Emmett, R & Nye, D 2017, *The environmental humanities: a critical introduction*, MIT Press.
22 Bahro, R 1994, *Avoiding social and ecological disaster: the politics of world transformation*, Gateway, Bath, p. 219.
23 Placing humans in the center of and above all other species; *Book of Genesis* 1:28.
24 Horkheimer, M & Adorno, T 2002, *Dialectic of the enlightenment*, Stanford University Press, Stanford.

humans can control and rearrange the material world purely as a matter of utility, with no moral or ethical constraints, duties or obligations. It is at the root of the equation of the natural environment with natural resources.

Prevailing in science is an atomistic (or reductionist) worldview that seeks to break complex objects of study into smaller and smaller parts. It makes the assumption that a complex system is nothing but the interaction of these parts. The universe is seen as a "clockwork" and the interaction of billiard ball–like objects.[25] As a consequence, scientific focus on the whole (the forest) is lost through hyper-specialization within science, which concentrates on the trees.

The Enlightenment's concern with personal autonomy created human rights. However, it also promoted a tendency to favor entitlement over responsibility, individuality over community, competition over collaboration and selfishness over altruism. In its radical form, individualism can lead to greed that denies any sense of responsibility, erodes social ties and citizenship and inhibits collective action.

Economism refers to the beliefs and myths collectively held about the economy. Just as all cultures have myths about nature and the proper human relationship to nature, our capitalist culture has created a mythical belief that the economy matters more than anything else. Economic analysis has a privileged place in society's institutions and in public decision-making. As a consequence, decisions, some with deep moral implications, are now determined primarily by income and price.

c) *Environmental Reductionism*

These characteristics have, over time, resulted in what I call environmental reductionism: a compartmentalized, fragmented and anthropocentric idea of the environment.

Cumulatively, the six mentioned characteristics of modernity have had the effect of damage (sic!) to what can only be described as a healthy human mind. Over time and each in their own way, anthropocentrism, individualism and economism have reinforced one another and nurtured the idea that a healthy environment is secondary to human well-being, that economy is more important than ecology and that consumer society is indispensable. Together, these characteristics of Western (and now global) culture have brought about the Anthropocene.

Seen in this light, environmental law could not do better than it has. However, it has its own characteristics that we may be able to identify in an effort to overcome them and describe the transformation of environmental law.

25 Isaac Newton's Principia Mathematica (1687) remains one of the most influential scientific texts ever written and further developed Descartes's image of a "clockwork" universe.

At present, its subject is a severely compartmentalized, fragmented and economically charged idea of the environment.

Compartmentalization

To get a sense of the modern compartmentalization of the environment, it may be instructive to focus on the way in which the media present environmental issues. News stories about the environment make a lot of headlines, but still more as human hardship stories (storms, floods, droughts) than as political news. It is fair to say that media attention to issues like climate change, oil and food prices has dramatically increased. However, the links between ecology and economy are only rarely made – usually only in terms of the costs of environmental measures that most people cannot, or will not, afford. Meanwhile, financial markets seem to operate in complete independence from the state of the environment.

The compartmentalized picture that the media delivers is paralleled by the way that governments treat the environment. Most countries have a Ministry for the Environment, but it is Treasury that determines the direction of public policy. There are environmental laws, but they are isolated from commercial laws. And there are law schools with environmental law programmes, yet 80% of the curriculum has no environmental component at all.

Moreover, the entire public discourse is compartmentalized. Many, although not all, public leaders in government or business perceive the environment as a special interest: very important, perhaps, but not really relevant to market needs and economic growth. They use the language of economics to hone their arguments on conventional theories of economic security. Small wonder, therefore, that environmental laws are written with economic security and competitiveness in mind.

Fragmentation

In contrast with compartmentalization, which refers to the conceptual "boxing off" of the environment from other policy areas, fragmentation refers to a focus on specific aspects of the environment itself, rather than its value as an integrated whole. Lawmakers do not normally think of the natural environment as a whole (including humans), but more as a generic word for natural resources (an economic term) that need to be protected. This is also true for New Zealand, for example, where one of the most progressive environmental laws was enacted in 1991. The name Resource Management Act (RMA) reflected an overall concern for managing natural resources. On the other hand, as will be discussed in the following chapter, the RMA introduced sustainability as a key concern which, if understood correctly, makes the preservation of ecological integrity paramount to all other interests that humans may have with respect to the environment.

Anthropocentric Utilitarianism

A final flaw in modern environmental law is its anthropocentric-utilitarian approach to the environment. Most legal definitions emphasize the utility value of the environment. Typically, this includes natural resources and amenity values, such as recreation and beauty.

The mentioned RMA stands out as a bit more ambitious in this context. The RMA's definition of the environment has non-anthropocentric elements ("Ecosystems and their constituent parts, including people and communities") coupled with the notion of "intrinsic values"[26] and the concept of *kaitiakitanga*, as well as anthropocentric elements ("natural and physical resources etc,"). The intention of the Act has been to accommodate both anthropocentric and non-anthropocentric interpretations.

While such ethical pluralism may have seemed sensible at the time, it has turned out to be counterproductive. If this most fundamental ethical stance on the human-nature relationship is left to choice, the old familiar paradigm is likely to prevail. This is what happened: the sustainability component of "sustainable management" has been reduced beyond recognition. The general trend has been to move from initial ecocentrism ("environmental bottom-line approach") back to the well-trodden anthropocentric path ("overall judgment approach"). However, in the absence of a benchmark of ecological sustainability, the application of the Act fails to promote tangible "sustainable" management, rather than the intangible "wise use and management" of the previous Town and Country Planning Act 1977.

By and large, administrators and judges have applied the RMA in a manner that limits or mitigates ecological damage but does not prevent it in the first place. This is consistent with environmental laws and their application all around the world.

5. Unravelling the Problem

So what to do? First of all, the deficiencies of compartmentalization, fragmentation and anthropocentrism associated with environmental law need to be acknowledged. To be sure, the reductionist concept of environmental protection was not without success, as mentioned earlier. A number of trees have been saved, but the forest is disappearing. The global commons – atmosphere, biodiversity, the oceans – are in rapid decline, and the human ecological footprint both *per capita* and in total getting larger. To not stop and reverse this disastrous overshoot seems almost incomprehensible, and yet our biggest problem at this point in time seems to be denial.

26 New Zealand Resource Management Act 1991, s 2(1)(a).

According to Sigmund Freud, denial is a defence mechanism in which a person is faced with a fact that is too uncomfortable to accept and rejects it instead, insisting that it is not true despite what may be overwhelming evidence.[27] Experimental research has shown that humans strongly favour avoidance of immediate costs over the risk of less immediate, long-term costs, even if they will be much higher.[28] That seems human, only too human. Denial at the collective level, however, can have disastrous effects. While politicians are still preaching some balancing of economic prosperity and environmental sustainability, both are quickly disappearing.

The idea of balancing is politically motivated, of course, but psychologically reveals denial as it suppresses proven reality. The economy and the environment are both in decline for the same reason: organizing the economy within ecological boundaries is too uncomfortable a task.

Unfortunately, not only are many politicians still in denial, but so too are many of our social institutions. In 1997, educationalist Chet Bowers wrote a revealing book entitled *The Culture of Denial*[29] that examines how Western educational systems reinforce the cultural beliefs that contributed to environmental destruction in the first place. Even universities (sic!) still and despite good intentions provide students with an overly fragmented view of life, compartmentalized into various disciplines, that creates a sort of mythic ambiguity around modernist culture. Bowers's thesis is that the fragmentation of the environmental movement, with all its specialists for everything, repeats itself in the fragmentation of modern academic disciplines. This way, the complexities of sustainability fall between the gaps.[30]

The absence of a unifying sustainability paradigm in our educational institutions has dire consequences. It perpetuates the belief that the environment is "the other", the specialist field that cannot compete with mainstream economics, management or law. A further consequence may be that the current weakness of environmental law will not disappear anytime soon.

To overcome the flaws in environmental law, mere reform is not enough. We do not need more laws, but different ones that are integrated into the entire legal system. Ecological approaches to law are based on ecocentrism, holism, and intra-/intergenerational and interspecies justice. From this perspective, the law will no longer favour humans over nature and individual rights over collective responsibilities. Essentially, ecological law seeks to internalize the natural living conditions of human existence and, in this way, informs the

27 Freud, S 2003, *Psychopathology of everyday life*, Dover, New York, NY.

28 Leiser, D & Azar, OH 2008, "Behavioral economics and decision making: applying insights from psychology to understand how people make economic decisions", *Journal of Economic Psychology*, vol. 29, p. 613.

29 Bowers, C 1997, *The culture of denial*, State University of New York Press, New York.

30 Bosselmann, K 2001, 'Sustainability and university: compatible agendas?' *Educational Philosophy and Theory*, vol. 33, p. 167.

entire spectrum of legal areas, such as constitutions, human rights, property rights, corporate rights and state sovereignty.

Ecological law is not really new. Its values and principles of safeguarding the natural environment have guided ancient cultures and indigenous peoples in all parts of the world and are also part of the pre-industrial history of Western civilisation. After all, if previous generations had not been successful in maintaining at least a degree of sustainability, the present generation would not be here. It is important, therefore, to recognize the history and continuity of ecological values and principles. They have also informed modern environmental law, albeit in a rudimentary form, hidden behind the dominant values of modernity (anthropocentrism, dualism, utilitarianism etc.).

In contemporary legal scholarship, the values and principles of ecological law are expressed in ecocentric jurisprudence (e.g., rights of nature, Mother Earth rights, eco-feminism and ecological legal theory), eco-constitutionalism and Earth system law for the Anthropocene.

6. Book's Content

It is in this vein that the chapters of this book have been written. Each chapter explores three interrelated themes: the relationships between science and jurisprudence, between "laws of nature" and human laws and between environmental law and ecological law.

The book's first part explores ideas for transforming international environmental law.

Chapter 1 argues that the concept of sustainable development, central to most treaties, has been eroded by interpretations that are ignorant of ecological realities. Ecological sustainability is conditional to social and economic sustainability (not the other way around).

Chapter 2 introduces Earth system science as the basis of sound decision-making. Planetary boundaries modelling (climate, oceans, biodiversity etc.) and guaranteed social foundations (food, income, equity etc.) together define the "safe and just space for humanity".

Chapter 3 explores Earth as a system and how it is related to human systems. Ecological and social systems are interrelated and cannot be dealt with in isolation from each other. The system approach to decision-making holds the key to dealing with complexities. In essence, we learn to (re-)imagine economic systems as embedded within ecological systems.

Chapter 4 shows that, and how, the systemic approach informs our understanding of sustainability as an overarching objective of law and governance. Its focus is on the (non-anthropocentric) concern for the integrity of ecological systems (as already expressed in many international agreements). Ecological integrity is best conceptualized as a *grundnorm* of national and international legal systems akin to the guarantee of human rights.

The **second part of the book** centers around the concept of state sovereignty. Based on the analysis of history and developmental changes of the concept, it shows the limitations of conventional theories and employs critical legal theory to define state sovereignty in the context of ecological realities (as discussed in the book's first part).

Chapter 5 outlines the evolution of sovereignty from its original theories and the Westphalian system to its modern global context (UN system, Anthropocene, new political thought).

Chapter 6 discusses contemporary theories of state sovereignty, including realism and neo-realism and the ecology-sovereignty debate with responses from liberal and neo-liberal theory. Following (Western) critical constructivism and indigenous (non-Western) scholarship, the chapter explores the potential of two foundational principles – i.e. the no-harm and the precautionary principle – for advancing state sovereignty.

Chapter 7 develops the duty to protect as the positive expression of the no-harm rule and in expansion of the human rights–based concept of responsibility to protect (R2P). In the context of environmental law (with associated rights and duties), it becomes clear that the duty to protect is transboundary and reflective of ecological well-being, not just human well-being.

The book's third part relates the sovereignty of the state to its environmental responsibilities. For the concept if state sovereignty to keep its promise of autonomy and freedom of citizens, it must be linked to responsibilities towards the preservation and restoration of the transnational Earth system.

Chapter 8 introduces trusteeship as an ancient, cross-cultural concept of responsibility for otherwise unrepresented entities. Building on the theory of the state as trustee of human rights and the literature on fiduciary duties, the chapter expands these duties to include the Earth system. As a trustee of humanity, the state can no longer ignore the ecological conditions that allow for the sustenance of humanity and enjoyment of human rights in the first place. Consequently, sovereignty must include the duties associated with Earth trusteeship.

The final chapter further defines the state's trusteeship duties with respect to the Earth system and shows how they can be institutionalized at national and international levels. In this regard, current developments at UN level are of particular importance: i.e. repurposing the UN Trusteeship Council and/or a World Environment Organization. The UN can take leadership here but is reliant on the support of individual member states. Whether this will happen depends on dialogues between civil society and governments, driven by a shared vision for a peaceful, just and sustainable future.

The overall thesis is that state sovereignty must, and can, be reframed to meet the challenges of the Anthropocene.

Part I

Transforming International Environmental Law

Chapter 1

In Search of Direction

1. Rethinking Sustainable Development

> We are facing a devastating pandemic, new heights of global heating, new lows of ecological degradation and new setbacks in our work towards global goals for more equitable, inclusive and sustainable development. To put it simply, the state of the planet is broken. Humanity is waging war on nature. This is suicidal . . . Now is the time to transform humankind's relationship with the natural world.[1]

This statement by Antonio Guterres, Secretary-General of the United Nations, is a call for transforming our relationship with the natural world. But how might this be possible, given the inherent limitations of sustainable development as an overarching framework?

Sustainable development is generally perceived as a normative anthropocentric concept.[2] It is a decision-making framework based on equitable principles for achieving human well-being, attempting to balance:[3]

1. A concern for the poor;
2. A concern for future generations; and
3. A concern for the environment.

The Brundtland Report emphasized that each of these concerns is intertwined with the other, although it did not appear to acknowledge any limit

1 Guterres A 2020, 'The state of the planet', conference presentation at Columbia University (2 December 2020); see also United Nations Environment Programme 2021, *Making peace with nature: a scientific blueprint to tackle the climate, biodiversity and pollution emergencies*, Nairobi, (https://www.unep.org/resources/making-peace-nature).

2 Dernbach, JC & Cheever, F 2015, 'Sustainable development and its discontents', *TEL*, vol. 4, no. 2, p. 247, 252.

3 Bosselmann, K 2013a, 'A legal framework for sustainable development', in K Bosselmann, D Grinlinton & P Taylor (eds), *Environmental law for a sustainable society*, 2nd edn, New Zealand Centre for Environmental Law Monograph Series: Volume One, Auckland, p. 167, 168.

DOI: 10.4324/9781032674049-3

to social and economic growth based on a finite natural environment.[4] Part I(3) paragraph 27 of the Brundtland Report suggests no absolute ecological limits but rather only relative limits that are imposed by "the present state of technology and social organisation of environmental resources".[5] The problem lies in our failure to recognize that social and economic systems are necessarily limited to operating within the boundaries of a finite physical planet. There can be no sustainable development without ongoing access to natural resources. We must commit to sustaining those ecosystems that produce the planet's resources. If these resources are used up and the supporting ecosystems destroyed, there can be no human development at all. Ecological integrity and "true" or strong sustainability must be the essential foundation on which all development is built.

While some substitution of natural resources and ecosystem services is possible and will actually be desirable in a sustainable world,[6] natural resources and natural systems carry out many functions that cannot be replicated by human technology. Even if they could be, we might not choose to live in a world where plastic trees replace real ones[7] or where human lives must be lived indoors in certain parts of the world because the climate has become too hot.[8]

We have known for a long time now that the economic value of nature's services is enormous but still largely unrecognized by the global economic system. This is the reason a growing number of economists now recommend estimating and placing a monetary value on ecosystem services to try and internalize their true value into the financial system. The reasoning is that if this can be done, then many unsustainable activities will be exposed as too costly to continue. Robert Costanza and others have estimated the global ecosystem service value to humans at $125 to $145 trillion per year.

4 World Commission on Environment and Development 1987, 'Brundtland report ("Our Common Future")', UNGA A/42/427 (4 August 1987).

5 At Part I, subpart III, para 27. It is interesting to note here that in a book marking the 20th anniversary of the Brundtland Report –Bugge, HC & Voigt, C (eds) 2000, *Sustainable development in international and national law*, Europa Law Publishing, Groningen – the editors (one being Hans Christian Bugge, personal assistant to Gro Harlem Brundtland and Secretary of the Commission) and the contributors to the book share the view that the Brundtland Report's concept of sustainable development was meant to assume a position of strong sustainability. However, this is not how governments and corporations have interpreted the definition of sustainable development in the report.

6 The natural resources and ecosystem services that humans use are often referred to using the economic term "natural capital".

7 Tribe, LH 1974, 'Ways not to think about plastic trees: new foundations for environmental law', *The Yale Law Journal*, vol. 83, no. 7, p. 1315.

8 Intergovernmental Panel on Climate Change 2021, 'Summary for policymakers', in V Masson-Delmotte, P Zhai, et al. (eds), *Climate change 2021: the physical science basis. Contribution of working group I to the sixth assessment report of the intergovernmental panel on climate change*, Cambridge University Press, p. 15.

According to the World Bank, total GDP for the world in 2019 was well over half that amount at $85 trillion (USD).[9] These kinds of economic exercises start to uncover and highlight the unacknowledged value of the environment. Costanza also estimates a loss of natural capital of $4.3 to $20.2 trillion per year due to human land-use change.[10] Once vital parts of ecosystems are lost, the resilience of the human socio-economic systems that rely upon them are weakened.[11]

Jared Diamond, in his book *Collapse: How Societies Choose to Fail or Succeed*, gives some sobering historical examples of the decimation of areas and societies that failed to use their own area's natural resources sustainably.[12] Diamond's premise is not that all historical collapses were a direct result of environmental destruction but that the failure to value and use the environment sustainably weakens societies and makes them more vulnerable to collapse. One of his starkest examples is that of the indigenous people of Easter Island who completely deforested their land, causing the collapse of their community. The casts of palm trees (the largest in the world at that time), found buried in the island's volcanic lava, show trees with diameters of up to seven feet. The trees were prized for their sap (used to make wine, honey and sugar), the trunks and fronds were used for building materials and the nuts provided a ready source of food. Diamond asks the question, why would any society destroy its own life supporting resource base? Yet the same question might well be asked by future generations of our own choices.[13]

9 The World Bank 2019, *GDP (current US$)*, (https://data.worldbank.org/indicator/NY.GDP.MKTP.CD).

10 Costanza, R, De Groot, R, Sutton, P, Van der Ploeg, S, Anderson, SJ, Kubiszewski, I, Farber, S, Turner, RK 2013, 'Changes in the global value of ecosystem services', *Global Environmental Change*, vol. 26, p. 152. In this paper, the research estimates show that global land use changes between 1997 and 2011 resulted in a loss of ecosystem services of between $4.3 trillion to $20.2 trillion per year. The researchers consider the estimates to be conservative and a necessary precursor to understanding and creating a more comprehensive "picture of the assets that support human well-being and humans' interdependence with the well-being of all life on the planet". See also Pelenc, J & Ballet, J 2015, 'Strong sustainability, critical natural capital and the capability approach', *Ecological Economics*, vol. 112, p. 36; Kubiszewski, I, Costanza, R, Anderson, S & Sutton, P 2020, 'The future value of ecosystem services: global scenarios and national implications', in KN Ninan (ed), *Environmental assessments: scenarios, modelling, and policy*, Edward Elgar.

11 Millennium Ecosystem Assessment 2005, *Ecosystems and human well-being: synthesis*, Island Press, Washington, DC.

12 Diamond, J 2011, *Collapse: how societies choose to fail or succeed*, 2nd edn, Penguin Group, New York.

13 Kahan, DM, Jenkins-Smith, H & Braman, D 2011, 'Cultural cognition of scientific consensus', *Journal of Risk Research*, vol. 14, no. 2, p. 147. This study suggests that forming risk assessments on matters like climate change is often based on personal and cultural values, not rational or empirical evidence.

At the time the Brundtland Report was prepared, two clear global themes had emerged.[14] The first was a growing awareness of development inequity in the world around distribution of the planet's natural resources. Of particular concern was the imbalance between the rich North developed countries and the poorer South developing ones with the prime task being to combat poverty in the developing countries. The second was the growing awareness that conventional development was leading to environmental degradation.[15] The commonly accepted definition of sustainable development in the Brundtland Report is:[16]

> Sustainable development is development that meets the needs of the present without compromising the ability of future generations to meet their own needs.

The sentence immediately following the definition must also be taken into account:[17]

> It [i.e. sustainable development] contains within it two key concepts:
>
> - The concept of "needs", in particular the essential needs of the world's poor, to which overriding priority should be given; and
> - The idea of the limitations imposed by the state of technology and social organisation *on the environment's ability* to meet present and future needs" [emphasis added].

The "environment's ability" to meet human needs is the forgotten and overlooked part of the Brundtland definition. If our needs are to be met by sustainable development, this places the focus squarely on protecting the earth's physical systems to achieve this. It cannot be overemphasized that there can be no sustainable development if development threatens those ecosystems that provide the living conditions on which we depend.[18]

14 Bosselmann, K 2020, 'Sustainable development law', in KN Scott, J Lindley, E Techera & A Telesetsky (eds), *Routledge handbook of international environmental law*, 2nd edn, Routledge, p. 31.

15 Meadows, D, Meadows, D, Randers, J & Behrens, W 1974, *The limits to growth: a report for the club of Rome's project on the predicament of mankind*, 2nd edn, Universe Books. The authors predicted that economic growth would not continue indefinitely because of physical limits to the world's physical resources.

16 World Commission on Environment and Development, see n 4, at Chapter 2.

17 World Commission on Environment and Development, see n 4, at Chapter 2.

18 Bosselmann, K 2013, 'Sustainable development and international environmental law', in S Alam, et al. (eds), *Routledge handbook for international environmental law*, Routledge, London, p. 671.

Since the Brundtland Report, and in our own Easter Island moment, the misapplication of the concept of sustainable development is causing ongoing destruction of the environment and the ongoing unsustainable use of natural resources.

While sustainable development is clearly focused on the anthropocentric notion of what is best for humans and how to fulfil our human "needs", the concept itself cannot be effectively operationalized without the ecocentric notion of carrying out all development activities within the confines of the planet's ecological and physical reality.[19] Bart Muys perhaps defines sustainable development most accurately as:[20]

> The increase of human prosperity (exergy content) and human well-being (exergy buffering) without the loss of ecosystem structure (exergy content) and ecosystem functioning (exergy buffering). In short it is development that does not degrade the biosphere.

a) Sustainability: Weak or Strong?

If we are now able to accept that the heart of sustainable development is strong or "true" sustainability, then what exactly does this mean? A simple definition of sustainable is "the ability to be sustained, supported, upheld or confirmed".[21] We instinctively understand that the basic rule of existence is the necessity to sustain the water we drink, the air we breathe and the soils our food comes from.

But sustainability is also something more complex. The term is subjective by nature and open to different interpretations. Sustainability is a value-based concept. Ultimately the decisions within society about what we *should* sustain and what we *should not* sustain are ethical and cultural ones. Our current value system over-prioritizes the economy at the expense of the environment, even though the environment is our life support system. Perhaps a good metaphor for this situation might be that of a group of astronauts out in space on a mission who are busy protecting and valuing their rocket fuel supply while ignoring the current state of their air supply.

The existing environmental situation has arisen because historically the human population has sat well below the planet's carrying capacity. Also,

19 Montini, M & Volpe, F 2016, 'The need for a new regulatory approach for the promotion of ecological sustainability', in L Westra, J Gray & A D'Aloia (eds), *The common good and ecological integrity*, Routledge, London. See also Bosselmann, n 18, at 671.

20 Muys, B 2013, 'Sustainable development within planetary boundaries: a functional revision of the definition based on the thermodynamics of complex socio-ecological systems', *Challenges in Sustainability*, vol. 1, no. 1, p. 41, 45.

21 Dictionary.com 2020, *Sustainability*, online edn.

there has been a lack of scientific knowledge about where ecological boundaries and tipping points into undesirable ecological states lie. Now, however, the human population presses up against what the planet can carry,[22] and we also have more knowledge of the physical constraints on economic growth via the use of natural resources. Pope Francis in his encyclical letter *Laudato Si'* points out the "growth" misconception running through the existing development model:[23]

> The idea of infinite or unlimited growth, which proves so attractive to economists, financiers and experts in technology . . . is based on the lie that there is an infinite supply of the Earth's goods, and this leads to the planet being squeezed dry beyond every limit. It is the false notion that an infinite quantity of energy and resources are available, that it is possible to renew them quickly, and that the negative effects of the exploitation of the natural order can be easily absorbed.

Internationally, the three-pillar model of sustainable development, sometimes called "weak sustainability", is generally applied. According to this model, sustainable development has three core elements – the ecological, the social and the economic – each of which is given equal weight when making development decisions. The meaning of the term "sustainable" in this weak approach immediately creates a problem for sustainable development. For example, sustaining our economy's growth as it currently functions involves consuming natural resources at unsustainable rates:[24]

> We are using more of the world's resources than can be replenished given the rate we keep taking them. Every year we are destroying more and more of the world's bio-capacity, which makes it harder for our ecosystems to even provide the same level of service as the year before. . . . [O]ur current way of living is ecologically unsustainable.

In reality, the economic pillar is the one given most weight in practice and has depleted (and continues to deplete) both natural and social capital, commonly referred to as "the Mickey Mouse version" of sustainable development:[25]

22 United Nations Department of Economic and Social Affairs 2019, *Population division world population prospects 2019: highlights*, ST/ESA/SER.A/423, United Nations, New York.
23 Francis, P 2015, *Laudato Si'*, Encyclical Letter, Vatican, 24 May 2015, at para 106.
24 Magallanes, CJI 2015, 'Forward: new thinking on sustainability', *New Zealand Journal of Public and International Law*, vol. 13, no. 1, p. 1. See also Millennium Ecosystem Assessment (see n 11).
25 Sustainable Aotearoa New Zealand 2009, *Strong sustainability for New Zealand: principles and scenarios*, Nakedize Publishing, Auckland, p. 8.

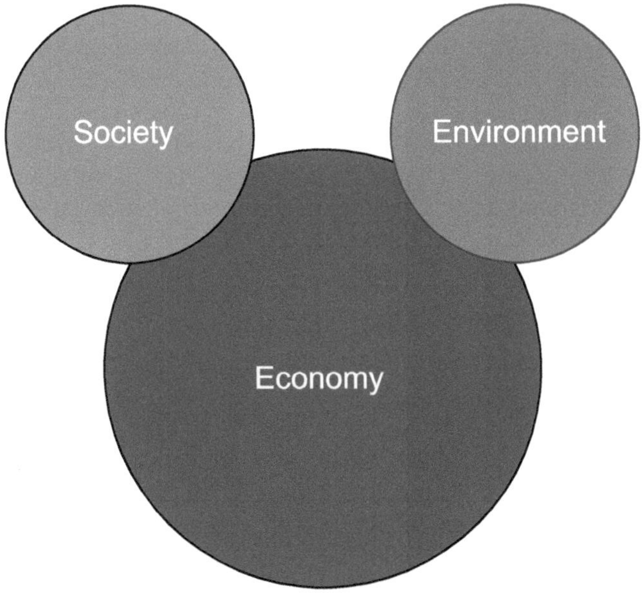

Figure 1.1 Mickey Mouse Economy

Source: Sustainable Aotearoa New Zealand, Strong Sustainability for New Zealand: Principles and Scenarios (Nakedize Publishing, Auckland, 2009) at 8

Given the strong bias we have towards economic development that reaps short-term tangible financial benefits compared to the often immeasurable and intangible long-term negative impact on the environment, the weak three-pillar approach has been unsuccessful in protecting the environment.[26] There is an inherent tension between the concepts of "sustainability" and "development" that the current application of sustainable development under the weak approach does not address. This failure facilitates the weakening of the world's socio-economic systems. The fundamental question about the priority of these three interests cannot be avoided if sustainable development is to be effective moving into the future.

So long as we continue to view the environment, the economy and human needs as equal components of sustainable development, we will perpetuate

26 We have crossed four of the nine planetary boundaries, which provides clear evidence of this failure. See Steffen, W, Richardson, K, Rockström, J, Cornell, SE, Fetzer, I, Bennett, EM, Biggs, R, Carpenter, SR, De Vries, W, De Wit, CA, Folke, C, & Sörlin, S 2015, 'Planetary boundaries: guiding human development on a changing planet', *Science*, vol. 347, no. 6223, p. 1259855. See, more recently, Steffen, W & Morgan, J 2021, 'From the Paris Agreement to the anthropocene and planetary boundaries framework: an interview with Will Steffen', *Globalizations*, vol. 18, no. 7, p. 1298, 1299, 1304.

the biggest obstacle to achieving economic and social justice and unwittingly encourage a race to the bottom to use up the planet's resources. Sustainability fundamentally requires an examination of some key questions of justice. Should those living today do so at the expense of others still to come? Should wealthy countries live at the expense of poorer ones? We must grapple not only with equity issues of human rights for the current population but also with what it actually means to ensure continuity of natural resources for future populations.[27]

b) History of Sustainability

Prior to the Brundtland Report, the term sustainability referred to the physical balance between a human society and the natural environment.[28] The concept of "living from the yield but not the substance" was well understood. Within Europe, whenever the main energy resource base, the forests, reached serious depletion rates, governments created laws to sustain that resource.[29] Prior to the Industrial Revolution, human need for an ongoing sustainable form of energy meant that most societies learnt to take care of and steward natural timber resources, the primary energy supply, in a way that enabled those resources to self-renew. Within the European context, we see the passing of laws that reflect this principle of sustainability.[30] For example, the Weimar Forestry Statute of 1775. Sustainability of resources was a fundamental norm of societies in the past, and from this, it can be presumed that sustainability is an environmental law norm that is well capable of being understood as a legal principle.

27 Becker, C, Ewringmann, D, Faber, M, Petersen, T & Zahrnt, A 2015, "Endangering the natural basis of life is unjust: on the status and future of the sustainability discourse", *Ethics Policy and Environment*, vol. 18, no. 1, p. 60. Becker proposes that the preservation of the natural basis of life is by itself a requirement of justice because it is a necessary precondition for lasting global societal order.

28 Hans Carl von Carlowitz coined the German term *Nachhaltigkeit* in 1714, which was translated by Adolphe Parade to *soutenir*, reflecting the Latin root *sustinere*, meaning to keep, preserve or sustain. The English version then came to be known as the word we use today, sustainability.

29 Bosselmann, K 2017, *The principle of sustainability: transforming law and governance*, 2nd edn, Routledge. See also Grober, U 2012, *Sustainability: a cultural history*, Green Books, Devon.

30 Parrotta, JA & Trosper, RL (eds) 2012, *Traditional forest related knowledge*, Springer, New York. See also Umwelt, BM & Recht 2003, *Mitteleuropa: Von den Groben rodungen des Hochmittelalters bis ins 21 Jahrundert*, Zurich, Schulthess. John Evelyn of England and Hans Carl Carlowitz of Germany both became leading advisers of good forestry practice fulfilling similar roles to those the world's leading economists occupy today. The key difference is that the philosophy was sustainability and not limitless growth.

In *Gabčikovo–Nagymaros Project (Hungry v Slovakia)*,[31] the International Court of Justice noted that:

> Owing to new scientific insights and to a growing awareness of the risks for mankind for present and future generations of pursuit of such interventions at an unconsidered and unabated pace, new norms and standards have developed. . . . [S]uch new norms have to be taken into consideration. . . . [T]his need to reconcile economic development with protection of the environment is aptly expressed in the concept of sustainable development.

While the court majority recognized the concept of sustainable development, Vice-President Christopher Weeramantry went further in his separate opinion, confirming the principle of sustainability (in its strong form) by noting that use of natural resources (development) and their preservation (sustainability) were bound together by "the need for human activity to respect the requisites for its maintenance and continuance".[32]

Clearly, the "requisites" are prescribed by ecological systems themselves, not by social or economic interests. Understood this way, the principle of sustainability gives content and direction to the concept of sustainable development. It requires the preservation and restoration of the integrity of ecological systems. The far-reaching legal implications of defining sustainability in these terms will be discussed in Chapter 4.

c) *The Sustainable Development Goals*

> We are determined to protect the planet from degradation, including through sustainable consumption and production, sustainably managing its natural resources . . . so that it can support the needs of the present and future generations.[33]

In September 2015, the Sustainable Development Goals (SDG) were agreed upon. They build on the previous Millennium Development Goals (MDG) and set the world on a new development agenda path for the period 2015–2030.

There are some important differences between the MDG and the process used to reach them, compared to the SDG. The MDG were formulated by a small specialist group through a top-down process involving very little civil society presence. The result was a narrowly focused group of eight goals, mainly concerned with alleviating poverty in developing countries. In

31 Gabčikovo–Nagymaros Project (Hungry v Slovakia) [1997] ICJ Rep 7.
32 At 18.
33 Transforming our world: the 2030 agenda for sustainable development GA Res 70/1 (2015).

contrast, the SDG have only been reached after a long and drawn-out process involving the participation of many parts of civil society.

It is fair to say that in preparation for reaching the SDG, the United Nations has facilitated perhaps the first truly cosmopolitan exercise in participatory global democracy, holding more than 50 country consultations, a worldwide online citizen survey and several global thematic consultations. Numerous experts and state and NGO initiatives also followed these consultations.[34] The SDG process took a number of years to complete and has produced 17 goals and 169 targets in a complex and broad global agenda focused on a much wider view of the role of sustainable development than the MDG had.

While the MDG are sometimes criticized for oversimplifying the meaning of "development", the SDG might be seen to suffer from the opposite problem. There is plenty of room for the goals to clash with each other. For example, an increase in agricultural land use to reduce hunger (goal 2) could easily clash with the need to stem biodiversity loss (goal 15). Challenging inequality (goal 10) will involve questioning the existing economic model. (Goal 8 promotes economic growth.)

Perhaps the complexity of the SDG more accurately reflects the complexity in the post-modern world. From a systems point of view, this may actually prove to be useful as pursuing the goals will certainly uncover and highlight the *connections* between the goals (the economy and poverty/inequality, and the economy and the environment) that could be ignored in the past.

There is certainly some cause for optimism in that the SDG reflect a very broad normative consensus for the world development agenda. Those NGOs and other actors that fought for the inclusion of particular goals have a special interest in fostering and following their implementation through to 2030. The goals themselves will be unachievable without the wider citizen push and political pressure to reach them.

Despite the relevance and importance of the planetary boundary framework, the SDG do not refer to the planetary boundaries. Nevertheless, the UN Secretary General did specifically refer to the planetary boundaries when introducing the goals in the synthesis report. Each of the nine boundary areas are recognized and represented in the SDG.[35] While many groups and citizens called for the specific inclusion of the planetary boundaries, there were considerable political barriers. Clara Brandi discusses these hurdles, noting that

34 Langford, M 2016, 'Lost in translation? The politics of the sustainable development goals', *Ethics and International Affairs*, vol. 30, no. 2, p. 167. The contributions to this roundtable emerged from a conference organised by Oxford University and the Norwegian Centre for Human Rights, University of Oslo, supported by the Norwegian Ministry of Foreign Affairs and the Oxford Martin School.

35 Climate change – goal 13, biosphere integrity – goal 15, land-system change – goal 15, freshwater use – goal 6, ocean acidification – goal 14, biochemical flows – goal 2, atmospheric aerosol loading and novel entities – goals 2, 3, 11, 12, 14 and 15.

on the one hand, poorer states saw them as limitations to their future development, and, on the other, wealthy OECD countries recognized that endorsing them would impose normative obligations concerning natural resource use and consumption in their own countries.[36]

Both Brandi and Rockström and others argue that rather than limiting development for the poorest, the outer planetary boundary framework, along with inner social floor boundaries, provide:[37]

> An indispensable precondition for poverty eradication and development . . . it is the consumption decisions and lifestyle choices of the global middle and upper classes that are contributing most to humanity putting the earth system at risk, which in turn puts the spotlight on their ecological footprint and on global inequalities.

Massimiliano Montini and Francisca Volpe point to the loss of opportunity to specifically include the planetary boundaries in the SDG as a missed chance to guide a paradigm shift away from the unsustainable mainstream development model towards a more ecologically sustainable future. They note that the SDG fail to provide a comprehensive definition of sustainable development and also fail to meaningfully define what "growth" actually means.[38] Goal 8 of the SDG aims to promote "sustained, inclusive and sustainable economic growth" without defining the phrase. Is it quantitative growth requiring increasing amounts of natural resources? Or is it a new kind of "qualitative" growth that is needed to decouple the economy from using up the environment and moving beyond the "business as usual" approach?

36 Brandy, C 2015, 'Safeguarding the earth system as a priority for sustainable development and global ethics: the need for an earth system SDG', *Journal of Global Ethics*, vol. 11, no. 1, p. 32, 33.

37 At 33. See also Leach, M, Raworth, K & Rockström, J 2013, 'Between social and planetary boundaries: navigating pathways in the safe and just space for humanity', in World social science report 2013: changing global environments, OECD Publishing, Paris. See also Rockström, J, Sachs, JD, Öhman, MC & Schmidt-Traub, G 2013, Sustainable development and planetary boundaries: a background report submitted to the high-level panel of eminent persons on the post-2015 development agenda, Sustainable Development Solutions Network, May 2013; Hajer, M, Nilsson, M, Raworth, K, Bakker, P, Berkhout, F, De Boer, Y, Rockström, J, Ludwig, K & Kok, M 2015, 'Beyond cockpit-ism: four insights to enhance the transformative potential of the sustainable development goals', Sustainability, vol. 7, p. 1651; De Schutter, O 2020, 'Report on the "Just transition" in the economy recovery: eradicating poverty within planetary boundaries', presented to the UNGA A/75/181/REV.1, 9 October 2020.

38 Montini, M & Volpe, F 2019, 'The need for an "integral ecology" in connection with the UN sustainable development goals', in F Pasquale (ed), *Care for the world: Laudato Si' and catholic social thought in an era of climate crisis*, Cambridge University Press, p. 62. See also, Montini, M & Volpe, F 2015, 'Sustainable development goals: much ado about nothing?', *Environmental Liability: Law, Policy and Practice*, vol. 4, p. 141, 142.

Despite these shortcomings, the 17 SDG and 169 targets represent global opportunities for change. Robert Costanza sees them as an important step in the transition process to a sustainable world because they open the door for "much-needed additional work".[39] Unlike the MDG, the SDG require substantial commitment and action from all states.[40] Costanza notes that the next important step will be "to create metrics for human and ecosystem well-being and to replace Gross Domestic Product (GDP) as the primary development goal for nations".[41]

> The recent single-minded focus on GDP growth has exacerbated inequality and environmental damage in many countries. . . . The new metrics should therefore incorporate insights from ecology and psychology to describe how natural, social, human, and built capital assets interact to contribute to sustainable well-being, based on the idea that the best system is one that achieves the overarching goal of a world that is simultaneously prosperous, equitably shared, and ecologically sustainable. There is compelling new research relating ecosystem services and natural and social capital to human well-being, which can be integrated with GPI [the "Genuine Progress Indicator" holding potential to replace GDP] to produce an expanded version that connects more directly with the SDGs.

Even though no single goal referring to planetary boundaries is included, they are the first scientific system to emerge for global ecosystem integrity, and the SDG can make profitable use of them as yardsticks for individual goal progress.

The SDG do attempt to cover the various components of the global ecological system. These are broken down and dealt with under individual and, in some cases, multiple goals. For example:[42]

1. Goal 2 addresses sustainable agriculture (the land-system change planetary boundary and the biogeochemical boundary);
2. Goal 6 addresses sustainable management of water (the freshwater use boundary);
3. Goal 7 addresses sustainable energy (the climate change boundary);

39 Costanza, R, Fioramonti, L & Kubiszewski, I 2016, 'The UN sustainable development goals and the dynamics of well-being', *Frontiers in Ecology and the Environment*, vol. 14, no. 2, p. 59.

40 Fukuda-Parr, S 2016, 'From the Millennium Development Goals to the sustainable development goals: shifts in purpose, concept, and politics of global goal setting for development', *Gender and Development*, vol. 24, no. 1, p. 43.

41 Costanza et al., n 39. See also Hák, T, Janoušková, S & Moldan, B 2016, 'Sustainable development goals: a need for relevant indicators', *Ecological Indicators*, vol. 60, p. 565.

42 Transforming Our World, n 33.

4. Goal 12 seeks to ensure sustainable consumption and production patterns (the novel entities boundary, stratospheric ozone and atmospheric aerosol loading boundaries);
5. Goal 13 requires urgent action to combat climate change and its impacts (the climate change boundary, also covered by goal 7);
6. Goal 14 requires conservation and sustainable use of the oceans, seas and marine resources (the ocean acidification boundary); and
7. Goal 15 aims to protect restore and promote sustainable use of terrestrial ecosystems, forests, desertification and biodiversity loss (the land system, biodiversity and biogeochemical boundaries).

In Johan Rockström and others' background research paper submitted to the High-Level Panel on the Post-2015 Development Agenda, they point out that rather than knowingly crossing planetary boundaries, the world can take the opportunity presented by the SDG to re-imagine the concept of sustainable development within a safe operating space by adopting improved technologies, stabilizing world population and protecting biodiversity:[43]

> We propose that the world should live within the planetary boundaries through the deployment of new sustainable technologies and new global rules of the game . . . which would comprise six major structural transformations to ensure the world continues to develop economically while staying within planetary boundaries.

The six major transformation areas suggested are all included within the SDGs. They are:[44]

1. A global energy transformation (goal 7);
2. Food security transformation (goal 2);
3. Urban sustainability transformation (goals 9 and 11);
4. Population transformation (goal 3, target 3.7: "universal access to sexual and reproductive healthcare services, including family planning, information and education and the integration of reproductive health into national strategies and programs";[45]
5. Biodiversity management transformation (goal 15); and
6. Private and public governance transformation (goal 16).

43 Rockström, n 37.
44 At 8–16.
45 The MDG did not attempt to tackle the delicate political issue of population growth at all, even though it is a key factor to creating a sustainable world. See also United Nations Department of Economic and Social Affairs, Population Division, n 22, at 9.

While the SDG do not clarify the meaning of sustainable development (strong or weak sustainability?), which is a lost opportunity, they do support the notion of ecological integrity and offer the potential to be a powerful citizen-backed blueprint supporting a transition towards protecting and sustaining the environment while striving for human prosperity.

2. Overcoming Anthropocentric Reductionism

a) Why Environmental Law Is Not Working

All law is a body or a system of rules that a community recognizes as regulating the actions of its members and that can generally be enforced by the imposition of penalties.[46] Environmental law[47] is no exception and is the specific regulation of the interactions of humans with the environment. Its purpose is to influence and change human conduct and activity where those activities do not follow socially agreed norms.[48] Law is created and determined by the cultural environment in which it evolves. Law simply reflects how we see ourselves and what we, as a society, consider to be important. This means that, generally, changes in the law occur only once a shift in those things we consider to be important has taken place. In other words, law historically lags societal change.

At present, international environmental law lacks coherence, effectiveness and structure. The scientific community is warning that human activities' impact on the earth system[49] are driving us away from the Holocene – the geological epoch that started 11,700 years ago and is characterized by its relative climate stability that has allowed contemporary human societies to strive and develop in a sustainable way.[50] We are entering a new geological era, the Anthropocene, which is considered unfavourable to the well-being and development of our modern human societies.[51] In the Anthropocene, our political institutions have an additional responsibility

46 *Oxford dictionary law*, 3rd edn, 2019, online edn.

47 The term "environmental law" is used here to include international and national environmental laws and governance issues.

48 Bosselmann, K 2010, 'Losing the forest for the trees: environmental reductionism in the law', *Environmental Laws and Sustainability: Special Issue of Sustainability*, vol. 2, no. 8, p. 2424, 2425.

49 University Corporation for Atmospheric Research, *The earth as a system*, UCAR Center for Science Education, (https://scied.ucar.edu/longcontent/earth-system).

50 Gerlak, AK, et al. 2018, *Earth system governance: science and implementation plan of the earth system governance project, UNU-IAS reports*, Earth System Governance, p. 31.

51 Gerlak et al., *Earth system governance*. See also Brook, BW, Ellis, EC, Perring, MP, Mackay, AW & Blomqvist, L 2013, 'Does the terrestrial biosphere have planetary tipping points?', *Trends in Ecology & Evolution*, vol. 28, no. 7, p. 396.

that until now only existed as a sentiment – the responsibility to care for the Earth.[52]

The Anthropocene introduces a new dynamic into environmental policy, law and governance and how it should evolve because it heralds a new period of *global* human-induced environmental change. This change highlights the failure of the existing legal system to adapt[53] – so far, environmental law has been largely problem specific rather than global in focus.

Now that human impact is no longer just local or national but transcends state boundaries with large, systemic and long-term environmental problems, the way environmental law is created and applied must be carefully re-evaluated.

Many of our human activities causing large and complex environmental issues are not socially unacceptable or even illegal but are deeply embedded in our modern way of life. They are not criminal, nor are they torts or civil wrongs. They do not violate national or international law. Essentially, the law is blind to these seemingly innocuous activities. An obvious example is climate change. All of us contribute to increasing the greenhouse effect by adding to the levels of carbon dioxide ($CO_{2)}$ in the air through the daily activity of driving our cars.

Environmental law faces the difficulty of actions occurring at one level (the local), where there are no obvious negative effects on those carrying out the activity, creating reactions and tipping points in macro-ecological systems at another location and another level (the global). To make matters worse, many of these problems can still only be largely detected through scientific knowledge, data and computer modelling, rather than our own senses.[54]

Science and law have been historically intertwined, and "coevolved over time".[55] But while a fundamental paradigm shift has occurred in the science of ecology, a corresponding shift in law has struggled to follow.[56] Instead of humans "evolving" within the Earth system, we now "evolve" the Earth system ourselves in ways that are often unseen and with unknown consequences.

52 The World Conservation Union, United Nations Environment Programme and World Wide Fund for Nature 1991, *Caring for the earth: a strategy for sustainable living* (October 1991), (https://portals.iucn.org/library/efiles/documents/cfe-003.pdf); Earth Charter Initiative 2000, *The earth charter*, (https://earthcharter.org/virtual-library2/the-earth-charter-text/).

53 Kotzé, LJ & Kim, RE 2020, 'Exploring the analytical, normative and transformative dimensions of earth system law', *Environmental Policy and Law*, vol. 50, no. 6, pp. 457–470. See also Kim RE 2013, 'Unravelling the maze of multilateral environmental agreements: a macroscopic analysis of international environmental law and governance in the anthropocene', PhD thesis, Australian National University.

54 DiMento, JF 2015, 'Protection of our earth: a half century of environmental law', Legal Studies Research Paper Series No. 94, University of California School of Law, p. 8.

55 Capra, F & Mattei, U 2015, *The ecology of law: toward a legal system in tune with nature and community*, Berrett-Koehler Publisher, Oakland, California, p. ix.

56 Capra & Mattei, n 55, at x.

The framework of law struggles to adapt to the pace of environmental change, incorporate the relevant science into the legal decision-making process and provide any meaningful brake on the activities causing the changes.[57]

International environmental law has developed in a fragmented and anthropocentric manner, without regard to the biological and geological reality of the Earth system. Our environmental laws are ill conceived and utterly inoperative. Government responses to the growing ecological crisis have frequently acknowledged the need to increase ambitious targets already in place with no measurable outcome. The last examples of this are the 2015 Paris Agreement, targeting a maximum of 2 degrees[58] (but preferably 1.5 degrees) surface temperature increase, and the 2015 Sustainable Development Goals. In other words, our governing bodies are attempting to achieve targets, but those efforts are immediately lost if not supported by a coherent global governance framework.[59]

Over the years, the global environmental legal order has been shaped by the adoption of numerous universal instruments that have progressively contributed to the circulation of fundamental principles. Although international environmental law has developed a certain level of coherence through the inclusion of these principles, the question remained whether its core value system contained a goal – in a sense of a unifying constitution-type core of norms. The 1972 Stockholm Declaration paved the way for international environmental law to reflect the global community's need to legislate on the sustainable protection of the Earth system. However, as the conference's final declaration suggested, its purpose was "to inspire and guide the peoples of the world in the preservation and enhancement of the human environment".[60] This instrument's lack of awareness of the ecological concerns is apparent, which is why it solely remained within the boundaries of human rights

57 For a recent scientific assessment see Bamber, JL, Oppenheimer, M, Kopp, RE, Aspinall, WP & Cooke, RM 2019, 'Ice sheet contributions to future sea-level rise from structured expert judgment', *PNAS*, vol. 116, no. 23, pp. 11195–11200. See also, Rose, G 2011, *Gaps in the implementation of environmental law at the national, regional and global level*, United Nations Environment Programme, Kuala Lumpur, p. 2. Rose refers to the suite of environmental laws created after the 1972 Stockholm Conference and then the shift in focus to "sustainable development" after the 1992 Rio Conference on Environment and Development. His assessment focuses on existing law and the gaps that exist in implementation between ambition and reality. See, more recently, United Nations General Assembly 2018, *Report of the Secretary-General on the Gaps in international environmental law and environment-related instruments: towards a global pact for the environment* A/73/419 (30 November 2018).

58 Conference of the Parties 2015, *The Paris Agreement*, U.N. Doc. FCCC/CP/2015/L.9/Rev/1, Article 2, (www.sustainabledevelopment.un.org/frameworks/parisagreement).

59 Bosselmann, K 2015, *Earth governance: trusteeship for the global commons*, Edward Elgar, Cheltenham.

60 Declaration of the United Nation Conference on the Human Environment UN Doc A/CONF.48/14 REV.1 (1974), part I para 3.

language. Ten years later, the 1982 World Charter for Nature (WCN), for the first time, recognized a global environmental ethic by affirming respect for nature as a whole.[61] However, the main drawback of the WCN was the lack of reference to the ethical responsibility of care for nature and all forms of life.[62] Therefore, even if the WCN contained the notion of ecological integrity as its core, it was not placed within a central category.[63]

The 1992 Rio Declaration reaffirmed Stockholm,[64] but what is more significant is the participation of an important number of non-governmental organizations (NGOs) and other non-state representatives carrying the view of civil society in the creation of this instrument. From this massive response to the emergence of a growing awareness of ecological integrity came the adoption of the Earth Charter in 2000. The Earth Charter was not adopted by states but by civil society groups[65] and is the first ecocentric global document to define the obligation of preserving Earth's ecological system.[66] The international environmental principles recognized before the Charter, such as sustainable development, polluter pays and public participation,[67] are also reaffirmed in the instrument. In contrast to the previous documents, the Earth Charter is, in its entirety, designed around the concept of ecological integrity.

There is a need for a coherent body of international environmental law that is based on a unifying constitution-type core of principles – such as ecological integrity and its corollary, planetary boundaries – which could be embedded in a global environmental constitution. These legally binding goal-oriented norms would serve to steer all environmental treaties and institutions toward a common direction, creating an effective purposeful legal and governance system. The international environmental order needs

61 Wood, H 1985, 'The United Nations World Charter for nature: the developing nations' initiative to establish protections for the environment', *Ecology LQ*, vol. 12, no. 4, p. 977.

62 See *World Charter for Nature* GA Res 37/7 (1982). The World Charter for Nature solely refers to an invitation to respect nature in principle 1: "Nature shall be respected and its essential processes shall not be impaired".

63 Bosselmann, K 2010, 'Outlook: the earth charter – a model constitution for the world?', in K Bosselmann & R Engel (eds), *The earth charter: a framework for global governance*, Kit Publishers, Amsterdam, p. 245. See also Bosselmann, K 2019, 'Towards a world constitutional order', in K Bosselmann & K Engel (eds), *The crisis in global ethics and the future of global governance: fulfilling the promise of the earth charter*, Edward Elgar Publishing, p. 39.

64 It is also significant to note all these instruments are soft law in nature. See Abbott, KW & Snidal, D 2000, 'Hard and soft law in international governance', *International Organisation*, vol. 54, no. 3, p. 421.

65 Earth Charter Initiative, n 52.

66 Earth Charter Initiative, n 52 at principle 5. Principle 5 states: "Protect and restore the integrity of Earth's ecological systems, with special concern for biological diversity and the natural processes that sustain life".

67 *Report of the United Nations Conference on Environment and Development* UN Doc A/CONF.151/26 (Vol 1) (12 August 1992), principles 4, 10, 16.

a constitution that will hold the environment – our foundation of life – and the integrity of the ecological systems as non-negotiable.[68] Without such a structure, we are losing sight of the long-term core, and the consequence is the environmental-protection gaps the current legal order generates.

The aim of this chapter is to expose the underlying or hidden cultural assumptions and foundations beneath existing environmental law. Once acknowledged and seen as social constructs that have little or no connection to the physical environment, it becomes possible to think about ways the law can be interpreted or might adapt to the existing Earth system to accommodate the new levels of complexity between humans and nature in the age of the Anthropocene.

This new human/nature relationship is sometimes described as *entangled*. The challenge before us is to entangle the law itself with the Earth system so that it becomes capable of recognizing and reacting to areas of danger. Environmental law already sits at the outer edges of the legal system. The Anthropocene pushes it further out still with the need for greater penetration into and interdisciplinary support from other areas of knowledge, such as the sciences.[69]

Environmental law has been effective in dealing with specific environmental problems located in one place with clear and recognizable offenders.[70] It has saved a few "trees" but not the "forest", which continues to be degraded by human activities. Specific successes are vastly outweighed by global Earth system failures like overwhelming biodiversity loss, climate change and ocean acidification.[71]

Environmental law shares many features with the rest of the law. For example, the use and consideration of primary and secondary source materials, such as treaties and legislation, and the reliance on precedent, rules and principles. Yet there are also important conceptual differences that must be

68 Bridgewater, P, Kim, RE & Bosselmann, K 2015, 'Ecological integrity: a relevant concept for environmental law in the anthropocene?', *Yearbook of International Environmental Law*, vol. 25, no. 1, pp. 61–78. See also, Kim, R & Bosselmann, K 2013, 'International environmental law in the anthropocene: towards a purposive system of multilateral environmental agreements', *Transnational Environmental Law*, vol. 2, p. 285, 307.

69 Environmental law is one of the newest branches of law with a commonly accepted starting point of 1969 – the year the US National Environmental Policy Act was enacted. See Biber, E 2017, 'Law in the Anthropocene epoch', *The Georgetown Law Journal*, vol. 106, no. 1; Percival, RV & Alevizatos, DC 1997, *Law and the environment: a multidisciplinary reader*, Temple University Press, Philadelphia, p. 208; Amirante, D & Bagni, S (eds) 2022, *Environmental constitutionalism in the anthropocene*, 1st edn, Routledge, London.

70 Bosselmann, n 48, at 2424. Many Western regions have increased protected areas and reserves. Urban air environments have improved, and many rivers and lakes are less polluted.

71 Bosselmann, n 48, at 2425. See also Narain, V & Vij, S 2016, 'Where have all the commons gone?', *Geoforum*, vol. 68, p. 21. This article examines the depletion of common pool resources through the process of urbanization and neo-liberal reforms in India since 1991.

recognized if environmental law is to develop in a way that will support a sustainable environment. Unlike other areas of law that are created by social and cultural parameters and deal with specific areas of human activity,[72] environmental law has a non-human component that is continuously adapting and changing in often unforeseen ways and infiltrates and intersects *all* areas of human activity.[73] The other areas of law could be considered pieces of the "legal cake"[74] while environmental law could be understood as the essential raw ingredient, such as flour, without which the cake itself cannot be made:[75]

> Providing a definition of environmental law itself is extremely difficult, for it is a vast, amorphous conglomeration of laws and regulatory systems that relate, directly and indirectly, to the environment. Indeed, it has been said that it encompasses, actually and potentially, everything that may ever be encompassed by law in general.

Environmental law and governance must recognize and incorporate the realities of human social systems and natural ecological systems, which sustain humanity, along with an understanding of ecological system tipping points and boundaries. This requires a legal methodology that is capable of sitting *outside* of the law observing the social and physical world while also functioning *inside* the framework of existing law.

The *subjects* of environmental law are not just one segment of society but all of us – including non-human legal and cultural creations, such as trusts, companies, nation states and the United Nations. The *object* or *objective* of environmental law is equally far reaching; it is the environment and its protection. This makes the failure to recognize an overarching environmental goal within environmental law all the more concerning.

Another paradox for environmental law is the need to set clear legal boundaries for an environment that often operates without boundaries, such as the air or the oceans.[76] It also must attempt to address long time spans that reach far beyond short political cycles and human lifetimes in order to protect the environment for future generations.

72 For example, tax law, family law or company law.

73 Little, G 2016, 'Developing environmental law scholarship: going beyond the legal space', *Legal Studies*, vol. 36, pp. 48, 49–61, 64–65, 68, 73 and 74. See also Etty, T 2022, 'Crossing (conceptual) boundaries of transnational environmental law', *Transnational Environmental Law*, vol. 11, p. 1.

74 Bosselmann, n 48, at 2427.

75 Little, n 71, at 54. See also Philippopoulos-Mihalopoulos, A 2011, 'Towards a critical environmental law', in A Philippopoulos-Mihalopoulos (ed), *Law and ecology: new environmental foundations*, Routledge, London, p. 18.

76 Bosselmann, n 48, at 2428.

b) The Human/Nature Divide

Environmental law has developed out of a very specific set of Western cultural ideas about the human/nature relationship that date back to the biblical book of Genesis and to the Enlightenment.[77] These ideas have shaped not just the law but also our current economic and social reality. The characteristics are:

1. *Duality*. An emphasis on opposing categories, such as the material world versus the spiritual, good versus evil, the arts versus the sciences, the economy versus the environment, individuality versus the community and humans versus nature.[78] The philosophy behind duality is that these opposing categories are irreducibly distinct.
2. *Anthropocentrism*. Out of the sense of duality grew the concept of anthropocentrism, which regards as fact that human beings occupy a position at the centre of the universe. This is described by Pelizzon and Ricketts as an "ontological fantasy".[79] In fact, humans are only one part of the complex ecosystem on Earth and are irrelevant to nature's systems existing beyond the Earth in the universe. However, having said this, anthropocentrism is alive and well as a *cultural and human historical reality* that permeates the law. It has resulted in a legal system that interprets everything in terms of human values, creating a kind of "human chauvinism" with respect to nature and other forms of non-human life.[80]
3. *Individualism*. This has been a vital ingredient in the creation of international human rights, technology and economic growth. Taken to extremes, however, individualism erodes the ability of a community to take collective action for the benefit of the group and increases selfishness and inequality.[81] The age of the Anthropocene introduces a non-compartmentalized complex and nuanced reality, which incorporates all the previously mentioned concepts but also their opposites. For example, along with individualism must now come collaboration, social responsibility and collective action.
4. *Materialism*. Descartes's mind/matter dichotomy saw nature as inert or dead and introduced the idea that humans can manipulate and control

77 At 2430.
78 At 2430.
79 Pelizzon, A & Ricketts, A 2015, 'Beyond anthropocentrism and back again: from ontological to normative anthropocentrism', *AJNRLP*, vol. 18, no. 2, p. 105.
80 At 109.
81 Bosselmann, n 48, at 2431. See also Schluter, M, Tavoni, A & Levin, S 2016, 'Robustness of norm-driven cooperation in the commons', *Proceedings of the Royal Society B: Biological Sciences*, vol. 283, no. 1822, p. 283. This article explores ways to discourage selfish individual overharvesting of common pool resources through innovative use of social norms.

the natural world with no moral or ethical constraints.[82] Materialism is reflected in most environmental law, which describes and compartmentalizes nature into packets of "natural resources" specifically for human use.[83]

5. *Economism.* All cultures operate around central myths that their own societies create and accept. Economism is the belief that the human-created financial system is always the most important consideration. In democratic election cycles, we see this play out where the primary topic of conversation revolves around economic growth. This myth calibrates the human relationship with nature. Where there is any competition between the environment and economic development, the environment invariably loses out because of the privileged position that economic considerations hold within our political and legal frameworks and institutions.
6. *Reductionism.* This is the technique of breaking a complex system down into its separate parts in order to understand how that system works.[84] The key flaw in this approach is the failure to appreciate the importance of the connections and relationships between those parts.[85] Modern systems theory takes the opposite approach to reductionism, considering the connections between the parts themselves to also be of essential importance in understanding how that system works and in predicting how it may change over time.
7. *Compartmentalism.* The separation of different aspects of life – for example, the economy and the environment – means that the links and relationships between them remain hidden and unnoticed. This creates a serious problem. It enables politicians to formulate schizophrenic policies in which each issue is considered separately and is not acknowledged as part of an overall, interlinked human/nature system.

82 Schluter et al., at 2430.

83 For example, section 1A of New Zealand's Crown Minerals Act 1991 sets out the purpose of the Act, which is to "promote exploration for, and mining of Crown owned minerals for the benefit of New Zealand."

84 Newton, I 1995, *Principia mathematica*, Andrew Motte (translator), Prometheus Books, Amhurst. Newton developed further Descartes's theory of a clockwork universe, meaning that the truth of a thing can be discovered through breaking it down to study its separate parts.

85 For example, geo-engineering, where instead of approaching the earth system as a complex interconnected system, an attempt is made to address a particular symptom, rather than the underlying cause with the likelihood of unintended consequences. Reductionism and compartmentalization of the Earth system is the opposite of the approach taken by Earth system science. Another example of a reductionist short-term solution is shore hardening or "armoring", which is a by-product of human development that leads to accelerated erosion, loss of beaches and tidal wetlands. See Prosser, DJ, Nagel, JL, Howlin, S, Marbán, PR, Day, DD & Michael Erwin, R 2018, 'Effects of local shoreline and subestuary watershed condition on waterbird community integrity: influences of geospatial scale and season in the Chesapeake Bay', *Estuaries and Coasts*, vol. 41, pp. 207–222.

To illustrate this idea of compartmentalization, consider that a country may agree to reduce its carbon emissions on the one hand while, on the other, espousing aggressive mining policies that provide incentives to dig up and sell more coal, oil and gas – the burning of which negates any attempt to reduce carbon emissions. The links between the destruction of important ecological systems and the economy are deliberately overlooked and ignored through viewing things in a compartmentalized way.

8. *Fragmentation.* While compartmentalization is used to refer to the separation of different aspects of life, fragmentation is used to refer to the separation of different parts of the environment (and environmental law) into separate boxes containing separate sets of rules.

Environmental law is fragmented in this way to deal with specific issues, such as pollution, the oceans, rivers and lakes, fisheries and forests. However, while some level of fragmentation is inevitable and necessary,[86] the lack of an overall view of the environment or an overarching environmental goal, idea or norm (or *grundnorm*)[87] leads directly to our current dilemma and the resulting environmental consequences.[88]

Public perception, rather than embracing a concern with the entire human-nature relationship, tends to focus on "environmental issues". As practical as this may appear, the plurality of environmental issues simply serves to reaffirm the illusion that environmental degradation can be dealt with through a process of separation and prioritization that fails to do justice to the broader reality. Moreover, this tendency can be related to that of short-term-oriented decision-making, hostile to complexities and to the idea that the environment concerns "everything", not merely natural resources.

Rakhyun Kim uncovered examples of the way piecemeal efforts to protect specific areas of the environment can lead to transferring environmental harm from one area to another, due to the lack of a holistic overview. This occurs because treaties and most environmental laws deal with environmental problems on a narrow sectorial basis. Treaties are considered to be autonomous agreements, which can inadvertently lead to improving one environmental system by degrading another.[89]

86 Some fragmentation is, of course, necessary to enable laws to be specific enough to be enforceable. For example, concerning the release of "contaminants" into the environment, see sections 2 and 138A, 15, 15B, 30, 43, 43F, 68, 69, 70, 107, 108, 131 of New Zealand's Resource Management Act 1991.

87 A *grundnorm* is a concept described by Hans Kelsen. He used the word to denote the basic norm order or rule that forms the underlying basis or foundation for a legal system.

88 Bosselmann, K & Botrel, M 2020, 'Constitutionalizing international environmental law', *Sciences Po Law Review*, vol. 18, p. 11, 14.

89 Kotzé & Kim, n 53, at 89. Another example of problem shifting is replacing gasoline with corn ethanol to mitigate climate change, causing water scarcity and eutrophication.

The transformation of climate change to ocean acidification is inadvertently facilitated by the United Nations Framework Convention on Climate Change (UNFCCC). Over the past 200 years, the oceans have absorbed about 40% of the excess atmospheric CO_2 that humans have emitted. Although this natural buffering effect has helped mitigate climate change, the extra carbon taken up by the oceans is making them more acidic. In other words, by design, the climate regime has been knowingly externalizing the costs of mitigating climate change, which has manifested partly as acidifying the ocean.

Adelheidour Jóhannsdóttir has conducted a study to determine why, despite increasing numbers of international laws to ensure biodiversity and ecological sustainability, losses continue unabated. A key finding is what she describes as *the significance of the default.*[90] This arises due to the starting point in our system of law: that environmental use, loss or damage is legal *unless* expressly forbidden. As the environment is unprotected as a whole, individual laws at the national and international level must be enacted to protect different aspects of the environment. This approach inevitably results in gaps or "defaults" in protection.

This happens, of course, because of the lack of an overarching norm or environmental goal operating to protect the environment in the absence of a specific law. Jóhannsdóttir's conclusion is that the significance of the default in the current legal system is large enough to diminish the probability of realizing ecological sustainability.[91]

9. *Utilitarianism.* The theory of utility value is that the best moral action is the one that maximizes happiness and value for the greatest number of people. For example, the environment is dealt with by law mainly in terms of the *benefits* it provides humans – such as "beauty" (by protecting reserves of land for human recreation and enjoyment) and the allocation of "natural resources" (an economic term that describes the utility value of parts of the environment for human use).[92]

The current approach of environmental law is to attempt to limit or mitigate environmental damage rather than to prevent it in the first place. This idea is consistent with national and international environmental law all over the world.

90 Jóhannsdóttir, A 2009, 'The significance of the default, a study in environmental law methodology with emphasis on ecological sustainability and international biodiversity law', Doctor of law, Uppsala University.

91 Jóhannsdóttir, 'The significance of the default'.

92 Bosselmann, n 48, at 2433. See also Bentham, J 2007, *An introduction to the principles of morals and legislation*, Dover Publications, New York. Bentham formulated the principle of utility, which approves of an action insofar as an action has an overall tendency to promote the greatest amount of happiness.

c) *New Zealand's Steps Towards Ecological Integrity*

The 1991 Resource Management Act (RMA) in New Zealand was the world's first legislation to apply the principle of sustainability. Its Section 5 described the Act's purpose as "sustainable management of natural and physical resources" to "meet the reasonably foreseeable needs of future generations" by "safeguarding the life-supporting capacity of air, water, soil and ecosystems".[93] However, the RMA omitted to clearly define sustainability as preserving the integrity of ecological systems as the overarching objective. This caused uncertainty and inconsistency. Initially, commentators, administrators and courts followed the so-called "environmental bottom-lines approach" reflecting strong sustainability. In time, though, the so-called "overall judgement approach" took over.[94] Rather than measuring all human activities against resilience and integrity of ecological systems (strong sustainability), decision-makers and judges increasingly aimed for balancing economic, social and environmental impacts (weak sustainability).[95]

In 2014, the Supreme Court of New Zealand, in a landmark case,[96] ruled that the overall broad judgment approach was not consistent with the purpose description of Section 5 RMA. The Supreme Court moved in the direction of strong sustainability by accepting that the environmental bottom-line approach needs to be followed in specified contexts.[97] Subsequent cases and court decisions, however, delivered mixed results. Eventually, this led to a widely held view that the RMA failed to achieve its purpose and needed to be replaced with a new environmental act. End of 2023, the RMA was replaced by the Natural and Built Environment Act (NBEA).

Remarkably, Section 3 NBEA describes its overarching aim in this way: "The purpose of this Act is to uphold Oranga o te Taio". Sec. 3 (3) explains Oranga o te Taio to include

> all of the following: a) the health of the natural environment; b) the relationship between the health of the natural environment and its capacity to sustain life; c) the relationship between the health of the environment and the health and well-being of people and communities; and d) the interconnectedness of all parts of the environment; and e) the relationship between iwi and hapu and te Taio that is based on whakapapa.

93 Section 5.
94 For example, North Shore City v Auckland Regional Council [1997] NZRMA 59, 94.
95 Bosselmann, K 2017, *The principle of sustainability*, 2nd edn, Routledge, London, pp. 73–82.
96 Environmental Defence Society Inc. v. New Zealand King Salmon Co. Ltd [2014] NZSC 38, [2014] 1 NZLR 593.
97 Bosselmann, n 93, at 76–79.

It is telling that Māori language was chosen to capture what seemingly cannot be fully expressed in English: namely, the interrelationships between nature and people. Oranga o te Taio is very different from the "natural environment" indicating segregation and separation so typical of (Western) environmental law. To further overcome traditional anthropocentrism, Section 5 NBEA prescribes "system outcomes" to ensure that

> the following aspects of the environment are protected or, if degraded, are restored: the ecological integrity, mana[98] and mauri[99] of air, water and soil; the coastal environment (including the coastal marine area and estuaries), wetlands, and lakes and rivers and their margins; and indigenous biodiversity.

The triad of ecological integrity, mana and mauri is of particular significance. It describes the essentials and inherent values of living systems in scientific-philosophical (ecological integrity) and conceptual (mana, mauri) terms. Far from human-centered utilitarianism, they reflect ecological wisdom. Humans and non-humans alike belong to the "community of life" (The Hague Principles)[100] or "Earth Community" (Earth Charter).[101] This brings human responsibilities rather than rights to the fore. Consequently, Part II of the NBEA ("Duties, responsibilities, and restrictions") sets out that everybody has an "environmental responsibility" (Section 13), duties to avoid adverse effects (Section 14) and restrictions relating to land (Sections 17, 18), coastal marine areas (Section 19), and rivers, lakes and water (Sections 20, 21). Taken together, the key elements of the NEBA signal a non-anthropocentric, ecological approach to law and policy.[102] This is, at least, the potential that New Zealand's new legislation holds and in line with the recognition of legal recognition nature.

In 2017, New Zealand became the first country to give legal personhood to a river. The Te Tawa Tupua Act recognizes the Whanganui River as an indivisible and living whole with legal personhood. The river's voice are guardians appointed by local iwi (Māori) and the government.[103] In essence, the river demands legally enforceable respect of its ecological integrity.

98 Meaning dignity, authority, status, spiritual power of all living things.

99 Meaning force, essence and energy of life; mana flows through all living things.

100 The Hague Principles for a Universal Declaration on Responsibilities for Human Rights and Earth Trusteeship (10 December 2018), principle 1.

101 Earth Charter Initiative 2001, *Earth charter*, preamble.

102 See 2016 Oslo Manifesto, *From environmental law to ecological law: a call for re-framing law and governance*, (https://elgaworld.org/oslo-manifesto).

103 Bosselmann, n 95, at 163–165; Bosselmann, K & Williams, T 2020, 'The river as a legal person: the case of the Whanganui River in New Zealand', in SA Ribeiro & VL Catalao (eds), *Water, sharing and peace culture*, International Center on Water and Transdisciplinarity,

New Zealand's moves towards ecological integrity are steps in search for a new direction. With its non-anthropocentric yet scientifically quantifiable characteristics, the concept of ecological integrity holds great promise as will be further explored in the following chapters.

d) *From "Tragedy" to Trusteeship of the Commons*

A key function of environmental law is to provide a set of norms that adequately address the various aspects and areas of the natural environment that need protection. One of the most discussed issues is the gap between ecological systems defying any national boundaries and legal systems divided up between nation states. States govern their territories but not areas outside national boundaries. These areas are known as "global commons". The United Nations Environment Programme (UNEP) defines the global commons as follows:[104]

> The "global commons" refers to resource domains or areas that lie outside of the political reach of any one Nation State. Thus, international law identifies four global commons namely: The High Seas; the Atmosphere; Antarctica; and Outer Space. These areas have historically been guided by the principle of the common heritage of humankind – the open access doctrine or the *mare liberum* (free sea for everyone).

Though not the first person to identify it, Garrett Hardin wrote a seminal article on the "tragedy of the commons".[105] This has generated continuing discussion and debate as to how the commons might best be protected. The article is essentially about the need for human population control on a finite planet if we expect to live what he describes as the "good life". Hardin notes that it is not rational or possible to maximize "the greatest good for the greatest number" without addressing a continually growing population

Brasilia, pp. 169–178. See also Martin, R 2023, 'The river as a separate legal person: implications for sustainability law and governance', *Environmental and Planning Law Journal*, vol. 39, p. 166.

104 United Nations Environment Programme, *IEG of the global commons: background*, Division of Environmental Law and Conventions, (https://cil.nus.edu.sg/wp-content/uploads/2015/12/Ses4-7.-UNEP-Division-of-Environmental-Law-and-Conventions-Global-Commons.pdf/). The need to address environmental issues of the global commons has been of concern for a long time now. A number of legal frameworks exist to deal with the global commons. For example, the United Nations Convention on the Law of the Sea (UNCLOS) contains parts that are dedicated to managing the world's oceans. The UNEP has stated that while there are some regulatory and institutional frameworks in place for the commons, there are also fundamental inconsistencies and gaps requiring immediate attention.

105 Hardin, 'The tragedy of the commons'.

seeking access to a limited finite pool of natural resources. His conclusion is that "ruin is the destination toward which all men rush, each pursuing his own best interest in a society that believes in the freedoms of the commons. Freedom of the commons brings ruin to all".[106]

Hardin refers to Aristotle's statement that "what is common to the greatest number gets the least amount of care".[107] The idea behind the statement is that people pay the most attention to what is their own and care less about what is commonly or communally held. Unfettered free use of the global commons allows each individual to externalize any costs associated with that use while, at the same time, internalizing all benefits they may reap. This, of course, is why the problem arises of taking more from the commons than is sustainable.

The introduction of property rights to regulate overuse of the commons is one solution. Harold Demsetz proposed a theory setting out three categories of ownership – communal, private and state. He suggests that private ownership is the best model to plan and to protect claims of future generations.[108]

Alexander Pearle takes a different approach and introduces a new category of commons, which he describes as *vital commons*. This refers to those things that cannot easily be compartmentalized, are essential to human existence and must support a massive population. His argument is that the traditional response of introducing private property rights as a solution to the tragic overuse of vital commons makes things considerably worse.

Pearle uses the example of the Ogallala Aquifer, which runs under and supplies ground water to eight states in the United States of America. The rate at which the water is currently being taken is unsustainable and causing a drop in the water table, while the population in the region and demand for the water continues to grow and shows no signs of slowing. He comments that the aquifer is most seriously compromised under the state of Texas, which has *by far the strongest conception of private property rights in groundwater* of the affected states.[109] A key reason property theory does not appear to work for vital commons is that there is no right to exclude another from use of those commons. Each landowner has a co-equal property right to pump groundwater with no limitation. Without the right to exclude, the commons

106 Hardin, 'The tragedy of the commons'.
107 Hardin, 'The tragedy of the commons'.
108 Demsetz, H 1967, 'Toward a theory of property rights', *American Economic Review*, vol. 51, no. 2, p. 347. See also Grinlinton, D & Taylor, P (eds) 2011, *Property rights and sustainability: the evolution of property rights to meet ecological challenges*, Martinus Nijhoff, Amsterdam.
109 Pearle A 2015, 'The tragedy of the vital commons', *Environmental Law*, vol. 45, no. 4, p. 1021, 1051. See also Texas Water Code §36.002 (2015), which states, "The legislature recognises that a landowner owns the groundwater below the surface of the landowner's land as real property".

remain overused. And, in this case, the strength of the property rights exacerbates the tragedy of the commons:[110]

> The absence of the right to exclude is what allows the tragedy of the privatised commons to exist. Without the right to exclude, privatisation creates the exact same circumstances as Hardin's tragedy of the commons: overuse is not curtailed by other users and continues unchecked until total exhaustion. . . . The next thing a landowner will do when her wells begin to run dry is ask why extraction is not regulated. Immediately, the most ardent proponents of private property and groundwater are transformed into "Marxist-statist-regulatory" advocates. Why? . . . [T]he externalities of cost have been internalised; they are no longer blind to or ignorant of them.

Pearle concludes his discussion by recommending that United States' federal law is needed to deconstruct private property rights to pump unlimited amounts of groundwater. He further suggests a well-funded commission for the aquifer with the ability to monitor and model groundwater resources and invest in efficiency-enhancing infrastructure. "Technology will not solve the problem, but it should be employed to mitigate and conserve every drop".[111]

Hardin viewed putting faith in our sense of ethics or morality for the use of common resources as admirable but not sufficient on its own to protect the commons. He also introduced the idea that the commons are *systems-sensitive* in terms of ethics and morality, providing two examples:[112]

> Analysis of the pollution problem as a function of population density uncovers a not generally recognised principle of morality, namely: *the morality of an act is a function of the state of the system at the time it is performed.* Using the commons as a cesspool does not harm the general public under frontier conditions because there is no public; the same behaviour in a metropolis is unbearable. . . .
>
> Hundred and fifty years ago a plainsman could kill an American bison, cut out only the tongue for his dinner, and discard the rest of the animal. He was not in any important sense being wasteful. Today, with only a few thousand bison left, we would be appalled at such behaviour.

This idea that our actions and how they are perceived are *systems sensitive* is one that is starting to be explored in looking for innovative ways to preserve

110 Pearle, n 109 at 1053, 1055.

111 At 1060.

112 Hardin, n 105, at 1245. Here, Hardin gives an example of putting something "into" the commons (pollution) not taking something out; however the principle of overuse is the same.

global public resources. It is now well understood that cooperation to protect global goods often works very well in small, closely connected social groups but breaks down and becomes difficult to achieve in larger groups, particularly at global or international levels.

A study by the Program for Evolutionary Dynamics at Harvard University[113] looked at experiments focusing on successful interactions and cooperation within small groups (and how to upscale these successes to large groups). The study proposed a first technical solution to the problem of accessing the power of the local to global reciprocity through the development of a novel online software platform to conduct large-scale economic game experiments.

The findings show that direct reciprocity can, in fact, be maintained within large groups *if each individual has even a very small number of pairwise interactions*. The conclusion reached is that developing theoretical models of interaction between pairwise and large group interactions is an important direction for future research in the protection of the global commons. There is an untapped potential for environmental law scholars to participate in similar future experiments of this kind by exploring regulatory models at national and international levels that might utilize such technology to protect the commons.

Elinor Ostrom's work on management of common pool resources (for which she received the 2009 Nobel Prize in Economic Sciences) identified three areas requiring further research that could lead to better legal and governance models protecting the commons:[114]

1. Comprehensive policy analysis of the existing management of common pool resources. Recognising that no "one-size-fits-all". Each resource and its connections and interactions with other resources and with human needs and use, require full discovery.
2. Empirical study into historical attempts to manage these common resources. What has worked? What has failed and why?
3. Research and work on developing better tools to understand self-governing institutions.

Ostrom stated that:[115]

> What one can observe in the world . . . is that neither the state nor the market is uniformly successful in enabling individuals to sustain long-term productive use of natural resource systems.

113 Hauser, O, Hendriks, A, Rand, D & Nowak, M 2016, *Think global, act local: preserving the global commons*, Scientific Reports 6, November 2016.

114 Ostrom, E 1990, *Governing the commons: the evolution of institutions for collective action*, Cambridge University Press, Cambridge at Chapter 1.

115 At 8.

Her conclusion was that there are no simple solutions. Rather, a mix of regulations, laws, market forces and community-based management will be required.[116]

e) *Redefining "Nature"*

> The Anthropocene confirms that society and nature are not two separate entities influencing each other, but rather there exists a socio-natural entanglement – that is, an irreversible, complex and increasingly hybrid socio-natural system.[117]

The tragedy of the commons dilemma illustrates clearly the entanglement of humans with the environment, which becomes more obvious as these common resources deplete.

Manuel Arias-Maldonado suggests that the environment or "nature" no longer exists on Earth in the untouched or wild sense. No part of nature is now unaffected by the human enterprise. We must, as a result, redefine our understanding of nature in a way that *includes* ourselves. The Anthropocene might just be what is required, enabling new conversations about the human/nature relationship.[118]

The Anthropocene starts with an acknowledgment that humans not only affect every aspect of nature but are also now a major force with formidable transformative power that can be used either to destroy or to preserve the environment. This requires that we re-evaluate the normative approaches towards the environment in law and governance. Paradoxically, it is the historical and cultural act of separation from nature that creates the distance that allows us to become aware of the entanglements and raises new possibilities for rearranging the socio-natural relationship. How do we correctly re-position human influence within these systems?

Climate change again is an early attempt to grapple with this new paradigm, in which the duality of the human/nature relationship has broken down:[119]

> From a philosophical point-of-view, nature is now human nature; there is no more wild nature to be found, just ecosystems and different states of human interaction, differing in wildness and humanness.

116 At 8. See also Berkes, F & Palmer, T 2015, 'Managing shared resources: collective community action is the best way to close the curtain on the tragedy of the commons', *Alternatives Journal*, vol. 41, no. 1, p. 67.

117 Arias-Maldonado, M 2016, 'Nature and the Anthropocene: the sense of an ending?', in P Pattberg & F Zelli (eds), *Environmental politics and governance in the Anthropocene, institutions and legitimacy in a complex world*, 1st edn, Routledge, London, p. 33.

118 At 1.

119 Ellis, EC 2011, 'Anthropogenic transformation of the terrestrial biosphere', *Philosophical Transactions of the Royal Society*, vol. 369, p. 1010, 1027. See also, Williams, M,

This raises an enormous responsibility and puts an end to the assumption of human exceptionalism while, at the same time, confirming the human ability to change the natural environment. It is recognition of this power which raises the moral and ethical implications that confront us in the Anthropocene:

- What are the *intentional* modifications we have made to nature?
- What are the *unintentional* side effects from these modifications?
- What are the influences of nature on humans as a result of these modifications? How does nature's response in turn then alter our courses of action?
- What frameworks (in terms of law and governance structure) are necessary to ensure the nature/human system is able to thrive in sustainable and healthy ways?
- What legal rules, norms or *grundnorms* will facilitate this aim?

Proceeding into the future entails rethinking how we are *inhabiting* the world. Any retreat from nature for humans is a cultural delusion, which could result in our species extinction if we fail to recognize and protect those ecological systems that sustain us.

Human domination of nature must become human stewardship of nature, which includes an understanding of the interconnections between social and natural systems and assimilates scientific information on reaching and passing ecological tipping points.

Control of the system is no longer the control of nature but the control of human nature. This is both the promise and the challenge of the Anthropocene.[120] As Arias-Maldonado pithily points out; "the experiment after all, can't be stopped. It might thus better be successful".[121]

> Sustainability is then taken as the central concept and practical goal around which the reflection on socio-natural relations revolves. In this regard, a post-natural sustainability involves a conscious control of complicated socio-natural relations and an acceptance of the role that science and technology have to play in our attempt to rearrange such relations.

Zalasiewicz, J, Haff, PK, Schwägerl, C, Barnosky, AD & Ellis, EC 2015, 'The Anthropocene biosphere', *The Anthropocene Review*, vol. 2, no. 3, p. 196, 197.

120 See for example, Baskini, J 2015, 'Paradigm dressed as epoch: the ideology of the anthropocene', *Environmental Values*, vol. 24, no. 1, p. 9, 16–18.

121 Arias-Maldonado, n 117, at 45.

Chapter 2

The Earth System Approach

Facing the possibility of overstepping our planetary boundaries, a key question we must ask ourselves is how we organize human endeavours in a way that create the right conditions for human and non-human life to flourish. What are the boundaries or safe operating space within which we must organize ourselves to achieve this goal? The current legal and institutional framework is inadequate for the task of keeping human impacts within planetary boundaries. It has been too focused on economic systems, neglecting the creation of equitable social systems and the wider ecological context within which everything else operates. As a result, we are faced with the continuous deterioration of global ecological systems such as the atmosphere, biodiversity and the oceans – but also human systems such as the economy, financial markets and societies. In order to reverse this trend, there needs to be recognition that ecological and human systems are now fully entangled and can only function in an interdependent fashion.

Protecting and restoring the integrity of both human and ecological systems must guide the way we design our legal and institutional framework. To appreciate this, we must first understand why existing arrangements are ineffective and insufficient. Fundamentally, there is a mismatch between the Earth system and national interests and also a mismatch between the national interests of wealthy countries and poorer ones.

The aim of this book is to set out, as clearly as possible, the requirements for a radical re-conception of environmental law and governance and the challenges faced in first, creating a safe operating space and second, bringing true and meaningful sustainable development, with ecological integrity at its core, into that safe space.

We must also recognize that continuing advances of knowledge in the sciences and in technology may alter the parameters of that safe operating space. We must be conscious of our hubris in assuming that after using up the planet's resources, technological solutions will always be able to

DOI: 10.4324/9781032674049-4

replace such overuse. Even if this were true, is it a world we would choose to live in?[1]

Not only is Earth system science the study of the physical processes of atmospheric chemistry, oceanic circulation, biodiversity, ecosystem physiology et cetera, but it is also the study of the complex interaction of human beings with the environment. Its core function is to work out how to retain the Eden-like Holocene state that has fostered human and ecological health. There is a strong focus on understanding the deeply embedded connections between the sub-systems and how these affect the global system. Earth system science contains a level of complexity well beyond the scope or understanding of any one discipline and reflects most accurately the true complexity of modern life. Undaunted, it attempts to uncover the socio-ecological system that already exists and is a moving target, constantly mutating in unexpected ways. It calls for a community of human effort from all directions and a flexibility in law and in democratic governance structures that can adapt and keep pace with the new knowledge and changing aspects of the earth system.

1. Living Within Planetary Boundaries

As human impact on the planet increases, the chances of achieving well-being for everyone and sustainability of natural resource use at global, national and local levels grows dimmer. We only have one planet, and yet, the Global Footprint Network calculates that we already use the equivalent of 1.75 Earths to provide for current annual resource use, with this measure set to rise to 2 Earths by the 2030s.[2] The calculation is based on how quickly the planet can regenerate what we actually use in a year. Whatever measure is used to determine Earth system resilience, it is clear that we are living on borrowed natural capital, which at some point must be repaid. The situation causes an ecological overshoot that, over time, steadily erodes the planet's

1 Tribe, 'Ways not to think about plastic trees', p. 1315, 1341. Tribe suggested that a perception that nature exists for itself should be given institutional expression, and a sense of human obligation towards the natural world should be developed.

2 Information provided is based on data collected from 2017 to 2021 from the Global Footprint Network's National Footprint and Biocapacity Accounts published in 2021. See Global Footprint Network, *Ecological footprint*, (www.footprintnetwork.org). The figure is averaged out over the whole global population. The average American uses 8 global hectares, compared to the global average of 2.77. It is this figure of 8 global hectares that allows some to calculate that it would take 5 Earths to sustain a population of seven billion at American levels of consumption. The United States does not consume the most on this measure. It is ranked eighth with Qatar on top with 14.7 global hectares (9.2 Earths), followed by Luxembourg (8 Earths), United Arab Emirates (5.6 Earths), Bahrain (5.4 Earths) and Australia (4.6 Earths). Others in the top 15 are Canada, Trinidad and Tobago, Mongolia and Denmark. See also McDonald, C 2015, 'How many earths do we need?', *BBC News* (16 June 2015), (www.bbc.com).

resilience levels and ability to support life, including our lives and those of future generations.[3]

International environmental law has attempted to stem the damage but has been largely unsuccessful, except at local and problem-specific levels. Vital questions environmental law scholars grapple with are: How can the law protect the natural environment both *from* humanity and *for* humanity? Has the time finally arrived to consider protecting the environment simply for its own sake and beyond our own human interests? And why is it that the body of law so far created does not actually protect the environment except in a sporadic and localized fashion?

These questions raise issues that range far outside the traditional purview of the law. Who are we as human beings? What is our place, and how do we fit into the natural world? Since Darwin, we have come to understand how closely embedded we are with all other life, and yet, the differences are highlighted too. We now have the power to dramatically alter the natural environment as evidenced by the fact that our activities appear to have created a whole new era of geology called the Anthropocene. Does this new power then carry new responsibilities of stewardship of the planet?

Andrew Revkin[4] describes this era as one of both our own making and our own choosing – a new and uncomfortable situation unknown to any other species. He sees our level of evolutionary development as being similar to the delicate juncture between adolescence and adulthood, a transition that is never easy and is slow and halting. As a species, we are beginning to recognize the difference between being in a fast sprint (our industrialization of the planet) and a long-distance marathon, in which we must be conscious of our limits and settle in for the long haul:[5]

> We are almost at that juncture that an individual human goes through from adolescence to adulthood. Adolescence is that pure muscle flexing "Wow! Look what I can do" period and, essentially the last couple of hundred years have been like that. We have celebrated our industrialisation and our potency. . . . [A]nd now, the indicators from science are that we

3 Intergovernmental Panel on Climate Change and Masson-Delmotte, V, Zhai, P, et al. (eds) 2021, Climate change 2021: the physical science basis. Contribution of Working Group I to the Sixth Assessment Report of the Intergovernmental Panel on Climate Change, Cambridge University Press. The models incorporate many linked ecological and social system processes. See also, Bradshaw, CJ, Ehrlich, PR, Beattie, A, Ceballos, G, Crist, E, Diamond, J, Dirzo, R, Ehrlich, AH, Harte, J, Harte, ME & Pyke, G 2021, 'Underestimating the challenges of avoiding a ghastly future', Frontiers in Conservation Science.

4 Andrew Revkin is a science and environmental writer, was a reporter at *The New York Times* from 1995 to 2009 and is a senior fellow for environmental understanding at the Pace Academy for Applied Environmental Studies at Pace University, New York.

5 Revkin, A 2011, 'Confronting the Anthropocene: a new era', (2 September 2011), (www.youtube.com).

are approaching limits. We are like a bacteria that's been put on a petrie dish and we now see that there is an edge to that dish.

Exacerbating the problem is that the current paradigm operates on the false assumption that limitless growth is possible on a finite planet. To correct this fallacy will require deep and difficult re-evaluations of almost everything about how we choose to live, our legal system, our financial system and our methods of local, global and social organization. Notwithstanding that the numbers of environmental treaties and soft law documents continues to grow,[6] the destruction of the natural environment continues at pace. Why is this so when almost everyone can agree that we must do our best to protect it? Why do our legal, financial and social tools seem helpless in the face of an increasingly worrying situation?

The idea that there will be dangerous, even catastrophic, consequences for humanity if we do not respect the boundaries and limits of the planet's ecosystems is not a new one. This view, although expressed in a different form, was common during the 1970s "limits to growth" discourse.[7] This idea failed to gain international traction, as evidenced by the Brundtland Report in 1987,[8] which introduced the concept of "sustainable development". This was then interpreted to mean that choices are to be made by equally balancing the interests of the environment, of people and of economic development. The creation of "sustainable development", sometimes referred to as "weak sustainability", has been extremely popular and internationally successful – precisely because of its ability to be all things to all people. However, it must arguably take a large piece of responsibility for why we continue the march towards and over the limits of the natural environment's ability to support and sustain us.

One of the difficulties for proponents of strong sustainability[9] at the time of the Brundtland Report was the lack of scientific knowledge and ability to measure ecosystem limits. A further concern was that accepting *any* ecological limits would stifle economic growth and consign the developing Third

6 Frank Biermann and others count over 900 environmental treaties in force. See Biermann, F, Abbott, K, Andresen, S, Bäckstrand, K, Bernstein, S, Betsill, MM, Bulkeley, H, Cashore, B, Clapp, J, Folke, C & Gupta, A 2012, 'Transforming governance and institutions for global sustainability: key insights from the earth system project', *Current Opinion in Environmental Sustainability*, vol. 4, no. 1, pp. 51–60. See also Kim, R 2013, 'Unravelling the maze of multilateral environmental agreements: a macroscopic analysis of international environmental law and governance in the anthropocene', PhD thesis, Australian National University. Kim collates a list of 747 multilateral environmental agreements.

7 Meadows, DH, Meadows, DL, Randers, J & Behrens, W 1972, *The limits to growth*, Universe Books, New York. See also Carson, R 1962, *Silent spring*, Houghton Mifflin, Boston.

8 World Commission on Environment and Development, 'Brundtland report (our common future)', UNGA A/42/427 (4 August 1987).

9 "Strong sustainability" here means making development decisions within ecological limits.

World to poverty and the inability to grow and develop in the same way that Western countries had.

These same issues arise again when considering the new science of planetary boundaries.[10] However, we now have the ability to measure the resilience of specific ecosystems and make normative choices as to where guardrails or boundaries of safety should be set. The focus on planetary limits this time around highlights *where* the bulk of resource consumption is taking place and clearly exposes huge social equity issues that exist not only between the developing and the developed world but also, more recently, between the haves and have-nots, showing a worrying and widening gap developing.

Social scientists are perceptibly more engaged in exploring ways to introduce questions of human and environmental ethics and values into the planetary boundary and sustainable development discussions,[11] which is leading to efforts to create models that can equalize the global social and environmental inequities that exist.[12] Unlike the earlier "limits to growth" discussions, the planetary boundary science highlights the issues with empirical information.

In 2015, the International Geosphere-Biosphere Programme and the Stockholm Resilience Centre published an updated dashboard of 24 indicators showing the dramatic acceleration of human impact on the planet and highlighting two key trends.[13] The first is the exponential acceleration of natural resource use since the 1950s, and the second is that, from the period of 1750 to 2010, while the BRICS countries (Brazil, Russia, India, China and South Africa) were showing a significant contribution to world production, the greatest share of consumption was still occurring in the wealthy Organization for Economic Cooperation and Development (OECD) countries, even though it has a much smaller proportion of the global population:[14]

> In 2010, the OECD countries accounted for 74% of global GDP but only 18% of the global population. Insofar as the imprint on the Earth System

10 Rockström, J, Steffen, W, Noone, K, Persson, Å, Chapin, FS, III, Lambin, E, Lenton, TM, Scheffer, M, Folke, C, Schellnhuber, HJ & Nykvist, B 2009, 'Planetary boundaries: exploring the safe operating space for humanity', *Ecology and Society*, vol. 14, no. 2, p. 32.

11 Wilson, I & Henning, PB 2015, 'A call to action for the systems science community', Proceedings of the 59th Annual Meeting of the International Society for the Systems Sciences, vol. I, Berlin, Germany, 2–7 August 2015.

12 See for example, Raworth, K 2012, *A safe and just space for humanity: can we live within the doughnut?*, Oxfam International, 13 February 2012, (https://www.oxfam.org/en/research/safe-and-just-space-humanity). See also Future earth: research for global sustainability, (www.futureearth.org).

13 At 86. These graphs were first published in Steffen, W, Sanderson, RA, Tyson, PD, Jäger, J, Matson, PA, Moore, B, III, Oldfield, F, Richardson, K, Schellnhuber, HJ, Turner, BL, & Wasson, RJ 2004, *Global change and the earth system: a planet under pressure*, 1st edn, IGBP Global Change Series, Springer, Germany.

14 Steffen, et al., n 13, at 91. Emphasis added.

> scales with consumption, most of the human imprint on the Earth System is coming from the OECD world. This points to the profound scale of global inequality, which distorts the distribution of the benefits of the Great Acceleration and confounds efforts to deal with its impacts on the earth system. . . . [Therefore, by treating "humans" as a single, monolithic whole, it ignores the fact that the Great Acceleration has, until very recently, been almost entirely driven by a small fraction of the human population, those in developed countries.

However, this started to change dramatically over the last decade. From 2010 to 2021, the BRICS GDP rose from US$12.6 to over US$25 trillion.[15] As result of this rapid economic progress, they were responsible for more than 42% of the world's CO_2 emissions in 2019,[16] with China standing as the top global emitter by the sole contribution of 10.06 GT of CO_2 and India being the third largest (2.65 GT).[17] Besides CO_2 emissions, China, India, Brazil and Russia are now four of the five countries with the largest ecological footprint in the world.[18] But although the extreme inequalities between the developed and developing countries have fallen, today's global injustice is at record levels, with 76% of total wealth in the hands of billionaires (top 10%)[19] and nearly half of humanity living on less than US$5.50 a day.[20]

> Despite the contribution of these and other developments to bringing many people in the non-OECD world out of absolute poverty, inequalities in income and wealth both within and between countries continue to be a significant problem, with consequences for individual and societal wellbeing.

15 Lin, J, Shen, Y, Li, X & Hasnaoui, A 2021, 'BRICS carbon neutrality target: measuring the impact of electricity production from renewable energy sources and globalization', *Journal of Environmental Management*, vol. 298, p. 113460 at 2.

16 BP 2021, *Statistical review of world energy*, 70th edn. See also, Pata, UK 2021, 'Linking renewable energy, globalization, agriculture, CO_2 emissions and ecological footprint in BRIC countries: a sustainable perspective', *Renewable Energy*, vol. 173, pp. 197–208.

17 By way of comparison, the USA sits as the second largest emitter of carbon dioxide with 4.71 GT in 2020. See Global Carbon Atlas, *World map fossil fuels emissions in 2020*, (http://www.globalcarbonatlas.org/en/CO2-emissions) (Accessed 2 February 2022).

18 Global Footprint Network 2018, *Has humanity's ecological footprint reached its peak?*, 9 April, (https://www.footprintnetwork.org/2018/04/09/has_humanitys_ecological_footprint_reached_its_peak/). The ecological footprint indicator was first proposed by Wackernagel, M & Rees, W 1996, *Our ecological footprint: reducing human impact on the earth*, The New Catalyst Bioregional Series, New Society Publishers. This is a reliable cumulative environmental indicator that allows simultaneous analysis of air, water and soil pollution in order to calculate human pressure on the planet.

19 Lucas Chancel and others, World Inequality Report 2022 (World Inequality Lab, 2022) at 11.

20 Steffen, et al., n 13, at 91.

Johan Rockström, director of the Potsdam Institute for Climate Impact Research, stated that our old sustainable development paradigm is fundamentally flawed and obsolete.[21] We now need to recognize that the economy has grown at the expense of both human and natural capital and come back to a logic in which the economy is used as a tool – for example, to eradicate poverty and hunger – and that this must occur within the limits of a safe operating space. If we now perceive that we have finite budgets for carbon, the hydrological cycle and phosphorus et cetera, we can see that these resources must be shared equitably amongst the people of the world in a truly sustainable fashion. Statements from developed countries, which have historically used up the bulk of the world's resources (and continue to do so), that their lifestyles are not up for negotiation become obsolete in the face of the new evidence.

The concept of planetary boundaries has been promoted by the world's top scientific journals and referred to in United Nations programmes, though not without experiencing resistance.[22] This is largely due to the climate change discourse, which Earth system science highlights as one of the key boundaries humanity should not cross.

2. Earth System Science

In 1986, the International Geosphere Biosphere Programme was formed and became the first major international scientific collaboration to conceptualize Earth as a single organism and system.[23] Earth system science attempts to understand and expand knowledge of how the planet works as a complete system, including the interacting physical, chemical and biological global – and, increasingly, also local – scale cycles and energy fluxes that make up the life-support system at the surface of the planet. This includes the impacts of humans, which means that we do not sit outside the Earth system but are an integral part of it.[24] Planetary boundary science grew out of Earth system science and represents a major paradigm shift in the way that science

21 Rockström, J 2015, 'Bounding the planetary future: why we need a great transition', *Great Transition Initiative* (April 2015), (https://greattransition.org/publication/bounding-the-planetary-future-why-we-need-a-great-transition).

22 Rockström, J 2015, *Planetary boundaries and the anthropocene* (27 November 2015), (www.youtube.com).

23 Biermann, F & Kim, RE 2020, 'The boundaries of the planetary boundary framework: a critical appraisal of approaches to define a "safe operating space" for humanity', *Annual Review of Environment and Resources*, vol. 45, pp. 497–521, at 501–504; Saunders, FP 2015, 'Planetary boundaries: at the threshold . . . again: sustainable development ideas and politics', *Environment, Development and Sustainability*, vol. 17, p. 823, 828.

24 Seitzinger, SP, Gaffney, O, Brasseur, G, Broadgate, W, Ciais, P, Claussen, M, Erisman, JW, Kiefer, T, Lancelot, C, Monks, PS & Smyth, K 2016, 'International geosphere-biosphere programme and earth system science: three decades of co-evolution', *Anthropocene*, vol. 12, p. 3.

approaches and understands the natural world.[25] Recognition of the importance of ecosystem and social system connections now places great emphasis on interdisciplinary work on how the overall Earth system functions.

a) Planetary Boundaries and the Safe Operating Space

Planetary boundaries define a safe operating space for humanity based on evolving understanding of the functioning and resilience of the planet. The physical conditions of the Holocene period have been recognized as most beneficial for human development. It is during the Holocene that most of our evolution has taken place; this is as a result of the stable global temperature remaining within a narrow band of plus or minus one to two degrees. The Holocene environment has predictable and stable seasons, within which humans have evolved from small nomadic hunter-gatherer groups to settled locations, developing agriculture, then industrialization and now the technological age. The Eden-like state of the Holocene has facilitated our ability to thrive, resulting in vast increases in human population numbers.

The underlying premise of planetary boundary science is that we have now entered a new geological age of our own making called the Anthropocene. In May 2019, the Working Group on the Anthropocene voted in favor of designating a new epoch starting around the mid–20th century,[26] on the grounds that the human-dominating presence in the natural world is of sufficient scale to have the potential to drive the Earth system out of the Holocene. Will Steffen, Earth system scientist and advisory member of the Working Group, and colleagues explained:[27]

> A continuing trajectory away from the Holocene could lead, with an uncomfortably high probability, to a very different state of the earth system, one that is likely to be much less hospitable to the development of human societies. The PB [planetary boundaries] framework aims to help guide human societies away from such a trajectory by defining a "safe

25 Steffen, W, Sanderson, RA, Tyson, PD, Jäger, J, Matson, PA, Moore, B, III, Oldfield, F, Richardson, K, Schellnhuber, HJ, Turner, BL & Wasson, RJ 2004, *Global change and the earth system: a planet under pressure*, Springer, Heidelberg, p. 7.

26 Subcommission on Quaternary Stratigraphy 2019, 'Working Group on the Anthropocene', Results of binding vote by AWG (21 May 2019), (http://quaternary.stratigraphy.org/working-groups/anthropocene/).The geological interpretation of the Anthropocene as a new epoch remains to be formally adopted within the competent chronostratigraphic body, the International Commission on Stratigraphy. The result of the voting was expected to take place in December 2022. See Working Group on the Anthropocene, Newsletter of the Anthropocene Working Group, *Report of activities 2020*, vol. 10 (Subcommission on Quaternary Stratigraphy, December 2020).

27 Steffen, W, Richardson, K, Rockström, J, Cornell, SE, Fetzer, I, Bennett, EM, Biggs, R, Carpenter, SR, De Vries, W, De Wit, CA & Folke, C 2015, 'Planetary boundaries: guiding human development on a changing planet', *Science*, vol. 347, p. 1, 2.

> operating space" in which we can continue to develop and thrive. It does this by proposing boundaries for anthropogenic perturbation of critical earth system processes. Respecting these boundaries would greatly reduce the risk that anthropogenic activities could inadvertently drive the earth system to a much less hospitable state.

The updated Planetary Boundaries framework (2023) identifies nine boundaries relevant to the Earth system[28] and stipulates that six of them have been crossed.[29] The boundaries are not set at the tipping points into unknown states. Rather, the human-determined values are set at a safe distance from a dangerous level. Determining a safe distance obviously involves normative value judgments on how societies choose to deal with risk and uncertainty:[30]

> Much of the uncertainty in quantifying planetary boundaries is due to our lack of scientific knowledge about the nature of the biophysical thresholds themselves. . . . This generates a zone of uncertainty around each threshold. . . . A boundary is designed to avoid the crossing of a critical continental to global threshold in an earth system process. Insufficient knowledge and the dynamic nature of the threshold generate a zone of uncertainty about its precise position, which informs the determination of where to place the boundary.

The safe operating space (green zone) sits below the zone of uncertainty and the area of high risk (red zone). Most of the conjecture in setting the boundaries has been due to incomplete knowledge about biophysical thresholds, which generates a "zone of uncertainty" around each threshold. A great deal of debate has occurred around where threshold levels should be and where boundaries should be set. Researchers have used the precautionary approach, pointing out that it would be unwise for human societies to push the Earth system too far away from Holocene conditions into an unknown state that is highly likely to be less hospitable to humans.

The boundary "novel entities" includes not just chemical pollution but also new types of technologically engineered materials and organisms and their transformation products, which have the potential to cause effects on

28 Climate Change, Biosphere Integrity, Land-System Change, Freshwater Use, Biochemical Flows, Ocean Acidification, Atmospheric Aerosol Loading, Stratospheric Ozone Depletion and Novel Entities.

29 https://www.stockholmresilience.org/research/planetary-boundaries.html Based on analysis in Persson, L, Carney Almroth, BM, Collins, CD, Cornell, S, De Wit, CA, Diamond, ML, Fantke, P, Hassellöv, M, MacLeod, M, Ryberg, MW & Søgaard Jørgensen, P 2022, 'Outside the safe operating space of the planetary boundary for novel entities', *Environmental Science & Technology*, vol. 56, pp. 1510–1521, and Steffen, et al., n 27.

30 Rockström, et al., n 10, at 34.

Earth system processes.[31] In 2022, 14 Earth system scientists, led by Linn Persson, concluded that the novel entities boundary is exceeded and elevated plastic pollution as an issue of high concern in this regard. They argued that even if production and release of emissions of novel entities were to be stabilized or reduced, the effects caused by the transgression will continue to pose a threat due to the persistence of many novel entities and their associated effects. In other words, we will never be able to return to the safe operating space of this boundary if we continue at this unsustainable pace of mass global production and use (mainly of plastics, pesticides and other industrial chemicals). As measures enabling the mitigation of current damages and avoid futures threats, Persson and colleagues encourage "a higher degree of circularity in product supply chains, material and product design, design for recycling, and safe and sustainable chemicals," as well as addressing "the issue of inequitable resource distribution and affluence".[32]

The biosphere integrity boundary highlights the current rate of species loss, which is primarily driven by human activity. Biodiversity loss is a separate boundary in the planetary boundary structure because non-human species maintain important ecosystem services for humans.[33]

The ocean acidification boundary shows rates of acidification occurring faster than any time in the last several million years. The biogeochemical boundary shows that changes in the global phosphorus and nitrogen cycles have induced unexpected biochemical shifts in rivers and lakes. Human impact on the nitrogen cycle is profound, with human activity converting more nitrogen into reactive forms than the entire world terrestrial processes.

The freshwater use boundary shows that humans are the stimulus behind altered global scale river flow, with 25% of the world's basins run dry before reaching the oceans, and large dams now substantially change natural flow patterns. The land-system change boundary identifies the removal of natural carbon sinks (driven largely by agriculture) with risks of undermining long-term sustainability.[34]

b) Social Science's Contribution to the Safe Operating Space

In line with the new systems thinking approach, the emergence of the "environmental humanities" within the social sciences has taken place. Although

31 Rockström, et al., n 10, at 34. See also, Hochella, MF, Mogk, DW, Ranville, J, Allen, IC, Luther, GW, Marr, LC, McGrail, BP, Murayama, M, Qafoku, NP, Rosso, KM & Sahai, N 2019, 'Natural, incidental, and engineered nanomaterials and their impacts on the Earth system', *Science*, vol. 29:363, no. 6434, p. eaau8299.

32 Persson, n 29, at 1517.

33 For example, non-human species pollinating crops for human agricultural/food purposes.

34 Agriculture occupies 38% of the Earth's surface, the largest single land use.

historically, the humanities focused on the human world only, Earth system science necessarily includes the human world and has led to growing participation from the humanities as environmental issues are now seen as "inescapably entangled with human ways of being in the world".[35]

The humanities' traditional stomping grounds are issues of human values, ethics, and justice and knowledge production. However, Deborah Rose and others point out that:[36]

> In bringing these questions into environmental domains, we are able to articulate a "thicker" notion of humanity, one that rejects reductionist accounts of self-contained, rational, decision-making subjects. . . . [T]he Anthropocene unmakes the idea of the unlimited, autonomous human and calls for a radical reworking of a great deal of what we thought we knew about ourselves and the humanities as fields of enquiry. How can our accumulated knowledge and practice, built up over centuries, be refashioned to meet these new challenges, and to productively rethink the human in more than human terms?

Two key tasks set out by Val Plumwood are to re-position "*the human*" within the environment and to re-position "*the environment*" within human cultural and ethical domains.[37] Nigel Clark also reframes the debate, seeing ethics as much more than a consideration of classic moral dilemmas but as a condition of social life itself.[38]

One of the criticisms of the planetary boundaries' safe operating space was a failure to identify some of these human issues. Kate Raworth took the planetary boundary concept further, combining it with the complementary concept of a social floor with "social boundaries".[39]

Raworth's expanded concept combined hard planetary boundary science with a social science foundation, forming an inner boundary and creating what is commonly referred to as "the doughnut". The space between the two boundaries creates a safe zone within which sustainable development can take place. The internal area represents an environmentally safe and socially just space. The framework brings a new approach to sustainable development, creating a closed system that is bounded at the upper limits by

35 Rose, DB, Van Dooren, T, Chrulew, M, Cooke, S, Kearnes, M & O'Gorman, E 2012, 'Thinking through the environment: unsettling the humanities', *Environmental Humanities*, vol. 1, p. 1, 2.

36 Rose, et al., 'Thinking through the environment'.

37 At 3. See also Plumwood, V 2002, *Environmental culture: the ecological crisis of reason*, Routledge, London.

38 Clark, N 2017, 'Geosocial formations and the anthropocene', *Theory, Culture and Society*, vol. 34, nos. 2–3, Special Issue 3 at 14.

39 Raworth, n 12.

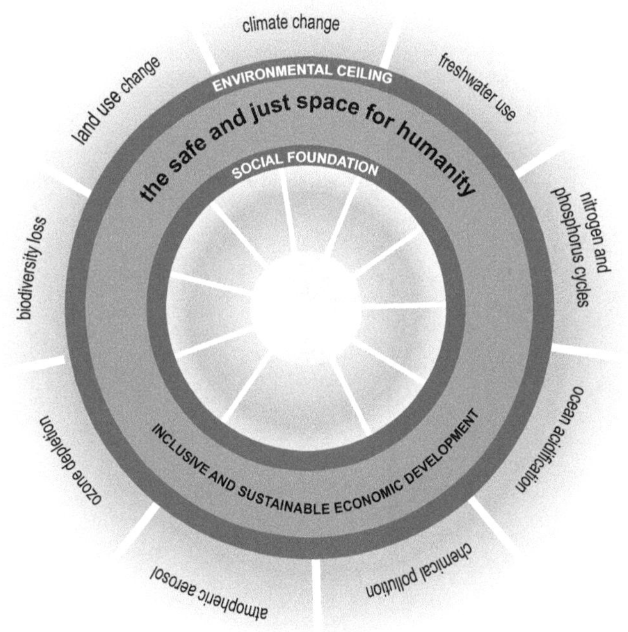

Figure 2.1 A Safe and Just Space for Humanity

Source: Raworth (2012), n 12, at 4. The material "Oxfam Discussion Papers, A Safe and Just Space for Humanity: Can We Live within the Doughnut?", Kate Raworth, February 2012, Figure 1. Reproduced with the permission of Oxfam, Oxfam House, John Smith Drive, Cowley, Oxford OX4 2JY, UK (www.oxfam.org.uk). Oxfam does not necessarily endorse any text or activities that accompany the materials.

environmental sustainability or ecological integrity and at the lower limits by human social needs. Raworth's position is that this implies no limits to human well-being but opens many potential new pathways within which sustainable development can take place.

Melissa Leach takes the safe operating space concept further still, by considering *how* pathways should be developed within that space:[40]

> There are likely to be many possible pathways in that space, which will be aligned with different cultures, visions and values, and with different costs, risks and distributions of power and benefits between social groups. So there will be a range of outcomes for social justice. This makes the process of adjudicating between them a deeply political one.

40 Leach et al., 'Between social and planetary boundaries', p. 84, 86.

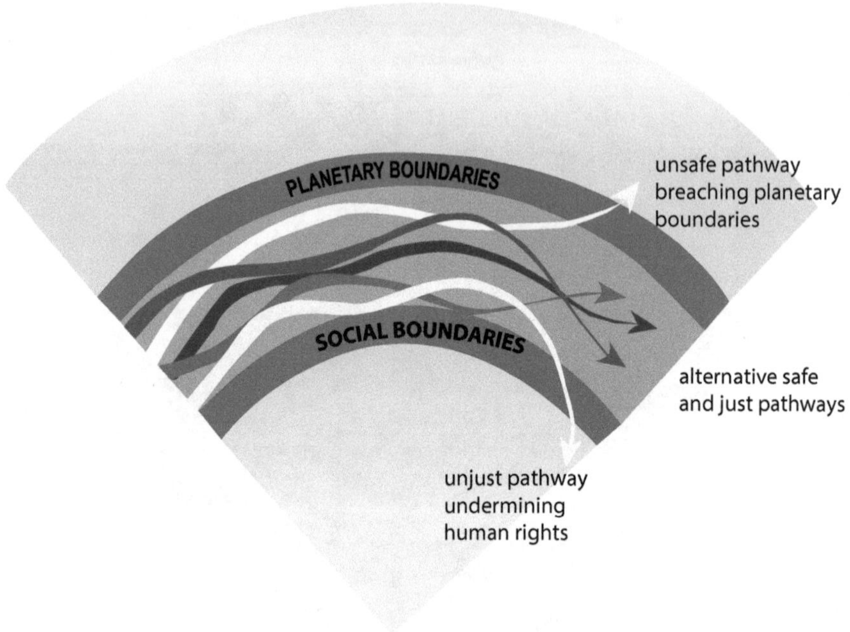

Figure 2.2 Possibilities Within the Safe and Just Operating Space – Diverse Pathways, Alternative Directions and Varying Distributional Outcomes

Source: Leach, et al.

The challenge ahead is no longer just one of working out planetary and social boundaries but also *which* pathways within those boundaries should be taken. Melissa Leach's warning is that choosing pathways is a deeply political process and will have profound impacts on the goal of achieving equitable distribution of natural and social resources.[41] When considering alternative pathways, she recommends implementing the three Ds (direction, diversity, distribution) to ensure sustainable development challenges are met in ways compatible with social justice:[42]

1. *Directions*: The first question to ask when considering any action is which direction is a particular pathway taking us? Is it towards one of

41 Leach, M, Reyers, B, Bai, X, Brondizio, ES, Cook, C, Díaz, S, Espindola, G, Scobie, M, Stafford-Smith, M & Subramanian, SM 2018, 'Equity and sustainability in the anthropocene: a social-ecological systems perspective on their intertwined futures', *Global Sustainability*, vol. 1, p. 1, 3.

42 Leach, et al., 'Equity and sustainability in the anthropocene'.

the boundaries? Do other pathways offer directions more likely to stay within the boundaries? Bringing attention to the direction of pathways focuses on the power relations that drive particular pathways and the value interests and behaviours they reflect.

2. *Diversity*: The second question is whether there is sufficient diversity of approaches within the safe operating space. Is the range of options being explored wide enough? Keeping several options open provides resilience against uncertainties and surprises that complex social environmental processes produce.
3. *Distribution*: Understanding distribution implications is essential for identifying which pathways promote social justice and enable more equitable sharing of the safe operating space. Who is likely to benefit from a particular pathway? Who will bear the risks and costs?

More recently, the Earth Commission,[43] with one of its leading scientists, Johan Rockström, introduced a new conceptual framework for defining a safe but also "just" operating space for all.[44] Given current social and societal inequalities, the risk of attempting to meet the needs of all may lead to crossing the safe Earth system limits on which we rely. Regarding the advancement of this proposed "corridor" framework, the authors defend:[45]

> These frameworks [the planetary boundaries and the doughnut economics], however, do not fully integrate safe and just, representing them with different dimensions (Earth system processes vs. social goals) and incomparable variables. How biophysically "safe" targets can be achieved while also meeting goals for human well-being and justice is difficult to explore in such frameworks, for example, determining a safe and just allocation of land for food production. Furthermore, these prior frameworks explicitly incorporate neither sub-global scales, interactions and feedbacks between variables, nor potential trade-offs between planetary targets and development and equity. An integrated framework is needed that aligns safe and just Earth system variables while also accounting for sub-global scales and interactions between Earth system processes.

Figure (a) represents the safe and just targets for each biophysical variable. The stricter of the safe and just target ranges for each variable defines the safe and just corridor, shown by the grey zone (see Figures (a) and (b)). Aiming

43 The Earth Commission was launched in June 2019 and gathers 19 expert commissioners in both natural and social sciences. See Earth Commission (https://earthcommission.org).

44 Rockström, J, Gupta, J, Lenton, TM, Qin, D, Lade, SJ, Abrams, JF, Jacobson, L, Rocha, JC, Zimm, C, Bai, X & Bala, G 2021, 'Identifying a safe and just corridor for people and the planet', *Earth's Future*, vol. 9, no. 4.

45 At 4. Emphasis added.

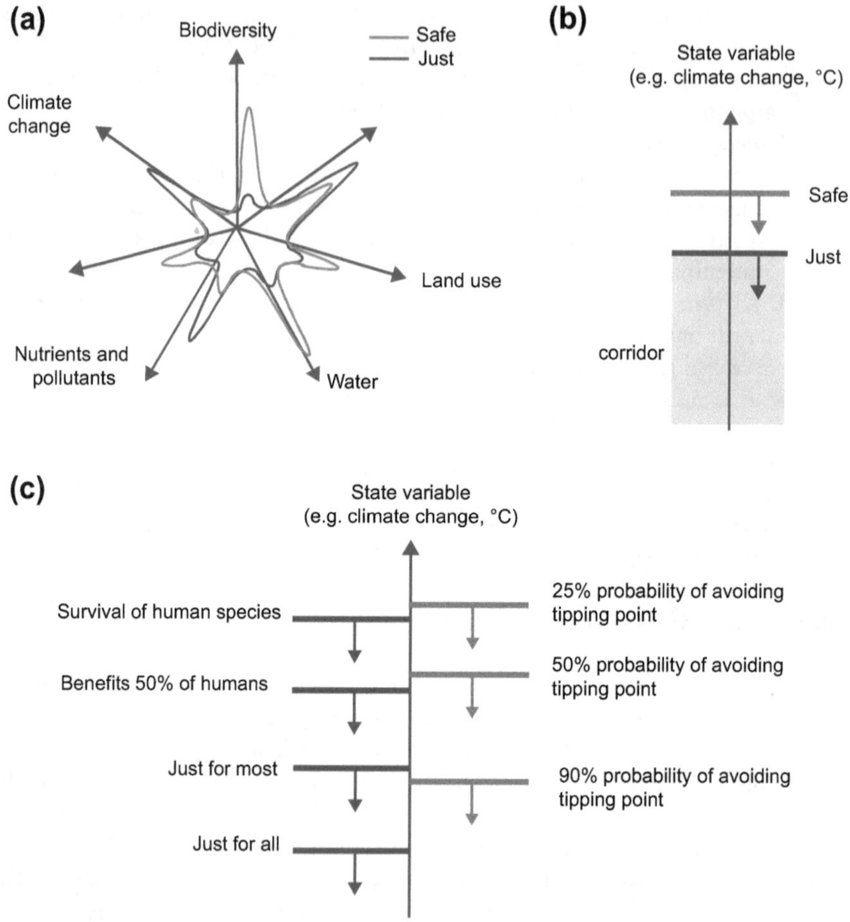

Figure 2.3 Integration of Safe and Just Targets Into the Corridor

Source: Rockström, et al., n 48, at 5.

to ensure that "no one will be left behind," Figure (c) identifies "a spread of safe and just targets corresponding to different physical risk tolerances and different understandings of environmental justice".[46]

This framework and its variables and targets are strictly experimental at this stage. Further studies are required moving forward, particularly to define the scientific targets for each Earth system regulating process and lever of transformation and considering the political implications of such an approach.

46 At 4.

c) *The Role of Law and Governance*

> What would a renewed analytical framework look like if we strive to contribute to a renewed institutional understanding of the Anthropocene? The short answer is a framework based on poly-centricity, and a deeper understanding of the interplay between networks, institutions and earth system complexity (including human-environmental-technological interconnections).[47]

This brings us to the important question of how international environmental law and governance fit into the Anthropocene and the sustainability debate and discourse, which are the focus for much of the rest of this chapter. How does the law hinder true sustainable practice, and how can it facilitate it? What exactly do we mean by the term "sustainability" within the law? Are there potentials in the law to correct the underlying assumption that the environment can sustain us indefinitely, regardless of how much we take from it, and what rights and responsibilities do we have towards the environment?

International environmental law is a relatively young branch of law that has grown out of a necessity to create protection for specific parts of the environment in a piecemeal and often local way. For example, in the developed world, most of the worst excesses of the Industrial Revolution have been addressed, such as cleaning up air pollution in large cities, removing lead from petrol and banning damaging synthetic pesticides where damage caused clearly outweighs benefits.[48] However, these individual improvements are not sufficient to prevent or address the global problem of continuing damage to major ecological systems.

One of the key reasons international environmental law has been ineffective in dealing with macro problems that spread themselves over space and time is that the basic design of international environmental law has no foundation or overarching principle or *grundnorm* of ecological integrity.[49] The planetary boundaries provide a bottom line to human activities in a way that the law currently does not. In this sense, the law, as it now functions, contributes to the problem. Exploring such overarching principles has promising potential to redress the defects in international environment law.

Within the law, there are historical roots for a foundational ecological bottom line, which, if operationalized, would complement and buttress the work

47 Victor Galaz Global Environmental Governance 2014, *Technology and politics: the anthropocene gap*, Edward Elgar, Cheltenham, p. 126.

48 Jones, K 2015, 'Planetary boundaries and the evolution of global environmental law', LLM thesis, University of Auckland, p. 33.

49 Bosselmann, K 2020, 'The framework of ecological law', *Environmental Policy and Law*, vol. 50, no. 6, p. 479, 479–480. See also Kotzé, LJ & Kim, RE 2022, 'Towards planetary nexus governance in the anthropocene: an earth system law perspective', *Global Policy*, vol. 13, p. 86.

carried out by the natural and social scientists in creating and then protecting the safe operating space.

Unlike other branches of the law, which do not necessarily need to look outside the boundaries of traditional primary and secondary legal sources, international environmental law deals specifically with the physical environment and the human intersection with that environment. It is argued here that the correct methodology for approaching environmental law is a systems theoretical one, which looks at environmental law from an external bird's-eye view, considering it in the wider context of the human *and* the physical world.[50] This approach immediately exposes the "gaps" between ecological and social realities, legal constructs and the global, economic and financial paradigm.

Like other disciplines, the complexity of the modern world now requires the law to accommodate pluralistic (anthropocentric and ecocentric) concepts within its framework. An underlying *grundnorm* of ecological integrity is ecocentric in nature, which is why it has been rejected by the anthropocentrically focused legal system. An interesting example of how the law's anthropocentric focus has developed internal distortions is that, along with humans, corporations are recognized as "legal persons" protecting economic interests, whereas the natural environment has no such legal protection. This has created a rather surreal situation in which the law is focused on protecting economic interests over and above the very life support system of the people conducting those economic activities. This surely must cause us to question and re-evaluate the core values underlying the law.

If "ecological integrity" (carefully defined to be legally effective) can be shown to be fundamental in terms of law and governance, this automatically calls for guardianship or trusteeship concepts to form part of international and state institutional arrangements.[51]

The idea that all systems, whether natural, social or legal, function best with a certain level of underlying integrity[52] is one that is worth exploring in this report. "Integrity" here is used to mean that which a particular system needs to maintain coherent order between stability and change and to function in a resilient manner without collapse.[53]

50 Westerlund, S 2008, 'Theory of sustainable development, towards or against?', in Bugge & Voigt (eds), *Sustainable development*, pp. 55–58. See also Collins, LM 2019, 'Environmental resistance in the anthropocene', *Oñati Socio-legal Series*, Forthcoming – Governing the Political: Law and the Politics of Resistance.

51 Bosselmann, K 2015, 'Mind the gap: state governance and ecological integrity', in L Westra, J Gray & V Karageorgou (eds), *Ecological systems integrity: governance, law and human rights*, Routledge, London, pp. 272–273. See also Garver, G 2020, *Ecological law and the planetary crisis: a legal guide for harmony on Earth*, 1st edn, Routledge, London.

52 At 276.

53 At 273.

The concept of "ecological integrity" is already well known in international environmental law. At least 23 international soft and hard law agreements contain specific reference to it.[54] Yet states generally ignore any commitments to ecological integrity. Environmental law has also failed (as explained by Staffan Westerlund)[55] because it has looked at sustainability from the perspective of the law instead of looking at the law from the perspective of sustainability. This has resulted in exercising the concept in a way that is empty of real meaning, with ecological integrity missing from its core.

Douglas Fisher reveals that after conducting an analysis of the methodology of judges, administrators and politicians who consider environmental matters, decisions are reached without specific environmental *points of commencement*. Instead, traditional assumptions concerning human rights to "the good life" and economic imperatives play the dominant (albeit sometimes unconscious) roles in the decision-making process. He concludes that the processes of legal reasoning need to reflect fundamental *grundnorms* in the form of the rule of law and of true sustainability, with an ecological core in the context of environmental governance.[56]

Victor Galaz very clearly defines the challenges ahead as being three-fold:[57]

1. Our mental models and causal beliefs are being seriously challenged by the complexity, scale and speed of global change.
2. Our analytical approaches [meaning political approaches] are increasingly failing us as we gain increasing insights about the anatomy of earth system change.
3. Our political institutions at multiple levels of social organisation are unable to effectively respond to novel risks and opportunities induced by interacting environmental, political and technological change.

Discussions about altering the existing structure of environmental governance must also deal with the historical and existing recognition of state sovereignty. The success of states advancing their own interests achieves nothing in the face of the global risk that every citizen and every nation is confronted with. One proposed model of governance which seeks to address this challenge is Rockström and others' "nested governance" approach.[58] This framework would consist of three tiers of planetary commons determined by their

54 At 274.

55 Westerlund, n 50, at 65.

56 Fisher, D 2013, *Legal reasoning in environmental law: a study of structure, form and language*, Edward Elgar, Cheltenham, p. 433.

57 Galaz, n 47, at viii.

58 Rockström, et al., 'Global commons in the anthropocene', *Proceedings of the National Academy of Sciences*.

scale, with a governance regime created for each tier.[59] Crucially, the consultative process for the creation and reform of these regimes must represent the views and needs of non-state stakeholders, and multiple knowledge systems would also play a significant part in the forming and operationalization of these regimes.[60] Ultimately, it is recognized that any new approach must give weight to global *and* local interests, as well as global citizenry. In other words, all interested stakeholders.

59 At 12.
60 At 12, 14.

Chapter 3

Dealing With Complexities

The Earth as a "system" requires an appreciation that its (natural and human-made) components interact and interrelate in a certain way. Exactly how they interact may not be known for some time yet, but the fact of their interrelatedness cannot be in any doubt, especially in the Anthropocene. This raises the issue of how to deal with "complex systems" and is the subject of system theory.

One critical aspect of system theory is to explain how large numbers of relatively simple entities organize themselves, in the absence of a central controller, into a collective whole that creates patterns, uses information and evolves. Insect colonies, immune systems, economic markets, the World Wide Web and so on have long been studied by complex systems scholars as being complex systems in nature. For instance, there is an extraordinary gap between the individual simplicity of an ant and the collective sophistication of a colony. Bourke and Franks, ant behaviour biologists, wrote, "[A solitary ant] will walk around and around in never decreasing circles until [it] dies of exhaustion",[1] but the social organization of an ant colony is developed in a way that collective cohesion increases the survival, well-being, and stability of the entire community.

Niklas Luhmann was one of the first legal scholars to introduce systems theory in social science analysis of societal systems. Modern society, he argued, is "a system comprised of a number of operatively closed and functionally distinct sub-systems such as economics, science, law, the mass media and so on".[2] Each sub-system is autonomous and observes the world in its own terms via its internal communications while contributing to the preservation of the system equilibrium.[3]

1 Franks, N & Bourke, AFG 1995, *Social evolution in ants*, Princeton University Press, Princeton, NJ.

2 Halsall, F 2012, 'Niklas Luhmann and the body: irritating social systems', *The New Bioethics*, vol. 18, p. 4, 5.

3 Luhmann, N 2012, *Theory of society, volume I*, R. Barrett (trans.), Stanford University Press, CA. See also Leach, M 2023, 'Seeking systems in earth system law: boundaries, identity and purpose in emergent field', *Earth System Governance*, vol. 15, p. 100162.

DOI: 10.4324/9781032674049-5

When it comes to the Earth as a "system", its foundations could be what Maturana and Varela referred to as autopoiesis.[4] For them, a system is autopoietic when capable of reproducing and maintaining itself through continuous regeneration of its own components, constituting a concrete unity in space (a network of interrelated component).[5] This autopoietic understanding of the Earth as a self-organizing system that maintains itself was the interpretation retained by Earth system science (and therefore Earth system law).

By using the concept of *complexity* in his social system theory, Luhmann refers to non-predictable and hence complex social systems which are not, in his words, either capable of being steered or fully describable:[6]

> This can mean that certain complex descriptions (for instance, of the system or its environment) can fail to do justice to the complexity of their object, reducing it to the simplified form of a model, a text, a map.

Therefore, dealing with complexities is not an exercise of adding up data from individual components – the oceans, the biodiversity, the atmosphere, human societies, economics, and so forth – hoping to get a picture of the whole Earth system. Instead, dealing with complexities requires a standard or benchmark that is valid for all components (or systems and sub-systems).

While the core research task for social system theory scholars is to understand and model the stability in the social system, the same is true for the Earth system. The benchmark is "integrity". In order to function sustainably, each of Earth's components has to maintain a degree of changeability and stability with respect to external pressures, best captured by its integrity.

System theory and complexity are poised to help us – and current and future leaders – make sense of planetary issues and address the challenges and opportunities we face in a new epoch of human history. How critical it is to think along the lines of system and complexity theories will be the cynosure of this chapter and the next.

1. Social and Ecological Complexities

Increasing levels of complexity in the economy, the environment and our human world (rising inequality) are increasing the risk of global collapse. The *Oxford English Dictionary* defines complexity as "the quality or condition of

4 Maturana, H & Varela, F 1973, *Autopoiesis and cognition: the realization of the living*, D. Reidel Publishing Company, pp. 78–79.

5 Maturana & Varela, *Autopoiesis and cognition.*

6 At 83.

being complex".[7] In the case of modern society, complexity levels are growing at high rates in a positive reinforcing feedback loop.

Joseph Tainter, a world-leading historian of the rises and falls of societies, tells us that sustainability is much more than simply a consequence of consuming less but, rather, is a function of learning to be successful at solving complex problems. He points out that, ultimately, governments that fail to solve complex problems lose their legitimacy and popular support.[8]

Tainter has conducted extensive research on civilizations throughout history, looking at the causes of their survival or collapse. He asserts that collapse can best be understood by understanding four interlocking factors.[9]

First, human societies are primarily problem-solving groups. For example, we come together in families, communities and nations because it efficiently solves many survival problems we would struggle to deal with alone.[10]

Second, we generally solve our problems by increasing the level of complexity. For example, in our methods of communication, we have now reached levels of technological complexity at which it is possible to stay connected while on opposite sides of the world. As complexity nearly always works well in the short term, there is a modern tendency to assume that all complexity must be good. However, according to Tainter, "Complexity is neither good nor bad but is either useful and affordable to a society or it is not":[11]

> Complexity is a long-term paradox of problem-solving. It facilitates the resolution of problems in the short run while undermining the ability to solve them in the long term. Maintaining a society or other kind of institution requires that the problem-solving system itself be sustainable.

Third, this increase in complexity requires that some additional form of high-quality energy must pay for it.[12] Today, we rely on fossil fuel, which is really a subsidy from the past, to maintain the complexity of our present society. One barrel of oil contains six gigajoules of energy. To put that into perspective, a healthy male adult peddling as fast as he can on an exercise bike attached to an efficient generator can produce 100 watt-hours of energy per hour. To produce the same amount of energy as that contained in a barrel

7 Oxford Dictionary 2019, *Complexity*, 3rd edn, online edn.
8 Tainter, J 1988, *The collapse of complex societies*, Cambridge University Press, Cambridge, p. 25, 27, 37, 121.
9 At 93 and 118.
10 At 37 and 93.
11 Tainter, J 2000, 'Problem solving: complexity, history and sustainability', *Population and Environment*, vol. 22, no. 1, p. 3, 36.
12 At 93.

of oil, he would need to pedal 40 hours a week for 8.01 years.[13] If we consider that one barrel of oil costs somewhere between $50 and $100,[14] we start to get a sense of the enormous energy subsidy that fossil fuel provides to maintain the level of complexity contained in modern life.

Fourth, eventually, our investment in higher levels of complexity to solve problems reaches a point of decline in marginal return,[15] which we do not usually consider in the decision-making process. Once we reach this point, both the resilience of the system and its ability to continue (to operate sustainably) are reduced. We generally forget we are currently paying for our complexity by using a surplus borrowed from the past that has a finite future and only accounts for the last 200 years of human evolution. Prior to that, energy was regarded as precious and treated as a resource to be used sustainably.

One prism through which collapse can be understood is recognizing that vast amounts of energy are needed just to tread water and maintain the status quo of our society's complexity. What happens when we hit the limits of fossil fuel? Can alternative renewables produce the same (and more) amounts of "work" needed to maintain existing levels?[16] On top of this, Tainter states that the resilience/integrity of the world system requires a buffer or surplus of energy to be available for unexpected disruptions in the system.

a) Societal Responses to Increased Levels of Complexity

Tainter gives three examples of societies from the past that responded to increasing levels of complexity in different ways.[17]

The Western Roman Empire

Through successive conquests, the Romans expanded very quickly. With each new province conquered, high returns or "surplus" in the form of peasant labour, taxes and land flowed into the Empire. As a result, it increased in size and level of complexity rapidly. By the second century AD, Rome's enemies had grown powerful, and Rome had reached the limits of its strategy of expansion by war and conquest. However, the administrative costs of managing a sprawling area still had to be paid, even though no further

13 Lee & Borden, A 2017, '"The energy in a barrel of oil" let the sun work: sustainable living in a petroleum world' (17 June 2017), (https://letthesunwork.com/).

14 MacroTrends 2022, 'Crude oil prices: 70 Year historical chart' (23 January 2022), (https://www.macrotrends.net/1369/crude-oil-price-history-chart).

15 Tainter, n 8, at 93.

16 The term "work" is here used in the technical sense. Energy is the capacity for doing "work". See Nave, R 2017, 'Work, energy and power', *HyperPhysics*, (http://hyperphysics.phy-astr.gsu.edu/hbase/index.html).

17 Tainter, n 11.

surpluses from conquests were available. In order to maintain itself, Rome debased its currency, used its now-unoccupied (and therefore unruly) army to wrest increasingly heavy taxes from an unhappy population and froze labour wages. Each of these steps negatively affected the well-being of the citizens upon which the survival of Rome depended. Legitimacy of power is always a delicate matter. As long as those in power must rely on force for compliance, most of the profits are consumed by the cost of coercion.[18] Lands were abandoned, productivity declined and the peasant population attempted to flee beyond Rome's borders. Eventually, the cost of maintaining Rome reached unsustainable levels, and collapse followed.

Byzantine

Byzantine's inability to pay for the cost of maintaining the level of complexity within its society is one of the few examples of a complex society simplifying voluntarily. During the seventh century, the Byzantines were facing extinction after having been weakened by the plague and repeated Persian invasions. It responded by dramatically simplifying its society, offloading an expensive, inefficient army and offering soldiers land that they could defend as their own. The economy contracted, and barter replaced the monetary economy. This strategy of simplification prevented further loss of land and societal collapse. Tainter points out that very few societies will voluntarily choose this option.

Europe

Europe was another prime candidate for collapse with ongoing skirmishes and wars amongst many cultural groups, which were supported and paid for by an impoverished peasantry. High costs and military stalemates should have created a classic collapse scenario. However, Europe "stumbled upon great subsidies".[19] By crossing the oceans in search for more resources, they were able to initially conquer foreign lands and then later colonize them, which provided enormous surpluses for Europe. In more recent times, since the beginning of the Industrial Revolution, the subsidies provided by fossil fuel further developed Europe's complexity and problem-solving ability. Internal competition has also forced the Europeans to continuously innovate new systems of finance and technology.

Our own society continues to increase in complexity. Modern life requires enormous amounts of energy to function. What will be our future? Our current lifestyles are subsidized mainly by fossil fuel. Immanuel Wallerstein holds

18 At 36.
19 At 36.

the view that today, we have a single capitalist world economy that encompasses the entire globe. This is the first time in human history that "there is only one historical system on the planet at a given time".[20] The problem of the Anthropocene is that this system has run out of space to find new surplus to easily maintain complexity. Our recent attempts to circumvent this problem by creating "artificial surplus" through debt and the financial system now has the capacity to threaten the whole system, as evidenced by the 2008 global financial crisis.

Before delving into a deeper discussion about energy in modern society, it is worth looking at the way causal loops work in systems so as to get a clearer picture of the hurdles we face in reaching and maintaining sustainability. The take-home message from this chapter and the next is that it is not possible to separate us from the environment. Make no mistake – the environment and our economy are currently at loggerheads. If growth (as we currently understood it) wins out, then, in the long term, we will lose.

b) Causal Loops and the World System

According to Karen Higgins, systems can be best understood through causal loops and feedbacks. Causal loop diagrams illustrate the complexities of a system, but equally help explain causes and consequences.[21] For example, cause and consequence may move in the same direction or in opposite directions, leading to either positive (reinforcing) or negative (balancing) effects. Depending on such feedback mechanisms, the system can either gain stability and integrity or lose its stabilizing characteristics and eventually become disintegrated (causing new consequences).

In this way, the capacity of a system to sustain growth can be measured.[22] Whether or not the system reaches its limits depends on the nature and speed of growth. Any overshoot will lead to collapse.[23]

In the same vein, Higgins explains the world system (comprising physical and human systems).[24]

The world system can enter a situation of overshoot and collapse, in which the elements of the system grow uncontrollably, overshoot their capacity and then decay. This second scenario tends to happen when there are delays in the

20 Williams, G 2013, 'Special contribution: interview with Immanuel Wallerstein – retrospective on the origins of world systems analysis', *American Sociological Association*, vol. 19, no. 2, p. 202, 206.

21 Higgins, K 2015, *Economic growth and sustainability: systems thinking for a complex world*, Elsevier Academic Press, United States of America, San Diego, p. 6.

22 At 8

23 At 9.

24 At 101.

system that are unrecognized, and the system overshoots the capacity of the system to sustain growth and then falls rapidly – creating societal collapse.

Even without detailed knowledge of systems thinking, the many components of the world system make it clear how interconnected each part of life really is in society. We can see, for example, that the economy and its growth or decay are intimately connected to both the size of the population and the amount of goods we purchase, which, in turn, is connected to the personal gratification we get from buying those goods. We see how population and its growth or reduction are connected to resource use, and access to these is connected to inequality and poverty. We can also imagine that environmental degradation, once the natural buffers and delays in the Earth system are overcome, will eventually regulate the size of the population and, in turn, the economy in an overshoot-and-collapse scenario. One causal element for this scenario to develop is the way how energy is generated and used.

Energy is a key driver for growth, yet it seems to be taken for granted and does not really feature in going about our daily business.

Joseph Tainter describes our relationship to energy as something akin to a fish's relationship to water. He refers to a talk given in 1920 by British scientist Sir Oliver Lodge, who asked his audience to imagine a deep-sea fish living on the bottom of the ocean:[25]

> It is surrounded by water; it lives in water; it breeds in water. Now, what is the last thing that fish would discover? I am inclined to believe that the last thing the fish would be aware of at all is water.

This aptly describes our relationship with energy. We have grown up in an era when energy is high quality, work dense and cheap in human labour terms. We are culturally accustomed to this situation and consider it normal. Yet imagine for a moment the amount of human labour and time it must have taken to build the great pyramids of Egypt without machinery powered by fossil fuel. Tainter points out that, over the course of human evolution, a surplus of high-quality dense energy is far from normal.

Nate Hagan states that it is important we grasp that it is energy, not money, that drives all growth in economies – a fact overlooked by classical economics. Energy underpins everything in the world system, with money being what he describes as "just a marker for energy".[26] One barrel of oil is the equivalent of approximately 10,000 human labour hours of work. Chris Martenson notes that all growth and prosperity are dependent on energy

25 Tainter, JA & Patzek, TW 2012, *Drilling down: the gulf oil debacle and our energy dilemma*, Copernicus, New York, pp. 186–189.

26 Hagens, N 2015, 'Turning 21 in the anthropocene: an invitation to participate in the future' (28 April 2015), (www.youtube.com).

surplus. In the case of economic growth and prosperity, nothing is more important than surplus energy:[27]

> While you run water, take hot showers and vacuum the floor, it's as if your house is employing the services of 50 extremely fit bike-riding slaves in the basement, ready to peddle their fastest, 24 hours a day, at the flick of a switch. When you jump in a car, depending on your engine, it's the same as a king harnessing up a carriage of 300 horses. This slave count, if you will, exceeds that of kings in times past.

When we consider replacing oil with other energy sources like the renewables, it has to be factored in that they are much less dense than oil in "work to output" ratios.

The commonly held view is that technology will save the day and provide us with an alternative to fossil fuel. This may, indeed, turn out to be the case, but there are a number of things to be considered. First, *technology does not create energy*. Technology can help us use energy more efficiently. It can increase productivity. It can replace human labour with mechanical labour, and it can entertain and connect us in new, faster and more innovative ways. Energy, according to the first law of thermodynamics, cannot be created or destroyed, only transformed from one form into another. The second law of thermodynamics determines what happens to energy when it is transformed. Every transformation results in a loss of at least a small amount of energy in the form of diffuse heat.[28]

> Technology can help us exploit what energy we do have more cleanly, cheaply and more efficiently, but it cannot create energy. And when we transform energy, we lose energy to the universe along the way in the form of diffuse heat. . . . [T]echnology has an enormous role to play in helping us to use our energy more wisely and with greater efficiency and utility, but these efforts will only slow the eventual day when our giant pile of free food is gone. . . . Nature will carry on whether we use up our energy stores wisely or shamefully, quickly or slowly, without any concern for how much or how little useful work we extract along the way.

The economic law of diminishing returns is in play with oil extraction and, according to Tainter, also new technology. Tainter and others recently conducted a study concerning the productivity of innovation in the United

27 Martinson, C 2011, *The crash course: the unsustainable future of our economy, energy and environment*, John Wiley and Sons, New Jersey, p. 128.
28 Martinson, n 27, at 182–183.

States based on patent data from the US Patent and Trademark Office.[29] The conclusions found that scientific fields undergo a fairly common evolutionary pattern, making breakthroughs in the early years (often by individual scientists) but, later on, requiring greater and greater numbers of scientists and resources in order to achieve a diminishing yield of breakthroughs:[30]

> It is widely believed that solar and wind energy will be needed to power industrial societies in the future, yet it appears that our investments and improving technologies in the sectors are producing diminishing returns, and that these sectors may be approaching technical maturity.

Tainter describes energy's positive feedback loop as an "energy complexity spiral". Energy causes complexity to increase, and higher complexity creates the need for more energy. Recent re-analysis of the "Limits to Growth" report (LTG), published 50 years ago in preparation for the Club of Rome's project on the predicament of mankind, calibrate how closely society is tracking the LTG business as usual (BAU) scenario.[31]

Notwithstanding a number of unforeseeable events, such as the global financial crisis in 2008 and the new fracking technology, Graham Turner concludes that, bearing in mind the limitations of computers in the 1970s, their systems analysis assessments are surprisingly accurate and on track. In discussing of the additional oil that new fracking technology now unlocks, he states that protagonists have misunderstood a crucial point:[32]

> They have essentially confused a stock with a flow. The key, as the LTG modelling highlights, is the rate at which the resource can be supplied, i.e. the flow and the associated requirements of machinery, energy and other inputs required to achieve that flow. Contemporary research into the energy required to extract and supply a unit of energy from oil shows that the imports have increased by almost an order of magnitude. It does not matter how big the resource stock is if it cannot be extracted fast enough or other scarce inputs needed elsewhere in the economy are consumed in the extraction.

29 Strumsky, D, Lobo, J & Tainter, J 2010, 'Complexity and the productivity of innovation', *Systems Research and Behavioral Science Journal*, vol. 27, p. 496.

30 At 503–504.

31 Turner, G 2014, 'Is global collapse imminent? An updated comparison of the limits to growth with historical data', MSSI Research Paper No. 4, Melbourne Sustainable Society Institute, University of Melbourne. See also Herrington, G 2021, 'Updates to limits to growth: comparing the World3 model with empirical data', *Journal of Industrial Ecology*, vol. 5, no. 3, p. 614.

32 Turner, at 11.

Turner's point is that the age of cheap oil is coming to an end, which the LTG authors flagged (as constraints on extraction rates and additional inputs needed) as indicators leading to collapse. The question of peak oil is less a question of how much oil is left and more a question of the cost of removing that oil. Energy return on energy invested (known as EROEI in the industry) has been declining for the past century from 100:1 down to below the range of 10:1. In other words, the cost of extracting oil is rising because we have accessed all of the easy options.[33] Energy constraints are well known to cause economic downturns.[34] There are direct and indirect links between oil and food prices associated with fuel transport, on-farm and processing distribution costs as well as feedstock and pesticide input costs.[35]

> The close alignment between the LTG BAU scenario and observed developments over the last four decades, as well as the correspondence and the underlying dynamics described above, portend of potential global collapse.[36]

A failure to recognize the transitory nature of the current energy age is due partly to our evolutionary psychology and partly to the level of complexity in the interconnections within the world system, which we do not yet fully understand or recognize. Tainter describes the place we have arrived at as one requiring serious discussions around energy resource use before constraints leave us few choices. Putting in place renewable energy infrastructure and changing energy habits takes time. A recent study by Silviu Nate and colleagues shows that many indicators for human well-being and quality of life are highly correlated with availability of energy and EROI,[37] as well as equity of distribution:[38]

> Time is of the essence. Society must quickly recognise that we are not in complete control, and it must also recognise what is and is not possible in the context of our dependent relationship with the physical world.

33 See Weißbach, D, Ruprecht, G, Huke, A, Czerski, K, Gottlieb, S, Hussein, A & Physik, A 2013, 'Energy intensities, EROIs and energy payback times of electricity generating power plants', *Energy*, vol. 52, p. 210.

34 King, N & Jones, A 2021, 'An analysis of the potential for the formation of "nodes of persisting complexity"', *Sustainability*, vol. 13, no. 8161, p. 3.

35 Turner, n 31, at 14.

36 Turner, n 31, at 14.

37 Nate, S, Bilan, Y, Cherevatskyi, D, Kharlamova, G, Lyakh, O & Wosiak, A 2021, 'The impact of energy consumption on the three pillar of sustainable development', *Energies*, vol. 14, p. 1372.

38 Nate, et al., 'The impact of energy consumption on the three pillar of sustainable development'. See also Lambert, J, Hall, CAS, Balogh, S, Gupta, A & Arnold, M 2014, 'Energy, EROI and quality of life', *Energy Policy*, vol. 64, p. 153.

c) *Human Evolutionary Biology and Psychology*

In 1987, the World Commission on Environment and Development stated that failure to manage the environment and sustain development was a problem that threatened to overwhelm all countries and could not be treated separately: "They are linked in a complex system of cause and effect".[39] Since that time, a vast quantity of articles, books, conferences and reports like this one have been produced, talking about how to live on the planet in a sustainable way. Why is there such a gap between our rhetoric and our actions when it comes to sustainability? Why is it so hard for us to grasp the full extent of the sustainability problem? And are we up to the challenge of handing a healthy planet on to future generations?

> Did selfishness – or sharing – drive human evolution? Evolutionary theorists have traditionally focused on competition and the ruthlessness of natural selection, but often they have failed to consider a critical fact: that humans could not have survived in nature without the charity and social reciprocity of a group.[40]

Strange as it may seem, answering these questions involves thinking about our own human nature. Who are we?

On the one hand, we have a strong survival instinct that focuses attention on ourselves, particularly when under threat or in survival mode. This part fosters survival of the fittest, short-term thinking and self-interest, to the exclusion of others.[41] The prime concern is what affects us directly:[42]

> As long as I get what I need – enough clean air or water or money – I can ignore that my actions prevent others from getting what they need.

This part of human nature reflects the mind of immediacy and self-protection.[43]

On the other hand, this genetically embedded aspect is offset by caring for others to live in and be part of communities, to be part of a cause or a

39 World Commission on Environment and Development, Brundtland Report ('Our Common Future') UNGA A/42/427 (4 August 1987), at part I, para 40.

40 Szalavitz, M 2012, 'Is human nature fundamentally selfish or altruistic?', *Time Magazine*, viewed 8 October 2012, (https://healthland.time.com/2012/10/08/is-human-nature-fundamentally-selfish-or-altruistic/).

41 Jenkins, M 2009, *Hobbes, socialism and human nature*, viewed 22 January 2009, Independent Labour Publications, (https://www.independentlabour.org.uk/2009/01/22/hobbes-socialism-and-human-nature/).

42 Higgins, n 21, at 15.

43 Higgins, n 21, at 15.

purpose that is larger than us.[44] This aspect of human nature reflects mediacy and altruism.

There is no denying that the way the world currently works, particularly our economic system, reinforces and rewards the individualistic aspect of human nature and focuses primarily on short-term gains in the present. The rewards are the spoils of what many perceive to be "the good life", made up largely of money and consumption of material goods and services (which, in turn, places a huge toll on the environment in terms of resource use and waste). Without structural change to the existing system, the altruistic part of our nature remains undeveloped and unexplored because it is not rewarded in a way that most of us consider "counts".

Karen Higgins, in her thoughtful and wide-ranging work *Economic Growth and Sustainability: Systems Thinking for a Complex World*, points out that the way we understand (and, as a result, behave in) the world – that is, the parts of ourselves we activate going about our daily business – goes to the very heart of the sustainability question and any chance we have of achieving a healthy planet that is not exhausted by the wants and needs of the present generation:[45]

> Sustainability is the ultimate state of dynamic balance and where competing concerns are blended in a harmonious dance of flow and change. . . . [C]hange is both possible and imperative. Such change requires courage and lifestyles that embrace stewardship; it requires collaboration among groups and profound alteration of individual behaviours.

d) Our "Mental Model" of the World

Mental models are the underlying skeleton of systems thinking. They are our perceptions and ideas about how the world works and are created through beliefs, experiences and culture. Along with the innate qualities discussed earlier, mental models also dictate our choices and behaviour. Jay Forrester notes that, generally, mental models are "fuzzy, incomplete and imprecisely stated".[46]

> It is imperative to get at least a sense of what beliefs and perceptions are driving our worldly system. We want to understand how these fuzzy but

44 Ross, WD 2011, *The Nicomachean ethics of Aristotle*, Pacific Publishing, Seattle. Aristotle considered the question "What is the purpose of life?" to be the most important question we face.

45 Higgins, n 21, at xix.

46 Forrester, J 1995, 'Counterintuitive behavior of social systems' (March 1995), Creative Learning Exchange, (http://static.clexchange.org/ftp/documents/system-dynamics/SD1993-01CounterintuitiveBe.pdf). See also Higgins, n 21, at 14.

powerful mental models undermine the goals of sustainability without our full awareness so that we can identify how to get there.[47]

While each of us has our own mental model, the discussion here is about an aggregate of common perceptions that underpin the structure of the world system. Some of these are a result of our biology and others are cultural beliefs. They are:

1. A predisposition towards short-term thinking.
2. A dominant interest in self. We attend most to things that arouse our emotions and touch us personally. As long as pollution and population problems do not affect us, it is possible to push them to the back of our minds.
3. Humans are predisposed to project a current situation into the future and to assume that past experience will dictate future experience in terms of sustainability. This mindset means that, for most of us living in developed countries, we believe we will always wake up each morning with enough food, water and energy.
4. There are evolutionary limits to human mental processing power, which also predisposes us to short-term thinking. "Old but familiar research places our short-term mental capacity for remembering lists at seven plus or minus two items – not enough to wrap our minds around the many issues of sustainability at the same time".[48] Regardless of whether this number is exact, it causes us to acknowledge that, as individuals, we cannot readily grasp highly complicated subjects; we tend to look at complex problems either a piece at a time or tied to something familiar.
5. Economic growth is essential to human happiness and will continue forever.[49]
6. Technology developments will replace all parts of nature that are lost through human consumption of natural resources and pollution and will create enough energy capacity to keep up with continuous economic growth.
7. Population growth and pollution growth are beyond our personal concern if they do not directly affect us.

Although it is possible to think of many more beliefs than those listed, these are fundamental to why we continue to grow the global economy,

47 Higgins, n 21, at 14.

48 At xviii. See also Miller, G 1956, 'The magic number seven, plus or minus two: some limits on our capacity for processing information', *Psychological Review*, vol. 63, no. 2, p. 81.

49 It should be acknowledged here that economic growth is necessary in developing countries with many people still living below the poverty line, but recent research shows this is not the case above a threshold level of income. See Kahneman, D & Deaton, A 2010, 'High income improves evaluation of life but not emotional well-being', *Proceedings of the National Academy of Sciences*, vol. 107, no. 38, p. 16489.

even though the effects "profoundly damage the environment".[50] They also explain why we continue to use energy as though it were infinite and why we place more CO_2 into the atmosphere without seeming to worry about the consequences. They explain why we can push the problems of population growth and pollution outside our immediate level of consciousness, particularly in the wealthy countries.[51] The problem with these beliefs is that they limit our understanding of how the world is actually working and reduce our chance to achieve sustainability.

In essence, the dominant state of mind asserts that economic growth, our seemingly stable environment and our resources will go on forever.

Using Higgins's mental model system,[52] we can detect two reinforcing loops, one for the economy and one for personal gratification. They create the belief that economic growth fuels human happiness and will continue forever. Even though the concept of economic growth is a fairly recent one, a life without growth now seems unthinkable. This mindset accepts the global economy growing larger, with more people having the ability to buy more products, which creates more global consumers, which results in more pollution, and on it goes. This is what Higgins calls a true growth cycle. In the gratification reinforcing loop, although more goods are purchased, the gratification is short lived and so must be continuously fed.

> Psychologist call this loop the "hedonic treadmill" and systems thinkers call it a "vicious circle". When individuals pursue a materialistic path towards happiness, the more they have, the less fulfilled they feel, and the more they want.[53]

The following chapter will explore the growth phenomena more fully and look at growth issues in relation to human population and its impacts on the natural environment.

2. Growth and Sustainability

We will first discuss the current economic situation and the basic workings of our financial system in relation to growth. This is followed by two short case studies, one on population and other on environmental impacts ("pollution"),

50 Higgins, n 21, at 16.
51 Higgins, n 21, at 16.
52 At 25.
53 At 27. See also Mogilner, C, Whillans, A & Norton, M 2018, 'Time, money and subjective well-being', in E Diener, S Oishi & L Tay (eds), *Handbook of well-being: noba scholar handbook series: subjective well-being*, DEF Publishers, Salt Lake City; Brickman, P & Campbell, D 1971, 'Hedonic relativism and planning the good society', in MH Appley (ed), *Adaptation-level theory*, Academic Press, New York.

to finally ask what have we learnt and what we can we do. The aim is to re-imagine capitalism so it could function in a system that is sustainable.

Prior to 1750, there was virtually no growth. Sparked by the Industrial Revolution, rapid growth became the driver of modernity and environmental degradation. This raises the question whether the last 275 years mark a unique episode in human evolution.[54] It is important to note that recent history has proven capitalism's remarkable capacity to evolve and adapt, which should caution us against thinking of capitalism as a static set of " 'structurally invariant' processes".[55] Jason Moore tells us that "capitalism does not act upon time and space. It actively produces these".[56] He views Karl Marx's idea that the real barrier of capitalist production is capital itself, as an entry point into changing our Cartesian understanding of "capitalism *and* nature" in favour of a new understanding of "capitalism *in* nature". David Weinstein takes the view that we should first try to alter the existing financial system to operate sustainably, but if that doesn't work, it is time to consider a new paradigm:[57]

> Part of the issue is going to be some tweaking of the system and part of the issue is knowing when you can't tweak any more and you're going to have to move to the next paradigm.

The fundamental problem with our mental model of the global economy is the illusion that unlimited economic growth is possible on a finite planet. The goal of all national economies is to achieve continuous economic growth. If this belief alone was the only issue we faced, that would be serious enough. However, it's also clear that we are not in a position to simply decide to stop growing the economy. We are in a prisoner's dilemma where to do so results in severe unemployment and deep recession. The economy works in a circular system. Capitalist economies continuously and aggressively search for efficiencies to obtain surplus profit from production (labour capital and resources). Efficiency improvements stimulate demand by driving down costs, which increases the supply of goods, generating a cycle of expansion and growth.

Improvements in efficiency and technology mean that fewer people are needed for employment to produce the same amount of goods/services over time. This has been one of the primary points of discussions at the annual meetings of the World Economic Forum in Davos. What do we do about the

54 Gordon, RJ 2012, *Is US economic growth over? Faltering innovation confronts the six headwinds*, National Bureau of Economic Research Working Paper Series No. 18315, Cambridge, MA, August 2012, (https://www.nber.org/papers/w18315.pdf) at 1.

55 Moore, J 2011, 'Ecology, capital, and the nature of our times: accumulation and crisis in the capitalist world-ecology', *American Sociological Review*, vol. 42, no. 1, p. 108.

56 At 108.

57 Stiglitz, J, et al. 2012, 'Financial instability mini-documentary' (15 April 2012), (www.youtube.com).

problem that our capitalist system has worked so well that we need fewer and fewer people to run it when the world still has a growing population? Machines and computers – including AI – now do the jobs many humans used to do, and this situation will continue to expand.

This also raises another problem in our economic system. If more people are unemployed, there are fewer people available with the funds to buy the goods and services that the world produces. This creates a situation in which demand shrinks, oversupply occurs and the global economy itself starts to shrink – in other words, a situation of no growth. All this occurs before we even begin to think about the problem that the planet's resources will not forever be able to sustain the current economic system. Our use of the world's sources and sinks outstrips the limits of the planet.[58] Attempts to deal with economic problems using traditional growth policies only leads to higher use of natural resources and more pollution.

As would have been expected after the 2008 global financial crisis (GFC) and many years of quantitative easing (QE), the global economy is not growing (despite everyone's best efforts).[59] Economic activity in the world economy remains lacklustre with little prospect for a turnaround in the foreseeable future. The COVID-19 pandemic and the widespread lockdowns that most countries around the world imposed since early 2020 threaten any potential chance of recovery.

Since the GFC, global growth has been sluggish. In the immediate aftermath, governments scrambled to prevent a recession by pumping large quantities of newly created money into the system. In the decades leading up to the GFC, real growth declined as the growth of complex financial instruments increased. This weakened the economy, making the whole system brittle and less resilient. Private debt grew to such high levels that once confidence dropped, the incapacity to repay that debt almost crashed the whole economic system.[60]

> They blindsided themselves to the role of rising debt and what is really the biggest Ponzi scheme in human history, which is what we've been going through in the last 20 years.[61]

58 Martinson, n 27.

59 QE is the tactic of central banks buying securities, like government bonds, with electronic cash that did not exist before, creating money and then injecting it into the financial system to stimulate growth. See United Nations Department of Economic and Social Affairs 2020, *World economic situations and prospects 2020*, United Nations, New York, p. viii.

60 Victor, PA & Jackson, T 2015, 'Toward an ecological macroeconomics', in PG Brown & P Timmerman (eds), *Ecological economics for the anthropocene*, Columbia University Press, New York, p. 240. See also Capra, F & Luisi, PL 2014, *The systems view of life: a unifying vision*, Cambridge University Press, Cambridge, p. 263.

61 Keane, S 2013, 'Financial instability mini-documentary', *New Economic Thinking, YouTube*, (www.youtube.com).

Steve Keen, one of the few economists who predicted the GFC, pointed out in advance that the exponential rise in private debt was unsustainable and would lead to a collapse in asset prices. "This is how bubbles grow and burst. Ignoring debt in this way is one of the great fallacies of modern economics".[62]

Since the GFC, the average growth rate in developed economies has declined by more than 54%, and the global unemployment has sharply increased to more than 210 million people. Joseph Stiglitz states that the dominant policy of the post-crisis period to kick-start growth through QE by major central banks has not been effective. Instead of banks lending the money into the real economy, much of it was simply parked at interest to create a less risky surplus for banks. When banks are given the freedom to choose, they choose riskless profit or even financial speculation over lending that would support the broader objective of economic growth.

Raghuram Rajan also flagged early that the creation of complicated instruments, like credit default swaps and mortgage-backed securities, made the global financial system much riskier. His views are that the long-term low interest rates and unorthodox monetary programmes used to try and stimulate growth in economies could lead to further turmoil:[63]

> My sense is that monetary policy can only do so much and beyond a certain point if you try to use monetary policy it does more damage than good.

Global economists are now confirming that the COVID-19 pandemic showed notable similarities in effects with the GFC in terms of economic activity, labour markets and so on.[64] A crucial divergent point, however, is that the recent pandemic has changed and keeps changing the world as we know it and the basic operations of our societies. While the COVID-19 crisis has acted as a catalyst accelerating certain sectors, such as science, technology and innovation (including healthcare and online communication sectors), many others sectors declined. Ultimately, economic inequality has worsened between those who can access digital tools and training or aptitude for exploiting them and those who cannot.

62 Cooper, C 2015, 'Six economists who predicted the global financial crisis', *In The Black*, viewed 7 July 2015, (www.intheblack.com).

63 Schuman, M 2014, 'A global financial guru who predicted the crisis of 2008 says more turmoil may be coming', *Time Magazine*, viewed 11 August 2014, (www.time.com).

64 Li, Z, Farmanesh, R, Kirikkaleli, D & Itani, R 2021, 'A comparative analysis of COVID-19 and the global financial crisis: evidence from US economy', *Economic Research*, vol. 35, pp. 2427–2441. See also Boskin, M 2020, 'How does the COVID recession compare?', *Project Syndicate*, (https://www.weforum.org/agenda/2020/08/how-does-the-covid-recession-compare). See also International Labor Organisation 2022, *World employment and social outlook 2022*, International Labor Organisation, Geneva.

As in all recessions, at this point of the spiral, social costs rise with higher unemployment (e.g. as more people need assistance in income and support through government transfer payments), and tax revenues decline as incomes fall. If we want to wean ourselves off this cycle, we must stop spending. This, in turn, means there must be cuts to public and social services affecting the poorest in the community first. The end result is that the population becomes dissatisfied and will generally look for leadership change.[65] Karl Marx recognized this aspect of capitalism early on. He also recognized that the rate of profit would fall even as the economy grew.

> In short, modern economies are driven toward economic growth. For as long as the economy is growing, positive feedback mechanisms tend to push this system towards further growth. When consumption growth falters, the system is driven toward a potentially damaging collapse, with a knock-on impact on human flourishing. People's jobs and livelihoods suffer. In a growth-based economy, growth is functional for stability. The capitalist model has no easy route to a steady state position. Its natural dynamics push it toward one of two states: expansion or collapse.[66]

In some of the soul-searching that has taken place since 2008, a number of gaps in our understanding of the economic system have emerged. First, economics looks at the elements of supply and demand without factoring in the role of banks, which is to create credit in the system. The non-recognition of the impact of banks creating commercial money (which, unregulated, led to levels of debt that proved unsustainable) seems to be a key reason most economists missed the coming financial collapse:[67]

> What is important to understand about market economies is that they have financial sectors that generate instability and that's because they generate credit and debt, which as far as the real sector is concerned comes out of nothing.

Second, classical economic models are built on the idea that the financial system is one that seeks an equilibrium when, in fact, there is much evidence suggesting the opposite. Economists became convinced that markets were mechanical and behaved according to "normal distributions".[68] Third,

65 Marx, K 1967, *Das Kapital: critique of political economy*, F Engels & E Untermann (eds), vol. III, Aristeus Books, St. Frederick, p. 250. See also Arrighi, G 2010, *The long twentieth century: money, power and the origins of our times*, Verso, New York, pp. 371–386.

66 Victor & Jackson, n 60, at 240. See also Capra & Luisi, n 64, at 263–267.

67 Stiglitz, JE 2010, 'Lessons from the global financial crisis of 2008', *Seoul Journal of Economics*, vol. 23, no. 3, p. 321.

68 Stiglitz, 'Lessons from the global financial crisis of 2008'.

economics assumes a "rational man" model, which does not recognize the spectrum of human psychology. Ultimately, economics is a social science and not one based on unchanging physical laws. The financial system is a human-made system. A further factor appears to have been reliance on the belief that Adam Smith's *invisible hand* (each person acting in their own self-interests) is sufficient to ensure an optimal and efficient marketplace:[69]

> In a free market, each individual makes choices by allocating their own resources as they see fit, voting on the perpetual democracy of the market that, in turn, controls the allocation of natural and human resources to best supply demand. The self-interest of individuals is harnessed by market mechanisms to serve the common good.

This does not work in our complex, interconnected and shrinking world. For example, if we all purchase the biggest vehicle we can afford, the world's carbon emissions problem will correspondingly expand. We can no longer pretend that pollution is an externality to the economic system. Another example is the banks' self-interest in maximizing their profits at the expense of the rest of the economy and the outcome of that choice. Steve Keen points out that a credit crisis is always preceded by deregulation of banks. He describes the deregulation policy of the last few decades as a "massive corporate governance failure of the financial system".[70]

Fourth, research coming out of the International Monetary Fund (IMF) eliminates the idea, long held in economics, that there is a trickle down of wealth from the richest members of society to everybody else. This is a belief that is not supported by real data. The IMF analysis shows that GDP growth actually declines as the gap between the rich and the poor grows wider:[71]

> A growing body of evidence suggests that rising influence of the rich and stagnant incomes of the poor and middle class have a causal effect on crisis, and thus directly hurt short- and long-term growth. In particular, studies have argued that a prolonged period of high inequality in advanced economies was associated with the global financial crisis by intensifying leverage, over extension of credit, and a relaxation of mortgage-underwriting standards.

69 Rosen, BA 2016, 'Potted review of economic theory: the complex evolving system', in J-P Close (ed), *AIREAS sustainocracy for a healthy city: the invisible made visible*, Springer International, New York, p. 2.

70 Stiglitz, n 67.

71 Dabla-Norris, E, Kochhar, K, Suphaphiphat, N, Ricka, F & Tsounta, E 2015, *Causes and consequences of income inequality: a global perspective*, International Monetary Fund Strategy, Policy and Review Department, Washington, DC, p. 8.

Case Study 1: Population

> Earth's population is growing like algae in a pond and is aging more rapidly than ever. Unlike Aristotle or Malthus who could not conceive of the miraculous technology that saved the day for us, we now face the sobering fact that population is an issue and that there are actual limits to Earth's capacities to sustain these massive numbers, even with technology.[72]

Both population and pollution currently sit outside our mental model of how the economic system works. One is seen as an "input" to the system, creating growth (population), and the other is seen as an output or externality (pollution). If we incorporate both into the world system model, we see two feedback loops that look like this:

> More people = more consumers = more economic growth.
> AND
> More people = more use of natural resources = more waste = more environmental destruction.

From the Industrial Revolution onwards, world population has grown at an exponential rate. Fossil fuels have allowed us to vastly improve health, standards of living and productivity, enabling many more of us to thrive than ever before. World population reached 1 billion in 1804 and tripled to 3 billion in 1959. By 1999, it had doubled to 6 billion, and 9.7 billion of us are likely to exist by 2050. The population growth rate is declining, but overall population is still rising.[73]

These global population figures hide the fact that most developed countries have declining population rates due to falling birth rates, and a small number of developing countries have high population rates and still high birth rates. Continued population growth until 2050 is almost certain, even with declining fertility rates. However, future population growth is highly sensitive to the paths and choices made now as relatively small changes projected over decades generate large differences in total population. Only nine countries are expected to make up more than half the world's projected population increase between 2019 and 2050; those countries are India, Nigeria, Pakistan, the Democratic Republic of the Congo, Ethiopia, the United Republic of Tanzania, the United States of America, Indonesia and Egypt.[74]

72 Higgins, n 21, at 56.

73 United Nations Department of Economic and Social Affairs 2019, *Population division world population prospects 2019: highlights ST/ESA/SER.A/423*, United Nations, New York, p. 5, (https://population.un.org/wpp/Publications/Files/WPP2019_Highlights.pdf).

74 At 12.

Region	Population (millions) 2019	2030	2050	2100
World	**7713**	**8548**	**9735**	**10875**
Sub-Saharan Africa	1066	1400	2118	3775
Northern Africa and Western Asia	517	609	754	924
Central and Southern Asia	1991	2227	2496	2334
Eastern and South-Eastern Asia	2335	2427	2411	1967
Latin America and the Caribbean	648	706	762	680
Australia/New Zealand	30	33	38	49
Oceania*	12	15	19	26
Europe and Northern America	1114	1132	1136	1120
Least Developed Countries	1033	1314	1877	3047
Land-locked Developing Countries	521	659	926	1406
Small Island Developing States	71	78	87	88

Figure 3.1 Population of the World, SDG Regions and Selected Groups of Countries, 2019, 2030, 2050 and 2100, According to the Medium-Variant Projection

Source: At 6

Higgins conducts a "business as usual" experiment using projected population figures which show CO_2 emissions growing by 23%, municipal solid waste growing by 87% and fossil fuel consumption growing by 23%. Loss of forest amounts to another 78 million hectares and drops in aquifer levels a further 3,583 cubic kilometres per year.[75]

Higgins also considers a scenario in which the world would take conscious steps to decrease population. However, reducing population raises difficult political, moral, legal and religious questions. The human right to reproduce is seen by many as sacrosanct. As a general rule, large numbers of children in poorer societies are seen as an asset increasing family wealth, whereas in developed societies, the cost of having a large family reduces family wealth. On the positive side, education in poorer countries around family planning and changing cultural values about having large families are starting to make inroads. Ultimately, the population problem boils down to a conflict between the "reproductive rights of the current generation and the survival rights of the next generation".[76]

A number of countries have experimented with population de-growth policies. In the 1980s, Iran initiated a policy of family-planning education and contraception before a marriage license could be obtained. The drop in Iran's fertility rate (from seven children per woman in the 1980s to two today) is the largest and fastest drop ever recorded and shows a strong link between

75 Higgins, n 21, at 106–107. Higgins includes sources used to calculate the figures.

76 At 139. See also Brown, L, Gardner, G & Halweil, B 2000, *Beyond Malthus: nineteen dimensions of the population challenge*, Earthscan, London.

education and reduced fertility rates.[77] China's one-child policy, which was started in the 1970s, reduced China's fertility rate to 1.702 in 2022.[78] Unfortunately, for political reasons, both countries are reassessing their population control policies.

Data shows that overall, the world population is ageing. Globally, the number of people over 60 will double by 2050 and triple by 2100. The number of people over 80 is expected to increase from 143 million in 2019 to 426 million in 2050 and to 881 million in 2100.[79] This has repercussions for the developed countries, where an ageing population creates a cycle of fewer people available for productive employment, creating a shortage of workers, which negatively affects the economy and reduces tax revenue right at the time when higher pension and health costs are coming on stream. In developed countries, public spending on pensions and healthcare is likely to hit 15 to 23% of GDP by 2030.[80]

Although there are obvious hurdles, there are also strong benefits to putting in place a single global population policy or goal that applies to all countries and would assist in evening out different countries' high and low population growth issues while pursuing the goal of decreasing population growth. The movement of people from over-populated areas to under-populated areas for employment would smooth the process, as would the right adoption policies, allowing a flow of children from high-fertility regions to low-fertility ones. None of the solutions are easy, but neither are they impossible:[81]

> Global values that promote *quality* of life for all could be helpful. . . . [I]n addition, people must know the dire and unintended consequences that unrestrained population growth has on environment, economy and society. None of us should consider ourselves exceptions to the population reduction goal.

77 See United Nations Department of Economic and Social Affairs 2019, *Population division world population prospects 2019: highlights ST/ESA/SER.A/423*, United Nations, New York, p. 31. See also Higgins, n 21, at 141.

78 MacroTrends 2022, 'China: fertility rate 1950–2022' (viewed 24 January 2022), (https://www.macrotrends.net/countries/CHN/china/fertility-rate). We note that China's population policy may have prevented around 400 million births. Unfortunately, through a culture promoting the value of males over females, China now has an imbalance in its gender ratio. In India, while government policies promote population control, internally, some groups still promote the birth of many children.

79 United Nations Department of Economic and Social Affairs, Population Division, n 77, at 18.

80 Higgins, n 21, at 56.

81 At 140.

Case Study 2: Pollution

Once we acknowledge population and pollution consequences and integrate these into our mental model of how the world actually works, the limits to growth become obvious. Pollution is a by-product of the global economy. As we buy more goods, we produce more rubbish and waste, which feeds back into the world system to slow down the economy, damage the environment and negatively affect us:[82]

> Acknowledging the consequences of population growth and increasing pollution must forever change how we view the world. No longer can we push them aside, for they have already pricked the shimmery bubble that contains our mental model. When we integrate them into our world view . . . we see the potential for disastrous outcomes.

The World Bank's *Getting Down to Earth* states that, as of 2022, "exposure to outdoor airborne pollutant particles . . . leads to an estimated 4.2 million deaths a year".[83] The latest World Health Organization data, as of 2021, also reports that around 92% of pollution-related deaths occur in low- and middle-income nations.[84] Regarding the disparity of the spread of pollution between high-income and low- and middle-income countries, Higgins states that in high-income countries:

> The truth is that because most of us have not yet felt substantial damage, we do not worry much about pollution or population. We just "kick the can" into the future.[85]

In 2018, the World Bank updated its 2012 What a Waste report that looks at the production of municipal solid waste (MSW) levels.[86] Based on these data, MSW levels reached 2.01 billion tonnes in 2016 and are expected to rise to 3.40 billion tonnes per year by 2050.[87] Again, global averages hide a

82 At 69.

83 The World Bank Group and International Bank for Reconstruction and Development 2022, *Getting down on Earth: are satellites reliable for measuring air pollutants that cause mortality in low-and middle-income countries?* International Development in Focus.

84 The World Health Organization, *Air pollution data portal*, (https://www.who.int/data/gho/data/themes/air-pollution).

85 Higgins, see 21, at 28.

86 Hoornweg, D & Bhada Tata, P 2012, *What a waste: a global review of solid waste management*, The World Bank's Urban Development and Local Government Unit of Sustainable Development Network, Washington, DC. For the latest edition, see Kaza, S, Yao, L, Bhada-Tata, P & Van Woerden, F 2018, *What a waste 2.0: a global snapshot of solid waste management to 2050*, Urban Development, World Bank, Washington, DC.

87 Kaza, et al., see 86, at 17–18.

bigger picture. The bulk of MSW is produced in the developed countries and correlates strongly with high rates of economic development and urbanization: "waste generation varies as a function of affluence".[88] Generation of MSW is projected to rise faster than population growth, which indicates that, as more people move out of poverty (through economic growth – the main driver of rising affluence), more people buy more goods that a ultimately discarded as waste.

The greenhouse gas/climate change problem is really a pollution "sink" problem. The planet is not able to dispose of the higher and higher levels of CO_2 that our fossil-fuelled lifestyle produces.[89] Do we really need to know how much of the world's 400 billion tonnes of agricultural, industrial, and human waste finds its way into our rivers, oceans, lakes, streams and ultimately into our bodies?

Systems thinking shows us clearly that unrestrained materialism and capitalism in its current form are in complete contradiction with ecological integrity. We cannot continue to produce and consume at the rate we are doing now. If we do, we will destroy the earth's delicate and complex ecological balance as well as our own well-being.

3. What Have We Learnt?

> The signs are everywhere around us. . . . [T]hese are symptoms of a world in overshoot, where we are drawing on the world's resources faster than they can be restored, and we are releasing wastes and pollutants faster than the earth can absorb them. . . . They are leading us toward global environmental and economic collapse-but there may still be time to address these problems and soften the impact.[90]

We have learnt that we are globally connected. We have also learnt that our economy is out of balance with the environment and with human health and well-being. Lord Nicholas Stern states that climate change is the greatest and most far-ranging market failure in the history of capitalism.[91]

Thomas Piketty's *Capital in the Twenty-First Century* also signals the failure of capitalism to stem the growing and socially corrosive worldwide

88 Hoornweg and Bhada Tata, see 86, at 8.

89 Intergovernmental Panel on Climate Change 2021, 'Summary for policymakers', in V Masson-Delmotte, P Zhai, et al. (eds), *Climate change 2021: the physical science basis.* Contribution of Working Group I to the Sixth Assessment Report of the Intergovernmental Panel on Climate Change, Cambridge University Press, In Press.

90 Meadows, et al., *A Synopsis: Limits to Growth: The 30-Year Update, 2002.*

91 Stern, N 2006, *The economics of climate change: the Stern review*, Her Majesty's Treasury, London.

inequality.[92] What are our options? We can disguise, deny and ignore the growing data, or we can limit the extent of the problem with new technology and efficiency (though the latter will only delay the outcome and not eliminate *the cause* of the problems). We could recognize the underlying cause as overshoot of the planet's ecological limits, which now requires radical changes to the structure of our economic system and our behaviour.

We can confront our situation with objectivity and integrity and acknowledge that:

- The laissez-faire system does not magically solve long-term systemic economic and environmental challenges.[93]
- Maximizing profit does not necessarily maximize human wealth. Capital and wealth need redefining for the twenty-first century.
- Robust circulation of capital through all levels of the economy is critical for resilience within the system and cannot be sacrificed for efficiency. There must be a balance between the two.[94]

John Fullerton, a former JP Morgan managing director with two decades of financial expertise and also the founder and president of Capital Institute,[95] sets out eight key principles for creating a new kind of capitalism called "regenerative capitalism" based on universal principles that underpin natural systems and also apply to human systems:[96]

1. *In right relationship.* Humans being in right relationship with the rest of the natural system. The scale of the economy must be in right relation to the limits of the biosphere in which it is embedded.
2. *Views wealth holistically.* Culturally. we must redefine wealth to include other forms of capital that are aligned with our core values, such as social, cultural, living, intellectual, material, spiritual, financial and experiential capital.[97]
3. *Innovative, adaptive, responsive.* An economic system that has resilience is one that is most adaptable to events and changes in the environment.

92 Piketty, T 2013, *Capital in the twenty-first century*, A Goldhammer (trans), Brilliance Audio, Grand Haven. See also Wilkinson, RG & Pickett, KE 2009, 'Income inequality and social dysfunction', *Annual Review of Sociology*, vol. 35, p. 493.

93 Oxford Dictionary 2019, *Laissez-faire*, 3rd edn, online edn. "A phrase expressive of the principle that government should not interfere with the action of individuals, especially in industrial affairs and in trade".

94 Berry, C, Ryan-Collins, J & Greenham, T 2015, *Financial system resilience index: building a strong financial system*, New Economics Foundation, London.

95 See Capital Institute, (www.capitalinstitute.org).

96 Fullerton, J 2015, *Regenerative capitalism: how universal principles and patterns will shape our new economy*, Capital Institute, Greenwich, p. 43.

97 See The International Integrated Reporting Council (www.integratedreporting.org).

4. *Empowered participation.* Empowered participation is enabling all sections contributing to the economy to negotiate for their needs and add their unique contributions to the nested larger holes in which they are embedded.
5. *Honours community and place.* Honours community and place through nurturing healthy and resilient communities. Diversity creates richness.
6. *Edge, effect, abundance.* Recognizing that innovation often comes from the edges of the system, not the centre.
7. *Robust circulatory flow.* Robust circulatory flow of money, information, resources and supports flushing out toxins in the economy and nourishing all participants.
8. *Seeks balance.* Regenerative systems are engaged in delicate harmonizing of multiple variables, not optimizing single ones. Balance of efficiency and resilience, collaboration and competition, diversity and coherence meeting small, medium and large organizations and needs.

Transforming our economy will be challenging and difficult. Each one of the ideas that follow needs substantial development from economists, bankers, legal scholars, taxation specialists, trade unions, employees, companies and others. Most of them are politically difficult, but they also represent an enormous opportunity to create a sustainable system. They include (but are not limited to):

- Implementing a carbon tax.
- Encoding a *grundnorm* of ecological integrity in international and national law to protect the environment.
- Re-examining the international money system. Should banks have the right to create commercial money? Should the creation of money be a public responsibility? Should governments *spend* money into the economy instead?[98]
- An international population policy with a single goal applying across all nations.
- Internalizing pollution costs into the economic system.
- Removing subsidies for all products and activities that damage the environment. Creating subsidies for those activities that sustain the environment through tax changes, tax credits and feed in tariffs.
- Aligning tax codes internationally, incorporating social and environmental costs and benefits.

98 See Positive Money (www.positivemoney.org). See also Teubner, G 2011, 'A constitutional moment? The logics of "hitting the bottom"', in P Kjaer & G Teubner (eds), *The financial crisis in constitutional perspective: the dark side of functional differentiation*, Hart Publishing, Bloomsbury, p. 3.

- Strengthening the trusteeship character of the World Health Organization to more effectively control the outbreak and impact of pandemic diseases.
- Creation of trusteeship institutions to protect the world's global commons, such as a World Environment Organization, to monitor and report and collect data on Earth's ecological systems.
- Re-evaluating our values around consumption and the cultural use of goods to symbolize our personal status.[99]
- Re-evaluating our values around freedom (and responsibilities) of speech and the role and influence of advertising and the media in a sustainable global society.
- Developing new metrics that go beyond GDP for measuring national and global wealth.

John Fullerton sets out a number of practical working examples operating at the edges of the economic system that are already experimenting with new models. These include the creation of B corps, micro-enterprises and micro-finance, slow food/energy/money organizations, impact investing, Global Alliance for Banking on Values (GABV) and NGOs.[100] Paul Hawken describes NGOs as "the largest movement in the world that no one saw coming":[101]

> "Usually set up by ordinary citizens . . . NGOs devote themselves to critical initial issues that require long-term attention and where neither market nor government solutions are viable on their own such as climate change, malaria prevention or even rethinking capitalism!

Fullerton points out that NGOs often enjoy a high degree of public trust, working across broad concerns of society. There are 1.8 million NGOs in the United States,[102] 3.3 million in India[103] and approximatively 216,000 in Russia.[104]

99 Braungart, M & McDonough, W 2009, *Cradle to cradle: re-making the way we make things*, Vintage Books, London.
100 Fullerton, n 96, at 83–91.
101 At 86.
102 Faulk, L, Kim, M, Derrick-Mills, T, Boris, ET, Tomasko, L, Hakizimana, N, Chen, T, Kim, M & Nath, L 2021, *Nonprofit trends and impacts 2021: national findings on donation trends from 2015 through 2020, diversity and representation, and first-year impacts of the COVID-19 pandemic*, Research Report, Urban Institute, October, p. 1.
103 International Center for Nonprofit Law, India (last updated on 11 February 2022), (https://www.icnl.org/resources/civic-freedom-monitor/india).
104 International Center for Nonprofit Law, Russia (last updated on 31 November 2021), (https://www.icnl.org/resources/civic-freedom-monitor/russia).

In discussing the United Kingdom's economic system, Professor Lord May states that the time has come to make the economy much more resilient.[105] Economic resilience is defined as:[106]

> The capacity of an economic system to adapt in response to both short-term shocks and long-term change and ecological, social and economic conditions while supporting the community to thrive within fair ecological limits.

Re-imagining an economic system that functions within ecological limits is the greatest challenge and also the greatest opportunity for our generation in the age of the Anthropocene.

105 Berry, et al., n 94, at 7.
106 Greenham, T, Cox, E & Ryan-Collins, J 2013, *Mapping economic resilience*, Friends Provident Foundation, York, p. 29.

Chapter 4

Ecological Integrity

> The unique insight of the systems science community is one crucial to these times, to this anthropocentric era in which we find ourselves. The era and its challenges demand the engagement of humanity to an unprecedented degree, and we feel the systems community must step forth to a vitally important role.[1]

1. Systems Thinking

Thinking about the law and its relationship to the environment, we need to step outside a specific area or discipline to fully appreciate the way the world works outside the framework and assumptions that permeate individual disciplines such as jurisprudence, for example. Instead, in the following, we focus on understanding how "systems thinking" works and how it can help us understand the convergence of environmental, economic, political and social problems within an overall macro-system framework. This is often described in systems thinking as looking at the "world system".[2] Systems thinking is not so much about focusing on quantitative data but rather focusing on the *trends* that data reveals and then placing those trends in the context of a world system model in order to understand where leverage points for changing the behaviour of the system[3] might reside:[4]

> A system is a network of multi-variables that are connected to each other through causal relationship and has certain behaviours, which we only

1 Wilson, I & Henning, PM 2015, 'A call to action for the systems sciences community', *Journal of the International Society for the System Sciences*, vol. 1, no. 1. See also Future Sharp (https://www.futuresharp.co/).

2 "World system" is used here to describe a system that includes both the physical and human world.

3 A leverage point is a place within a complex system where a small shift in one thing can produce a large change across the entire system. See Meadows, D 1999, *Leverage points: places to intervene in a system*, The Sustainable Institute, (http://donellameadows.org/archives/leverage-points-places-to-intervene-in-a-system/).

4 Haraldson, HV 2004, 'Introduction to systems and causal loop diagrams: reports in ecology and environmental engineering', *Lund University*, vol. 1, p. 11. See also Grant, WE 1997,

DOI: 10.4324/9781032674049-6

> can characterise through observation as a whole. The principal attribute of a system is that we can only understand its behaviour by viewing it as a whole.

The goal in introducing any change is to create greater resilience and integrity in the world system as a whole. For the purposes of these three systems chapters, the terms "resilience" and "integrity" are used interchangeably. The resilience/integrity of any system is its ability to survive and thrive in a variable environment.

Understanding the world system's leverage points and which ones are most likely to create greater integrity in the system is vital to our ability to live sustainably without crashing and collapsing the whole system. If we do not achieve this, we threaten the future of our children and our ability to thrive on the planet. Confidence in achieving this can come from the creation of a more accurate mental model[5] of how the world system works. It requires a more complete mental picture of the connections and interdependencies between a number of key issues, such as human population size, energy and its use and pollution/waste.

Donella Meadows, even while spending her whole adult life constructing and explaining systems thinking, also warned of the necessity of being able to transcend *all* paradigms. She described this as the highest leverage point in any system: to be able to stay flexible realizing that all paradigms are limited and can only ever be merely a hazy reconstruction of reality. She noted that it should be kept in mind that our understandings are "tremendously limited in comparison to the immense and amazing universe that is far beyond human comprehension".[6]

> Everyone who has managed to entertain that idea, for a moment or for a lifetime, has found it to be the basis for radical empowerment. If no paradigm is right, you can choose whatever one will help to achieve your purpose. If you have no idea where to get a purpose, you can listen to the universe. . . . [I]t is in this space of mastery over paradigms that people throw off addictions, live in constant joy, bring down empires, found religions, get locked up or "disappeared" or shot, and have impacts that last for millennia.[7]

Ecology and natural resource management, systems analysis and simulation, John Wiley and Sons, Toronto, p. 373.

5 The term "mental model" is used here to mean the model we create from our experiences, cultures and behaviours and which generally dictates our choices. See Higgins, *Economic Growth and Sustainability*, p. 14.

6 Meadows, n 3, at 19.

7 Meadows, n 3, at 19.

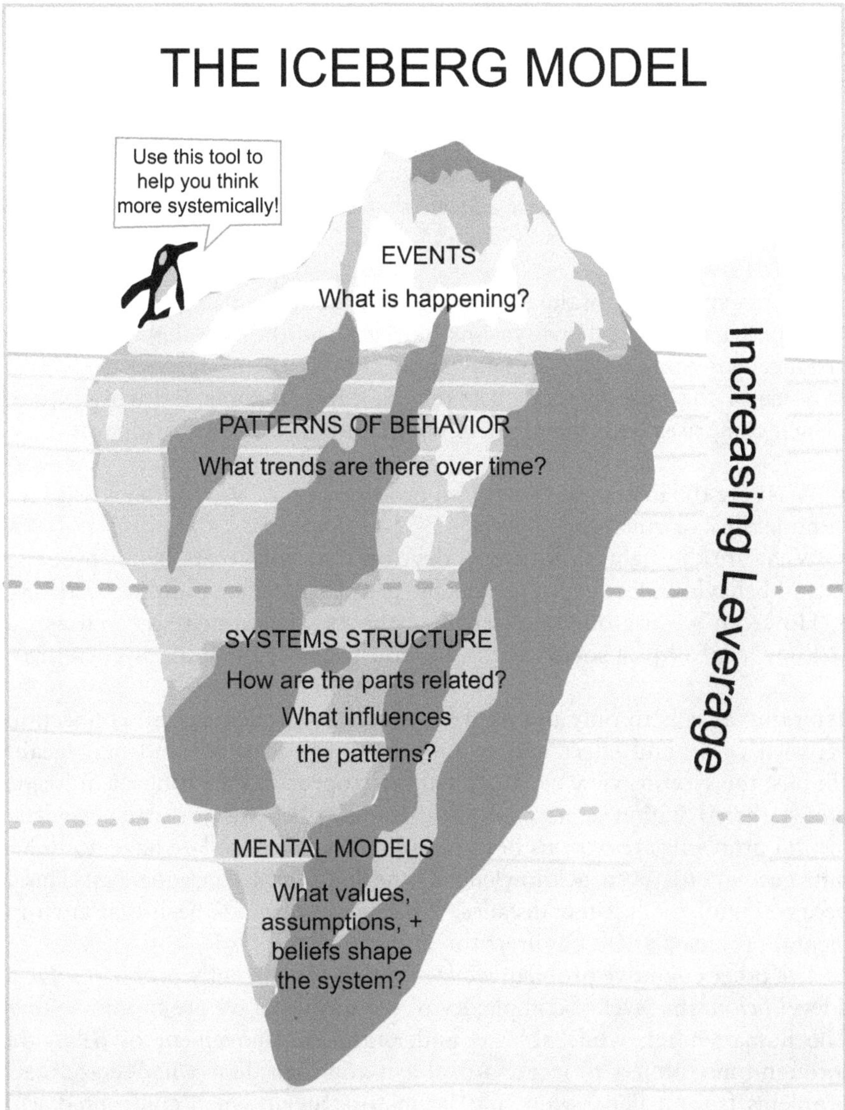

Figure 4.1 The Iceberg Model

Source: Meadows, D, 'The iceberg model' (http://donellameadows.org/systems-thinking-resources)

Peter Senge, another of the system community's most creative thinkers, describes a good entry into systems thinking in the following way:

> Are you part of a family? If so, you will know you live within a complicated and delicate web of family relationships. You will also instinctively know that each family member is capable of producing many unintended consequences through their actions that have the capacity to reverberate throughout that family's "system".[8]

The sheer complexity of the interchanges within that small group of relationships perhaps best explains systems thinking and the idea that a system can produce many unintended and unwanted consequences.

Some of the introductory questions we can ask about the world system (which comprises both the *physical* world and the *human* world) are:

- What are the interacting parts and processes of the system that create sustainability or collapse?
- What are the right pathways to develop that will create better processes and behaviour, leading to greater integrity/resiliency within the system?
- How can we use our knowledge of the existing system, as well as our knowledge of past societies, to consciously create the future we want?

Tempting as it is to only use the reductionist approach to find connections between cause and effect and to look at things in small and manageable chunks, the systems view can augment this approach by setting the information gathered within a larger holistic framework. Many existing environmental problems are with us because solutions taken to date have not taken into account (or even acknowledged) the long-term consequences. This is because, until the last few decades, the general view has been that environmental problems are not a direct threat to society.

The other cognitive problem we face is that we currently problem solve at a level *below* the level of complexity of the problems we are trying to solve. The human mind, while able to understand the movement of behaviour through time, prefers to freeze a problem and then dissect it. We approach problems from a linear view and begin to struggle when confronted with complex dynamic behaviour that includes more than two to three dynamic variables. This is why system thinking tools and computer system modelling can help and why systems constantly seem to surprise us.

There is also the additional problem of the human tendency to look for someone to blame for environmental and other problems – whether it is politicians, the banks or the wealthiest people in our society soaking up vast

8 Senge, P 2014, *Introduction to systems thinking*, viewed 5 August 2014, (www.youtube.com). Peter Senge is the author of *The Fifth Discipline*, senior lecturer at MIT and founder of the Society for Organizational Learning.

amounts of capital, leading to inequity and tension. In systems thinking, we give up any assumptions that someone is responsible for the problem encountered. Rather, the problems are a result of *the structural dynamics and behaviour set-up by the system itself*. Systems thinking is understanding the relationships and patterns between the different components in a network of relationships. While psychologically, it is more comfortable to find a scapegoat, no one *deliberately* creates these problems. They are systems problems. In other words, they are undesirable characteristic behaviours produced by the very system structure we have unwittingly put in place. They only yield to change once we ask ourselves the question "What is the system?" Once recognizing the system as the source of the problem, we then, in Donella Meadows's words, must "find the courage and wisdom to restructure it".[9]

a) The Basics of Systems Thinking

> Long before we were educated in rational analysis, we all dealt with complex systems. We are complex systems – our bodies are magnificent examples of integrated, interconnected, self-maintaining complexity.[10]

Humans are adept solvers of simple problems, but, as already mentioned, systems thinking provides us with better tools for understanding complex problems.[11] It requires that we move beyond looking at events in isolation at a particular point in time and start looking for a system that is made up of interacting parts that often function simultaneously. Systems diagrams allow us to move beyond the restriction of a linear language like English, in which we can only talk about one step in a system at a time. Systems thinking looks at how "effects" loop back to influence the original cause. It considers the interactions that shape system behaviour *as time passes*.[12]

A system is defined as "an interconnected set of elements that is coherently organised in a way that achieves something".[13] From this definition, we can see that all systems have three things:

1. Elements;
2. Interconnections; and
3. A function or purpose.

9 Meadows, DL 2008, *Thinking in systems: a primer*, Chelsea Green Publishing, Vermont, p. 4.
10 At 3.
11 Our usual response to a problem is to apply a fix that shows swift results and restores something to its original condition. Although we do not recognize it, we are often solving a symptom and not a cause within a system. This is sometimes called an end-of-pipe solution. Generally, end-of-pipe solutions deal only with the obvious short-term problem without taking into account long-term consequences. For example, dealing with the impact of acid rain by initiating liming programmes to rebalance pH levels without dealing with the cause of the acidity effects.
12 Meadows, n 3, at 6.
13 At 11.

Systems exist all around us. A school is a system, a university is a system, a city is a system, a business is a system and the national and global economy is a system.

The planet is one large system with many sub-systems at many levels.

A systems map tells a story. The *elements* of a system are the easiest parts to identify because they are often (but not always) the visible parts of the system. For example, a sports team is a system with elements such as a coach, the players, the field and the ball.[14] A university is a system with the elements being the students, the lecturers and the buildings. Elements can also be intangible things like the values of the university and its academic success and university pride.

The *interconnections* of a system are the *relationships* that hold the elements of the system together. For example, the interconnections of the sports team system discussed here are the team's strategy of play, the rules of the game, the players' interactions and communications with each other and the coach. Also, the laws of physics that set physical boundaries for the motions of the players and the ball. In the university system, the interconnections are the flow of knowledge from the lecturers to the students (which is also the overall goal and function of the system), the standards for admission, examination grading, budgets, internal politics and communications, money flows, internal standards and rules. If we look at a natural system like a plant, the interconnections are the chemical signals or flows of information that allow one part of the plant to respond to what is happening in another part. When the plant's leaves lose water on a hot day, the drop in pressure in the water-holding vessels in the leaves signal the roots to take up water through the soil instead.[15]

The *function/purpose* of the system is often the hardest part to discover. The best way to find it out is to watch a system over a period of time and see how it behaves:[16]

> If a government proclaims its interest in protecting the environment but allocates little money or effort toward that goal, environmental protection is not, in fact, the government's purpose. Purposes are deduced from behaviour, not from rhetoric or stated goals.

b) Bathtub Dynamics

Donella Meadows uses the example of a bathtub to understand system behaviour over time.[17] A "stock" is the stored quantity of element(s) in a

14 At 11.
15 At 14.
16 At 14.
17 At 17.

system.[18] There is an inflow of water, the quantity or stock of water and an outflow. Stocks change over time due to the actions of the flow.

For example, when a bathtub is full and has the taps turned off and the plug in place, we have an unchanging undynamic system. However, if the plug is removed, the water (the stock) runs out, and the level of water (stock) reduces until the bathtub is empty. If we imagine a full bathtub once more but remove the plug and turn the inflow tap on at the same time so the rate of water flowing out is equal to the rate of water flowing in, we now have a system in "dynamic equilibrium" – the stock does not change although it is continuously flowing through the system. A sustainable renewable energy system properly conceived and managed has the ability to operate in dynamic equilibrium.

Now, if we imagine increasing the inflow tap so the amount of water coming in is greater than the amount of water going down the drain, the level of water in the bathtub will slowly rise. This is, for example, our current position with CO_2 in the atmosphere. We are putting more CO_2 into the air than the planet can naturally remove through its systems.

Within, for example, an energy system, we can see that non-renewable fossil and mineral resources (coal, oil and gas) are "stock limited": that is, eventually, they will run out. Renewable energy resources are "flow limited": only able to regenerate at a certain rate. From a system's point-of-view we could say that:[19]

1. Every renewable resource should be used at or below the rate at which it can regenerate itself;
2. Every non-renewable resource should be used at or below the rate at which a renewable substitute can be developed; and
3. Every pollution stream should only be emitted at or below the rate at which it can be absorbed or made harmless.

c) *Feedback Loops*

A further characteristic of stocks is that they tend to change slowly, even when inflows and outflows in the system change suddenly. To some extent, inflows and outflows can be independent of each other and out of balance for a period of time.

18 Meadows, n 9, at 188. Further, "stocks are the elements of any system which are an accumulation of material or information that has built up in a system over time".

19 Meadows, D 2013, 'Donella Meadows lecture: sustainable systems' (viewed 9 May 2013), (www.youtube.com).

This means that stocks act as "delays" or buffers in systems. Delays or lags between a cause and consequence can have an enormous impact on a system, mainly because we find it difficult to recognize the difference between a delay in a system and a system that is functioning in a state of equilibrium. Delays are often subtle or ignored completely and nearly always underestimated.[20] Once we understand the dynamics of stocks and flows and their behaviour over time, we are well on the way to understanding more about the behaviour of complex systems.[21]

System thinkers look at the world as a series of stocks, along with the mechanisms for regulating levels of those stocks by manipulating flows. They see the world as a collection of feedback processes:[22]

> Systems of information feedback control are fundamental to all life and human endeavour, from the slow pace of biological evolution to the launching of the latest space satellite. . . . [E]verything we do as individuals, as an industry or as a society is done in the context of an information feed-back system.

A feedback loop is formed when "changes in a stock affect the flows into or out of that same stock".[23] The two common feedback loops are *balancing feedback loops* and *reinforcing feedback loops*.

Balancing feedback loops are equalizing or goal-seeking structures in systems and can be sources of both stability and resistance to change. Balancing loops push behaviour towards a particular state and then work to maintain that state.[24]

Reinforcing feedback loops, on the other hand, self-enhance, leading to exponential growth or to collapse over time.[25] Reinforcing feedback loops generate growth behaviour or decay behaviour, driving a system in the direction that it is already heading. Reinforcing feedback loops are sometimes called *virtuous* or *vicious cycles* and have the potential to create both healthy growth and destruction. Reinforcing leaps can be found in a system in which an element has the capability to reproduce itself, as, for example, populations

20 For example, prior to the global financial crisis, complex strategies to bundle and sell dubious debt along with relaxed credit requirements for home mortgages seemed initially beneficial to growth but had disastrous consequences years later. These consequences were unrecognized as a problem at the time because of the delay in the system between cause and consequence.

21 Meadows, n 3, at 19.

22 Forrester, J 1961, *Industrial dynamics*, The MIT Press, Cambridge, p. 15.

23 Meadows, n 9, at 25.

24 Kirkwood, CW 2013, *System dynamics methods: a quick introduction*, Arizona State University: Systems Dynamics, 12 January.

25 Meadows, n 9, at 289.

or economies can do. Understanding the feedback loop awakens us to the idea that a system can cause its own behaviour.[26]

The many feedback loops in a system pull against each other, trying to make stocks grow, die off or come into balance. As a result, complex systems do not approach goals smoothly or remain steady or grow as expected.[27]

d) Resilience

The resilience/integrity of any system is its ability to thrive in a variable environment. For the purposes of understanding the basics of systems thinking, we have been looking at each part of a system in a reductionist manner, but it is important to understand that the resilience of a system generally arises out of "a rich structure of many feedback loops that work in different ways to restore a system even after a large perturbation".[28]

> Ecosystems are also remarkably resilient, with multiple species holding each other in cheek, moving around in space, multiplying or declining over time in response to weather and the availability of nutrients and the impacts of human activities.[29]

Resilience is quite different from the idea of a system remaining constant over time. Resilient systems tend to be dynamic, exhibiting oscillations and cycles of change and involving a process of climax, collapse and rebirth. Resilience in a system can be hard to detect unless the systems limits are exceeded, or its balancing loops are damaged. It is common for resilience to be sacrificed in systems by humans in order to achieve stability. An example of this would be the narrowing of genetic crop variability to grow our food.[30]

How do we change systems to get less of what we *don't* want and more of what we *do* want? This is where an understanding of leverage points within a system becomes important.[31]

> Leverage points are places within a complex system where a small shift in one thing can produce big changes in everything.

Jay Forrester has pointed out that even though we understand intuitively where to find leverage points (in our world system, "growth" is a leverage

26 At 34.
27 Meadows, n 3, at 13.
28 Meadows, n 9, at 76.
29 At 76–77.
30 At 79.
31 Meadows, n 3, at 1.

point), we often try to push change in the *wrong direction*.[32] The classic example is the current attempt to increase GDP growth to solve large systemic environmental and social problems when, rather, breaking down the existing paradigm to re-imagine different *kinds* of growth (and new measurements for these) is needed, along with accepting that negative growth in some parts of the world system will be necessary (for example, the fishing of exhausted or close to exhausted fish species in the oceans).[33] Our mental model of growth as we now conceive it is woefully inadequate. Both population and economic growth have environmental and social costs (poverty and environmental destruction), which we ignore in classical economics focusing only on benefits.

The following is a list of Donella Meadow's 12 points of key places to intervene in any system, in increasing order of effectiveness.[34]

Places to Intervene in a System

(in increasing order of effectiveness)

12. Constants, parameters, numbers (such as subsidies, taxes, standards).
11. The sizes of buffers and other stabilizing stocks, relative to their flows.
10. The structure of material stocks and flows (such as transport networks, population age structures).
9. The lengths of delays, relative to the rate of system change.
8. The strength of negative feedback loops, relative to the impacts they are trying to correct against.
7. The gain around driving positive feedback loops.
6. The structure of information flows (who does and does not have access to information).
5. The rules of the system (such as incentives, punishments, constraints).
4. The power to add, change, evolve, or self-organize system structure.
3. The goals of the system.
2. The mindset or paradigm out of which the system – its goals, structure, rules, delays, parameters – arises.
1. The power to transcend paradigms.

Points 1, 2 and 3 are the hardest leverage points with which to create change, but, if successful, they are also the most effective in doing so. Our unstated assumptions and deepest-held beliefs about how the world works

32 Forrester, n 25, at 65.
33 Meadows, n 9, at 146. The dynamics of growth are discussed in Chapter 7.
34 Meadows, n 3, at 2.

will be the focus of the next chapter, along with a closer look at an integrated world system:[35]

> Every nation and every man instantly surround themselves with a material apparatus which exactly corresponds to . . . their state of thought. Observe how every truth and every error, each thought in some man's mind, clothes itself with societies, houses, cities, language, ceremonies, newspapers. Observe the ideas of the present day. . . . [S]ee how timber, brick, lime and stone have flown into convenient shape, obedient to the master idea reigning and the minds of many persons. . . . [I]t follows, of course, that the least enlargement of ideas . . . would cause the most striking changes of external things.

2. Ecological Integrity

a) Presence in International Law

Aldo Leopold, in his book *A Sand County Almanac*, is credited with the origin and meaning of the term "ecological integrity" when he wrote that a "thing is right when it tends to preserve the integrity, stability and beauty of the biotic community".[36] The term "ecological integrity" has come to hold normative ethical value, but can it be found within the law? The answer is yes, the term can be found in a growing number of both international and national instruments. Figure 4.2 shows a selection of environmental instruments containing reference to the concept of ecological integrity.[37]

The notion of ecological integrity made its first appearance in international law in 1978 in the Great Lakes Water Quality Agreement, which was signed by both Canada and the United States "to restore and maintain the chemical, physical, and biological integrity of the waters of the Great Lakes".[38]

The first multilateral agreement to include ecological integrity was the Convention on the Conservation of Antarctic Marine Living Resources, which recognizes in its preamble "the importance of safeguarding the

35 Ralph Waldo Emerson "War" (lecture delivered in Boston, March 1838) as reproduced in Emerson, RW 1887, *Emerson's complete works*, vol. XI, Houghton, Mifflin & Co, Boston, p. 177.

36 Leopold, A 1986, *A sand county almanac (outdoor essays and reflections)*, 7th edn, Ballantine Books, New York.

37 Kim, RE, Bosselmann, K & Mauerhofer, V 2020, *Planetary boundaries and post-2015 sustainable development goals: safeguarding ecological integrity as a priority goal and a Grundnorm of international law*, Working Paper 2020, WWF UK, the Planetary Boundaries Initiative on the Sustainability Development Goals, pp. 26–28.

38 Great Lakes Water Quality Agreement, United States-Canada, 1978,30 U.S.T. 1383, T.A.I.S. No. 9257 (signed 22 November 1978, entered into force 22 November 1978), art 2.1.

Year of Ado priori.	Title	Location)	
1980	Convention on the Conservation of Antarctic Marine Living Resources	Preamble	RECOGNISING the importance of safeguarding the environment and protecting the integrity of the ecosystem o f the seas surrounding Antarctica;
1982	World Charter for Nature	I. General Principles	4. Ec:osystems and organisms, as well as the land, marine and atmospheric resources that are utilized by man, shall be managed to achieve and maintain optimum sustainable productivity, but not in such a way as to endanger the integrity of those other ecosystems or species with .which they coexist.
1990	Protocol Concerning Specially Protected Areas and Wildlife to the Convention for the Protection and Development of the Mali ine Environment of the Wider Caribbean Region	Preamble	Conscious of the grave threat restrictions on fish and wildlife consumption; (ii) tainting of fish and wildlife flavour posed by ill-conceived development options to the integrity of the marine and coastal environment of the Wider Caribbean Region,
1992	Rio Declaration on Environment and Developme	Preamble	Working towards international agreements which respect the interests of all and protect the integrity of the global enviroritnental and drcelopmental system,
		Principle 7. State Cooperation to Protect Ecosystem	States shall cooperate in a spirit of global partnership to consenre, protect and restore the health and integrity of the Earth's ecosystem. In view o:f the different contributions to global environmental degradation, States have common but differentiated responsibilities. The developed countries acknowledge the responsibility that they bear in the international pursuit of sustainable development in view of the pressures their societies place: on the global environment and of the technologies. and financial resources they commud
1992	Agenda: 21	Chapter 10 Integrated Approach to the Planning and Management of Land Resoure	10.1. Land is 110falally defined as a physical entity in terms of its topography and spatial nature; a broader integrative view also includes natural resources: the soils, minerals, water and biota that the land comptises. These components are org:anized in ecosystems which provide a variety of services essential to the maintenance of the integrity of life-support systerns and the productive capacity of the enviromnent.
		Chapter 16 Environmentally Sound Management of Biotechnology	16.4. Governments at the appropriate level, with the assistance of international and regional organizations and with the support of non-governmental organizations. the private sector and academic and scientific institutions., should improve both plant and animal breeding and micro-organisms through the use of traditional. and modern biotechnologies. to enhance sustainable agricultural output to achieve food security,: particularly in developing countries, with due regard to the prior identification of desired characteristics before modification, talcing into account the needs of farm.ers, the socio- economic. cultural and environmental impacts of modifications and the need to promote sustainable social and economic development, paying particular attention to how the use of biotechnolog3r will impact on the maintrance of environmental integrity. 16.22. The aim of this programme is to pre-vent. halt: and reverse enviromnental degradation through the appropriate use of biotechrtolonr in conjunction with. other technologies, while supportin.g safety procedures as' an integral component of the progrimine Specific objectives include the inauguration as soon. as possible of specific programmes with specific targets: [...] c.. To apply biotechnologies and their products to protect environmental integrity with a view to long-term ecological security
		Chapter 18 Protection of the Quality and Supply of Freshwater Resources	18.38. Three objectives will have to be pursued concurrently to integrate water-quality elements into water resource management: a. Maintenance of ecosystem integrity, according to a management principle of preserving aquatic ecosystems. including hying resources, and of effectively protecting them from any form of degradation on a drainage basin. basis;
		Chapter 31 Scientific and Technological Community	31.9. The objective should be to develop, improve and promote international acceptance of codes of practice and pidelines relating to science and technology in which the integrity of life-support systems is comprehensively accounted for and where the important role of science and technology in reconciling the needs of environment and development is accepted. [...]
1994	Convention Establishing the Association of Caribbean States	Preamble	Convinced of the critical importance of presening the environment of the region and, in particular, their shared responsibility for the preservation of the environmental integrity of the Caribbean Sea, by deploying the collective capabilities of their peoples in developing and exploiting its resources on an environmentally sound and sustainable basis, in order to enhance the quality of life of present and future generations of Caribbean peoples;

Figure 4.2 Selected International Environmental Instruments With References to Ecological Integrity

environment and protecting the integrity of the ecosystem of the seas surrounding Antarctica".[39] Since 1980, more than a dozen multilateral environmental agreements make reference to the integrity of ecosystems either in the preamble or in the operative part of the document.

As well as those instruments in which the term is specifically referred to, there are also a growing number of other important multilateral environmental agreements in which, although the term itself is not used, the underlying concept is one of ecological integrity. In Article 2 of the UNFCCC, the primary function of the Convention is "to prevent dangerous anthropogenic interference with the climate system".[40] Article 1.2 of the Vienna Convention for the Protection of the Ozone Layer sets out its primary objective of safeguarding the "integrity of the ozone layer".[41] Article 1.1(4) of the United Nations Convention on the Law of the Sea requires the protection of the "integrity of the marine environment".[42]

The concept of ecological integrity has also been included in the preamble of the Framework Agreement for the Conservation of the Living Marine Resources of the High Seas of the South Pacific:[43]

> With these goals in mind, the coastal states in question agreed to establish the South Pacific Permanent Commission (SPPC), to coordinate their maritime policies and to promote the adoption of measures to preserve the environment and protect the integrity of the South Pacific's marine ecosystem.

The preamble to the South Pacific Fishery Resources Convention states that its signatories are:[44]

> Conscious of the need to avoid adverse impacts on the environment, preserve biodiversity, maintain the integrity of marine ecosystems and minimise the risk of long-term or irreversible effects on fishing.

39 Convention on the Conservation of Antarctic Marine Living Resources, 1329 UNTS 48 (signed 20 May 1980, entered into force 7 April 1982), preamble.

40 United Nations Framework Convention on Climate Change 1771 UNTS 107 (opened for signature 4 June 1992, entered into force 21 March 1994), art 2.

41 Vienna Convention for the Protection of the Ozone Layer 26 I.L.M 1516 (signed 22 March 1985, entered into force 22 September 1988), art 1.2.

42 United Nations Convention on the Law of the Sea 1833 UNTS 3 (adopted 10 December 1982, in force 16 November 1994), art 1.1.(4).

43 Framework Agreement for the Conservation of the Living Marine Resources of the High Seas of the South Pacific (signed 14 August 2000, not yet in force) at preamble. It is commonly known as the Galapagos Agreement. See also Bosselmann, K 2022, 'A normative approach to environmental governance: sustainability at the apex of environmental law', in D Fisher (ed), *Research handbook on fundamental concepts of environmental law*, Edward Elgar Publisher, Cheltenham.

44 Convention on the Conservation and Management of High Seas Fishery Resources in the South Pacific Ocean (Auckland, 14 November 2009, in force 24 August 2012), preamble.

The Convention on Wetlands of International Importance Especially as Waterfowl Habitat refers in Article 3.12 to the "wise use" of wetlands and in Article 3.2 to the "ecological character" of wetlands.[45] The European Union's Water Framework Directive[46] has a current ecological objective for surface water to be of a "good ecological status".[47] More generally, the outcome document *The Future We Want* from the United Nations Conference on Sustainable Development in Rio de Janeiro (commonly known as Rio +20) includes the following aspirational statement:[48]

> We call for holistic and integrated approaches to sustainable development, which will guide humanity to live in harmony with nature and lead to efforts to restore the health and integrity of the Earth's ecosystem.

As well as these and other bilateral and multilateral environmental agreements, most of the significant international environmental soft law documents contain the concept of ecological integrity, demonstrating its quality as a legal norm. Article I(4) of The World Charter for Nature sets out as one of the core principles:[49]

> Ecosystems and organisms, as well as the land, marine and atmospheric resources that are utilised by man, shall be managed to achieve and maintain optimum sustainable productivity, but not in such a way as to endanger the integrity of those other ecosystems or species with which they coexist.

The preamble to The Rio Declaration on Environment and Development refers to protection of the integrity of the global environment and developmental system. Principal 7 also states:[50]

> States shall cooperate in a spirit of global partnership to conserve, protect and restore the health and integrity of the Earth's ecosystem.

45 Convention on Wetlands of International Importance especially as Waterfowl Habitat T.I.A.S., 996 U.N.T.S. 245 (signed 2 February 1971, in force 21 December 1971). It is commonly known as the Ramsar Convention.

46 The European Union is a region with transboundary environmental laws that go beyond the usual separate distinction between national and international laws.

47 European Council, Directive 2000/60/EC of the European Parliament and of the Council establishing a framework for Community action in the field of water policy (200) OJ L327, 22 December 2000. This directive of the European Parliament and Council established a framework for community action in the field of water policy. See also Josefsson, H 2012, 'Achieving ecological objectives', *Laws*, vol. 1, p. 39, 44. See also Josefsson, H 2015, 'Good ecological status: advancing the ecology of law', Doctor of laws dissertation, University of Uppsala.

48 UNGA RES 66/288 The Future We Want: Our Common Vision (2012) at [40].

49 UNGA A/RES/37/7 World Charter for Nature (28 October 1982), art I(4).

50 *The Rio Declaration on Environment and Development* UN Doc A/Conf.151(Vol 1) (12 August 1992), principle 7.

Section 10.1 of Agenda 21 acknowledges eco-services provided by ecosystems that are essential to the maintenance of the integrity of life-support systems and productive capacity of the environment.[51]

The Earth Charter places the concept of ecological integrity at its heart:[52]

> Protect and restore the integrity of Earth's ecological systems, with special concern for biological diversity and the natural processes that sustain life. (a) Adopt at all levels sustainable development plans and regulations that make environmental conservation and rehabilitation integral to all development initiatives. (b) Establish and safeguard viable nature and biosphere reserves, including wild lands and marine areas, to protect Earth's life-support systems, maintain biodiversity, and preserve our natural heritage. (c) Promote the recovery of endangered species and ecosystems. (d) Control and eradicate non-native or genetically modified organisms harmful to native species and the environment, and prevent introduction of such harmful organisms. (e) Manage the use of renewable resources such as water, soil, forest products, and marine life in ways that do not exceed rates of regeneration and that protect the health of ecosystems. (f) Manage the extraction and use of non-renewable resources such as minerals and fossil fuels in ways that minimise depletion and cause no serious environmental damage.

Principle 6 requires the prevention of "harm as the best method of environmental protection and when knowledge is limited apply a precautionary approach". Principle 7 requires the adoption of "patterns of production, consumption, and reproduction that safeguard Earth's regenerative capacities, human rights, and community well-being". Principle 8 advances "the study of ecological sustainability" and promotes the "open exchange and wide application of the knowledge acquired". The Charter holds uncertain legal status because it is a civil society and not a state-sanctioned document. It does not meet the threshold for soft law, but it is unsatisfactory to dismiss it as a nullity – it is still a significant document. Indeed, if considered within a paradigm of ecological law, it can be seen as a core articulation of an emerging ecological *grundnorm*.[53] It was prepared as the more ambitious alternative to The Rio Declaration through a global civil society process and has now been formally endorsed by over 2,000 national and international organizations, including the International Union for the Conservation of Nature (IUCN) and the United Nations Educational Scientific and Cultural Organization (UNESCO).

51 *Agenda 21: Programme of Action for Sustainable Development* UN Doc A/Conf.151/26 (14 June 1992) at s 10.1. Sections I6.4 and I6.22 also refer to the maintenance of environmental integrity with respect to biotechnology and long-term ecology security. Section I8.38 makes reference to ecosystem integrity for the management of aquatic ecosystems.

52 The Earth Charter Initiative 2000, 'The earth charter', principle 5, (https://earthcharter.org/).

53 Bosselmann, n 43, at 98.

The IUCN's Draft International Covenant on Environment and Development also aims to achieve "environmental conservation [as] an indispensable foundation for sustainable development".[54] Article 2 sets out a requirement to maintain and restore "the integrity of the earth's ecological systems".[55] Article 9 acknowledges the scientific concept of resilience and recognizes the finite capacity of natural and human systems to cope with environmental stress and disturbance.[56] While the covenant is still in draft form, it is regularly updated and represents many years of work by leading environmental scholars from around the world. It is ultimately intended by its authors to become a codification of international environmental law. It represents "the most accurate portrayal of the present corpus of existing and developing international environmental law".[57]

It is clear from the international agreements and instruments referred to here that there is no shortage of statements about the need to protect and sustain the environment using the concept of ecological integrity. Clearly it holds the potential to flesh out and underpin the concept of sustainable development in a way that can protect the sustainability of the planet's ecological systems or at least those systems that humans rely on and need.

b) Defining the Legal Concept

In the age of the Anthropocene, a period characterized by rapid non-linear change caused by humans, the concept of ecological integrity can no longer be understood as a return to conditions of pristine nature before human interference or even to a position of stasis and stability, which the concept of sustainability on its own might suggest.[58] Human influence now affects every aspect of the environment, and so ecological integrity must be understood in the context of socioecological or human *and* nature systems.

Ecosystems themselves are loosely defined dynamic associations of biotic and abiotic components. Our knowledge for maintaining them is incomplete, which makes the task of preserving ecological integrity challenging. Furthermore, attempting to maintain ecosystems within a stable range is not necessarily good for ecosystems as they tend to periodically cycle through different

54 International Union for the Conservation of Nature 2015, *The draft international covenant on environment and development*, 5th edn, IUCN, Gland, art 1.

55 Article 2.

56 Article 9.

57 Birnie et al., *International law and the environment*, p. 103.

58 Rockström, J, Polasky, S, Rockström, J, Galaz, V, Westley, F, Lamont, M, Scheffer, M, Österblom, H, Carpenter, SR, Chapin, FS, III, Seto, KC, Weber, EU, Crona, BI, Daily, GC, Dasgupta, P, Gaffney, O, Gordon, LJ, Hoff, H, Levin, SA, Lubchenco, J, Steffen, W & Walker, BH 2021, 'Our future in the Anthropocene biosphere', *Ambio*, vol. 50, pp. 834–869. See also Burdon, PD 2023, 'Ecological integrity', in *The Anthropocene: new trajectories in law*, 1st edn, Routledge, London.

states with multiple modes of functioning. It is the dynamic processes of the ecosystems themselves that ensure the resilience of the system. Resilience is used here to mean "the capacity of an ecosystem to withstand a disturbance and maintain the same basic processes and structures".[59] Tarsha Eason and others comment that establishing ecological integrity must take into account the economic, technical, social and also legal dimensions in play:[60]

> Sustainability relates to finding a set of system conditions that can support the social and economic development of human and ecological systems without major reversible environmental consequences. . . . Its trajectory must remain within a region of acceptable variability for all of its critical dimensions. Resilience, then, is the ability of the system to remain within this region over time while under pressure from external forces and its own internal dynamics.

The law generally operates best from a position of legal certainty. However, with respect to environmental law, the environment is a moving target. It is constantly evolving and changing, which means that the possibility of establishing complete legal certainty regarding the management of ecosystems is illusory.[61] This requires that any definition of ecological integrity must strike a balance between a level of certainty for legal enforceability and the capability for flexibility:[62]

> Ecosystems will always be more complex than any assessment or management system. Therefore the legal system must be selective, when reducing this complexity. Through selectivity, the legal system addresses the ecosystems complexity, and reduces it to a manageable, legal system complexity, differentiating the legal assessment system from the ecosystem, but also establishing coupled systemic path dependence between the systems.

For the purposes of a legal definition of ecological integrity that can be recognized and used as a "global environmental constitutional norm",[63] ecological integrity might be defined as:[64]

> The combination of the biodiversity and ecosystem processes that characterise the area at a given point in time. Maintenance of ecological integrity

59 Garmestani, AS & Allen, CR (eds) 2014, *Social-ecological resilience and the law*, Columbia University Press, New York, p. 5.

60 Eason, T, Flournoy, AC, Cabezas, H & Gonzalez, MA 2014, 'Incorporating resilience and innovation into law and policy', in AS Garmestani & CR Allen (eds), *Social-ecological resilience and the law*, Columbia University Press, New York, pp. 299–300.

61 Josefsson, n 51.

62 Josefsson, n 51.

63 Bridgewater, et al., 'Ecological integrity', p. 4.

64 At 12.

> assumes a continued delivery of goods and services from the ecosystem or ecosystems present in the area.

This definition suggests ecological integrity as an objective, non-anthropocentric category that makes any ecosystem functions for delivery of goods and services conditional to its maintenance.

To return now to considering ecological integrity from the global position, the Earth as a whole can be understood and conceptualized as a single social-ecological system. Essentially, this is what the planetary boundary framework does. The Holocene period represents the only geological time period that we know for certain is capable of supporting human life, and this is certainly true at the level of population that the planet now carries.[65]

The planetary boundaries framework provides the safe operating space within which global ecological integrity can be operationalized. It does this not by focusing on the boundaries' actual limits per se (these must be fluid enough to accommodate updating, depending on scientific knowledge and physical, social or economic factors that cause change), but by helping estimate the safe space within which human development can occur.

The key challenge in operationalizing ecological integrity within sustainable development is to recognize and respect the social, economic and ecological processes that create resilience and self-generation within the ecosystems themselves.

c) Ecological Integrity as a Grundnorm

> We stand at a critical moment in Earth's history. . . . [H]umanity must choose its future. . . . [W]e are one human family and one Earth community with a common destiny. We must join together to bring forth a sustainable global society founded on respect for nature, universal human rights, economic justice, and a culture of peace. Towards this end, it is imperative that we, the peoples of Earth, declare our responsibility to one another, to the greater community of life, and to future generations.[66]

"Legal theory has a decisive role to play in defining and defending the values and ideals that sustain our way of life".[67] The philosophy of the law, sometimes referred to as general jurisprudence, is the investigation of the foundations of the law. What gives law its authority over and above any other set of social norms? Does law consist only of a collection of human-made rules

65 United Nations Department of Economic and Social Affairs 2019, *Population division world population prospects 2019: highlights ST/ESA/SER.A/423*, United Nations, New York.

66 The Earth Charter Initiative, n 56, at preamble.

67 Wacks, R 2014, *Philosophy of law: a very short introduction*, 2nd edn, Oxford University Press, Oxford at preface.

and norms, or does the law also consist of universal values in accordance with nature?[68]

The purpose of this chapter is to explore, from a jurisprudential point of view, how the law can better protect the environment. It does this by considering the jurisprudential context for a fundamental norm or *grundnorm* of ecological integrity, which would have the capacity to inform and colour *all* existing law.

In the new age of the Anthropocene, it becomes imperative to establish ecological integrity as holding fundamental normative status within the law in the same way that human rights have done.[69] After all, human rights are unachievable without a healthy environment that can sustain life. Set out next is a discussion of the work of some of the law's leading theorists – Hans Kelson, Immanuel Kant, Robert Alexy and John Finnis – so as to explore the foundations from which ecological integrity could be held to hold fundamental normative value.

Hans Kelsen was a legal positivist who developed the "pure theory of law" that proposes a hierarchy of norms, each of which gains its authority and validity from another higher norm within the legal system. He recognized that this process could not continue forever and that the validity of all legal norms must ultimately be based on a final *grundnorm* or basic norm, which should be presupposed. By definition, the authority and validity of the *grundnorm* cannot rely on any higher norm and must simply be accepted. Kelsen believed that this *grundnorm* exists only in "juristic consciousness"[70] and holds no content. His chief concern was to construct the law as a closed system of hierarchically ordered and binding norms separate from all other social systems, such as politics or morality.[71] However to do this, he needed to transcend the positive law system itself and rely on an extra-legal or transcendent norm, which could be understood as the ultimate "ground" for the validity of the entire legal system:[72]

> All norms whose validity can be traced back to one and the same basic norm constitute a system of norms, a normative order. The basic norm is

68 At 129.

69 The Universal Declaration of Human Rights is generally regarded as something like a constitution in the field of human rights with its norms achieving acceptance as customary law binding all states. Also, the Agreement Establishing the World Trade Organization contains principles such as free trade, which have also achieved the status of superior norms that override other norms and bind most states.

70 Bindreiter, U 2002, *Why Grundnorm? A treatise on the implications of Kelsen's doctrine*, Kluwer Law International, The Hague, p. 219.

71 At 3.

72 Kelsen, H 1967, *Pure theory of law*, M Knight (trans), 2nd edn, UCLA Press, Berkeley, p. 195.

> the common source for the validity of all norms that belong to the same order – it is the common reason of validity. . . . [I]t is the basic norm that constitutes the unity in the multitude of norms by representing the reason for the validity of all norms that belong to this order.

Kelsen's *grundnorm* has been interpreted to allow judges and courts in countries where there have been successful revolutions to use the *grundnorm* concept to change the law and validate a new constitution.[73]

In Kelsen's thinking, the constitution of a country (whether written or by custom) is not itself the *grundnorm*,[74] but if a constitution is changed or created (by specific means or by custom) and if jurists then begin to deduce the law from that new constitution which is followed by those affected, then the *grundnorm* will reflect this change and can again be presupposed.[75] For example, if proper constitutional processes are followed requiring that all actions must be in accordance with ecological integrity, and if this requirement is accepted and adhered to by those persons affected, then the *grundnorm* would once again provide the foundation for the legal effectiveness of that new ecological constitutional requirement.

As a positivist, Kelsen emphasized the separation of law and morality. This means that Kelsen himself would have viewed a norm protecting ecological integrity as a moral *grundnorm* but not a legal *grundnorm*.

While Kelsen's chief concern was to use the empty *grundnorm* concept to deal with the issue of legal validity and authorization, Immanuel Kant approached the validity of law issue from the very different starting point of individual freedom. For Kant, self-rule and the duty-based rights and actions that flow from that self-rule establish autonomy. He considered that *all* law must be such that rational persons hypothetically consent to it:[76]

> The reason that one has a duty, for Kant, to enter into a "juridical state of affairs" is that moral freedom involves both the "negative" freedom of the will from "determination by sensible impulses" and the "positive" freedom of a will, which is determined by reason itself; negative freedom is thus instrumental to positive freedom.

73 Harris, JW 1971, 'When and why does the Grundnorm change?', *Cambridge Law Journal*, vol. 20, no. 1, p. 103. The use of the *grundnorm* concept has occurred in Pakistan, Uganda and Southern Rhodesia (now Zimbabwe).

74 Kelsen, H 1945, *General theory of law and state*, Harvard University Press, Cambridge, pp. 208–211.

75 Harris, n 73, at 118.

76 Riley, P 1973, 'On Kant as the most adequate of the social contract theorists', *Political Theory*, vol. 1, no. 4, p. 450, 453. See also Kant, I 1996 [1797], *The metaphysics of morals*, MJ Gregor (ed), Cambridge University Press, Cambridge.

Kant's famous "categorical imperative" is "Act only according to that maxim by which you can at the same time will that it should become a universal law".[77]

Kant saw the relationship between the individual and the state as a social contract,[78] in which the state's primary role is to carry out the rational will of its people, and, in return, the individual, as a matter of reason, obeys the law.[79]

> Everything in nature works according to laws. Rational beings alone have the faculty of acting according to the conception of laws, that is, according to principles, i.e. have a will. Since the deduction of actions from principles requires reason, the will is nothing but practical reason. . . . [T]he will as a faculty to choose that only which reason independent of inclination recognises as practically necessary, i.e. good.

Kant's idea of a *grundnorm* (though he did not use this term) is found in his 1797 work *The Metaphysics of Morals*, which commences with a treatise on the philosophy of law as the source of validity for all positive law.[80]

> Thus it is possible to conceive of an external legislation comprising positive laws alone, but then this legislation would have to be preceded by a natural law that established the legislator's authority.

According to Kant, reason dictates that people leave a state of nature and move into a civil or legal state of affairs by "subjecting oneself to a publicly lawful, external coercion".[81] Unlike others of his time, he imagined that states would also eventually start to move into a juridical relationship of some kind with other states or into what he called "the cosmopolitan juridical state", foreseeing the creation of an international body similar to the United Nations.[82] Kant is the only author of his time who anticipated the development of international law and attempted to set out a legal model at both the national and international levels.[83]

77 Kant, I 1993, *Grounding for the metaphysics of morals*, J Ellington (trans), 3rd edn, Hackett Publishing, Indianapolis, p. 30.
78 Horn, C 2016, 'Kant's political philosophy as a theory of non-ideal normativity', *Kant-Studien*, vol. 107, no. 1, p. 89.
79 Kant, n 77, at 30. Kant's notion of "the idea of a social contract" comes from what he calls the platonic ideal *respublica noumenon*, which is an eternal norm for all civil constitutions.
80 At 18.
81 Alexy, R 2002, *The argument from injustice: a reply to legal positivism*, SL Paulson and BL Paulson (trans), Clarendon Press, Oxford, p. 116.
82 Kleingeld, P 2016, 'Kant's moral and political cosmopolitanism', *Philosophy Compass*, vol. 11, no. 1, p. 14. Kleingeld examines the idea of cosmopolitanism and "world citizenship" in Kant's work.
83 Byrd, S & Hruscha, J 2010, *Kant's doctrine of right*, Cambridge University Press, Cambridge, p. 1.

Kant's *grundnorm* is a natural law recognized by means of reason.[84]

> An original contract . . . is in fact merely an idea of reason which nonetheless has undoubted practical reality for it can oblige every legislature to frame his laws in such a way that they could have been produced by the united will of the whole nation and to regard each subject in so far as he can claim citizenship as if he had consented within the general will.

One of the key concerns with Kant's philosophy is his seeming refusal to condone any individual rights against the power of the state or to condone any form of revolution against the state. Yet this stance must be understood against the background of his premise that the state is simply an extension of the people. Christoph Horn explores this issue more deeply and comments that:[85]

> It turns out, I think, that Kant's political normativity is not just a kind of "applied ethics": an application of his conception of morality to the field of institutions, as many of his readers assume. Contrary to such an interpretation, in my view, Kant has formulated a non-ideal form of normativity according to which "non-ideal" means a weaker version of normativity which can be lived up to by human beings, which is appropriate to specific situations and which is intended for a long-term effect, namely that of a historical development.

Kant firmly believed that rights can only be insured under a juridical state of *Rechtsstaat.*[86] This belief flows from a consideration that a sovereign (or a legislature) should only create laws that people could have given themselves.[87]

For Kant, sovereignty *is* the united will of the people:[88]

> Kant insists on political principles "akin in spirit to the laws of freedom which a people of mature rational powers would prescribe for itself even if the people is not asked literally for its consent". . . . [T]his hypothetical

84 Kant, I 1991, "On the common saying: 'This may be true in theory: but it does not apply in practice'", in HS Reiss (ed), *Kant: political writings*, HB Nisbet (trans), 2nd edn, Cambridge University Press, Cambridge, p. 79.

85 Horn, n 78, at 91.

86 *Rechtsstaat* has no true English counterpart but refers here to the state based on justice and integrity.

87 Riley, n 76, at 452. See also Mysicka, S 2015, 'Environmental justice and the Rawlsian social contract theory', *Filosofie Dnes*, vol. 1, no. 7, p. 39.

88 Riley, n 76, at 452. "Social contract" here means an act by which people constitute a state which has legitimacy and to which people will surrender their freedom in order to be members of that community. Kant describes such a contract as "an idea of reason" or an eternal norm for a constitution.

consent can restrict abuses in a way that actual consent might not . . . consent can be treated as a standard.

Christopher Horn observes here that:[89]

> Kant is thinking in terms of legal progress . . . in short: in terms of a balance between law and morality. Does Kant here not conceive of a gradual historical realisation of freedom, even though, in Kant's view, it is only the sovereign who is able and entitled to make political changes in that direction? Yes, but what is being considered here is only the historical progress of the moralisation of rulers and subjects (qua individuals). The progress of the law, which allows for the hope that the overall political state of the world will improve, is preferable only insofar as in its course, individual agents become more moral. In this we have an explanation for the irritating fact that for Kant, there are no rights protecting the individual against the state. . . . Kant's theory of non-ideal normativity is personalised and context specific.

Leaving aside this aspect of Kant's theory, the relevant question for us here is whether ecological integrity can be included as a "dictate of reason" in Kant's natural law basic norm. Apart from creating legal certainty, Kant's basic norm is exclusively concerned with achieving lasting peace. Kant lived during a time when security and peace were the prime concerns. The age was not one in which the global population was fast using up finite ecological budgets and pressing up against global ecological boundaries. The concept of humans having the capacity to affect and change the world's Earth systems like the air and the oceans was unforeseen.

Nevertheless, Kant did envisage a human social and political evolution through the pressure of the law. As a matter of reason, there is a strong argument to be made that Kant's basic norm would today include sustainability and the protection of ecological integrity. He would certainly have recognized the threat to both freedom and peace that failure to do so leads to.

Kant's concept of a fundamental norm holds clear jurisprudential potential to protect the ecological integrity of the planet on the basis that no rational human (or nation state) could imagine a world where sustaining and protecting the planet *is not a prior duty* to any further activity, duty or right that those persons or those states may hold.[90]

89 Horn, n 78, at 109.

90 Demiray, MR 2015, 'Natural law theory, legal positivism and the normativity of law', *The European Legacy*, vol. 20, no. 8, p. 807, 822. Demiray alludes to the Kantian distinction between "morality" as commonly understood and the more universal morality of "reasoned justice".

In his book *The Argument from Injustice*,[91] Robert Alexy comments that the basic norm is the most significant instrument for resolving the circularity of the concept of legal validity.[92]

> One can say that the move into the realm of the law is accomplished with the basic norm, and that there are moral or other extra-legal reasons for making this move.

His work uncovers and explores the dual nature to the law involving the two principles of justice and certainty. On the one hand, he accepts that a modern society can only be effectively organized by means of positive law. Yet, on the other hand, the principle of justice requires that the law should be "morally correct" (here meaning it should be just). This exposes the law's two natures: the "real" (the factual dimension of norms and their social efficacy) and the "ideal" (the requirement for moral correctness or justice). He makes reference to the Radbruch formula, which, in its most simple form, states that *extreme injustice is not law* and rejects the positivist idea that any content can be law.[93]

Alexy considers that the *grundnorm* or basic norm will work best when modified by taking the "argument of injustice" into consideration. That which is extremely unjust will be contrary to basic human rights, and this basic form of justice has universal validity. Where such rights are incorporated into a constitution, they will become legally binding.

Alexy also sees that there are two different perspectives from which we can approach what the law is: the "restricted" view and the "comprehensive" view. Under the restricted view, what the law is depends only on positive law and what is socially efficacious or a matter of social fact. From the comprehensive view, what law is depends on what it is correctly taken to be. This view constitutes the participant's perspective:[94]

> Positivism reflects quite well the observer's perspective. From this perspective what the law is depends exclusively on what has actually been issued and is socially efficacious. By contrast the participant's perspective

91 Alexy, n 81, at 95.

92 At 114.

93 Robert Alexy also refers to a decision in 1968 concerning statutory injustice. The 11th Ordinance of 25 November 1941 (issued pursuant to the statute on Reich citizenship) enabled a Jew holding German citizenship to be stripped of citizenship on the grounds of race. The Federal Constitutional Court concluded that citizenship was never lost because the Ordinance's conflict with justice was to such an intolerable degree that it must be held null and void and invalid from the outset.

94 Alexy, R 2015, 'Inclusive non-positivism', *Joaçaba*, vol. 16, no. 2, p. 283, 292. See also Barroso, LR 2015, 'Major transformations in contemporary law and the teachings of Robert Alexy', *Panorama of Brazilian Law*, vol. 3, nos. 3–4, p. 107.

> presupposes non-positivism. For a participant, the law is what it is correctly taken to be. What it is correctly taken to be depends, however, not only on social facts but also on moral reasons. In this way, normative arguments make their way into what the law is as soon as the participant's perspective is taken up. What is more, this perspective must be taken up for law is possible without observers but not without participants.

The addition of "content" to the basic norm, even at this minimal level and with the conditions suggested, takes Alexy away from the positivist Kelsenian approach and brings him closer to Kant and to traditional concepts of natural law.[95]

John Finnis, the leading contemporary natural law philosopher, delves into and reinvigorates the natural law tradition in his exceptional book, *Natural Law and Natural Rights*.[96] Like Alexy, he emphasizes the importance of positive law and social facts in any successful well-functioning society, but he also states, "There is no proper place for a positivism outside natural law theory".[97] Finnis asserts that natural law theory is fully positivist if by that we mean a system that provides a complete account of the concept of law, its institutions, sources of positive law and also the Rule of Law:[98]

> The development of modern jurisprudence suggests . . . that no theorist can give a theoretical description and analysis of social facts without also participating in the work of evaluation, of understanding what is really good for human persons, and what is really required by practical reasonableness.

By "practical reasonableness", Finnis means the rational and reasonable deliberations and choices that shape freely chosen actions and communities.

> So the philosophy of law finds the grounds for accepting the justice of fundamental principles of law and the authoritativeness of private and public juridical acts in the bearing of those principles and acts on the common good.[99]

95 Vinx, L 2007, *Hans Kelsen's pure theory of law: legality and legitimacy*, Oxford University Press, Oxford, p. 58 refers to Alexy's *The Argument from Injustice* (n 81) and objects to Alexy replacing Kelsen's analytical basic norm with substantive moral principle on the basis that law will not be capable of carrying out its core function if the conceptual difference between law's validity and its content is blurred.

96 Finnis, J 2011, *Natural law and natural rights*, 2nd edn, Oxford University Press, Oxford.

97 Finnis, J 2014, 'What is the philosophy of law?', *American Journal of Jurisprudence*, vol. 59, p. 133, 138.

98 Finnis, n 96, at 3.

99 Finnis, n 97, at 134.

Finnis sees the principal concern of natural law as tracing the way that sound laws "in all their positivity"[100] are derived from unchanging universal human principles that have force arising from "their reasonableness and not from any originating acts or circumstances".[101]

While law has its own distinct domain,[102] it nevertheless is underpinned by broader principles of moral and political philosophy that it cannot avoid when facing ethical and political challenges of the complex modern era, including environmental challenges.

Inadequate attention to the "long-term conditions of a sustainable" society[103] results, in Finnis's view, in errors of "practical thought", which are incompatible with political order and the rule of law.[104]

> Practitioners of the philosophy of law may be especially susceptible to this kind of error, to the extent that they envision legal systems simply as sets of norms rather than as the principals, norms and institutions adopted by a people . . . in more or less adequate fulfilment of its moral responsibility to do so.[105]

Natural law theory takes the view that it is not possible to have a complete theory of law without understanding how law can be rationally binding. This automatically requires examining laws' normative foundations. "A good theory of law should offer an explanation of how it came to arise".[106]

Like Kant and Alexy, Finnis carefully dissects the debate around morality and the law, stating that natural law has always been primarily concerned with the question of law's rationality, not its morality. The theme of natural law jurisprudence is that the essence of law concerns shared rational standards for action, not the imposition of a moral test on legal validity:[107]

> The principal concern of a theory of natural law is to explore the requirements of practical reasonableness in relation to the good of human beings who, because they live in community with one another, are confronted with problems of justice and rights, of authority, law, and obligation. And the principal jurisprudential concern of a theory of natural law is thus to identify the principles and limits of the Rule of law and trace the ways in which sound laws in all their positivity and mutability are to be derived . . . from unchanging principles.

100 Finnis, n 96, at 351.
101 Finnis, n 96, at 351.
102 Finnis, n 96, at 141.
103 At 142.
104 At 142.
105 At 142.
106 Crowe, J 2016, 'Natural law theories', *Philosophy Compass*, vol. 11, no. 2, p. 91, 94.
107 Finnis, n 96, at 351.

Finnis starts his natural law theory from an "Aristotelian foundation", which is to ask the question "What constitutes a valuable worthwhile and desirable life?"[108] From there, he arrives at seven basic forms of "goods" for human flourishing. These are:

1. Life;
2. Knowledge;
3. Play;
4. Aesthetic experience;
5. Sociability;
6. Practical reasonableness; and
7. Religion.[109]

Finnis contends that each of these is universal. To flourish, we require these basic goods, which are prized by all human societies at all times. Each has intrinsic value. They are neither facts or metaphysical propositions, nor are they deduced from anything else; they are simply self-evident. For example, "knowledge" is self-evidently preferable to ignorance. "Life" is self-evidently better than death. Self-preservation is a primary drive for human motive and action. Finnis uses the term "life" here to mean "every aspect of the vitality (vita, life), which puts a human being in good shape for self-determination".[110] He is at pains to point out what he sees as the modern mistake of trying to find a basic form of human well-being in experiences such as pleasure, peace of mind and happiness (all of which flow from one or other of the basic goods in any case). In his view, to imagine that "experience" is a basic good is to misunderstand human history and to mis-locate what is ultimately, truly worthwhile in one's life. Finnis sees the process of "participation" in the basic goods as signifying "a fullness of life, a certain development as a person, a meaningfulness of one's existence" that goes well beyond the ephemeral nature of experience alone.[111]

Having established the basic goods, Finnis then combines these with the following nine requirements for "practical reasonableness":

1. The active pursuit of goods;
2. A coherent plan of life;
3. No arbitrary preference among values;
4. No arbitrary preference among persons;

108 Wacks, n 67, at 17.
109 The term "religion" here means the human desire for some form of spiritual or transcendental experience.
110 Finnis, n 96, at 86.
111 At 96.

5. Detachment and commitment;
6. The limited relevance of consequences: efficiency within reason;
7. Respect for every basic value in every act;
8. The requirements of the common good; and
9. Following one's conscience.

From this natural law framework, we can start to perceive how protection of ecological integrity and sustainability of the environment are vital components for the attainment of the basic goods. None are achievable without a fully functional, ecologically healthy planet and a deep appreciation of the requirements of practical reasonableness to achieve this goal.

An argument for the foundational importance of ecological integrity in natural law terms is fairly straightforward. It is rational and reasonable to assume that humanity will not wish to destroy itself and will wish to fulfil the basic goods that allow humans to flourish.

It now becomes clear that *any* laws which facilitate damage to the planet and to ecological integrity place the global community of humans at risk and must be contrary to the principles of natural law and practical reasonableness. Here is the legal philosophy underpinning positive law that requires all law (both existing law and still to be created law) to be in alignment with the ecological requirements of Earth.

Is environmental law capable of being re-imagined in a way that will enable it to contribute to meeting the environmental challenges of the 21st century?[112] The unavoidable entanglement of humans and the environment along with the awareness of planetary boundaries has prompted renewed concern and interest in the theoretical foundations of the law and its lack of recognition of a fundamental norm of ecological integrity.[113]

The narrow focus, as in this chapter, on legal philosophy, while vitally important to operationalizing ecological integrity in the law, cannot create the needed change alone. The fundamental transition in our approach to the environment is one of culture and social values. Law itself does not determine social values but only expresses those values through the prism of specific technical rules and standards.

Aldo Leopold made the need for societal change clear when he observed that "No important change in human conduct is ever accomplished without an internal change in our intellectual emphasis, our loyalty, our affections

112 Gaines, SE 1997, 'Re-imagining environmental law for the 21st century', *University of Chicago Legal Forum*, vol. 1997, pp. 231–292, 288.

113 Carlarne, C 2015, *Delinking international environmental law and climate change*, Ohio State Public Law Working Paper No. 286, Ohio State University, 22 January, (http://ssrn.com/abstract=2553876).

and our convictions".[114] This also requires the focus of legal scholars to expand:[115]

> To address the root of the problem . . . environmental law needs a more expansive society-based conception of law, one that activates law as a social institution engaged broadly with the habits and customs, the expectations and aspirations of people and organisations in their daily lives. Environmental lawyers then need a fresh and bold re-imagination of their mission to hone and use their persuasive and analytical skills and creative ways to alter the social dynamic underlying environmental change and to ferment a deep commitment to effective stewardship of resources.

In terms of international documents, the Earth Charter recognizes and encourages these fundamental changes in our values, institutions and ways of living.[116]

Staffan Westerlund points out that legal rules and principles outside the environmental law field counteract and override environmental law due to the strong anthropocentric focus of the law. He remarks that a modern perspective on environmental law must take the whole legal system into account:[117]

> Each and every legal principle has to be reassessed from this perspective in order to avoid "legality" to prove hazardous for mankind.

The problem with simply looking to a legislative body or authority to create more positive law for each instance in which an ecological system is under threat is that human knowledge of ecosystem functioning (and their adaptive capacities) is still limited. We have much to learn. The overarching *grundnorm* or grounding norm concept can bypass this knowledge obstacle by underpinning *all* positive law with a requirement of sustainability and ecological integrity. It can also encourage a social change of perspective from viewing our environment as just a natural resource for our use to viewing it as one of human stewardship to protect the planet that protects and sustains us.

114 Leopold, A 1991, 'The ecological conscience', in SL Flader & JB Callicott (eds), *The river of the mother of god and other essays by Aldo Leopold*, University of Wisconsin Press, Wisconsin, p. 338.
115 Gaines, n 112, at 289. See also Lanni, S 2023, 'Nature as grundnorm', in *Greening the civil codes: comparative private law and environmental protection*, 1st edn, Routledge, London.
116 The Earth Charter Initiative, n 56. See also Bosselmann, K 2010, 'Outlook: the Earth charter – a model constitution for the world?', in K Bosselmann & R Engel (eds), *The Earth charter: a framework for global governance*, Kit Publishers, Amsterdam.
117 Gaines, n 112, at 292.

At this point, we find ourselves arriving back full circle to Kant's duty-based ethics. Now we must ask:

- What are our duties to ourselves, our community and to future communities?
- How, as a matter of rational reason, can a sustainable and healthy environment be achieved?

The challenge for international environmental law is to first recognize the aspects of law that encourage our capitalist society's overuse of the environment[118] and, secondly, to find the tools that will require the law to respect the ecological boundaries of the planet.[119] As Jürgen Habermas conceives, the legitimacy of the law must depend on an uncontaminated democratic process of discourse by which law should be made. Consequently, a sense of global responsibility and democracy involving all global citizens and states is central to the process.[120]

118 Trubek, DM 1972, 'Max Weber on law and the rise of capitalism', *Wisconsin Law Review*, vol. 1, no. 1, p. 720. Weber recognized that in order to thrive, capitalism needed control of natural resources and certainty through a highly normative legal order, which would be upheld by the state.

119 Gaines, n 112, at 291.

120 Wacks, n 67, at 104.

Part II

Examining State Sovereignty

Chapter 5

The Concept of State Sovereignty

1. The Evolution of State Sovereignty

The question as to what constitutes a state – or, more precisely, a sovereign state – is one that has captivated the attention of many international relations scholars, political theorists and international law jurists over the course of almost 400 years. From the Westphalian treaty system of 1648 to the Berlin conference in 1884–1885 and the present-day multilateral arrangement under the auspices of the United Nations, the entire concept of a sovereign state has morphed into a creature which became somewhat unrecognizable to early philosophers such as Aristotle and even renaissance thinkers like Jean Bodin and Hugo Grotius. With the rise of environmental multilateralism towards the latter part of the 20th century, states are now forced to hastily develop climate solutions which, in most occasions, occur outside their own territorial space. The dramatic shift, however, took place in the post–Cold War era, with Francis Deng's theory of a sovereign being a responsible institution under the framework of what is now known as "the responsibility to protect". Although this responsibility to protect permitted humanitarian intervention to prevent human rights abuses where the state in question is unwilling or unable to act, this theory questions whether a modern 21st-century state is now being saddled with trusteeship or other eco-related responsibilities in an ever-changing globalized world. This section offers a historical analysis of the sovereignty of yesterday in order to obtain a glimpse of the sovereignty of tomorrow.

a) The Classical Thinkers

There was a point in time when the world was not arranged in the format of sovereign states as we know them today.[1] Prior to the Peace of Westphalia

1 Parmar, SS 2017, 'Understanding the concept of 'sovereignty', *International Journal of Law*, vol. 3, no. 1, p. 31.

DOI: 10.4324/9781032674049-8

in 1648, the concept of national borders was not that well developed.[2] Throughout history, particularly during the medieval period, kingdoms were ruled by elites, kings and princes without any defined territory. Back in the mid–17th century, the world was seen as an "intimidating place" where natural borders such as seas, rivers, deserts and mountains separated so-called countries.[3] In fact, early-modern theories of the state rarely made any references to the concept of territory.[4] Support for these early theories of the state gained traction from the views of canonical political theorists such as Bodin and Grotius, who opined that when it came to the exercise of sovereign power, the primary subject was people as opposed to the territory.[5] It was during the 17th century that territorial competence and property in land became the centre of political life.[6] Locke, for instance, thought that property in land was a prior condition for the creation of sovereignty.[7] German philosopher Gottfried Leibniz similarly argued, "[S]overeign is he who is a master of a territory".[8] These ideas surely shaped the Peace of Westphalia, a time when the world began to connect the dots between sovereignty and territory.[9] Nowadays, the early theories of a state have become outmoded as current international law requires the possession of a defined territory as just one of the hallmark characteristics of a sovereign state.[10] Therefore, to fully grapple with how sovereignty works, it is pertinent to examine the classical models of sovereignty, which are, in essence, the early views expounded by jurists such as Bodin, Grotius, Hobbes and Vattel.

The classical model of sovereignty views states as having authority to govern and represent their people on strictly their own terms.[11] Conventional accounts traced the classical model back to Bodin, a 16th-century French jurist, who defined sovereignty as "power absolute and perpetual", "supreme" and "subject to no law".[12] Bodin expressed a clear preference for a monarchy (namely, a male figurehead) over other constitutional forms.[13] Accordingly, in his manuscript *Les Six Livres de la Republique* (1576) Bodin

2 Hickey, W 2020, *The sovereignty game: neo-colonialism and the Westphalian system*, Springer Nature, Singapore, p. 4.
3 Hickey, n 2, at 18.
4 Bartelson, J 2014, *Sovereignty as symbolic form*, Routledge, Oxon, p. 25.
5 Bartelson, *Sovereignty as symbolic form.*
6 Fitzmaurice, A 2014, *Sovereignty, property and empire, 1500–2000*, Cambridge University Press, Cambridge, p. 123.
7 Fitzmaurice, *Sovereignty, property and empire, 1500–2000.*
8 Bartelson, n 4, at 28.
9 Bartelson, n 4, at 28.
10 Montevideo Convention on the Rights and Duties of States, 165 LNTS 19 (1933), art 1.
11 Criddle, EJ & Fox-Decent, E 2016, *Fiduciaries of humanity: how international law constitutes authority*, Oxford University Press, New York, p. 5.
12 Criddle & Fox-Decent, *Fiduciaries of humanity.*
13 Bartelson, n 4, at 20.

stated, "[H]e [the king] is absolutely sovereign who recognises nothing, after God, that is greater than himself".[14] For Bodin, the sovereignty of states comprised one thing: namely, to make and give laws to each of the citizens and subjects.[15] The monarchy was therefore seen as a calling from God and sovereignty as an internal power to illustrate the power of a superior over an inferior.[16] Bodin's purpose was therefore to establish order in a world full of turmoil.[17] So profound was Bodin's interpretation of sovereignty that it gained widespread appeal as a practical roadmap towards the Peace of Westphalia, even decades after his death in 1596.[18] This classical model as expressed by Bodin may have influenced the work of Thomas Hobbes. The conventional Hobbesian account presents political authority as static, in that once sovereignty is posited, it becomes absolute and exclusive.[19] Hobbes also brings in the embodiment of a Godhead to justify the absolute authority within a given state.[20]

Elements of the classical model can also be found in the work of Grotius, a Dutch jurist, who succeeded Bodin. Grotius, widely considered to be the founder of modern international law, defined sovereignty as a state's power to act without being "subject to the legal control of another".[21] Some two centuries later, Swiss international lawyer Emer de Vattel also tended to agree with the absolutist powers of the state, as proposed by both Bodin and Grotius, when he asserted that every state "possesses an absolute independence on all the others".[22] Where Vattel (who followed the philosophy of Locke, Pufendorf and Wolff) diverted was when he looked outwardly, placing the state at the centre of international relations.[23] By the time of the publication of his treatise in 1758, Vattel was already viewing the world as a collective entity, with states being the only legitimate subjects of international law.[24] Vattel's own view of the world probably coincides with the world we know of today, with sovereign states being incorporated into an international order

14 At 19.
15 Parmar, n 1, at 32.
16 Parmar, n 1, at 32.
17 Parmar, n 1, at 32.
18 Criddle and Fox-Decent, n 11, at 5.
19 Zucca, L 2015, 'A genealogy of state sovereignty', *Theoretical Inquiries in Law*, vol. 16, p. 399, 401.
20 At 411.
21 Grotius, H 1925, *The law of war and peace*, vol. 102, FW Kelsey (trans), as cited in Criddle and Fox-Decent, n 11, at 6.
22 de Vattel, E 1758, 'The law of nations: or principles of the law of nature applied to the conduct and affairs of nations and sovereigns' (1758) as cited in Criddle and Fox-Decent, n 11, at 6.
23 Boucher, D & Kelly, P 1994, 'The social contract and its critics: an overview', in D Boucher & P Kelly (eds), *The social contract from Hobbes to Rawls*, Routledge, New York, p. 1, 13.
24 Criddle and Fox-Decent, n 11, at 5.

under the auspices of the United Nations, with the legal standing to bring disputes before the International Court of Justice.

Early philosophers such as Aristotle had already debated what constituted a state (also read as "sovereign state"). In 350 BC, Aristotle put forth the view that the state is a creation of nature, and man is by nature a political animal.[25] It follows that since man is a political animal, man by nature is the sole architect of the state. For Aristotle, the state was an order. (Centuries later, Kelsen would agree with this.)[26] A state is compared to a composite living being, which, like any other whole, is made up of many parts.[27] Thousands of years after this Aristotelian viewpoint emerged, classical thinkers were still harping and offering varying notions on how a state is perceived. For instance, a Hobbesian account of a state was that of an artificial man which possesses greater strength and power than any natural man. It is the soul which animates this artificial man, which triggers the concept of sovereignty.[28] This must be compared to Vattel, who advanced the idea of a state being a moral person having an understanding and a will peculiar to itself, also susceptible to obligations and rights.[29] Vattel's conception of a "moral" state with rights and obligations is consistent with the theory of a modern-day state and would be constantly revisited throughout this paper. Then there were some early thinkers who interlinked the state with an omnipotent force. This divine command theory had an easy job instilling obedience by the subjects of the state since disobedience would be met with divine punishment.[30] Hobbes was one who was in favour of this divine command theory as it brought God into the equation to justify the exercise of absolute authority within the frame of the national state. God (vicariously, through his representative) was therefore seen as the sole authority that motivated people to obey human laws out of fear.[31] On this theory, Hobbes may have been inspired by the 13th-century Italian poet Dante, who held the view that political authority stood on theological grounds.[32] These early philosophers who were advocates of the divine command theory would have perceived states not only as a product of human artefact and will but also something which was natural to the extent that they facilitate God's purpose of preservation of mankind.[33] Hegel, an 18th-century German philosopher who

25 Aristotle 2000, *Politics*, B Jowett (trans), Infomotions, Inc, p. 2.
26 Kelsen, H 1945, *General theory of law and state*, Harvard University Press, Cambridge, p. 283.
27 Aristotle & Jowett, n 25, at 37 and 40.
28 Boucher & Kelly, n 23, at 15.
29 Boucher & Kelly, n 23, at 15.
30 Zucca, n 19, at 410.
31 At 411.
32 At 402.
33 Boucher & Kelly, n 23, at 13.

succeeded Hobbes, was not that rigid. (He was also not purely secular either.) Although Hegel believed that religion was not the core basis of a state, he still considered the state God's sanction for man on Earth.[34] Hegel went on to define a state as "an ethical order in which individuals realize their capacities and potentialities".[35] Hegel certainly never indicated pure secularity like Machiavelli.[36] It was Machiavelli, noted as one of the first secular thinkers of his time, who put forth the idea that a state captures the actual ability of a political authority to rule rather than its moral or theological fitness to do so.[37] Machiavelli was also the first student of politics who conceived of the state in a modern way: i.e. it is neither the rule of God on Earth nor the institutional embodiment of reason.[38] Machiavelli, therefore, was the bridge between a secular and a non-secular state.

Within a space of about 200 years from Hobbes to Hegel, we therefore see the state being interpreted in three different forms – an artificial man, a moral person and an ethical order. Then came along Karl Marx, who challenged the Hegelian political theory. Marx considered the state a part of the "superstructure ideology" which served the ruling class.[39] In that sense, states were not entirely ethical since the "superstructure", which was made up of the institutional rules and laws which guide the conduct within the society, helps maintain a stable system in which the power over production and enjoyment of products is unequally allocated.[40]

From this analysis, it appears that the definition of a state, by its very nature, is a very elusive one and ultimately depends on the era, social conditions and political climate which the topic may be subject to. As Kelsen said, "[A] definition of the state is made very difficult by the variety of objects which the term commonly denotes".[41] Kelsen added that "the state" can be used in a broad manner to refer to "the society". Alternatively, using a narrower and more frequent interpretation, the state can also denote a particular organ of society such as the government, a nation or the territory which is inhabited.[42] Even Aristotle, in his treatise *Politics*, asked himself, "What is a state?" to which he replied (again to himself), "[A]t present this is a disputed question".[43] Thousands of years later, we are still asking ourselves this same

34 Hickey, n 2, at 10.
35 Boucher & Kelly, n 23, at 23.
36 Hickey, n 2, at 10.
37 Zucca, n 19, at 404–405.
38 At 405.
39 Hickey, n 2, at 13.
40 Stone, A 1985, 'The place of law in the Marxian structure-superstructure archetype', *Law & Society Review*, vol. 19, no. 1, p. 39, 47–48.
41 Kelsen, n 26, at 181.
42 Kelsen, n 26, at 181.
43 Aristotle & Jowett, n 25, at 37.

question, and the likelihood is that, just like Aristotle, we will receive the same response. Until we accept that the concepts of the state and state sovereignty continue to evolve before our eyes, we will be handicapped in our attempt to pin down one politically correct answer. We must therefore avoid placing "state sovereignty" in a pigeonhole and continue to deliberate the broad spectrum of the subject's forms and its practical basis in modern-day politics.

b) The Westphalian System

For generations, historians and other scholars have tended to converge around the idea that Western political thought shaped the creation of European empires and the abuses associated with those empires.[44] To put it simply, the concept of a state, and how we perceive it even today, is entirely a Western construct. The Peace of Westphalia is the historical circumstance that justifies this reasoning. As Hickey put it, Westphalia developed from ethnocentric Western ideological perspectives and has been the default position over the past four centuries.[45] This section will summarize the events that led up to the Peace of Westphalia and why it still bears an impact in our modern-day society.

In essence, Westphalia was the product of the Reformation: a religious war (also known as the Thirty-Years' War which occurred from 1618 to 1648) that splintered Catholic Europe.[46] These wars demonstrated that the legitimacy of states rested on religious piety or, to put it another way, a non-secular order.[47] Westphalia was the struggle of the Protestant Church for political existence, against the Catholic grip on power, especially in the region that is now known as modern-day Germany.[48] The Peace of Westphalia was brought about by a conference arranged between the warring factions of France, Habsburg Germany, Sweden, Denmark, Dutch Spain and Holy Roman principalities in the spring of 1648.[49] Although the peace resulted in the recognition of an independent Protestant Church, ironically, Westphalia was established to counter the influence of religion on the nation-state (namely, the influence of the Catholic Church).[50] From this perspective, Westphalia can be seen as a direct assault against Hobbes and the divine command theory that placed God at the centre of a nation-state. The upshot of Westphalia is that it manifested a shift in the purpose of the supreme sovereign under the classical model. That purpose was to be the

44 Fitzmaurice, n 6, at 1.
45 Hickey, n 2, at 21.
46 At 5. See also History, *The Reformation*, (www.history.com).
47 Fitzmaurice, n 6, at 10.
48 Hickey, n 2, at 5.
49 At 1.
50 At 5 and 25.

protector of human dignity. On this, Pufendorf, a natural law theorist and native of Saxony,[51] was recorded as saying, "Let the people's welfare be the supreme law".[52] Pufendorf's statement must be taken in context: The Peace of Westphalia was designed at a time when the creation of a peaceful order and the identity of nation-states were considered to be the most paramount.[53] That being said, the Peace of Westphalia was more concerned with the relationship between sovereign states and not what constitutes a nation-state so to speak. (The latter point was developed much later.)[54] So even though the peace agreements established state borders, these borders were quite independent from the notion of a nation.[55] These borders were not even religious as Germany itself was still a mix of Protestant and Catholic. (As Hickey points out, nowadays, Germany may be one quarter atheist.)[56] Here, the views of Hegel, who was born more than a century after the Peace of Westphalia, are once more important. For Hegel, a state can exist even if there are two or more religions, once there is a morality (i.e. Hegel's "ethical order") which unifies the community.[57] In the end, however, Hegel was dissatisfied with the Westphalian solution because it divided the German empire into independent states, thereby surrendering its status as a secure state.[58] For Hegel, a state had real meaning, and that meaning was to protect the culture, ethnicity and national identity of its people.[59] The Peace of Westphalia did the opposite of that as the divisions failed to unite the common bonds and homogeneity of a given society. With globalization and the cross-border movement of persons with different skills, ethnic backgrounds, cultures and religious (and secular) convictions, Hegel's conception of a state would be totally out of sync with a 21st-century state. Notwithstanding this fluidity today, Westphalia set the tone for the demarcation of borders worldwide and still remains ever present in our world today.

c) *The Principle of Non-Interference*

One of the main features surrounding the Westphalian system of nation-states is non-interference in the internal affairs of another state. Throughout history, this has been the traditional line of defence for states – regardless of their size

51 Fitzmaurice, n 6, at 105.
52 Car, CL & Seidler, MJ 1994, *Political writings of Samuel Pufendorf*, Oxford University Press, New York, p. 242 as cited in Criddle & Fox-Decent, n 11, at 10.
53 Bosselmann, K 2020, 'Environmental trusteeship and state sovereignty: can they be reconciled?', *Transnational Legal Theory*, vol. 11, p. 47, 48.
54 Hickey, n 2, at 9.
55 Hickey, n 2, at 9.
56 Hickey, n 2, at 9.
57 At 10.
58 At 11.
59 At 13.

or global influence – when called upon by members of the international community to take bold action on a particular domestic issue. In most cases, the action requested is perceived by the receiving state as falling within its "sovereign" remit and responsibilities. These actions are usually directed towards matters such as, for example, prohibiting human rights abuses, the restoration of power to a duly elected government, curtailing nuclear programmes, the unlawful annexation of territory, the release of political prisoners and the holding of free and fair elections. This idea of non-interference bears all the hallmarks of "Westphalian sovereignty".[60] Westphalian sovereignty refers to political organization based on the exclusion of external actors from authority structures within a given territory.[61] The foundation of this sovereignty not only bolsters the state's superficial powers, but also provides a "shield of justification" for a state to reject foreign meddling. The Westphalian model is therefore built on the exclusivity principle and the eagerness of an individual nation-state to protect its own internal vested interests.[62]

Evidence of the 17th-century Westphalian sovereignty can be found in the 1945 United Nations' Charter, which expressly prohibits the United Nations (UN) from interfering in matters which are essentially within the domestic jurisdiction of any state.[63] The exception to this prohibition are matters which fall under Chapter 7 of the Charter which involve threats, breaches to peace and acts of aggression.[64] Nowadays, many developing countries strongly uphold this principle of non-intervention under the Charter because it is a critical political tool which can be wielded against unilateral interventions by powerful states.[65] In addition to sovereign exclusivity (i.e. a state's exclusive jurisdiction in their internal affairs), the UN also promotes the sovereign equality of all member states.[66] These two principles are correlated because it presumes that decisions not to intervene are based on mutual respect for a state's sovereignty. In addition to the UN, the Westphalian sovereignty of non-interference and sovereign equality can also be found in the 1975 Helsinki Final Act, a political agreement signed by 35 governments from Europe, the United States and Canada.[67] On this point, Westphalia is seen as a stumbling block to international cooperation on pertinent issues

60 Bartelson, n 4, at 80.

61 Krasner, SD 1999, *Sovereignty: organized hypocrisy*, Princeton University Press, New Jersey, p. 3.

62 Hickey, n 2, at 37.

63 United Nations, *Charter of the United Nations*, 24 October 1945, 1 UNTS XVI, art 2(7).

64 United Nations, *Charter of the United Nations*.

65 Eckersley, R 2007, 'Ecological intervention: prospects and limits', *Ethics & International Affairs*, vol. 21, no. 3, p. 293, 298.

66 Charter of the United Nations (1945), art 2(1).

67 Organisation for Security and Co-operation in Europe (OSCE) 1975, *Conference on security and co-operation in Europe (CSCE): final act of Helsinki* (opened for signature on 1 August 1975).

which currently affect all states. Since 2020, the two most pressing problems the entire world faces are a health crisis (COVID-19) and an ecological crisis. Using Hickey's phraseology, these two issues can be identified as "public goods" problems: namely, problems which have a negative effect on the planet that no one country wants to take ownership of.[68] Let us take for example the COVID-19 pandemic, which has preoccupied all our thoughts, efforts and actions for a year (at the time of writing). In 2020, at the UN General Assembly, President Trump called for China to be held accountable for the infections and deaths caused by the pandemic since the Hubei Province was the source of the outbreak.[69] In response, China denied this assertion and accused the United States of mismanagement and failure to take the pandemic seriously.[70] This is a classic situation of a "blame game approach", in which each country denies the ownership of a "public goods" problem (in this case, COVID-19). The reality is that the world will never be the same after COVID-19, and no one country can, in a purely national effort, overcome the virus.[71] A more humane approach in this scenario would be for the two largest economies in the world to collaborate in a meaningful way to restrict the spread of the pandemic and to avoid future outbreaks.[72] This can be justified on this simple premise – that's what sovereigns do. The difficulty with this humane approach is that it acts contrary to the Westphalian model, which we still blindly subscribe to and which, by its exclusivity syndrome, threatens our global welfare and security.

The tenet of this argument can also apply to global warming (the ecological crisis). Global warming squarely falls within Hickey's definition of a "public goods" problem because it threatens all humanity, and no one state wishes to take ownership of it. To be objective, no individual state can fully claim ownership for global warming since all states are responsible for it, albeit to varying degrees. Throughout the quarter of a century of the COP negotiations on climate change, the position of developing states and small island states (SIDS) has been that they have borne the full brunt of global warming because of the disproportionate amount of greenhouse gases which have been pumped into the atmosphere by the developed industrialized nations. Over the course of 25 years, due to the continuous warming

68 Hickey, n 2, at 26–27.

69 'UN General Assembly: US-China tensions flare over coronavirus', *BBC News* (viewed 22 September 2020), www.bbc.com. See also 'US President Donald Trump says UN "must hold China accountable" for COVID-19', *ABC News* (viewed 23 September 2020), (www.abc.net.au).

70 Horsley, JP 2020, 'Let's end the COVID-19 blame game: reconsidering China's role in the pandemic', *Brookings*, viewed 19 August 2020, (www.brookings.edu).

71 Kissinger, HA 2020, 'The coronavirus pandemic will forever alter the world order', *The Wall Street Journal*, online edn, New York, 3 April.

72 Horsley, n 70.

of the Earth and the shift in its planetary boundaries, one has to question whether the modus operandi of these negotiations has been effective. The treaties negotiated under the COP process (e.g. the Kyoto Protocol and the Paris Agreement) are arguably weak and fragile, in that they lack enforcement and state accountability.[73] This begs the question whether we as human beings are fit enough to truly negotiate with global warming. Such an act is almost on par with negotiating with the rain (as to when it will fall) or sun (as to when it will shine).[74] In an esoteric sense, global warming and climate change are abstract concepts which cannot be negotiated. Since there is no brick wall up in the sky to prevent greenhouse gases from crossing national borders, what is required is a collective and comprehensive action on the part of states. To put it simply, states cannot compromise on the climate.

The Westphalian system is bolstered on the archaic mindset of "every man (woman) for himself (herself)". This is synonymous to an "us versus them" syndrome which leaves no room for global cooperation.[75] The words of 17th-century poet John Donne are quite apt because they contemporaneously contradict this Westphalian outlook. Donne is credited as saying "[N]o man is an island" but "every man is a piece of the continent". His ode compared people to countries and argued for the interconnectedness of all.[76] Two hundred years after Donne, the Westphalian saga continued. It spread globally throughout the 19th and 20th centuries, largely through imperialism, mainly in Africa, the Americas and Asia.[77] The Berlin Conference, which carved up Africa between 1884 and 1885, has been described as "the most confident expression of the projection of European sovereignty upon non-European peoples".[78] After the Berlin Conference, the European powers recognized King Leopold II in his personal capacity as the sovereign of the Congo Free State. As time passed, while the European colonizers often neglected to apply the concept of sovereignty to those colonized, ironically, the latter began to demand their independence based on the same Westphalian trappings. These trappings included national independence, sovereign statehood, national interest and non-interference.[79] Thus, we had a situation in which, after colonization, non-European states desired full membership into the sovereign state system on the basis of the political and legal ideologies of Western states.[80] Consequently Westphalia is an old colonial relic

73 Bosselmann, n 53, at 49. See also Hickey, n 2, at 41–42.
74 Bosselmann, n 53, at 55.
75 Hickey, n 2, at 20.
76 Ha, T-H 2016, 'John Donne's solemn 400-year-old poem against isolationism is resonating today', *Quartz*, viewed 25 June 2016, (www.qz.com).
77 Hickey, n 2, at 17.
78 Fitzmaurice, n 6, at 278.
79 Kissinger, H 2014, *World order*, Penguin Press, New York, pp. 6–7.
80 Jackson, R 2007, *Sovereignty: evolution of an idea*, Polity Press, Cambridge, p. 146.

whereby the newly "independent" countries replicated the governance structures of their colonizers.

This does not mean that the Westphalian principles are being challenged in these modern times. An example of such a challenge is the European Union (EU) where Europe set out to depart from the state system (which it designed) to an arrangement of pooled sovereignty.[81] With the UK officially exiting the EU in 2020 and the lack of a unified COVID-19 health protocol adopted by EU countries, one is left to wonder whether Europe is slowly reverting to familiar territory where "every state stands on its own". Notwithstanding this, and even in the face of a pandemic, there are still fair grounds to debate that the world may be slowly transitioning from an old Westphalian type sovereignty to a new model of sovereignty where borders are no longer territorial, and political authority is more decentralized and dispersed. Arguments in favour of this new model are rooted in globalization aided by instantaneous communication, which nurtures a single space, thereby rendering territorial borders (sooner or later) irrelevant.[82]

Despite all these odds, even if Westphalia represents a bygone vestige, it is still present with us today. Although the Westphalian system has practically claimed "every square foot of the planet", it can no longer deliver on its original peace mandate.[83] This led Kissinger to declare it "the blueprint" and "the scaffolding of the international order . . . as it now exists".[84] One possible positive spinoff (if one may so call it) about Westphalia could be attributed to the views of Travers Twiss, an English jurist. Twiss argued that following the Thirty Years' War, there was an increase in the number of treaties implemented between states, and this enabled, for the very first time, a detailed study of the theory of the law of nations, which eventually became known as "international law".[85] In this regard, Twiss was able to pick up where Grotius left off. After all this, Westphalia still represents an outmoded form of governance and should be abandoned on the grounds that it is a major impediment to the resolution of the current ecological crisis and an anathema to all "public goods" problems.[86]

2. The Global Context of Sovereignty

The challenge that many political and legal theorists face today is how to define sovereignty in this ever-changing world in which we live. As discussed, it is crucial to start off on the footing that sovereignty is "closet Eurocentric"

81 Kissinger, n 79, at 7.
82 Bartelson, n 4, at 61 and 72.
83 Hickey, n 2, at 17 and 41.
84 Kissinger, n 79, at 6 and 27.
85 Fitzmaurice, n 6, at 232.
86 Hickey, n 2, at 23 and 37.

and a decisive factor in the making of modern Europe.[87] Outside Europe, the word "sovereignty" first found its place in New Zealand on 6 February 1840. Under the English version of the Treaty of Waitangi, the local Māori chiefs ceded to Her Majesty, the Queen of England, "absolutely and without reservation all the rights and powers of Sovereignty".[88] When Hōne Heke, an influential Māori chief, was about to sign the treaty, William Colenso asked Consul William Hobson, "Your Excellency, do you think the Chiefs really understand all aspects of the treaty?" To this, Hobson replied, "If they don't it's not my fault."[89] History and the translations themselves reveal that there were stark differences between the English and Māori versions of the Treaty of Waitangi. From the Māori's perspective, they expected the treaty to be a start of a new relationship with Britain and the chiefs – one in which each party would play an equal role in the governance of New Zealand.[90] The Treaty of Waitangi example illustrates that the indigenous Māori found it difficult to grapple with this "Eurocentric" notion of sovereignty, and, as a result, the term was widely misconstrued by the signing chiefs.

Indeed, in the 20th century, especially post–European colonization, the term "sovereignty" came to be associated with the language of political independence and autonomy.[91] This serves to illustrate what Bodin sought to point out: that sovereignty is an abstract concept that possesses no singular phenomenal form but instead is made visible or perceptible to us through diverse manifestations.[92] "Sovereignty" (also to be read as "state sovereignty", unless stated otherwise), therefore, is not fixed but is evolving, taking on different personas over the centuries.[93] For these reasons, we cannot impose the ideas of 17th-century sovereignty on a 21st-century world.

a) Territorial Sovereignty and the Anthropocene

Under the traditional conception of sovereignty, every state is regarded as internally and externally sovereign within their given sphere.[94] This means that a state can exercise absolute authority over its territory – otherwise known as territorial sovereignty. Territorial sovereignty became ever more popular during the 17th and 18th century in Europe with the development of

87 Bartelson, n 4, at 3. See also Jackson, n 80, at 1.
88 Orange, C 2013, *The story of a treaty*, Bridget Williams Books Ltd, Wellington, p. 39.
89 At 28.
90 At 40.
91 Matthews, D 2021, 'Reframing sovereignty for the Anthropocene', *Transnational Legal Theory*, vol. 12, no. 1, p. 44, 58.
92 Walker, N 2013, 'Sovereignty frames and sovereignty claims', in R Rawlings, P Leyland & AL Young (eds), *Sovereignty and the law*, Oxford University Press, Oxford, p. 19, 22.
93 Jackson, n 80, at 1.
94 Parmar, n 1, at 3.

cartography and the increasing use of artificial lines on maps, which shaped a common understanding of the nature of political power.[95] Even the UN engenders respect, to some extent, for a state's territorial sovereignty. The UN Charter recognizes that member states refrain from the threat or use of force against the territorial integrity of another state.[96] This is in addition to the previously discussed "non-intervention" article found at Article 2(7) of the Charter.

Geographically, especially after the entry into force of the Law of the Sea Convention in 1994, it became widely accepted that territorial sovereignty extended beyond the physical landmass and included a state's internal waters, territorial waters, air space over territorial waters and exclusive economic zone. Under international law, a coastal state has the sovereign right to exploit the natural resources (whether living or non-living) in its exclusive economic zone (EEZ).[97] This was not the first time the UN recognized the rights of states to have full sovereignty over their own natural resources. In December 1962, the UN General Assembly passed a resolution (hereinafter referred to as "the 1962 Resolution") which acknowledged that nations have permanent sovereignty over their natural wealth and resources, and this sovereignty must be exercised "in the interest of their national development and of the well-being of the people of the State concerned".[98] Who determines the criteria of "national development" and "well-being of the people" is most likely the state (unless the exercise of rights over natural wealth and resources is pursued under a democratic vote such as a referendum). Giving the state "the final word" on how to utilize the nation's natural wealth and resources may not always be in the best interest of its citizens, especially if multinational corporations or third-party actors are in a position to easily influence domestic environmental policy. To add to this, even if sovereign nations have the power to freely consider what is necessary or desirable for their citizens, their actions may not always represent the will of the people unless the state consults their citizens in advance on the proposed action. These limitations, so described, are not surprising since the 1962 Resolution upholds one of the foremost principles on which the entire UN Charter is based: namely, the sovereign equality of all member states.[99] This means that sovereign states are at liberty to do what they want with their "natural resources" in the name of "sovereignty", and all other states must fall in line and mutually respect this fact. If one state violates the rights of another

95 Matthews, n 91, at 65.

96 Charter of the United Nations, art 2(4).

97 United Nations Convention on the Law of the Sea 1833 UNTS 3 (adopted 10 December 1982, entered into force 16 November 1994), art 56(1)(a).

98 United Nations General Assembly Resolution 1803 (XVII) "Permanent Sovereignty over Natural Resources" (14 December 1962), at [1].

99 At [5].

state to do what they wish with their natural resources, this is articulated as being contrary to the spirit and principles of the UN Charter.[100] According to the 1962 Resolution, this will restrict the development of international cooperation and the maintenance of world peace.[101] The conclusion to be arrived at is that all states have a right to exploit their own natural resources, and third-party states should not intervene. However, if a third-party state decides to intervene in a state's sovereign affairs, it does so with the risk of losing an international partner and possibly disrupting world peace.

Thirty years after the 1962 Resolution, the UN adopted the Rio Declaration on Environment and Development (Rio Declaration). The Rio Declaration, similar to the 1972 Stockholm Declaration, which was adopted ten years prior, gives the sovereign state the right under international law to exploit its own resources, on the condition that activities within their jurisdiction or control do not cause damage to the environment of other states or areas beyond the limits of national jurisdiction.[102] Under the Rio Declaration, this "right to exploit" is made pursuant to national "environmental" and "development" policies.[103] Conspicuously absent under the Rio Declaration was the specific criterion for the state to consider the "well-being" of their people when exercising its sovereign right to exploit resources. (One could argue that a state, by pursing national policy, is also taking into consideration the welfare of the people, but, as previously argued, this may not always be the case.) It becomes evident, after close examination, that the Rio Declaration, together with the 1962 Resolution and the 1972 Stockholm Declaration, are premised on the territoriality of sovereignty: i.e. a state's ultimate right to do whatsoever it pleases with the natural "resources" found within its spatial boundaries. The fact that sovereignty is defined partly by its territoriality remains uncontroversial.[104] This theory of sovereignty by territory, however, is totally out of sync with modern-day conceptions such as the Anthropocene, in which the Earth is moving away from the stable epoch of the Holocene to an era of unbalanced, erratic ecological collapse. To take the position that the state is a unit of analysis that can be delineated and thereby disconnected from the environment fails to recognize that political borders are effectively porous and not necessarily barriers.[105] The advent of the Anthropocene illustrates that a state's "immobile" territory is subject to and affected

100 At paragraph [7].
101 At paragraph [7].
102 United Nations, Report of the United Nations Conference on Environment and Development UN Doc A/Conf 151/26/Vol. I (12 August 1992), Annex I, Principle 2.
103 United Nations, Report of the United Nations Conference on Environment and Development UN Doc A/Conf 151/26/Vol. I.
104 Matthews, n 91, at 64.
105 Wijsman, K, 'State sovereignty in a time of global environmental problems: a move towards dynamism?', *Academia*, (www.academia.edu) at 7. See also Nordblad, J 2021, 'On the

by a range of transformations brought about by geological alterations and state-led initiatives.[106] An example of geological alterations is the melting of Antarctic ice sheets, which leads to sea level rise, which ultimately leads to devastating effects, even on those states situated thousands of nautical miles away. A similar analogy can be drawn using state-led initiatives – such as when wealthy, industrialized countries pump tonnes of greenhouse gases into the atmosphere, thereby causing severe climatological disruptions to the remote Pacific islands. The thing about the Anthropocene is that it slowly creeps up on us, both voluntarily and involuntarily, and its consequences cannot immediately be seen with the naked eye. Yet it is not the short-term repercussions that are worrying, but rather the long term. This requires states to become more vigilant and forward thinking and not myopic when it comes to their perception of sovereignty. Sovereignty should no longer be perceived as the "Rio Declaration" model of sovereignty, which asks, "How should we exploit our natural resources which fall squarely within our jurisdiction?" or "How should we exploit these resources in such a manner which is consistent with our environmental and development goals?" Rather, sovereignty should ask, "How can we manage our natural spaces and biodiversity in a manner that promotes the ecological well-being of not only our citizens but those living abroad?" This chapter therefore accepts that the Anthropocene draws attention to those aspects of the Earth that fall outside the typical sovereign boundaries.[107] As a result, a modern-day account of sovereignty should be reframed and not ignore the disastrous consequences of the Anthropocene.[108] As Matthews accurately points out, sovereignty fails to address how sovereign powers interact with the geological, earthly and putatively inanimate "natural" sphere.[109]

b) The UN System of Sovereignty

The Anthropocene offers one perspective on developing a theoretical understanding of what sovereignty is and how the notion should respond to physical and geological changes to the Earth. However, there are other modern-day perspectives which have implications on how we, as global citizens, view sovereignty. The issue as to whether sovereignty entails a responsibility is an additional perspective and will be discussed in the next chapter.

The attempt to come to grips with the concept of sovereignty, especially in this modern era, is a complicated one. Such a task has often been evasive

difference between Anthropocene and climate change temporalities', *Critical Inquiry*, vol. 47, p. 328.

106 Matthews, n 91, at 66.

107 At 65.

108 At 46.

109 At 59.

mainly due to the interchangeable usage of the term and the mutable nature of the subject. The difficulty with defining sovereignty is that it is such a Protean word with an inherent ambiguity.[110] Following this line of reasoning, Kelsen was recorded as stating:[111]

> The term "sovereignty", while denoting one of the most important concepts of the theory of national and international law, has a variety of meanings, a fact that causes regrettable confusion in this theory.

As Kelsen points out, part of the reason why the term sovereignty is inherently ambiguous is possibly due to the fact that it captures a wide range of reference.[112] Carré de Malberg adds:[113]

> [T]he unwieldy range of the sovereignty term, and the consequent danger of conceptual confusion, is exacerbated by the lack of sufficient discrimination in our natural language.

Throughout the medieval era in Europe and even in the ancient Far East, the use of the word "sovereign" would have been more aligned to the head of a kingdom or a dynasty. During the 16th century, at the time of the establishment of Catholic missions and European colonization in Africa, there also existed several kingdoms in West and West Central Africa.[114] So, generally speaking, when one considers "sovereign" or even "sovereignty", one would tend to think of simplistic and historic descriptions such as "kingdoms", "authority" or "supreme power". Yet to coin an actual phrase or sentence defining sovereignty can be seemingly difficult. The *Cambridge Dictionary*, for instance, defines sovereignty as "the power of a country to control its own government".[115] As accurate as this *Cambridge* definition may be, it is restricted in scope as it confines sovereignty to a localized space. Robert Jackson, professor emeritus in political science, went on to define sovereignty as "a distinctive configuration of state authority".[116] Whilst this definition is also helpful, it similarly does not consider the external relationships that sovereignty has with other states. For example, when Neil Armstrong planted

110 Bartelson, n 4, at 43.
111 Bartelson, n 4, at 43.
112 Walker, n 92, at 23.
113 de Malberg, RC & Maulin, E 2004, *Contribution à la théorie générale de l'Etat, spécialement d'après les données fournies par le droit constitutionnel français*, Paris Dalloz, vol. 1, p. 79, as cited in Walker, n 92, at 23.
114 Bennett, HL 2019, *African kings and black slaves*, University of Pennsylvania Press, Philadelphia at Prologue.
115 Cambridge Dictionary, *Sovereignty*, online edn, (www.dictionary.cambridge.org).
116 Jackson, n 80, at 5.

the United States (US) flag on the moon in 1969, did that mean that the US claimed "sovereignty" over the moon – an international entity outside its domestic jurisdiction? Using the *Cambridge* or Jackson definition, it may have been the intention of the US to control or to have authority over the moon, but establishing a long-term government or a colony on the moon back in 1969 would have been a bit far-fetched. On the other hand, it could be argued that although Armstrong's gesture may have implied territorial ownership, in the end, it was purely symbolic because the 1967 Outer Space Treaty (which provides that space shall be "the province of all mankind") was in force at the time of the landing of Apollo 11.[117] The idea of sovereignty being symbolic was first put forth by Bartelson, who argues that sovereignty is merely a perspective of an object rather than a representation of fact.[118] To put it another way, sovereignty is all about perception and optics. It is all about how a state flexes its muscles or influences power. So even though the Outer Space Treaty specifies that the use of the moon is for the benefit of all countries,[119] the installation of the US flag was perhaps psychological. Its purpose was to convey a message to all other states of the world that the US was the de facto superpower and, by extension, the owner of the Earth's only natural satellite. This message was expected to stand, even though no nation could claim sovereignty over the moon.[120] It must also be recalled that the flag planting transpired at the time of the Cold War, when the rivalry (including the space race) between the US and the Soviet Union was at an all-time high. This argument of symbolism may also appeal to Marxists, who maintain that sovereignty is a fiction to conceal the uneven distribution of powers between classes in capitalist societies.[121]

Comparing the *Cambridge* and Jackson definitions, the moon example illustrates that sovereignty is an interplay between states. To place it under a broader banner, sovereignty is not about an individual state per se but about the interaction of a group of states. As a result, a more modern school of thought is to examine what sovereignty has to offer externally. Consistent with this approach, one could look at sovereignty as the central organizing principle of the system of states.[122] Within this central organization, the principle of "sovereign equality" prevails. This means that every state, regardless of its size, political structure, socio-economic background, influence or

117 Ali, Y 2015, 'Who owns outer space?', *BBC News*, viewed 25 September 2015, (www.bbc.com).

118 Bartelson, n 4, at 13–14.

119 Treaty on Principles Governing the Activities of States in the Exploration and Use of Outer Space, including the Moon and Other Celestial Bodies, 18 U.S.T. 2410, 610 U.N.T.S. 205 (opened for signature 27 January 1967, entered into force 10 October 1967), art 1.

120 Article 2.

121 Bartelson, n 4, at 16.

122 Parmar, n 1, at 31.

military strength, is equal to the other states of the world.[123] This approach to sovereignty is streamlined into the UN model as set out in its Charter, which was created some 300 years after Westphalia. Accordingly, while the fact of sovereignty is derived from the actual structures of power within the state (as articulated by Jackson), the norm of sovereignty is essentially embedded in an international legal order.[124] One can look at it from another perspective. Before a nation enters into statehood, it must first pass the rigorous test laid out under the Montevideo Convention: namely, a permanent population, a defined territory, a government and the capacity to enter into relations with other states.[125] Once these criteria are established, the state can claim it is de facto sovereign. In this globalized world, being inducted in this "Hall of Sovereignty" means little or nothing to a state until it interacts with an international order, which nowadays is the UN. A classic example is South Sudan, the newest member state of the UN, which gained independence on 9 July 2011 and joined the UN on 14 July 2011.[126]

Once South Sudan was recognized as an independent nation, it became de facto sovereign. However, by joining the UN five days later, its de facto sovereignty was given more credence as it then became a member of a larger body: i.e., a community of nation-states. It is this magnetic pull towards the UN immediately upon the recognition of statehood that serves as the rationale behind the argument that sovereignty is essentially embedded in an international legal order. A state becomes "sovereign" because other states in the international community widely perceive it to be. And just like joining any club, all members of the UN must abide by certain rules. Although these rules are quite detailed, they include, inter alia, settling disputes by peaceful means and – as we have previously seen – refraining from the use of force against the territorial integrity or political independence of any state.[127] In this vein, states are construed as being self-contained entities within an international system which is self-regulating.[128] Such an observation is consistent with most international relations theories, which assume the international system is composed of states, and what makes these states what they are is their sovereignty.[129] In other words, sovereignty is a necessary fact of international political life.[130]

123 Parmar, SS 2019, 'Sovereignty and trans-boundary environmental issues: a search for co-existence', *SSRN Electronic Journal*, p. 4.

124 Bartelson, n 4, at 48.

125 Montevideo Convention, n 10, art 1.

126 UN News, *UN welcomes South Sudan as 193rd member state*, viewed 14 July 2011, (www.un.org).

127 Charter of the United Nations, art 2(3) and art 2(4).

128 Bartelson, n 4, at 41.

129 At 48.

130 At 48.

The converse is also true in that we need sovereign states for a self-regulating international system to thrive and exist. If one was to think about it, the UN would not be able to function without the cooperation of sovereign states and the diplomats representing those states. On this point, a definition of sovereignty inspired by Carré de Malberg is worth mentioning: "sovereignty" refers to the supreme character of a state's power, which enables it to act on the international level and to interfere with other sovereigns.[131] From this perspective, it is implied that for a state to possess "sovereignty", it must engender the respect and comity of other states. In this sense, international diplomacy and the ability to positively engage with the community of nations are what determine whether a state is sovereign or not. This is what true modern-day sovereignty is all about: a state's willingness to take initiative and to be a "mover and shaker" on matters which affect all humanity. Today, the world needs to "move" and "shake" in unison on the threat posed by the COVID-19 pandemic (health crisis) and global warming (ecological crisis) – two noticeable "public goods" problems. Both the pandemic and global warming traverse national boundaries without the need of a visa. In order to confront both problems, states (as self-contained entities) are required to collaborate with each other in good faith within an international system which is self-regulating (i.e. WHO or UN respectively). The establishment of COVAX – a coalition of 172 countries which seeks to "guarantee rapid, fair and equitable access" to vaccines "for people in all countries"[132] – provides evidence of a global response to tackle the current COVID-19 health crisis. Consistent with the call for global action, the World Health Organization (WHO) has already voiced concern against vaccine nationalism, in which wealthy countries secure vaccine stocks while the Global South struggle to do so. This led microbiologist Dr Siouxsie Wiles to state that countries should act ethically towards each other and that "it was impractical for wealthy countries to allow poorer ones to fall behind in vaccinations".[133]

What all this signifies is that a global response to "public goods" problems demand global and ethical leadership. Although COVID-19 has affected most, if not all states, few global leaders stand out. One of these leaders would be Jacinda Arden, whose country, New Zealand, has been acknowledged as having the best response to the management of the coronavirus.[134]

131 Troper, M 2016, 'The modern state and the concept of authority', in R Cotterrell & M Del Mar (eds), *Authority in transnational legal theory: theorising across disciplines*, Edward Elgar Publishing, Cheltenham, p. 75, 83.

132 Krueger, AO 2020, *Can poor countries avoid a vaccine bidding war?* viewed 7 January 2020, (www.gavi.org).

133 Weekes, J 2021, 'Mutating virus prompts alert call', *The New Zealand Herald*, Auckland, 2 February, p. A3.

134 Dziedzic, S 2021, 'New Zealand tops Lowy Institute list as country with best response to coronavirus, Australia sits eighth', *ABC News*, 28 January.

On this point, it has been reported that the United States and the world found New Zealand's response and Arden's leadership on the handling of the pandemic as exemplar.[135] Arden has certainly carved out a reputation for herself and New Zealand, which is arguably one of the safest places in the world to live during this global health crisis. The circumstances are not that clear for the climate crisis, and it is still premature to suggest that a global leader has emerged. When the US formally withdrew from the Paris Agreement on 4 November 2020, one was left to wonder whether the world would look towards China or the EU as world leaders on climate action. However, the suspense did not last that long as on 20th January 2021, the same day as his inauguration, President Biden signed an executive order to have the US re-join the Paris Agreement. On that occasion, Biden stated that the US "must lead" a global response to climate change. Paving the way for global co-operation, Biden also admitted that the US was not capable of meeting the challenges of the climate crisis and COVID-19 on its own.[136]

In effect, today, sovereignty can be viewed as a state's brand, in that it is less about what a state *is* and more about what it *does*.[137] Sovereignty depicts a state's ability to lead in a world fraught with global problems and the persuasiveness to encourage others to follow in their footsteps. Seen in this light, sovereignty is a form of consciousness. Our thoughts on a particular president or prime minister shape our reality of the country they govern. State sovereignty then becomes more in line with the character of the state than its territorial boundaries.[138] Katinka Wijsman could not have summed it up better: States are not a monolithic entity but come in diverse constellations.[139]

Sovereignty in its mature form, therefore, consists of a new "social imaginary".[140] This social imaginary achieves three main tasks. First, it offers a perception that is shared by large groups, if not the entire society. Secondly, it gives a shared sense of legitimacy. (In this case, it legitimises sovereignty.) Thirdly, it incorporates a sense of normal expectations that we have for each other.[141] These three elements, when placed side by side, illustrate the social relationship between an ordinary person and the determination of sovereignty.

135 Walls, J 2020, 'Gates's plea to Arden on vaccine', *The New Zealand Herald*, Auckland, 4 November, p. A3.
136 *Biden signs 'existential' executive orders on climate and the environment*, viewed 27 January 2021, (www.bbc.com).
137 Wijsman, n 105, at 7.
138 At 5–6.
139 At 5–6.
140 Walker, n 92, at 21.
141 Taylor, C 2004, *Modern social imaginaries*, Duke University Press, North Carolina, pp. 23–24.

c) *The Political Context of Sovereignty*

Another subject which academic and scholars fiercely debate is whether sovereignty is purely a political or a legal concept – or perhaps a mixture of both. One political and legal theory is that the endurance of sovereignty over the centuries is based on fetishism – that is, ascribing inherent powers to an inanimate object.[142] This term fetishism, as designed by Bartelson, is interpreted as an obsession whereby we worship "sovereignty" as if it has magical powers that can unilaterally emancipate us from our miseries. This school of thought perceives sovereignty as something which is man-made and intangible, yet still capable of shaping our political reality.[143] Caribbean constitutional jurist Simeon McIntosh agrees with this school of thought that sovereignty is a political subject. McIntosh stated:[144]

> In contemporary political theory, the term "sovereign" expresses the idea that there is a final and absolute political authority in the community. It is a theory or assumption about political power: a way of thinking and speaking about political power in a defined community.

On arriving at this idea of sovereignty as "political power", McIntosh was influenced by Hegel, who conceptualized the state as an organic unity which is sovereign.[145] Applying this political theory to the United Kingdom (UK) appears to be problematic. In the UK, the Parliament is supreme as it is the highest source of authority to make laws without restriction.[146] On this, Hobbes opined that absolute and uncontrollable power need not be vested in a single individual but could be enjoyed by a group such as the British Parliament.[147] This must be contrasted with the Queen, who is the sovereign, even though she has no political or executive role.[148] Despite this paradox, the Queen, as sovereign, is a symbol for national identity and gives a sense of stability and continuity to her citizens.[149] The problem that arises is that under the Hegel/McIntosh political theory, it would be incorrect to claim that the Parliament and the Queen are sovereign over the rest of the state as this would ignore the state's fundamental unity.[150] The driving force behind

142 Bartelson, n 4, at 40.
143 Bartelson, n 4, at 40.
144 McIntosh, SCR 2002, *Caribbean constitutional reform: rethinking the west Indian polity*, The Caribbean Law Publishing Company, Kingston, p. 308.
145 McIntosh, *Caribbean constitutional reform.*
146 The UK in a changing Europe 2021, 'What is sovereignty' (viewed 21 September 2021), (www.ukandeu.uk).
147 Parmar, n 1, at 32.
148 The Royal Family, *The role of the monarchy*, (www.royal.uk).
149 The Royal Family, *The role of the monarchy.*
150 McIntosh, n 144, at 308.

this theory is that sovereignty, in a political sense, is indivisible and is posited with the state alone. For these reasons, it can be argued that the indivisibility of a sovereign is essential since the quality of being supreme cannot be attributed to more than one actor within the same polity.[151] Walter Bagehot, a 19th-century writer on British politics, would disagree with this argument. According to Bagehot, the secret of the unwritten English constitution lay in having two kinds of institutions: the dignified and the efficient. The dignified, such as the monarchy, held everyone's respect. Meanwhile, the efficient, such as the House of Commons (the Parliament), did the real work.[152] In the end, Walker provides a glimpse of a neutral approach that can ease any misgivings and misunderstandings. This approach is that sovereignty only makes sense when taken in its own particular context.[153]

The next school of thought is that sovereignty is purely a legal concept.[154] This view is in alignment with that of Kelsen, who asserts that sovereignty is nothing but the quality of a legal order.[155] Kelsen reasoned that a state is a "political organization" and, by extension, an organization is an order. He added that the power of a state is organized by positive law.[156] Thus, there is no dualism of law and the state since there is only one legal order which regulates the state.[157] One form of legal order is a written constitution, which specifically sets out the structure of government and the powers of the state.

The last school of thought, which most theorists agree on, is that the concept of sovereignty refers to either a political fact or a legal norm.[158] This can be summed up as the two versions of an essentialist's view on sovereignty: namely, (1) sovereignty is nothing but a legal norm, and (2) sovereignty is nothing but a "brute political fact".[159] Morgenthau, a German/American political scientist, sought to harmonize this relationship by arguing that sovereignty is both a political fact (as a direct result of Westphalia) and a legal norm.[160] Due to how sovereignty shaped our own reality, sovereignty can be seen as two sides of the same coin. For this reason, it is accepted that "sovereignty" is a merged subject that represents part of our common-sense understanding of politics and law.[161]

151 Bartelson, n 4, at 47.
152 Lewis, A 1977, 'Dignified and efficient', *New York Times*, online edn, archives, New York, 9 June.
153 Walker, n 92, at 22.
154 Troper, n 131, at 82.
155 Bartelson, n 4, at 43.
156 Kelsen, n 26, at 190.
157 At 191.
158 Bartelson, n 4, at 42.
159 At 41.
160 At 45.
161 Jackson, n 80, at 5.

To conclude on this point, we have not moved very far from where we left off. A definition of sovereignty still eludes us, notwithstanding the fact that it is ever present in our midst. As one political scholar opined, the debate on whether sovereignty is factual or normative becomes rather inconsequential.[162] As a result, it does not matter what sovereignty is; what matters is rather *that* sovereignty is.[163] With this in mind, sovereignty becomes a mystical contraption, one that only makes complete sense when it is placed within an international sphere. To borrow a few words from French philosopher Raymond Aron, sovereignty is "an original fact of the international system".[164]

Some academics are tempted to argue that we have arrived at a stage of post-sovereignty, when states have been replaced by colossal multinational corporations such as Facebook, Microsoft and British Petroleum (who some persons claim are "sovereign" in their own right). The flaw with this argument is that these multilateral corporations lack territorial sovereignty and need the permission and protection of the states in whose jurisdiction they wish to operate.[165] That being said, there is no compelling evidence that we have already entered a post-sovereign world.[166]

162 Bartelson, n 4, at 48.
163 Bartelson, n 4, at 48.
164 Bartelson, n 4, at 48.
165 Jackson, n 80, at 155.
166 At 151.

Chapter 6

Sovereignty and International Environmental Law

1. Introduction

In a 2005 register, the United Nations Environment Programme (UNEP) recorded more than 272 international treaties and other agreements related to the environment.[1] The first of such treaties was the Convention Concerning the Use of White Lead in Painting, which was adopted by the International Labour Organization in Geneva in 1921. According to these figures, this amounts to an average of almost three treaties/agreements concerning the environment being adopted every year. This average may not represent the current state of affairs since it does not consider the environmental treaties or agreements that have been adopted post-2005, including, but not limited to, the Nagoya Protocol on the Access of Genetic Resources and the Paris Agreement adopted in 2010 and 2015 respectively. Nevertheless, and despite 100 years of negotiating a plethora of international legal texts pertaining to the environment, one can only conclude that states have not diverted the ecological crisis.

One would have hoped that, given the amount of effort undertaken by sovereign states over the years in shaping international environmental law norms, we would have been living on a more secure and sustainable planet. In fact, the opposite is true, and it becomes evident that over the last century (and counting), states are doing something considerably wrong with regard to addressing the dire state of the environment. It is reminiscent of Albert Einstein's definition of insanity, which is doing the same thing over and over again expecting different results. The paradox of this is that we continue to request that states resolve our planetary dilemma by adopting and ratifying environmental law instruments, when they are the main culprits of our ecological destruction.[2] The questions which then arise are: (1) What is the

1 United Nations Environment Programme 2005, *Register of international treaties and other agreements in the field of the environment*, UNEP/Environmental Law/2005/3, 30 December.
2 Smith, M 2011, *Against ecological sovereignty: ethics, biopolitics, and saving the natural world*, University of Minnesota Press, Chicago.

DOI: 10.4324/9781032674049-9

utility of international environmental law, when sovereign states use it as a tool to satisfy their own narrow political agendas? (2) Can non-state actors, such as civil society, non-governmental organizations (NGOs) and individuals, play a critical role in the development of an international environmental law jurisprudence? (3) If non-state actors were given such a role, would that impede on state sovereignty as we know it? and (4) Has the shaping of these "international environmental norms" over the decades placed an undue burden on states, thereby compromising their sovereignty?

2. The Neorealist Viewpoint

In attempting to determine the utility of international environmental law to states, it is worthwhile to consider the school of thought put forward by neorealists in international relations (IR) theory. Neorealists argue that the state is imbued with high autonomy and is the central actor of international politics.[3] The neorealists paint a very bleak picture of a state of disorder and global anarchy in which every state is fighting for survival and security, and morality and ethical behaviour have no place.[4] Within this school of thought, the stage is set for the "Wild West" as states are considered selfish entities, not altruistic, myopic and focused on short-term economic and/or development goals. Quite naturally, Trump's political rhetoric of "America First" appeals to this neorealist ideology. Hobson compares a neorealist's view of states as being "billiard balls" stacked on a pool table.[5] Using this analogy, the purpose of a state is to not to be bullied around by other billiard balls (states), lest they fall into the pit of destruction. As every state is fighting to survive, neorealists believe that states are rational egoists that have no incentive to take action to protect the environment, even if their action causes damage to other states.[6] In critique of this stance, holding such a position directly offends the no-harm rule under principle 2 of the Rio Declaration – a rule that is widely recognized as a principle of customary international law.[7] Notwithstanding this, the neorealist tradition is grounded on the fact that states are inclined to engage in the unrestrained exploitation of natural spaces, species and ecosystems in complete disregard for international environmental law.[8]

3 Hobson, JM 2000, *The state and international relations*, Cambridge University Press, Cambridge, p. 2.
4 Eckersley, R 2004, *The green state: rethinking democracy and sovereignty*, The MIT Press, Cambridge, p. 23.
5 Hobson, n 3, at 2.
6 Eckersley, n 4, at 22.
7 See also *Trail Smelter Arbitration (United States v Canada)* (1941) 3 U.N. Rep. International Arbitration Awards 1905.
8 Eckersley, n 4, at 23.

Realists and neorealists do not dismiss outright the fact that states enter into environmental treaties or declarations. However, they offer various pessimistic arguments relating to the substance of the treaties themselves and the ease with which such treaty objectives can be thwarted. In terms of treaty substance, it is common to find, during the negotiation process, compromises being struck between diplomats representing states. In some cases, these compromises (sometimes made behind "closed doors") appear as "trade-offs" which do not directly concern the environmental treaty which is the subject of negotiation but may well overlap into other external matters. As a result, by the time the treaty is formally adopted, it represents a "watered-down" text that fails to maximize the potential to address global environmental concerns. Eckersley refers to such negotiations as not being "the product of free and fulsome deliberation" but rather "strategic bargaining that reflects narrowly conceived geopolitical interests".[9]

In relation to thwarting treaty objectives, neorealists warn it cannot be assumed that multilateral cooperation occurs – e.g. under environmental law treaties – and if, for some reason, it did occur, it would not successfully address our global ecological crisis.[10] This line of thinking introduces a state of play in which states, motivated by their own selfish pursuits, sign on to international environmental law treaties with some indifference as to whether or not they will comply with all the obligations contained therein. Added to this, neorealists argue that states are not mandated to enter into multilateral treaty arrangements to protect the global environment.[11] It is this point that strikes at the core of what is perceived as traditional state sovereignty: the fact that government administrators are free to decide whether or not they wish to join up to treaties.[12] Even if states willingly decide to enter into a multilateral treaty arrangement, they are free to withdraw by giving the requisite notice – as seen with the United States, which officially withdrew from the Paris Agreement in November 2020.[13]

Having said all this, there is one critical analysis regarding the neorealist theory which ought to be made. Since neorealist theory is anchored on the premise that we live in a world of global anarchy where survival and security are the paramount objectives of all states, the rise of the Anthropocene and the instability it brings to our ecosystems force states to rely heavily on environmental multilateralism. An example of this is sea level rises, triggered by global warming and melting ice-sheets, which disrupt the territorial

9 Eckersley, n 4, at 23.

10 Eckersley, n 4, at 23.

11 Eckersley, n 4, at 22.

12 Hathaway, OA 2008, 'International delegation and state sovereignty', *Law and Contemporary Problems*: *The Law and Politics of International Delegation*, vol. 71, no. 1, p. 115.

13 On 20 January 2021, President Joe Biden, by executive action, moved to reinstate the US to the Paris climate agreement.

integrity, causing an existential threat to small island and low-lying states. Under these circumstances the need to preserve the environment would be regarded by such states as a matter of high priority.[14] Using this realist backdrop, low-lying and small island states may be required by force to enter into various environmental treaties because their own survival depends on it. Not only would the survival of these states be at stake but also their sovereignty. In the very near future, it is predicted that vulnerable low-lying island states such as Tuvalu, Kiribati and the Maldives are likely to become entirely submerged. This could possibly lead to two scenarios – or perhaps a combination of both. First, countries will experience a wave of climate-induced migration, which could ultimately lead to the death of sovereignty in these islands. Secondly, in an attempt to "preserve sovereignty", it could arguably lead to the creation of a new category of state called "the deterritorialized state". Rayfuse defines a deterritorialized state as a state that consists of a government entity that would continue to represent the rights of its citizens at the international level and vis à vis their new host state or states.[15] The idea of a deterritorialized state has been compared to what Maxine Burkett defines as ex-situ sovereignty, in which the existing government of a state could continue to exist outside the confines of its territory, especially when the land may become uninhabitable due to climate change.[16]

The creation of a deterritorialized state can be opposed on many practical and legal grounds. One opposing legal argument is that, under the Montevideo Convention, a disappearing state that no longer possesses a defined territory can be disqualified as a state under international law.[17] The practical reality of this legal argument is that citizens of a state which has become uninhabitable on account of climate change will not only be labelled "climate refugees", but they also run the risk of losing their cultural attachment to their homeland.[18] Additionally, such a state will also cease to retain control of their vast maritime zones and fisheries resources – all of which may likely fall under the jurisdiction of neighbouring states.[19] In the interests of survival, it therefore becomes the imperative for governments of small-island and low-lying states to enter into multilateral arrangements in order to preserve

14 Eckersley, n 4, at 22–23.

15 Rayfuse, R 2011, 'Life after land', *New York Times*, online edn, New York, 18 July, (https://www.nytimes.com/2011/07/19/opinion/19rayfuse.html).

16 Arcanjo, M 2019, *Has climate change rendered the concept of sovereignty obsolete?*, A Climate Institute Publication, viewed 17 January 2019, (http://climate.org/wp-content/uploads/2019/01/Has-Climate-Change-Rendered-the-Concept-of-Sovereignty-Obsolete.pdf) at 5.

17 *Montevideo Convention on the Rights and Duties of States*, opened for signature 26 December 1933, 165 LNTS 19 (entered into force 26 December 1934), art 1(b).

18 Arcanjo, n 16, at 5–6.

19 Rayfuse, n 15.

their long-term sovereignty. Seen in this light, these states, even though preoccupied with survival and security, will strive to ensure that the environmental multilateral system will prevail in their favour, thereby debunking the pessimistic myth of neorealists.

3. The Ecology-Sovereignty Debate

After a thorough examination of the ecology-sovereignty literature, there appear to be two perspectives which dominate this particular debate.[20] The first argues that the advancement of an international environmental law agenda effectively erodes the concept of state sovereignty. This is true to the extent that the evolution of environmental norms, global institutions and pressures from stakeholder groups (e.g. citizens, civil society and NGOs) all pose practical limits on the autonomy of states. Since the traditional role of all states has been that of an "environmental exploiter"[21] with no incentive to take action to protect the environment, this first debate would undoubtedly appeal to neorealists. The reason is that for a neorealist, a state cannot claim it is "sovereign" if it is bound by international rules which diminish its right to unreservedly exploit the natural resources situated within its territorial space. To sum up this argument, environmental interdependence restricts the ability of governments to achieve their objectives unilaterally, and it is this interdependence that threatens state sovereignty.[22]

This then begs the question is sovereignty at odds with ecology? In other words, is it possible to have a new prototype state that could prioritize ecological goals without surrendering its sovereignty? At this point, the second debate is activated. According to this second debate, the emergence of multilateral institutions for environmental protection do not inevitably erode state sovereignty but may even strengthen it.[23] States are therefore seen as enablers which, when acting collectively, expand rather than restricting the menu of choices available to them. So, while international environmental law regimes may limit the scope of states to act unilaterally, they can also facilitate and promote collective state-based problem solving. In this regard, a distinction is made between "formal" sovereignty and "operational" sovereignty. Formal sovereignty refers to the state's legal supremacy and independence while

20 Conca, K 1994, 'Rethinking the ecology-sovereignty debate', *Millennium Journal of International Studies*, vol. 23, no. 3, p. 701.

21 Eckersley, n 4, at 20.

22 Levy, MA, Keohane, RO & Haas, P 1993, 'Improving the effectiveness of international environmental institutions', in MA Levy, RO Keohane & P Haas (eds), *Institutions for the Earth: sources of effective international protection*, Massachusetts Institute of Technology, Cambridge, p. 397, 415.

23 Conca, n 20, at 702. See also Schrijver, NJ & Desai, BH 2021, 'State sovereignty in the planetary management of natural resources', *Environmental Policy and Law*, vol. 51, p. 13.

operational sovereignty is defined as the legal freedom of the state to act under international law.[24] Formal sovereignty is not threatened by international environmental law because a state will always remain "sovereign" over its internal affairs. However, formal sovereignty by itself cannot prevent climate change or the raging Anthropocene.[25] On the other hand, international environmental law, and the institutions created by it, constrain operational sovereignty because once a state interacts with the international system – which is self-regulating – it does not have carte blanche or unfettered powers to do whatsoever it pleases. Notwithstanding this, by acting collectively, states can increase the "menu" of choices available to them, which will, in turn, facilitate viable solutions to global problems. That is the true purpose of international environmental law and its institutions – to improve the quality of the planetary environment.[26] In this sense, operational sovereignty, once used effectively, has the power to reverse the effects of climate change as the benefits attained by states utilizing these enhanced problem-solving capacities (even when yielding part of their "operational" sovereignty) override the benefits (if any) of states willing to act on their own. This leads to the second IR debate of liberal theory.

4. Liberal Theory and Neoliberalism

At the extreme end of the IR debate are the liberals and radical pluralists who claim that state autonomy is on the decline due to the influence of state interdependence and the increase in non-state actors.[27] As a result, and contrary to the position of neorealists, states are not primarily interested in subjects of "high politics" such as security and survival, but rather, they are more willing to prioritize other matters such as economics, welfare and ecological issues.[28] In terms of state theory, there is a thin line to be drawn between liberal theory and neoliberalism. A contemporary debate on neoliberal theory suggests that as globalization increases, so does the interdependence of nations. So, although "state sovereignty" (i.e. operational sovereignty) becomes limited, the strength of the nation-state remains important since global concerns – such as the dire state of the environment and climate change – can be resolved through cooperation.[29]

The concept of interdependence and its correlation to the decline of state autonomy is a core construct of liberal/neoliberal theory. States have often

24 Levy et al., n 22, at 417.
25 At 416.
26 At 417.
27 Hobson, n 3, at 2.
28 At 82.
29 Bonanno, A 2004, *The legitimation crisis of neoliberalism: the state, will-formation, and resistance*, Palgrave Macmillan, New York, pp. 148–149.

been conceptualized as being "independent" of each other in a legal sense, thereby granting credence to the traditional view of state sovereignty.[30] However, there is a difference between complete isolation and engagement with others. The difference is that with engagement, states can still perform acts without conceding their actual independence – i.e. "formal sovereignty". The mere fact that a state can elect whom it wishes to engage with or which treaty it wishes to be bound by is evidence of the preservation of a state's formal sovereignty. According to political theorist Kenneth Waltz:[31]

> [T]o say that a state is sovereign means that it decides for itself how it will cope with its internal and external problems, including whether or not to seek assistance from others.

From a neoliberal perspective, environmental multilateralism does not challenge state sovereignty but rather justifies it. The very act of states "flexing their muscles" and holding on to tactical political "red lines" while negotiating a treaty is evidence of a state exercising its sovereignty. For a neorealist, this type of strategic bargaining is counterproductive in establishing a robust international environmental law regime. However, such actions cannot detract from the fact that a state, while in negotiating mode, is exercising its sovereign rights. The same applies post-negotiations, when a state signs or ratifies an international treaty. Entering into multilateral arrangements that restrict what states can do is not purely an abrogation of sovereignty. On the contrary, it is a voluntary exercise of sovereignty based on the principle of liberal contractualism.[32] The fact that states can decide to enter into reservations regarding the contents of a particular article or section of a treaty also serves to illustrate the non-abrogation of a state's sovereignty. (In marked contrast to liberal and neoliberal theory, neo-Marxists and global political ecologists have critiqued liberal contractualism on the basis that multilateralism and globalization have conspired to undermine sovereignty.)[33]

Neoliberals therefore contend that realists have a very fanciful understanding or, at the very least, ignore the significant developments in environmental multilateralism.[34] For neorealists, states are "passive bearers" and have no international agential power to determine policy or to shape an international system free from the shackles of international structural

30 Fowler, MR & Bunck, JM 1995, *Law, power, and the sovereign state: the evolution and application of the concept of sovereignty*, Pennsylvania State University, University Park, p. 37, 86.

31 Waltz, KN 1986, 'Political structures', in RO Keohane (ed), *Neorealism and its critics*, Columbia University Press, New York, p. 153.

32 Eckersley, n 4, at 30.

33 Eckersley, n 4, at 30.

34 At 28.

constraints.[35] The neorealist state-centrism philosophy thus denies the importance of the state, for example, taking global action against climate change.[36] Neoliberals will counter that neorealists cannot merely overlook the fact that there exists a highly sophisticated, structural network of multilateral treaties, declarations and soft law documents spanning the space of a century. While neorealists may claim that this "network" may not be working at its optimal level, neoliberals set out to prove that it provides a means to coordinate and harmonize inter-state relations, thereby gaining a better understanding of transboundary problems.[37] This is the defining argument of neoliberal institutionalism: that environmental regimes are effective and that they provide a framework for certainty which ultimately serves the rights of sovereign states as enablers.[38]

In summarizing, there are a few differences between these two IR schools of thought, especially in relation to their outlook on state sovereignty. For the realist, state sovereignty is the problem because it points the finger at states themselves as the root cause of the failure of environmental governance. On the other hand, for the neoliberal, state sovereignty is viewed as the solution to the extent that multilateralism serves to foster collaboration among states, which, in turn, enhances a wide range of choices for the protection of the environment.[39] Despite this difference of perception of state sovereignty, both realists and neoliberals tend to agree on one thing: that states have played a traditional role in the destruction of the environment.[40] But is this certain? Is the liberal theory a saviour of our ecological crisis, or has it contributed to the downward spiral of the planet's demise? Academic Yuval Harari answers this question in the negative. For Harari, liberalism has no answer to the ecological collapse that we are currently facing. Although, in a general sense, liberalism cherishes liberty, politically speaking, liberalism is associated with free elections, democracy, free trade agreements and globalization.[41] Liberalism, with its focus on economic growth, pays no heed to the global ecosystem and can be blamed for our ecological predicament. As Kathryn Gwiazdon aptly put it, "[T]he barbarity of our reigning global economic system, guided by neoliberalism and free market, is destroying the foundations of life".[42]

35 Hobson, n 3, at 17.
36 At 1.
37 Eckersley, n 4, at 28 and 30.
38 At 29.
39 At 29.
40 At 33.
41 Noah Harari, Y 2019, *21 Lessons for the 21st century*, Vintage, London, pp. 21–26.
42 Gwiazdon, KA 2019, 'From stardust to sacred sands: protecting life on Earth through a human story of ethics, care and the cosmos', in PD Burdon, K Bosselmann & K Engel (eds), *The crisis in global ethics and the future of global governance: fulfilling the promise of the Earth charter*, Edward Elgar Publishing Limited, Gloucestershire, p. 48, 53.

So, whilst the realist theory has dominated the political conversation over the years, it is in the interest of states to look beyond this approach. The challenge of looking beyond will avoid what Eckersley describes as "the tragedy of the commons"[43] or, to put it in a broader perspective, the ecological destruction of the planet. Yet thinking outside the realist realm unto liberal theory does not mean that our planetary dilemma is resolved.[44] This then raises another question – if not realist or liberal theory, what then?

5. Critical Constructivism

Constructivism was introduced in the IR landscape towards the end of the Cold War, at a time when theories such as realism and liberalism were more mainstream.[45] Since then, constructivism represents a point of departure from the classical realist/liberal (or neorealist/neoliberal) theories concerning the behavioural patterns of states as they relate to international law and politics. Constructivism recognizes that in traditional IR theory, state behaviour can be seen as either conflictual (neorealist) or increasingly cooperative (neoliberal). Here, constructivism, mainly through the work of its leading theorist Wendt, attempts to build a practical bridge between neorealists and neoliberals. In essence, constructivism sees the world as socially constructed.[46] Wendt argues that, in international politics, states are purposive actors with a sense of Self, and just as there cannot be a society without people, there also cannot be a "states system" without states.[47] Juxtaposing these arguments, Wendt concludes that "states are people too" in that they acquire identities which are relatively stable.[48] To illustrate social construction at work, one example which is utilized is a situation in which 500 British nuclear weapons appear to be less threatening to the United States than five North Korea nuclear weapons.[49] What is at stake here for the United States is not the nuclear weapons per se but the social context: i.e. who owns them. Critical constructivists therefore reject the notion that the state system can be studied in isolation, and one must examine the broader picture in world politics such as, for example, changes in identities and interests of states, a shift in domestic

43 Eckersley, n 4, at 22.
44 At 24–25.
45 Theys, S 2017, 'Constructivism', in S McGlinchey, C Scheinpflug & R Walters (eds), *International relations theory*, E-International Relations, Bristol, p. 36. Theys, 'Constructivism'.
46 Theys, 'Constructivism'.
47 Wendt, A 1999, *Social theory of international politics*, Cambridge University Press, Cambridge, p. 194.
48 Wendt, *Social theory of international politics*.
49 Theys, n 45, at 36.

politics, the role of moral norms, culture and NGO activity.[50] Constructivists are therefore more concerned about what goes on before and after regime formations and the relational aspect between states. Due to this, constructivists will avoid adopting a rational actor model as seen in traditional IR theory (e.g. as with realists).[51] Further characteristics and behavioural patterns adopted by constructivists will be discussed in the ensuing paragraphs.

a) Identities, Interests and Norms

Reverting to our small island/low-lying states example, although survival (in terms of the existential threat to their territorial sovereignty) may be their priority in a neorealist sense, these states are able to bridge the gap to become more engaged in the championing of climate change treaties because it is in their interest to do so. Take, for example, the Bahamas, an AOSIS member state,[52] which may be more interested in limiting global warming to 1.5 degrees Celsius above pre-industrial levels while the US and Israel may be more concerned with the diplomatic manoeuvring regarding the outcome (or no outcome, as the case may be) of a new Iran nuclear deal. The inescapable conclusion that can be drawn is that the identity of being a small state implies a set of interests that are different from those which bear the identity of a large state.[53] For small island/low-lying states, their identities are clearly defined not by the traditional neorealist ideals but by the stark reality of the ravaging Anthropocene and the effect that it would have on their territorial sovereignty.

Identities are critical for constructivists as they anticipate states aligned to certain identities would comply with norms associated with that identity. A norm only becomes an expected behaviour when that norm is adopted and internalized by a critical mass of relevant state actors.[54] This is how alliances of small island states, such as AOSIS, came together to develop climate change strategies as it is the right thing to do for the survival of all humanity. This same spirit of togetherness is perhaps needed when forging ahead with the Global Pact, which proposes the adoption of a legally binding treaty on, inter alia, the duty of states to take care of the environment. This is the bridge that constructivists seek to build – a bridge which moves states away from the position of anarchy to collaborators to, eventually, ecological trustees.

Although Wendt asserts that state identities are relatively stable, some constructivists argue that, over time, states' identities and interests may change.

50 Eckersley, n 4, at 33–34.
51 At 34–35.
52 Alliance of Small Island States (www.aosis.org).
53 Theys, n 45, at 37.
54 At 38.

It is perceived by some that states are reflexive actors which do not follow simple scripts.[55] Part of the reason for so doing may be a change in administration after a freely held democratic election, which may alter a state's identity or interests. (The Trump-Biden transition in the US may be a classic example of this.) States may also change their understanding of an external environment or situation in ways which may transform their view of their own interests and identities.[56] Once it is acknowledged that states have different interests and identities which are all relatively stable but which may alter from time to time, the next issue is how these varying conditions impact states' engagement in environmental multilateralism. It can be argued that states seek membership in environmental treaties arrangements for symbolic reasons – mainly, the optics. Unless for very compelling domestic reasons (or, in some instances, for reasons not so compelling), no state wants to be seen as the one that opted out of a climate agreement – a subject which is by all measures the most crucial issue in our present lifetime. The Paris Agreement illustrated that there was consensus among nearly all nations on the single subject of climate change, with 191 countries (out of 197) being States Parties.[57] What is noticeable about the Paris Agreement is that its States Parties include the top three global greenhouse gas emitters – namely China (28%), the United States (recently re-joined, at 15%) and India (7%).[58] To probe deeper into the socio-political context, one is left to ponder why the top three global greenhouse gas offenders would join a multilateral arrangement like the Paris Agreement. Is it out of a sincere obligation to the planet, or is it a political move to save face? While we may never be able to directly answer this question, constructivists assert that most states observe international treaties most of the time because treaties possess a certain degree of legitimacy. This assertion holds even if there is an absence of a world police force to enforce the obligations under the treaty.[59] Added to this argument, it is noted that even powerful states (in this case, China, the US and India) wish to join on to a treaty in order to gain recognition and approval from the international community as "the major player".[60] Although a state is not legally obligated to disclose its true intentions of joining an environmental treaty (or any treaty for that matter), the reality is that on an all-important issue such as climate change – which affects not only the future generations but also the generation unborn – it would be imprudent for any state to act

55 Eckersley, n 4, at 35.

56 Eckersley, n 4, at 35.

57 'Paris Agreement: status of ratification', UNFCCC, (www.unfccc.int).

58 Blokhin, A 2020, 'The 5 countries that produce the most carbon dioxide (CO_2)', *Investopedia*, last modified 1 December 2021, (https://www.investopedia.com/articles/investing/092915/5-countries-produce-most-carbon-dioxide-co2.asp).

59 Eckersley, n 4, at 41.

60 At 39.

outside the parameters of norms generally embraced by other members of the international community. As convincing as this may sound, there will always be a climate critic, the "odd state out" or the neorealist, which does not see climate change as being suited to the realm of international diplomacy and international politics.

b) *Wendt's Three Cultures of Anarchy*

A question that has been raised throughout this debate is whether there is a tendency of states to cooperate with each other while (1) negotiating multilateral environmental treaties and (2) performing their obligations under international environmental law. This question, in essence, considers whether the neoliberal approach works in theory or, in the inverse, if the neorealists' view is practical and not unrealistic. Obtaining a better understanding of this question requires the unravelling of Wendt's "three cultures of anarchy" and the scope of its application in the environmental law context. According to Wendt, international politics is defined by three cultures of anarchy – the Hobbesian culture, the Lockean culture and the Kantian culture. For the purpose of this section, these cultures will be explored in that order.

Under the Hobbesian culture, states are considered enemies, and they engage in a "no-holds-barred" approach when it comes to power politics.[61] Although it has become the common practice of IR theorists to refer to such an engagement as "realist", there is no necessary connection between a Hobbesian anarchy and realism.[62] For constructivists, however, there is a natural inclination to link the two subjects, especially since constructivism searches for a better understanding of Hobbesian anarchy. The logic behind Hobbesian anarchy is "war of all against all"[63] – a theme which resonates quite well with realists who cling to the security and survival of a state at any cost. Under the Hobbesian culture, state actors cannot count on each other for help, thereby instilling state suspicion and negating any form of cooperation.[64] Although Hobbesian culture paints a bleak picture of states at war, in theory, it can apply to states sitting around a negotiating table discussing the state of the environment.

Lockean culture strives to find a middle ground as it is based on state rivalry as opposed to pure enmity. As rivals, states are expected to act as if they recognize and respect another state's sovereignty.[65] This expectation can be found in today's international system, where almost all states have

61 Wendt, n 47, at 259 and 262.
62 At 259.
63 At 265.
64 At 265.
65 At 279.

the comfort of knowing that the majority of (if not all) states recognize their sovereignty.[66] Wendt argues that when states recognize each other's sovereignty as a right, then we can speak of sovereignty not only as the property of individual states but also as an institution shared by many states.[67] This argument corresponds with a modern-day understanding of sovereignty in which states act collectively to combat climate change, a phenomenon that does not discriminate between territorial boundaries.

In order to understand how states conduct themselves in an international setting, it is important to first distinguish between enemies and rivalries: i.e. Hobbesian culture versus Lockean culture. When states are enemies, they are only likely to cooperate with each other when they are implicitly or explicitly coerced. On the other hand, when states are rivals, because they are more competitive in nature but respect each other's sovereignty, they will comply (be it by cooperating in international negotiations or fulfilling obligations) mostly out of self-interest.[68] This brings us to the next question – can the shallow, narrow-minded interests of states reverse the Anthropocene? On this, Eckersley opines that international cooperation, especially as it relates to climate change, cannot be reduced to material self-interest but can only be understood in the context of mutual internalization of shared norms.[69] This leads us to the third limb of Wendt's theory – the existence of the Kantian culture of anarchy.

When it comes to international environmental law and environmental multilateralism, the Kantian culture, which is based on a role structure of state friendship, is applicable and ought to be carefully studied. Realizing that, in IR theory, "friendly" images are scarce, thereby leaving the concept somewhat "undertheorized", Wendt encourages us to think systematically about the nature and consequences of friendships in international politics.[70] When states relate to each other as friends, they tend to comply principally because of shared, internalized understandings.[71] As a result, under the Kantian culture, we would expect that moral and ethical reasoning are paramount and would influence political communication and decision-making among friendly states.[72] Such a quality of reasoning is pertinent because any discussion of the preservation of the environment and safeguarding the integrity of the planet must be underpinned by moral and ethical values. As climate change is a concern common to all, it can only be effectively treated by "friendly states" which have a shared and mutual understanding of its

66 At 281.
67 At 280.
68 Eckersley, n 4, at 44.
69 Eckersley, n 4, at 44.
70 Wendt, n 47, at 298.
71 Eckersley, n 4, at 44.
72 Eckersley, n 4, at 44.

devastating implications. There is no room for compromise, complacency or acts of self-interest when it comes to securing a sustainable planet for future generations. In carrying out their environmental law obligations, states, as friends, must therefore be altruistic and consider the welfare of others within the international community. For the Kantian culture model to work, Wendt suggests that a universal collective security approach be adopted under the banner "all for one and one for all".[73] Although when speaking about "universal collective security", Wendt had in mind military power and national security (or the balancing of world powers), the same approach can be applied to climate change, which also implicates the territorial sovereignty and security of states.

In practice, the Kantian model of friendships among states is not devoid of criticism. In the real world, scholars (especially realists) see friendships in international politics as an alien concept or a utopian ideal. Realists would assert that the most we can expect from states is to act on the basis of interests.[74] Wendt even goes on to say that "history suggests that few states remain friends for long anyway".[75] Yet given the nature of friendships as we know it, there are times when friends disagree, but that does not mean that all love is lost. Like when President Biden recently cancelled the Keystone XL pipeline, which pumps oil sands from Alberta to Nebraska, and this was met with disappointment from Justin Trudeau, the Canadian prime minister.[76] The cancellation of Keystone XL did not result in Canada taking extreme actions, be they military or political, to disturb its friendly neighbour. What is expected from this political tiff is that the two leaders will be able to come together to freely exchange ideas on matters of mutual understanding, such as the role both countries could play in becoming global climate leaders.

Despite these shortcomings, Wendt still holds on to the idea that the contemporary international system is mostly Lockean (rivalry), with increasing Kantian (friendship) elements.[77] Once we agree with the incremental take of this position, there still remains some promise for states to act in unison on issues which affect the welfare of all.

c) *Cultural Norms and Civil Society Perspectives*

Culture also plays a significant role in the discourse on domestic politics and state behaviour. Bhutan's 2015 Gross National Happiness (GNH) Survey

73 Wendt, n 47, at 301.

74 At 298.

75 At 298.

76 Arvin, J 2021, 'More than 20 Republican-led states sue Biden for cancelling the Keystone XL pipeline', *Vox*, viewed 18 March 2021, (https://www.vox.com/22306919/biden-keystone-xl-trudeau-oil-pipeline-climate-change).

77 Wendt, n 47, at 43. See also Eckersley, n 4, at 47.

Report found that 79.15% of the persons interviewed felt "highly responsible" for conserving the natural environment.[78] That finding must be read in tandem with the fact that, under their constitution, every citizen is a trustee of the kingdom's natural resources and environment for the benefit of the present and future generations.[79] Even prior to the enactment of the constitution and the GNH Survey Report, it was well established that Bhutan had integrated spirituality and compassion into both the personal and institutional levels of governance.[80] It is these two ideals – "spirituality" and "compassion" – that define the manner in which each Bhutanese citizen views the environment. By adopting a framework founded on actions such as empathy and kindness, the state of Bhutan is promoting a type of "covenantal ethics" which is lacking in the sphere of global environmental governance.[81]

Former Prime Minister of New Zealand Jacinda Arden, in her maiden speech to the United Nations General Assembly, spoke about the importance of *kaitiakitanga*, a Māori word meaning guardianship. Ardern explained that *kaitiakitanga* captures the fact that we (states) have been entrusted with our environment, and we all have a duty of care towards it.[82] What the prime minister was in effect saying was that the challenge of climate change requires us to look beyond the domestic and on to the global.[83] These words coming from a world leader illustrate that, at a state level, New Zealand has accepted the cultural norms of its indigenous population and plans to fully implement it into policy. This is made evident by the passage of the Te Urewera Act (2014), the Te Awa Tupua (Whanganui River Settlement) Act (2017) and the Record of Understanding/Te Anga Putakerongo (2017) for Mount Taranaki, which recognize certain ecosystems, a national park, a river and a mountain respectively as legal persons. In this regard, New Zealand has set targets to reduce greenhouse gas emissions to 30% below 2005 levels by 2030. Under the Climate Change Response (Zero Carbon) Amendment Act 2019, the country also set a target of zero greenhouse gases emissions by 2050.[84] Sovereign states like Bhutan and New Zealand are just two examples in which

78 'A compass towards a just and harmonious society: 2015 GNH survey report', *Centre for Bhutan Studies*, viewed 5 July 2016, at 212, (www.grossnationalhappiness.com).

79 Constitution of the Kingdom of Bhutan 2008, s 5(1).

80 'A compass towards a just and harmonious society', n 78, at 5.

81 Bosselmann, K & Taylor, P 2019, 'Promoting global ethics: The Earth trusteeship initiative', in PD Burdon, K Bosselmann & K Engel (eds), *The crisis in global ethics and the future of global governance: fulfilling the promise of the Earth charter*, Edward Elgar Publishing Limited, Gloucestershire, p. 279.

82 Ardern, J 2018, *Prime Minister of New Zealand 'New Zealand National Statement to United Nations General Assembly'*, UN General Assembly, New York, 28 September.

83 Bosselmann, K 2019, 'Can kaitiakitanga save the planet?', *Newsroom*, viewed 20 December 2019, (https://www.newsroom.co.nz/ideasroom/can-kaitiakitanga-save-the-planet).

84 Climate Change Response (Zero Carbon) Amendment Act 2019, s 5Q(1)(a).

cultural norms/indigenous perspectives influence state behaviour and positions in the international environmental law architecture.

It is generally accepted that sovereign states which commit themselves to reducing their greenhouse gas emissions under international environmental agreements (be it the Kyoto Protocol or the Paris Agreement) are the same ones that are generating the world's ecological problems.[85] This statement questions whether we as global citizens still have faith in the state-led multilateral machinery to negotiate us out of this Anthropocene. To put it in another perspective, do we have the confidence in states, either individually or collectively, to uphold their responsibilities as ecological trustees? The purpose of this chapter is not to demand that states tackle a financial crisis which threatens the viability of our economies and capital institutions. On the contrary, we are demanding that states resolve an ecological crisis which threatens the very existence of our species as homo sapiens. Negotiating our way out a financial crisis and an ecological crisis are two different subjects which require two distinct approaches. Over the years, especially from our experience with the 2007 financial crisis, it is largely perceived that states have placed a greater priority on the economy than on ecology. Statements such as "if the environment were a bank, it would have been saved by now" are true testaments of this harsh reality.[86] The indifference of states to take proactive action when it comes to safeguarding the integrity of the planet has provoked a line of thinking which suggests that the state is not the original source of motivation when it comes to the setting of environmental policy. The true source of motivation, or inspiration if one may so call it, are non-state actors such as NGOs, civil society, academia, think tanks and even individuals.[87] By acting as a check and balance within the states system, non-state actors play a significant role in the culmination of global environmental policies. We have seen the effects of this in the New Zealand context, where the Māori worldview has influenced the state's agenda on granting legal personality to natural spaces. Individuals such as Swedish activist Greta Thunberg and her classmates, who organized a school climate strike movement dubbed Fridays for Future, have also played their part is cultivating this conscious awareness on an international scale. Non-state actors are also referred to "fundamental actors" since they may not have the ultimate power to move certain issues beyond international politics. Yet non-state actors are influential in that they can help frame storylines for these issues, like the existential threat posed by climate change and the Anthropocene.[88] Critical IR scholarship therefore

85 Eckersley, n 4, at 33.

86 This statement has been attributed to US Senator Bernie Sanders.

87 Eckersley, n 4, at 82. See also Lüdert, J 2023, *Non-state actors at the United Nations: Contesting sovereignty*, Routledge, London.

88 Theys, n 45, at 107–108.

seeks to re-evaluate mainstream theories like realism which position states as the dominant force in international politics.

Since the rise of non-state actors in the 1990s, there has been a conscious awareness which gravitates towards the preservation of the natural environment for the future generations. This expansion of consciousness, in the form of environmental activism outside the state apparatus, has contributed in some form or fashion to the development of critical international instruments pertaining to the environment. One of the most recent of these instruments is the Hague Principles for a Universal Declaration on Responsibilities for Human Rights and Earth Trusteeship ("the Hague Principles"). Launched in December 2018, primarily by members of global civil society, the Hague Principles challenge states to think outside the proverbial box by supplementing our conventional human responsibilities towards each other with more contemporary human responsibilities towards the Earth community and Earth system at large.[89] The Hague Principles are based on three core responsibilities: our responsibilities for the Earth, our responsibilities to the community of life (of which human beings are a part) and our responsibilities to human rights.[90] It demands that states, together with their citizens, share responsibilities as trustees of the Earth and the integrity of Earth's ecological systems.[91] The Hague Principles, by and large, are an epitome of this expansion of consciousness in the 21st century. It is an international document which portrays the idea of states acting, either individually or collectively, as ecological trustees. As it is a soft law document, the test we are faced with is how to transfer this original idea of global civil society to states for the necessary political action. Even though environmental activism is on the rise, especially within the ranks of non-state actors, the world has not yet reached a stage at which they can act independently of states. At this present moment, whether we like it or not, sovereign states are the endgame, meaning that all our efforts towards a sustainable planet inevitably culminate with them.

6. International Environmental Law Versus State Sovereignty

As previously discussed, states, over the course of the century, have been involved in negotiating treaties which have had a direct and an indirect impact on the environment. For the purpose of this research, it is what transpired over the last 50 years that is of particular concern. Whilst the

89 Earth Trusteeship 2018, 'The Hague Principles for a Universal Declaration on Responsibilities for Human Rights and Earth Trusteeship' (10 December 2018), (www.earthtrusteeship.world).

90 The Hague Principles, principles 1 to 3.

91 The Hague Principles, principle 1.2.

1960s were viewed as a time of optimism, it was the decade after – especially with the convening of the 1972 UN Conference on the Human Environment – that offered hope for greater corporation on environmental issues.[92] The 1970s can be described as a new "dawn of awakening" or a renaissance period since it led to the development of a rich corpus of international environmental norms. For instance, states are now being obligated to react to environmental problems that occur beyond their national jurisdiction. Professor Tomuschat acknowledged this fact when he stated the following:[93]

> The international community is conceived of as a kind of authority that closely follows world events and bears responsibility for maintaining an orderly and peaceful international environment and for ensuring decent conditions of existence to every human being.

The subsequent sections will carefully evaluate two of these norms (the no-harm rule and the precautionary principle) and the tensions they placed on state sovereignty.

a) The No-Harm Rule

It is well recognized that international environmental law is one of those areas of law in which there are a steadily expanding number of obligations which result in the imposition of quite significant duties on states.[94] One of the first forms of such obligations emerged in the Stockholm Declaration of 1972, which stipulates:[95]

> States have, in accordance with the Charter of the United Nations and the principles of international law, the sovereign right to exploit their own resources pursuant to their own environmental policies, and the responsibility to ensure that activities within their jurisdiction or control do not cause damage to the environment of other States or of areas beyond the limits of national jurisdiction.

92 World Commission on Environment and Development, Brundtland Report ('Our Common Future') UNGA A/42/427 (4 August 1987) at 13.

93 Tomuschat, C 1993, 'Obligations arising for states without or against their will', *Collected Courses of the Hague Academy of International Law*, vol. 241, p. 195, 222.

94 Fitzmaurice, M 2017, 'Legitimacy of international environmental law. The sovereign states overwhelmed by obligations: responsibility to react to problems beyond national jurisdiction?', *Heidelberg Journal of International Law*, vol. 77, p. 339, 340.

95 Declaration of the United Nations Conference on the Human Environment ('Stockholm Declaration') UN Doc. A/Conf.48/14/Rev. 1 (16 May 1972), principle 21.

Twenty years later, the Rio Declaration declared an almost identical formulation of the aforementioned Stockholm principle.[96] This principle, which is known as the "no-harm rule", is a widely recognized principle of customary international law and has its roots in "good neighbourliness"[97] and the Latin maxim *sic utere tuo non laedas*. This maxim sets out the general obligation of states to ensure that activities within their jurisdiction and control respect the environment of other states.[98]

In theory, the legal jurisprudence surrounding the no-harm rule even predates the Stockholm and Rio Declarations. In the seminal *Trail Smelter* case, the arbitral tribunal found that Canada was responsible in international law for the discharge of fumes containing sulphur dioxide from their Trail Smelter, which caused injury in the state of Washington.[99] This was followed by the International Court of Justice's (ICJ) judgment in The *Corfu Channel* case. In that case, the ICJ ruled that Albania had an obligation to notify British warships (or any other ships flying a state's flag) of the existence of minefields in its territorial waters and of the imminent danger that they would have exposed.[100] The logic behind this rule is that a state must not knowingly allow its territory to be used in such a manner that would be contrary to the rights of other states.[101] Although the *Corfu Channel* case was not a strict environmental law case per se, its application can be linked to the no-harm rule and the general spirit behind the obligation of states contained in the Stockholm and Rio Declarations. Needless to say, the no-harm rule has been subsequently applied and approved by the ICJ post–the *Corfu Channel* case. It was the ICJ's advisory opinion on the *Legality of Threat or Use of Nuclear Weapons* where the Court cemented the no-harm rule as enshrined in the Stockholm and Rio Declarations. There, the ICJ stated:[102]

> The Court also recognizes that the environment is not an abstraction but represents the living space, the quality of life and the very health of human beings, including generations unborn. The existence of the general obligation of States to ensure that activities within their jurisdiction and control

96 United Nations General Assembly 1992, *Report of the United Nations conference on environment and development*, UN Doc A/Conf 151/26/Vol I, 12 August, Annex I, at principle 2. The only difference in the Rio Declaration is that it speaks to "environmental and development policies" whilst the Stockholm Declaration focuses on "environmental policies".
97 Fitzmaurice, n 94, at 342.
98 Crawford, J 2012, *Brownlie's principles of public international law*, 8th edn, Oxford University Press, Oxford, p. 359.
99 *Trail Smelter Case (United States v Canada)* (1941) 3 UN Reports of International Arbitral Awards 1905 at 1965.
100 *The Corfu Channel Case* (Merits) [1949] ICJ Rep 4 at 22.
101 *The Corfu Channel Case* (Merits) [1949] ICJ Rep 4 at 22.
102 *Legality of Threat or Use of Nuclear Weapons* (Advisory Opinion) [1996] ICJ Rep 226 at 29.

respect the environment of other States or of areas beyond national control is now part of the corpus of international law relating to the environment.

Implicit in the no-harm rule is the corresponding principle of prevention,[103] whereby a state is duty bound to prevent, reduce and control the risk of environmental harm to other states.[104] In the 2010 *Pulp Mills* case, the ICJ endorsed the principle of prevention when it pronounced that a state is obliged to use all means at its disposal to avoid activities taking place within its territory causing significant damage to the environment of another state.[105] Five years later, the Court in the *Certain Activities carried out by Nicaragua in the Border Area* and *Construction of a Road in Costa Rica along the San Juan River* cases restated the rule as articulated in *Pulp Mills* case.[106] All this must be read in tandem with the International Law Commission's (ILC) Draft Articles on Prevention of Transboundary Harm from Hazardous Activities (also called "Prevention Articles").[107] Article 1 of the Prevention Articles applies to "activities not prohibited by international law which involve a risk of causing significant transboundary harm through their physical consequences".[108] The use of the word "significant" is critical, and, according to the ILC commentary, "[A]ny hazardous and by inference any ultrahazardous activity which involves a risk of significant transboundary harm is covered".[109] Although both the Stockholm and Rio Declarations speak to some degree of harm to be attributed to the environment of another state, they fail to clarify where the threshold lies.[110] This is why the guidance on what constitutes a "significant" harm becomes pertinent. Here, the ILC commentary explains:[111]

> It is to be understood that "significant" is something more than "detectable" but need not be at the level of "serious" or "substantial". The harm must lead to a real detrimental effect on matters such as, for example, human health, industry, property, environment or agriculture in other

103 Fitzmaurice, n 94, at 342.

104 Brownlie, I 2012, *Principles of public international law*, 7th edn, Oxford University Press, Oxford, pp. 275–285. See also Birnie, et al., *International law and the environment*, p. 143.

105 *Pulp Mills on the River Uruguay (Argentina v Uruguay) (Judgment)* [2010] ICJ Rep 14 at [101].

106 *Certain Activities carried out by Nicaragua in the Border Area (Costa Rica v Nicaragua) and Construction of a Road in Costa Rica along the San Juan River cases (Judgment)* [2015] ICJ Rep 665 at [118].

107 *Report of the international law commission to the general assembly on its fifty-third session*, 2001, vol. II, no. 2, YILC 146.

108 At 146.

109 At 149.

110 Fitzmaurice, n 94, at 344.

111 Report of the Commission to the General Assembly on its fifty-third session, n 107, at 152.

States. Such detrimental effects must be susceptible of being measured by factual and objective standards.

Despite this, the ILC prefaces this comment by acknowledging that the term "significant" is "not without ambiguity" and that a determination as to what is "significant" should be made in each specific case.[112] To make matters a bit more complex, a further comment by the ILC under article 17 mandates a state to immediately notify another state of an emergency situation due to the "the seriousness of the harm involved".[113] In other words, and in accordance with the Prevention Articles, a state is obligated to take measures to prevent "significant" transboundary harm, which includes giving immediate notice to the state likely to be affected as this is justified on the "seriousness" of the harm involved. This led Fitzmaurice to clearly demarcate two distinct headings pertaining to the obligation of prevention: namely, (1) the classical obligation of prevention and (2) the obligation of prevention concerning emergency situations, which goes further than the classical obligation and is even more burdensome for states.[114]

Furthermore, the idea of a "serious" threshold was applied in the *Trail Smelter* case, in which the tribunal pronounced that it would interfere so long as the case involved a "serious magnitude" and that the injury was established by clear and convincing evidence.[115] This was subsequently made evident in the *Lake Lanoux* arbitration, in which the tribunal relied on the notion of "seriously".[116] As both the *Trail Smelter* case and *Lake Lanoux* arbitration arose out of a similar forum, one is left to wonder whether a precedent has been set using the "serious" threshold in UN arbitral proceedings.

After careful evaluation, it is widely accepted that the obligation of prevention is well entrenched in international environmental law. Whilst this hypothesis appears in some sense to be accurate, it cannot be said with the same degree of conviction that there are no legal problems relating to its implementation.[117] Fitzmaurice argues that the content of such an obligation is "unpredictable and woolly" and will undoubtedly lead to the imposition of significant burdens on states.[118] In the face of an obscure execution of an obligation, a state may be uninformed on how to act or be less inclined to act in the midst of uncertainty. A worst-case scenario is that a state my desire

112 Report of the Commission to the General Assembly on its fifty-third session, n 107, at 152.

113 At 169.

114 Fitzmaurice, n 94, at 349.

115 *Trail Smelter Case*, n 99, at 1964–1965 and 1970.

116 Report of the Commission to the General Assembly on its fifty-third session, n 107, at 152. See also *Affaire du Lac Lanoux (Espagne v France)* (1957) 12 UN Reports of International Arbitral Awards 281.

117 Fitzmaurice, n 94, at 349.

118 Fitzmaurice, n 94, at 349.

to opt out of the obligation all together. It also does not help if the no-harm rule/prevention principle, as burdensome as it is, encroaches on the concept of traditional state sovereignty to the extent that it restricts what a state can do within its own jurisdiction in the name of not causing transboundary environmental harm to other states.

b) The Precautionary Principle

In contrast to the no-harm rule or "preventive principle", the precautionary principle is designed to provide the basis for early international legal action to address serious environmental threats in cases in which there is ongoing scientific uncertainty with regard to the causes of these threats.[119] One scholar highlights that the precautionary principle was first expressly articulated in the mid-1980s.[120] It was perhaps however not until around 1992, with the adoption of the Rio Declaration, that it featured in international law. Principle 15 states:[121]

> In order to protect the environment, *the precautionary approach* shall be widely applied by States according to their capabilities. Where there are threats of serious or irreversible damage, lack of full scientific certainty shall not be used as a reason for postponing cost-effective measures to prevent environmental degradation.

In the same year the Rio Declaration was adopted, the precautionary principle was also incorporated into other environmental treaties, such as the United Nations Framework Convention on Climate Change (UNFCCC) and the Convention on Biological Diversity (CBD). The UNFCCC provides that states should take "precautionary measures" to anticipate, prevent or minimize the causes of climate change and to mitigate its adverse effects.[122] The CBD, to some extent, replicates the language of the Rio Declaration by specifying that where there is a threat of significant loss of biodiversity, the lack of scientific certainty should not be a reason for postponing measures to avoid or minimize that threat.[123] Once again, the precautionary principle, as articulated in the UNFCCC and the CBD, encroaches on traditional

119 Beyerlin, U 2007, 'Different types of norms in international environmental law: policies, principles and rules', in D Bodansky, J Brunnée & E Hey (eds), *The Oxford handbook of international environmental law*, Oxford University Press, Oxford, p. 440.

120 Beyerlin, 'Different types of norms in international environmental law'.

121 Report of the UN Conference on Environment and Development, n 96 (emphasis added).

122 *United Nations Framework Convention on Climate Change* (opened for signature 9 May 1992, entered into force 21 March 1994) 1771 UNTS 107, art 3(3).

123 *Convention on Biological Diversity* (opened for signature 5 June 1992, entered into force 29 December 1993), at the preamble. By comparison, the CBD describes the threat as a

sovereign rights of states. In order to combat runaway global climate change, the UNFCCC recognizes that states must take certain precautionary measures within their national jurisdictions to reduce and prevent the emission of greenhouse gases into the atmosphere. Similarly, the CBD reaffirms that even though states have sovereign rights over their biodiversity, they are responsible for conserving and using them in a sustainable manner.[124] In addition to this, the CBD provides that contracting parties promote the notification and exchange of information on activities under their jurisdiction which would significantly affect the biodiversity of other states. In order to achieve this, states are encouraged to enter into bilateral, regional and multilateral arrangements to address the cross-border threats to biodiversity.[125]

It is worth mentioning that the discussion surrounding the application of the precautionary principle does not exclusively apply to the sphere of international environmental law, and its general acceptance as a principle is often debated in other specialized areas of international law (e.g. WTO trade law in the *Biotech* and *Beef Hormones* cases).[126] Furthermore, the precautionary principle has emerged in some national systems as a tool for domestic policy making. A recent example of this was seen in New Zealand, when the government took "a precautionary approach" by halting its quarantine-free travel bubble with New South Wales due to a surge in COVID-19 cases in the Australian state.[127] Such an application may not have ultimately come as a surprise, given the country's position in the *Nuclear Tests* case and the words of Judge Weeramantry (in his dissenting opinion) to the effect that the precautionary principle is of relevance to New Zealand.[128]

That being said, the precautionary principle has been described as "an attempt to codify the concept of precaution in law".[129] Even if it can be argued that the principle is codified in international environmental law, can we be satisfied that the precautionary principle is a well-established rule under customary international law? On this question, Crawford notes that the precautionary principle is probably the best known of the "still evolving legal principles of environmental protection".[130] Although such a conclusive

"significant" loss of biodiversity whilst the Rio Declaration uses the phrase "serious or irreversible" damage.

124 *Convention on Biological Diversity.*

125 Article 14(1)(c).

126 For more on this debate, see Fitzmaurice, n 94, at 358–360.

127 Gabel, J 2021, 'NSW travel bubble paused', *The New Zealand Herald*, Auckland, 23 June, p. A2.

128 Request for an Examination of the Situation in Accordance with Paragraph 63 of the Court's Judgment of 20 December 1974 in the Nuclear Tests Case (New Zealand v. France) [1995] ICJ Rep 288 at 343.

129 Wiener, JB 2007, 'Precaution', in D Bodansky, J Brunnée & E Hey (eds), *The Oxford handbook of international environmental law*, Oxford University Press, Oxford, p. 599.

130 Crawford, n 98, at 357.

statement was made almost a decade ago, the truth remains that the possibility of its application today is not that remote. As Fitzmaurice argues, the principle is not static but evolving.[131]

One of the main problems of the precautionary principle is that it is difficult to define.[132] As Sands observes, there is "no clear and uniform understanding of the meaning of the precautionary principle among states and other members of the international community".[133] This observation is clearly made out in the *Beef Hormones* case. Even though made outside the context of international environmental law, the United States and Canada argued that the precautionary principle is only "an approach" due to the lack of one consistent formulation.[134] The supporters of those who argue that the principle is an "approach" have taken the view that the precaution is not legally binding.[135]

Returning to the developments in international environmental law, jurisprudence arising from the International Tribunal for the Law of the Sea (ITLOS) also failed to provide a definitive status on the precautionary principle. In the *MOX Plant* case, Judge Wolfrum (in his separate opinion) stated that the customary international law status of the precautionary principle was "still a matter for discussion".[136] The *MOX Plant* case therefore gave preferential treatment to the phrase "prudence and caution", a phrase that was previously applied in the *Southern Bluefin Tuna* cases.[137]

The case law and scholarly literature surrounding this subject suggest that there is some difficulty in applying the precautionary principle in practice.[138] First, the precautionary principle has been cited as having two forms: one weak and one strong. The weak formulation is found in the Rio Declaration and the strong in the 1982 UN World Charter for Nature, which states that "where potential adverse effects are not fully understood, the activities should not proceed".[139] Secondly, some experts are of the view that the precautionary principle is best applied on a case-by-case basis, which in turn defies the concept of fairness and consistency.[140] To illustrate this, one example is

131 Fitzmaurice, n 94, at 360.

132 At 357.

133 Sands, P 2003, *Principles of international environmental law*, 2nd edn, Cambridge University Press, Cambridge, p. 272.

134 Fitzmaurice, n 94, at 349. This was also recognized in the *Southern Bluefin Tuna* cases *(New Zealand v Japan) (Australia v Japan)* (Request for provisional measures) [1999] ITLOS Case No 3 and 4, Reports 280.

135 Fitzmaurice, n 94, at 356.

136 *The MOX Plant Case (Ireland v United Kingdom)* (Provisional Measures) [2001] ITLOS Reports 95 at 133.

137 At 84. See also *Southern Bluefin Tuna* cases, n 134, at 77.

138 *Southern Bluefin Tuna* cases, n 134.

139 Fitzmaurice, n 94, at 360.

140 At 368.

principle 15 of the Rio Declaration, which provides that "the precautionary approach shall be widely applied by States according to their capabilities". This implies that some states should apply the rule while others, which are not capable, should not. This is the type of unpredictability that Fitzmaurice probably had in mind when she argued that the principle lacks consistency partly due to the operation of the notion of "common but differentiated responsibilities", which advocates for a varied application of the principles of international environmental law in developed and developing countries.[141] However, whether the principle can itself be a mandate for action or provide definitive answers to all questions of environmental policy must be doubted.[142]

In summary, there appears to be some controversy over how to articulate or define a precautionary principle in law.[143] As it presently stands, there has not been a dramatic shift in the pendulum in favour of the certification of the precautionary principle as a customary rule. Just as the precautionary principle itself epitomizes, there appears to be a cautious approach by states, scholars and courts to labelling the rule as a general principle of international law. In the face of this dilemma, some states may be hesitant to make an early intervention on matters within their jurisdiction that pose a serious threat to the environment of other states. This is even more so given the fact that the principle imposes considerable burdens on states.[144] That being said, states may be more compelled to retain their traditional "territorial" sovereignty than to be responsible to other states under international environmental law. This is an undesirable position as the precautionary principle, which is based on the foreseeability of risk of environmental harm to other states, incorporates a sense of responsibility to other states.[145]

141 At 368.

142 Brow at 211–213.

143 Böckernförde, M 2003, 'The operationalization of the precautionary approach in international environmental law treaties: enhancement or façade ten years after Rio', *Zeitschrift Für Ausländisches Öffentliches Recht und Völkerrecht*, vol. 63, p. 313, 314.

144 Fitzmaurice, n 94, at 361.

145 Brownlie, I 2012, *Principles of public international law*, 7th edn, Oxford University Press, Oxford, p. 278.

Chapter 7

The Duty to Protect

When it comes to global ecological protection, state sovereignty is often villainized.

> The "conventional" reading of sovereignty is perceived as privileging
>
> states' authority over their own resource management, thus allowing states to circumvent environmental regulations that do not coincide with the "national interest" or the objectives of economic development. Some scholars consider the state itself as the primary source of global environmental degradation and the main obstacle to effective environmental protection. From this state-centric environmental perspective, sovereignty is considered an impediment to concerted international ecological protection, or an underlying cause of the world's environmental woes.[1]

But is this conceptualization (and indeed, demonization) of sovereignty simply a failure of both interpretation and imagination? Supporters of the conventional view either assert or appear to assume that, by its very nature, state sovereignty:

1. Is a static concept that shields states from assuming a positive duty to protect the global environment; and
2. Is irreconcilable with such a duty.

This chapter sets out to question whether these assumptions are correct, in the hope of proving that "sovereignty need not be such an obstacle".[2] Rather,

1 Kamieniecki, S & Granzeier, MS 1998, 'Eco-cultural security and indigenous self-determination: moving toward a new conception of sovereignty', in KT Litfin (ed), *The greening of sovereignty in world politics*, MIT Press, Massachusetts, p. 260.
2 Thakur, R 2002, 'Intervention, sovereignty and the responsibility to protect: experiences from ICISS', *Security Dialogue*, vol. 33, no. 3, pp. 323–330.

DOI: 10.4324/9781032674049-10

by interrogating, contextualizing and deconstructing the theories, interpretation, practice and evolution of international law and the modern nation-state in an increasingly interconnected and interdependent world, it is entirely possible to suggest that those assumptions are outdated, and a new "sovereignty frame" should be adopted.

To explore this contention, the following analysis explores the extent to which states are subject to existing or emerging duties with respect to environmental protection. It further considers the urgent need to re-interrogate the normative theory, functions and legitimacy of the state within the dominant neoliberal paradigm in order to overcome its privileging of economic growth and to steer a new course in pursuit of Earth integrity. This requires a normative re-set and the reframing (and reclaiming) of state sovereignty, legitimacy and accountability by reference to Earth trusteeship. The transformation required may seem idealistic and, indeed, in practical terms, involves just that – acceptance and implementation of a likely controversial and thus brave but critical ideological shift. With mounting evidence of widespread ecological devastation across our Earth system, we humans (will) have no choice but to make the shift or confront an increasingly uninhabitable world. We must hope we still have time to choose the former.

1. The Need to Widen the Frame

a) *The Current Conceptual Frame*

The modern concept of sovereignty is generally ascribed two dimensions: internal, by reference "to the exclusive competence of the state to make authoritative decisions of the government with regard to all people and resources within its territory",[3] and external, by reference to "the legal identity of the state in international law, an equality of status with all other states, and the claim to be the sole official agent acting in international relations on behalf of a society".[4] Unwillingness on the part of states to dilute their claims to territorial integrity and political independence – an absolutist approach to territorial sovereignty – in particular "has led to a status quo where domestic interests are put ahead of international cooperation on issues requiring uniform global attention",[5] thereby frustrating the cooperative spirit and action necessary to address the global ecological (and existential) crisis we face.

3 At 328.
4 At 328.
5 Nijs, L 2016–2017, 'Sovereignty in international environmental law: an outdated principle? The case of stratospheric aerosol injections and distributive justice', Master's thesis law and technology, Tilburg University, p. 25.

Significantly, neither internal nor external dimension "invites a reckoning with a non-anthropocentric framing of our planetary reality" or "helps situate human activity within the functioning of [planetary] systems, making clear that the forms of economic[6] and political organisation that the species adopts has profound impacts on the systemic functioning of the earth".[7] Indeed the "manmade patchwork system of nation-states"[8] stands in apparent contradiction to the "seamless web of nature"[9] within which we live: "the Earth system cannot be divided up into territories . . . any territory exists in an indivisible global environment".[10] With its assurances of equality among states, territorial integrity and political independence pursuant to Articles 2(1) and 2(4) of the Charter of the United Nations (which admittedly preceded current understandings and concerns around the environment), this superimposed web of nation-states which overlays the Earth's surface has been characterized – or, more accurately, blighted – by a narrow, self-interested, anthropocentric, rights-based, ecologically insensitive approach to state sovereignty.[11] This approach, Matthew argues, is repeated and recirculated within the scholarship on sovereignty, which "constitutively inure[s] us from ecological and environmental challenges".[12] Indeed, he notes:

> [T]he dominant discourse on sovereignty – expansive and heterogenous though it may be – remains strangely incurious about what, by any reasonable measure, is one of the most pressing political, legal and cultural challenges of our time. Today's preeminent constitutional theorists write as if sovereignty – as both concept and practice – were entirely unaffected by our entry into the new climatic regime; as if the changing composition of the atmosphere, rising seas, the shifting zones of habitability for basic food

6 Matthews, D 2021, 'Reframing sovereignty for the Anthropocene', *Transnational Legal Theory*, vol. 12, no. 1, p. 55.
7 Matthews, 'Reframing sovereignty for the Anthropocene'.
8 Litfin, KT (ed) 1998, *The greening of sovereignty in world politics*, MIT Press, Massachusetts, p. 3.
9 Litfin, *The greening of sovereignty in world politics*.
10 Bosselmann, K 2019b, 'Large-scale acquisitions of the commons: the need for Earth governance', in L Westra, K Bosselmann & V Zambrano (eds), *Ecological integrity and land uses: sovereignty, governance, displacements and land grabs*, Nova Science Publishers, pp. 285–300, 6.
11 This can be contrasted with Thakur's description of UN membership (writing on R2P): "When you sign the UN Charter, the international community welcomes the signatory state as a responsible member of the community of nations. On the other hand, the state itself, in signing the Charter, accepts the responsibilities of membership flowing from that signature. There is no transfer or dilution of state sovereignty. But there is a redefinition of sovereignty as it shifts from being a right of exclusivity to a responsibility of both internal functions and external duties. The UN is the symbol and the arena for the shared management of pooled sovereignty." See Thakur, n 2, at 331.
12 Matthews, see n 6, at 45.

stuffs, the reformation of landscapes and coastlines, mass extinctions, and the threat of systemic environmental collapse had no bearing on sovereignty and the claims to plenary authority made in its name.[13]

Whilst the concept of state sovereignty has "framed out" the Earth system within which it operates, it has not always "framed out" accountability of the state to non-citizens. Indeed:

> [T]he notion that sovereigns are accountable not only to their own citizens, but also to noncitizens, can draw on a long history. It has antecedents in sixteenth-century political, philosophical and legal scholarship on sovereignty and the state (and even further back). . . . These scholars articulated and developed theoretical and legal justifications for casting responsibilities on sovereign others, thus challenging the perception of sovereignty as being free from any obligations or limitations. For instance, the eighteenth-century scholar Emer de Vattel referred to the earth as belonging to all humankind, therefore obliging sovereigns to preserve their natural resources and share them with others. Similar arguments were voiced by Hugo Grotius during the seventeenth century.[14]

These early conceptions of sovereigns as trustees for humanity were susceptible to imperial manipulation, however. [Introduction: Sovereignty as trusteeship for humanity] recalls that

> Because sovereignty over a territory bears with it the responsibility to use natural resources in a manner that benefits all of humankind, and to share them with other nations, sovereigns who failed to uphold those responsibilities were rightfully subject to a takeover by other sovereigns. The concept of sovereignty as trusteeship also served to justify a paternalistic approach towards conquered nations and native peoples, which in turn reinforced their exploitation. In other words, the concept of sovereignty as trusteeship was deeply embedded within the brutal imperialism of past centuries.[15]

Sovereignty can also be viewed as a political aesthetic.[16] From this viewpoint, it is a framing device which "determines what is seen, heard and

13 Matthews, see n 6, at 45.

14 Braudo, Y, et al. (eds) 2015, 'Introduction: Sovereignty as trusteeship for humanity – Historical antecedents and their impact on international law', *Theoretical Inquiries in Law*, vol. 16, no. 2, p. i.

15 Braudo, et al., 'Introduction'.

16 Matthews, D 2021, *Earthbound: the aesthetics of sovereignty*, Edinburgh University Press, Edinburgh.

felt – determining in advance what registers legally and politically".[17] On the flipside, it anaesthetizes us to "the challenges we need to address", including ecological challenges.[18]

For these reasons, it "is not surprising, therefore, that for many decades it has been abandoned by most scholars, lawyers, and policymakers".[19] Indeed, "the introduction of the system of sovereign rights to natural resources" as a means to correct the global colonial system "in which foreign political powers and private individuals and companies unjustly appropriated natural resources occurring on territories of colonised people" became the new sovereignty frame, representing "the single most profound and consequential international reform concerning ownership, control, and use of land and natural resources"[20] and indeed, global environmental protection.

b) Thinking Beyond the "Sovereignty Rut"

The so-called "sovereignty rut",[21] which has served to exclude the broader Earth system and non-citizens from the sovereignty frame, has led to state impotence, indifference and/or immunity with respect to addressing ongoing global ecological decline. However, the interpretation and practice of state sovereignty should not be seen as static. Onwe and Nwogbaga note:

> [O]ver the years, the scope and perceptions of the concept have: varied from ancient to modern interpretations; changed from resting on individuals to being an exclusive preserve of states; while the rationale and dimensions of the idea have taken diverse perspectives.[22]

And as Litfin writes, "sovereignty is not a static organising principle, but rather a historical institution whose norms and practices have changed significantly over time".[23] And will continue to out of necessity, for, as Arcanjo notes, the possible disappearance of low-lying small island states as a result of sea level rise directly challenges traditional notions of, and the ability to exercise, sovereignty. He submits that "by reframing how sovereignty is conceived to view it as a political act, and the state itself as a social construction,

17 Matthews, D, Birrell, K & Lindgren, T 2022, 'Sovereignty in the anthropocene', *Griffith Law Review*, vol. 31, no. 3, p. 435, 444.
18 At 445.
19 At 445.
20 Gumplova, P 2020, 'Sovereignty over natural resources: a normative reinterpretation', *Global Constitutionalism*, vol. 9, no. 1, p. 5.
21 Matthews, see n 6, at 46.
22 Onwe, S & Nwogbaba, D 2015, 'Conceptual issues and theoretical analysis of sovereignty', *Research on Humanities and Social Sciences*, vol. 5, no. 3, p. 19.
23 Litfin, n 8, at 9.

opens the door for cooperation between nations when it comes to recognising and legitimising authority".[24] Indeed, the successful reimagining of sovereignty in the case of climate change "will require not only a reorientation of regional states' perception of each other, but also a new understanding of the place of human societies as a wholly-owned subsidiary of the natural world".[25]

Just as sovereignty has never been static, it has never been unconstrained. As Purdy and Fielding state, "Few ever argued that the powers of governments were notionally boundless. . . . Political thought always included the idea that governments existed to serve the interests of those who lived under them".[26] Today, "constitutional sovereignty holds that the power and authority of the state are . . . contingent and constrained" through the separation of powers, rule of law and accountability to the people, whilst internationally, "states are constrained by globally legitimated institutions and practices"[27] and a "condition of any one state's sovereignty is a corresponding obligation to respect every other state's sovereignty".[28] To varying degrees, states have expressly accepted (through international organizations, laws and obligations) or been subjected to (for example, through the influence of powerful nations, pressure groups, public opinion and globalization) limitations to their sovereignty.[29] Gumplova further notes:

> Contemporary international law reinvented after WWII articulates a number of rules and limits on state sovereignty. Internally or domestically, international law accords an extensive set of individual rights to all human beings and imposes legal duties and obligations on states to fulfil them. Externally or internationally, there are rules which recognise fundamental equality of the right to self-determination and sovereignty of states and prohibit the use of aggressive force and intervention in the internal affairs of other states. When perceived as a system which not only distributes sovereignty as a legal entitlement but also as a system which extensively regulates its internal and external exercise, international law can be interpreted

24 Arcanjo, M 2019, *Has climate change rendered the concept of sovereignty obsolete?*, A Climate Institute Publication, viewed 17 January 2019, (http://climate.org/wp-content/uploads/2019/01/Has-Climate-Change-Rendered-the-Concept-of-Sovereignty-Obsolete.pdf) at 8.

25 Habib, B 2015, *Climate change and the re-imagination of state sovereignty*, viewed 8 November 2015, (https://www.e-ir.info/2015/11/08/climate-change-and-the-re-imagination-of-state-sovereignty/).

26 Purdy, J & Fielding, K 2007, 'Sovereigns, trustees, guardians: private-law concepts and the limits of legitimate state power', *Law and Contemporary Problems*, vol. 70, p. 165, 167.

27 Thakur, see n 2, at 328.

28 At 329.

29 Onwe and Nwogbaba, n 22, at 22.

> as a system articulating a relatively coherent notion of justice for the world organised into sovereign territorial states.[30]

Alternatively, as Litfin writes,

> International environmental regimes . . . alter the function of boundaries by untying the bundle of rights conventionally associated with full territorial sovereignty. . . . If territory provides the container for state sovereignty, then transnational environmental problems and efforts to address them seem to be reshaping the container.[31]

But do any of these constraints on the exercise of state sovereignty – or reshaping of the container – give rise to a positive duty to protect the environment in law? Eckersley submits that

> [T]he issue specific regimes, declarations and strategies that have proliferated as part of the evolving processes of environmental multilateralism have gradually redefined the rights and responsibilities that are attached to sovereign statehood, which have produced new discourses on the underlying purpose of the state.[32]

Matthews also proposes that the existing sovereignty framework does not preclude us from finding other bonds to Earth and exploring these as "generative possibilities for thinking both beyond and with sovereignty in new ways".[33] This may require "shifting to a language of obligation rather than continuing to affirm the 'age of rights'".[34]

Consideration of how the evolution of the "no-harm" principle, environmental human rights, eco-constitutional law and rights of nature may be invoked suggest an emerging (albeit anthropocentric) duty, to which we now turn.

2. Duty to Avoid Harm to Other States

The obligation not to harm the environment of another state has developed in uneasy tension with the principle of "permanent sovereignty over natural resources" (PSONR). The traditional view in international law whereby "States were regarded to have an exclusive right to exploit the

30 Gumplova, n 20, at 8.
31 Litfin, see n 8, at 11.
32 Eckersley, R 2004, *The green state: rethinking democracy and sovereignty*, The MIT Press, Cambridge, p. 208.
33 At 446.
34 At 446.

natural resources within their territories and also to make laws relating to their environment"[35] is well reflected in UN General Assembly Resolution 1803 (XVII) of 14 December 1962 on Permanent Sovereignty over Natural Resources, which provided that the international community must respect the rights of peoples and states over their natural wealth and resources and that those rights were to "be exercised in the interest of their national development and of the well-being of the People of the State concerned".[36] PSONR was

> further confirmed and developed in a series of charters and resolutions dealing with human rights, international economic order, social progress, development, and the environment, . . . including [t]he Human Rights Covenants from 1966, the Charter of Economic Rights and Duties of States (1974) and the Declaration on the Establishment of a New International Economic Order (1974)[, which] are the most important international law instruments through which resource sovereignty was affirmed *erga omnes*. . . . As a result of these treaties and legal instruments, permanent sovereignty over natural resources legally protects the right of states to unlimited control, free exploitation and disposal of natural resources in their territories, to choose their economic system without outside interference, and also to regulate and nationalise foreign investment.[37]

The PSONR "frame" can be well understood in its historical context as "a response to the historical injustice of colonial appropriation of natural resources based on violence, domination, and dispossession of natural resources by foreign powers".[38] Sovereign territorial rights were seen as "a key component of political self-determination and a bulwark against predatory powers"[39] but also "an *economic expression of state sovereignty*".[40] The allocation of PSONR to territorial collectives was a means to "correct [the] global colonial system" and provide these collectives "a legal tool against foreign companies or powers and their efforts to exploit resources for their own benefit and to establish extensive property rights not subjected to regulation by local jurisdictions".[41]

35 Parmar, SS 2019, *Sovereignty and trans-boundary environmental issues: a search for co-existence*, Dharmsahastra National Law University, February 2019, p. 6.

36 United Nations General Assembly Resolution 1803 (XVII) (14 December 1962), art 1.

37 Gumplova, P 2014, 'Restraining permanent sovereignty over natural resources', *Enrahonar Quaderns de Filosofia*, vol. 53, p. 93, 96.

38 Gumplova, see n 17, at 2.

39 At 3.

40 Gumplova, n 20, at 102. Emphasis added.

41 Gumplova, n 20, at 4.

Furthermore, as well as a human right, "Domestic economic development based on resource exploitation was also seen by many developing countries as a necessary prerequisite for redressing global economic disparities between developed and newly independent and developing countries".[42]

The privileging of territorial sovereignty has meant that there are fewer instances of international treaties and arrangements relating to transboundary environmental issues, and much of the law on this issue is customary and often silent on the limitations of such rights when exploitation results in harm to a neighbouring state.[43] Parmar maintains that where there are limits, they are often "ambiguous and unclear"[44] and must be understood "within the context of territorial sovereignty".[45]

The PSONR frame has similarly limited the application of the customary international law principle *sic utere tuo ut alienum non laedas*, which has been applied to transboundary environmental harm. The Arbitral Tribunal in the *Trail Smelter* arbitration declared:

> No State has the right to use or permit the use of its territory in such a manner as to cause injury by fumes in or to the territory of another or the properties or person therein, when the case is of serious consequence and the injury is established by clear and convincing evidence.[46]

However, the doctrine of state responsibility for environmental harm has proven both reactive and limited in its application, favouring the freedom of "property holders" – the state – with the victims of environmental harm subject to the burden of demonstrating a duty of care, *actual* (notably not merely the risk thereof) and serious damage and causation.[47]

The no-harm principle, which is supported by the general principle of good neighbourliness,[48] is enshrined and expanded in Principle 21 of the 1972 Stockholm Declaration, which provides that

> States have the sovereign right to exploit their own resources pursuant to their own environmental policies, and the responsibility to ensure that

42 At 10.
43 Parmar, see n 35, at 2.
44 Parmar, see n 35, at 2.
45 Parmar, see n 35, at 2.
46 *United States v Canada, Arbitral Trib.*, 3 U.N. Rep. Int'l Arb. Awards 1905 (1941), cited in Parmar, n 30, at 7. The effectiveness of the no-harm rule is less clear vis-à-vis long term, cumulative environmental impacts or cases of the over-exploitation of resources within territorial limits but which may be unsustainable to the world community as a whole and may disturb the natural environment of neighbouring states.
47 Eckersley, n 32, at 219.
48 Wapner, P 1998, 'Reorienting state sovereignty: rights and responsibilities in the environmental age', in KT Litfin (ed), n 8, at 278.

> activities within their jurisdiction or control do not cause damage to the environment of other States or of areas beyond the limits of national jurisdiction.

Although rearticulating the principle of PSONR, Principle 21 notably refers only to "damage" (not "serious" damage) and extends the scope of protection by including "areas beyond the limits of national jurisdiction". Principle 2 of the 1992 Rio Declaration reaffirmed this, although it weakened the emphasis on environmental policies by adding "and development policies".

A more forgiving interpretation of the no-harm rule focuses attention on its (normative) constraints to absolute sovereignty and that, in seeking

> a balance between rights and responsibilities, [it] remind[s] states that, while they have authority over their own territories, ecosystems transcend political boundaries and extend obligations. Sovereignty, thus conceptualised, is "restricted". Resources within one's boundaries are interconnected with environmental systems in other states, and thus states must pay heed to the extraterritorial ramifications of activities within their borders and, . . . their activities in global common areas.[49]

This evolving idea of state sovereignty better reflects an interdependent world "where national boundaries are increasingly permeable",[50] as a result of which "traditional notions of territoriality, independence and non-intervention are losing some of their meaning".[51]

The responsibility of states for harm beyond their borders is similarly recognized under Article 1 of the International Law Commission's (ILC) draft Articles on Responsibility of States for Internationally Wrongful Acts, which provides that "[e]very internationally wrongful act of a State entails the international responsibility of that State". An "internationally wrongful act of a State" consists of an act or omission that is "(a) attributable to the State under international law; and (b) constitutes a breach of an international obligation of the State".[52] The commentary to the draft Articles notes that "[i]ncreasingly it has been recognised that some wrongful acts engage the

49 Wapner, 'Reorienting state sovereignty'.

50 Ferreira-Snyman, A 2010, 'Intervention with specific reference to the relationship between the United Nations Security Council and the African Union', *The Comparative and International Law Journal of Southern Africa*, vol. 43, no. 2, pp. 139, 140.

51 Ferreira-Snyman, 'Intervention with specific reference to the relationship between the United Nations Security Council and the African Union'.

52 Draft Articles on Responsibility of States for Internationally Wrongful Acts in Report of the International Law Commission on the Work of Its Fifty-third Session, UN GAOR, 56th Sess., Supp. No 10, UN Doc, A/56/10 (2001), art 2.

responsibility of the State concerned towards several or many States or even towards the international community as a whole".[53] In support of this, in the *Barcelona Traction*[54] case the International Court of Justice (ICJ) noted:

> [A]n essential distinction should be drawn between the obligations of a State towards the international community as a whole, and those arising vis-à-vis another State in the field of diplomatic protection. By their very nature the former are the concern of all States. In view of the importance of the rights involved, all States can be held to have a legal interest in their protection; they are obligations *erga omnes*.

Consequently, "Every State, by virtue of its membership in the international community, has a legal interest in the protection of certain basic rights and the fulfilment of certain essential obligations".[55] In this respect, the Court instanced "the outlawing of acts of aggression, and of genocide, as also . . . *the principles and rules concerning the basic rights of the human person*,[56] including protection from slavery and racial discrimination".[57]

The significance of the linking of rights with responsibilities is testament to "a common understanding about the problematic nature of state sovereignty as it relates to environmental challenges"[58] and "a normative commitment to restrict the freedom of individual states when one state's actions adversely affects another's".[59] However, although supportive of a duty in this regard, "[t]ranslating such understanding and commitment into practice has proved difficult"[60] because, as Wapner contends, "States have a tremendous amount of experience upholding sovereignty in the international sphere . . . [whilst] there is much less experience with and support for the notion of responsibility".[61] PSONR as a prerequisite for post-colonial self-determination, economic (now "sustainable") development in particular, has limited the sovereignty frame through an expansive interpretation of the rights and prerogatives it is thought to justify.

A way forward, Gumplova suggests, is to reinterpret the PSONR frame by reading in "environmental sustainability and ecological stewardship standards[,] in the same way that human rights constrain the exercise of

53 At 33, para (4).
54 *Barcelona Traction* Case (Belgium v Spain) [1970] ICJ Rep 3 at 32, para 33.
55 Report of the International Law Commission, see n 47, at 33, para (4).
56 Emphasis added.
57 *Barcelona Traction* case, at 49, para 34.
58 Wapner, n 48, at 279.
59 Wapner, n 48, at 279.
60 Wapner, n 48, at 279.
61 Wapner, n 48, at 279.

state power over its citizens".[62] Eckersley suggests that this may already be happening:

> [despite] the state's traditional record of environmental destruction and its more recent, but not entirely successful, efforts toward more ecologically rational utilitarian management. . . . [I]t is also possible to find not insignificant examples of states acting either individually or collectively as "ecological trustees", upholding a wider range of ecological values in the service of environmental protection.[63]

Like Gumplova, Eckersley maintains that "sovereign territorial rule is not necessarily ecologically problematic *if it is contextualised and qualified* by, say, ecological standards of membership, ecological standards of democratic legitimacy, or new ecological rights and responsibilities of states".[64] Simply by reading "territorial integrity" to include "ecosystem integrity", "the territorial dimension of sovereignty might be made to work for the environment insofar as it might enable political communities to . . . halt practices in other states that threaten to undermine domestic ecosystem integrity".[65]

3. An Emerging Environmental Duty

a) Human Rights Instruments

Just as there is no mention of the environment in the Charter of the United Nations (reflecting that, at the time of its drafting, peace and security were of principal concern, not the correction of global ecological abuses), there is no explicit, substantive right to environmental quality in the Universal Declaration on Human Rights 1948 (UDHR)[66] or in the International Covenant on Civil and Political Rights.[67] The environment is, however, mentioned with relevance to the full realization of rights set out in other international human rights instruments, most commonly health,[68] and cases have been brought

62 Gumplova, n 20, at 95.
63 Eckersley, n 32, at 33.
64 At 232.
65 At 233.
66 Universal Declaration of Human Rights (10 December 1948) UN Doc GA/Res/217A (III).
67 International Covenant on Civil and Political Rights (16 December 1966) 999 UNTS 171.
68 International Covenant on Economic, Social and Cultural Rights (ICESCR) (16 December 1966) 993 UNTS 3, Article 12, which references "the improvement of all aspects of environmental . . . hygiene". See also United Nations Convention on the Rights of the Child (7 March 1990) E/CN.4/RES/1990/74, Article 24(2), which refers to "the dangers and risks of environmental protection". Susan Glazebrook notes that Article 28 of the UDHR provides that everyone is entitled to "a social and international order in which the rights and freedoms set forth in [the UDHR] can be fully realised." She cites support for the propositions

successfully in this regard. Accordingly, in respect of the right to health,[69] the United Nations, through the Committee on Economic, Social and Cultural Rights in General Comment 14,[70] has stated:

> [T]he right to health embraces a wide range of socio-economic factors that promote conditions in which people can lead a healthy life, and extends to the underlying determinants of health, such as . . . healthy environment.

There is a similar lacuna in the European Convention on Human Rights, which has not been addressed through the creation of a standalone right to environment, despite repeated recommendations by the Council of Europe's Parliamentary Assembly to this effect[71] (which have been rejected by the Committee of Ministers, the Council's statutory decision-making body.) This "has not . . . discouraged applicants from seeking to invoke the Convention in the name of environmental protection",[72] a trend expected to continue (particularly in relation to climate change) following the *Urgenda* judgment[73] of the Dutch Supreme Court. European Court of Human Rights Judge Tim Eicke suggests that this precedent is particularly notable in light of the fact that the 2015 Paris Agreement contains no substantive provision making the link between climate change and human rights; the ECHR is not "specifically designed to provide general protection of the environment as such; to that effect, other international instruments and domestic legislation are more pertinent",[74] and, as noted earlier, the Council of Europe's Committee of Ministers has so far declined to provide for a standalone right to environment.

Whether a more "interventionist" or expansive approach to human rights cases involving environmental issues can be expected from the European Court of Justice (ECJ) remains to be seen. Previously, whilst expressly

that "order" can be seen as encompassing the environment, and environmental stress has been recognized as a catalyst for threats thereto through civil unrest and threats to territorial and resource security. In this regard, it is submitted that of greater relevance to an "international order" supportive of the full realization of the UDHR's rights and freedoms is the interpretation and exercise of state sovereignty. See Glazebrook, S 2009, 'Human rights and the environment', *Victoria University of Wellington Law Review*, vol. 40, no. 1, p. 293, 295.

69 ICESCR, see n 69, art 12(1).

70 UN Committee on Economic, Social and Cultural Rights (CESCR) *General Comment No. 14: The Right to the Highest Attainable Standard of Health (Art. 12 of the Covenant)*, Adopted 11 August 2000, UN Doc. E/C/12/2000/4.

71 European Court of Human Rights Judge Tim Eicke, 'Human Rights and Climate Change: What role for the European Court of Human Rights', Inaugural Annual Human Rights Lecture, Department of Law, Goldsmiths University, 2 March 2021.

72 Eicke, n 71, at 19.

73 *State of the Netherlands v. Urgenda Foundation* ECLI:NL:HR:2019:2007, Judgment (Sup. Ct. Neth. 20 December 2019).

74 *Krytatos v Greece,* No 41666/98, § 52, ECHR 2003 VI (extracts).

acknowledging that "in today's society the protection of the environment is an increasingly important consideration", the ECJ has demonstrated a reluctance to stray into matters that might be seen to fall within the state's margin of appreciation. Similar concerns have been expressed with regard to definitional issues, where the ECJ has cautioned that "it has not always been easy to identify the existence and/or content of these 'commonly accepted standards' or any 'evolving convergence'" (insofar as they may be different).[75]

Substantive environmental rights do, however, appear in other regional instruments.[76] Examples include Article 11 of the Additional Protocol in the Area of Economic, Social and Cultural Rights 1989 (Protocol of San Salvador) to the American Convention on Human Rights, which provides that states should "protect, preserve and improve the environment" and that citizens have the right to "live in a healthy environment",[77] and Article 24 of the African Charter of Human and Peoples' Rights 1981 states that citizens have a right to a "general satisfactory environment favourable to their development".[78] However, their use and development have been limited.[79]

b) *Right to a Healthy Environment Under International Law*

Although there is no express right to a quality environment under international human rights instruments, commentators have considered whether there is sufficient support for the existence of such a right under customary international law. In considering this question, Glazebrook notes that the Stockholm Declaration "evidences a clear view, at that time, that there was a human right to an environment of quality".[80] To this effect, Principle One states:

> Man has the fundamental right to freedom, equality and adequate conditions of life, in an environment of a quality that permits a life of dignity and well-being, and he bears a solemn responsibility to protect and improve the environment for present and future generations.

Although, as a declaration, it did not establish a new environmental right under international law, "it was of considerable influence especially in terms

75 Eicke, n 71, at 19.

76 Turner, S 2014, 'A global environmental right', in *Routledge explorations in environmental studies*, Routledge, London, p. 25.

77 Organization of American States (OAS) Additional Protocol to the American Convention on Human Rights in the Area of Economic, Social and Cultural Rights ("Protocol of San Salvador") (16 November 1999), A-52, Article 11(2).

78 Organisation of African Unity (OAU), African Charter on Human and Peoples' Rights ('Banjul Charter') CAB/LEG/67/3 rev. 5, 21 I.L.M. 58 (adopted 27 June 1981, effective October 1996). 21 ILM. 59, Article 24.

79 See here Turner, n 76, at 25.

80 Glazebrook, n 68, at 297.

of the way that established human rights such as the right to life and right to health went on to be interpreted and developed".[81] However, a qualification (and tension) was soon introduced by the concept of sustainable development under the Rio Declaration and subsequent Johannesburg Declaration,[82] with humans "at the centre of concerns", implying that "the environment is only there for (proper) human use".[83]

Against this, a fundamental duty to preserve the ecosystem was recognized (albeit by only 25 heads of state) in the Hague Declaration on the Environment 1989,[84] which also recognized the right to live in dignity in a viable global environment. United Nations General Assembly Resolution 45/94 of 1990 recognized that environmental protection is indivisible from the achievement of full enjoyment of human rights by all[85] and, thus, the right of all individuals to "live in an environment adequate for their health and well-being".[86] And the 1994 Draft Principles on Human Rights and the Environment proposed a standalone right "to a secure healthy and ecologically sound environment".[87]

In an advisory opinion of the International Criminal Court in 1996, although not discussing a general human right to the environment, the Court nevertheless recognized that "the environment is not an abstraction but represents the living space, the quality of life and the very health of human beings, including generations unborn".[88] And in the 1997 *Danube* case,[89] Vice President Weeramantry wrote, in a separate opinion, that he "saw the protection of the environment as being very much a question of human rights",[90] saying it was:

> a vital part of contemporary human rights doctrine, for it is a *sine qua non* for numerous human rights such as the right to health and the right to life itself. It is scarcely necessary to elaborate on this, as damage to the

81 Turner, n 76, at 25.
82 World Summit on Sustainable Development, *Johannesburg Declaration on Sustainable Development* (4 September 2002) A/CONF.199/20.
83 Glazebrook, n 63, at 298.
84 Hague Declaration on the Environment (1989) 28 ILM 1308, at 1309.
85 See The Need to Ensure a Healthy Environment for the Well-Being of Individuals, G.A. Res. 45/94 (14 December 1990), U.N. GAOR, 45th Sess., Supp. No. 49A, at 178, U.N. Doc. A/45/40.
86 The Need to Ensure a Healthy Environment for the Well-Being of Individuals, at [1].
87 *Draft Principles on Human Rights and the Environment* E/CN.4/Sub.2/1994/9 Annex I (1994), at part I para 1.
88 *Legality of the Threat or Use of Nuclear Weapons* (Advisory Opinion) [1996] ICJ Rep 226, at para 29.
89 Case concerning the *Gabcikovo-Nagymaros Project* (Hungary v Slovakia) [1997] ICJ Rep 7 (*Danube* case).
90 Glazebrook, n 68, at 302.

> environment can impair and undermine all the human rights spoken of in the Universal Declaration and other human rights instruments,[91]

(This view, however, arguably strengthens the case for an expanded interpretation of the rights to life and health rather than declaring a new substantive environmental right.)[92]

Glazebrook further notes that "[r]eference was also made to the value systems of various cultures which revealed the universal love of nature, the desire for its preservation and the need for human activity to respect the requisites for its maintenance and continuance".[93] Whilst not amounting to the creation of law or of precedential effect, the Judge Weeramantry's opinion, emanating from the ICJ (albeit as a separate judgment), is of persuasive value regarding the state of the law.[94]

In 2002, a joint expert seminar[95] recognized the role of environmental protection as a precondition for the effective enjoyment of human rights[96] and that "the growing recognition of a right to a secure, healthy and ecologically sound environment, either as a constitutionally guaranteed right or as a guiding principle of national and international law, ought to be supported".[97] But these conclusions were not incorporated into the Johannesburg Declaration of the same year, which focused on development.

Ultimately (and notwithstanding further references to a right to the environment in various regional instruments[98] and numerous state constitutions[99] discussed further later in this chapter), the intermingling of the right to environment with the right to development – "with consequent uncertainty as to its existence as a stand-alone right"[100] – together with its uncertain parameters[101] and "soft" law heritage,[102] have hampered its universal acceptance. To this end, the weight of opinion remains that currently there is no globally accepted substantive environmental right,[103] though one may be emerging.[104]

91 Separate Opinion of Vice-President Weeramantry in the *Danube Case*, n 89, at 91–92.
92 Turner, n 76, at 26.
93 Glazebrook, n 68, at 302, citing the Separate Opinion of Vice President Weeramantry in the *Danube* case, n 89, at 108–109.
94 Turner, n 76, at 24.
95 Office of the High Commissioner for Human Rights 2002, *Meeting of experts on human rights and the environment* (www.unhchr.ch).
96 At [5] and [12].
97 At [18].
98 Including, for example, the African Charter on Human and Peoples' Rights, see n 73, and the Protocol of San Salvador, n 78, art 15.
99 Turner, see n 76.
100 Glazebrook, n 68, at 311.
101 Though Glazebrook notes, "I consider, however, that the differences can be exaggerated. The basic concept is common to most formulations of the right", at 305.
102 At 310.
103 Turner, n 76, at 1.
104 At 29.

Strong support for the latter view is evidenced in the United Nation's Human Rights Special Procedures: Framework Principles on Human Rights and the Environment 2018 (Framework Principles), which "set out the basic obligations of States under human rights law as they relate to the enjoyment of a safe, healthy and sustainable environment".[105] The United Nations Special Rapporteur on Human Rights and the Environment, John H. Knox, contends that:

> Many of the obligations are based on treaties or binding decision from human rights bodies, while others draw on statements of human rights that have authority to interpret human rights law but not necessarily to issue binding decisions. Coherence of interpretations of human rights bodies is strong evidence of the converging trends towards greater uniformity and certainty in the application of human rights law to the environment. These trends are further supported by State practice, including in international environmental instruments and before human rights bodies.[106]

To this end, Knox concludes that the Framework Principles should be accepted as a reflection of actual or emerging international human rights law.[107]

Among other things, the Framework Principles accept that human beings are part of nature, human rights are intertwined with the environment, and states should ensure a safe, clean, healthy and sustainable environment in order to respect, protect and fulfil human rights (and that doing so will ensure a safe, clean, healthy and sustainable environment).[108] Principle 11 obliges states to establish and maintain substantive environmental standards, including effective legal and institutional frameworks. Principle 19 recognizes the need for global cooperation in good faith "to establish, maintain and enforce effective international legal frameworks in order to prevent, reduce and remedy transboundary and global environmental harm that interferes with the full enjoyment of human rights". Once agreed, no state should ever seek to withdraw from any of its international obligations to protect against transboundary or global environmental harm; states should continually monitor whether their international obligations are sufficient, and when they are not, states should quickly take the necessary steps to strengthen them "bearing in mind that the lack of full scientific certainty should not be used to justify postponing effective and proportionate measures to ensure a safe, clean, healthy and sustainable environment".[109]

105 Knox, JH 2018, *United Nations human rights special procedures: framework principles on human rights and the environment 2018 – the main human rights obligations relating to the enjoyment of a safe, clean, healthy and sustainable environment*, Final Report, UN Doc. A/HRC/37/59, at 3.

106 Knox, *United Nations human rights special procedures.*

107 Knox, *United Nations human rights special procedures.*

108 At 5 and 6.

109 At 38.

The recognition of procedural environmental rights under international customary law is less contentious.[110] Indeed, in 2016, the World Commission on Environmental Law of the IUCN and UNEP determined that the basic norms of procedural environmental rights are part of the "Environmental Rule of Law".[111] These do not guarantee any particular level of environmental protection; rather, they entitle individuals to challenge decision-making, be furnished with information, and participate in decisions relating to the environment and thus "represent a practical and functional hybrid between human rights law and environmental law".[112] The purpose and focus of the United Nations Economic Commissions for Europe Aarhus Convention are solely related to procedural environmental rights and are thus among the most important developments in this field.[113] One of its most "innovative features" is that it gives standing to members of the public to make complaints to the Convention's compliance committee, which enables "individuals and NGOs to place pressure on their home states to provide procedural rights that conform to the treaty regime's developing standards".[114] In practice, procedural environmental rights feature most prominently in relation to the carrying out of environmental impact assessments where there is a risk of environmental harm.[115]

c) *Nationally Recognized Environmental Rights*[116]

Constitutionally entrenched environmental rights are widespread and take various forms:

> [S]ome are enforceable, some are directive principles of state policy, designed to galvanise, though not compel, legislative activity to protect the

110 Turner, n 76, at 29.

111 Robinson, NA 2018, 'Environmental law: is an obligation Erga Omnes emerging?', conference presentation at the panel discussion at the United Nations, 4 June 2018, 1 pm–2.45 pm, Conference Room 12, p. 4, 5.

112 Turner, n 76, at 24.

113 Turner, n 76, at 24.

114 United Nations Economic Commission for Europe, Aarhus Convention on Access to Information, Public Participation in Decision-Making and Access to Justice in Environmental Matters (Aarhus Convention), 2161 UNTS 447, 38 ILM 517 (1999), art 15.

115 Turner, n 76, at 24.

116 Kotzé has adopted a broader conception of environmental constitutionalism that encompasses notions of environmental care, not just environmental rights. To this end, he sees such constitutional provisions as "a method to dictate the content of laws, a way to establish moral and ethical obligations with respect to the environment and as a legal grounding and authority to require actual performance of these obligations". In O'Gorman, R 2017, 'Environmental constitutionalism: a comparative study', *Transnational Environmental Law*, vol. 16, no. 3, vol. 6 at 437–438, citing Kotzé, LJ 2012, 'Arguing global environmental constitutionalism', *Transnational Environmental Law*, vol. 1, no. 1, p. 199, 208. O'Gorman notes that "such an understanding of environmental constitutionalism goes

> environment. They can be express or implied from other guarantees, notably the right to life, the right to dignity, or sometimes more specific rights such as the right to health. They can refer to just one part of the environment (such as water, flora, fauna, natural resources), or to the environment generally. Typically, they qualify the right with adjectives purporting to establish a goal, or at least a benchmark: the right may be to a healthful environment, or one that is clean, safe, adequate, harmonious, balanced, or otherwise desirable.[117]

In terms of a standalone right to environment and "[i]n spite of the limited development of substantive environmental rights on an international level, there has been a significant growth of constitutional substantive environmental rights at the national level".[118] Over three quarters of the world's constitutions include explicit references to substantive environmental rights or responsibilities for the protection of the environment,[119] and over 30 contain procedural environmental rights.[120] At least 144 constitutions impose a state obligation to conserve or protect the environment, and (although of questionable legal enforceability) at least 86 constitutions charge citizens with protective duties.[121] The very first constitution to protect environmental rights was Portugal's in 1976, which provides that "[e]veryone shall possess the right to a healthy and ecologically balanced human living environment and the duty to defend it" and goes on to "charge the state" with fulfilling the obligation in eight specific ways.[122] Even in the absence of a provision

> directly articulating the government's obligation to protect the environment . . . the basic human rights concept that there can be no right in the

beyond a focus on specific rights and instead sees value in the articulation of environmental concerns within a constitutional document as having the potential to influence a wider range of public and private interactions." At 438. However, O'Gorman maintains that "the myriad ways in which environmental constitutionalism manifests . . . is indicative of the ambivalence of its constitutional status, which in turn calls into question the appropriateness of their constitutional elevation. It is submitted that this diversity of expression can be traced back to a central weakness: the lack of a clear political or social value which anchors environmental constitutionalism in the same way as traditional first- and second-generation fundamental rights", at 458.

117 Daly, E 2012, 'Constitutional protection for environmental rights: the benefits of environmental process', *International Journal of Peace Studies*, vol. 17, no. 2, p. 71.

118 Turner, n 76, at 26.

119 Boyd, DR 2012, *The environmental rights revolution: a global study of constitutions, human rights, and the environment*, UBC Press, Vancouver, p. 6. See also Turner, n 71, at 26.

120 Boyd, n 119, at 66.

121 At 11 and 17.

122 Constitution of Portugal (1976), art 66. See also the Constitution of Columbia (1991), art 79: "Every person has the right to enjoy a healthy env", and The Constitution of Kenya

absence of a corresponding duty can be used to infer that the government has an obligation to protect the environment.[123]

The constitutional entrenchment of environmental rights is significant to the extent that constitutions inform and constrain government behaviour:

> Constitutions generate a set of inviolable principles and more specific provisions to which future law and government activity more generally must conform. This function – which, as if to highlight its centrality to the concept is commonly given the namesake constitutionalism – is vital to the functioning of democracy. Without a commitment to higher law, the state operates for the short-term benefit of those in power.[124]

Although the idea that the entrenched status of constitutions makes them difficult to amend (thereby assuring them their "higher law" status) may be questioned,[125] the inclusion of substantive environmental rights therein arguably reveals a degree of common commitment to recognize minimum environmental standards of living. Even though Europe does not have a constitution, many of its member states have environmental provisions within their own,[126] and although the United States has not amended its constitution, many states have done so, and their constitutions now contain environmental provisions.[127]

Not all constitutionally entrenched environmental rights are justiciable, but even so, they have been deployed successfully in support of other justiciable constitutional rights (particularly the rights to life and health) to secure protection of the environment.[128] However, the overall effectiveness of

(2010), art 42(a): "Every person has the right to a clean and healthy env, which includes the right to have the env protected for the benefit of present and future generations".

123 Boyd, n 119, at 11.

124 Elksins, Z, Ginsburg, T & Melton, J 2009, *The endurance of national institutions*, Cambridge University Press, Cambridge, p. 41.

125 Since "[b]etween 1990 and 2000, over half of the world's national constitutions were amended and of those, 70 percent adopted completely new institutions." See here Turner, n 76, at 26.

126 At 61.

127 Shelton, D 2007, 'Environmental rights in the state constitutions of the United States', in I Larmuseau (ed), *Constitutional rights to an ecologically balanced environment*, Gent, Belgium, V.V.O.R, p. 106.

128 Turner summarizes these at 27, including: "stopping an environmental authority from authorising the discharge of polluted groundwater into local rivers (State of Montana, USA), the ordering of a clean up of a polluted river that led to World Bank funding for a sustainable development project (Argentina), declaring that an ordinance by a local authority to convert an area of wetlands from recreational use to commercial use was unconstitutional (Peru), ensuring that a governmental authority take measures to protect endangered sea turtles within a national park (Costa Rica), making an order that certain timber license

constitutional environmental rights[129] has been limited to cases of severe environmental pollution or degradation at a local level, seldom cases in relation to national development projects.[130] This may be because, although

> [m]any constitutional systems have imbued courts with power of judicial review . . . some have shied away from the endeavour out of fear of treading too deeply and irreversibly into the waters of policy and line drawing that are more appropriately relegated to politically accountable legislatures.[131]

Daly maintains that

> courts refrain where there is a lack of judicially discoverable and manageable standards for resolving political questions; or the impossibility of deciding without an initial policy determination of a kind clearly for non-judicial discretion; or the impossibility of a court's undertaking independent resolution without expressing lack of respect due coordinate branches of government.[132]

Determining "the contours of the right to live in an environment free of pollution, and enforce that judgment against public and private actors who have different views and who are beholden to a public that may be equally divided" has been a particular obstacle to constitutional adjudication: how "clean" must the environment be, and how can a court determine what is "safe"?[133] The "uncertain boundaries of substantive environmental rights" thus "force courts onto a tightrope" when they seek to interpret and enforce them:

> If they read the rights too narrowly, they risk damage to the environment which could have deleterious effects on the ecosystem and the dignity and health of the population for generations to come. Over-enforcing [them], however, may unduly limit development and economic progress that could

agreements should be cancelled (Philippines), rejecting a challenge to a government ban on highly polluting vehicles (Nepal) and annulling a development plan for new businesses in the vicinity of a lakeland area (Slovenia)."

129 With regard to the effectiveness of constitutionally entrenched procedural rights, Turner finds that this remains highly dependent "on the system of laws and regulations that implement such rights and the admin and judicial infrastructure in the country concerned." See Turner, n 76, at 24.

130 At 28. Cf more activist courts, e.g. India.

131 See Daly, n 117, at 72.

132 At 76.

133 At 74.

> have benefited the local population and perhaps nation as a whole. . . . [H]ow much sustainability, how much development?[134]

In addition to concerns around the risk of judicial overreach, the adjudication of substantive environmental rights is inherently anthropocentric and unlikely to be capable of effecting environmental protection on a global scale: what is clean, safe or healthy is measured according to human health on a case-by-case basis, not vis-à-vis the ecosystem (as part of the wider Earth system) itself.[135] Indeed, the reductive anthropocentricity of Western human rights and constitutions "has been one of the main reasons for the ongoing failure of environmental law and governance to respond to the ecological crisis".[136]

Ultimately, the constitutionalization of environmental objectives may be "by definition anti-ecological". To the extent that constitutionalism is "designed to protect individual liberty from state oppression", it thus "still views nature as a resource, available for human ownership and consumption and as something separate from humanity and it is in this anthropocentric context that environmental commitments have evolved".[137] In the absence of a reorientation pursuant to an overarching ecocentric ethic, Townsend thus questions whether "[t]he constitutional limit on government in the interest of protecting the freedoms of the individual is potentially incompatible with the goals of environmental protection".[138]

A contrary view regarding the largely symbolic or aspirational value of environmental constitutionalism is offered by Weiss, who argues that a contrajudicative analysis reveals that many state obligations are entrenched more as constitutional directive principles, which are not designed to be given effect by direct judicial enforcement.[139] By overlooking the fact that constitutional directive principles are the most common method of entrenching environmental constitutional obligations, "the picture of environmental constitutionalism is both descriptively inadequate and normatively unattractive".[140] Constitutional directive principles address concerns about institutional competency and legitimacy of the courts and thereby respond to demands for accountability,

134 At 77.

135 At 74. See also Alves, F, Costa, PM, Novelli, L & Vidal, DG 2023, 'The rights of nature and the human right to nature: an overview of the European legal system and challenges for the ecological transition', *Frontiers in Environmental Science*, vol. 11.

136 Bosselmann, K 2015, 'Global environmental constitutionalism: mapping the terrain', *Widener Law Review*, vol. 21, p. 171, 174.

137 Lupin Townsend, D 2020, *Human dignity and the adjudication of environmental rights*, EE Elgar, Cheltenham, p. 10.

138 At 8.

139 Weiss, LK 2018, 'Environmental constitutionalism: aspiration or transformation?', *International Journal of Constitutional Law*, vol. 16, no. 3, p. 836, 7.

140 At 16.

expertise and flexibility by allocating responsibility for giving effect to values to political branches and by assigning a prominent role to legislation in particular.[141] Thus, it is important to read environmental constitutionalism as comprising not just rights (and their judicial enforcement) but also directive legislation within which constitutional legal norms are further found and enforced. The significance of and potential for environmental constitutionalism is revisited next in relation to arguments for a planetary integrity *grundnorm*.

d) Relevance of "Responsibility to Protect"

In exploring the question of whether states owe a duty to protect the environment in international law, the concept of "responsibility to protect" (R2P), notwithstanding its uncertain legal character,[142] has relevance for several reasons: (1) It normatively reformulates sovereignty as responsibility[143] (as opposed to rights),[144] and, consequently, its "evolution from a culture of impunity to a culture of national and international accountability"[145] and a "minimum content of good international citizenship";[146] (2) It confirms that sovereignty is conditional (rather than absolute); (3) It speaks to the possibility of duties to citizens beyond territorial borders; and (4) It provides that, where the responsible state defaults in its responsibility, "a residual, fallback responsibility also lies with the broader community of states".[147] In signing the UN Charter, Thakur writes, "[T]he state itself . . . accepts the responsibilities of membership flowing from that signature" and thus "to the international community through the UN".[148] The fact that R2P "was endorsed unanimously at the UN Summit of World Leaders as the central organising principle for responding to mass atrocity crimes"[149] was perhaps its less threatening appeal to a "re-characterisation of sovereignty",[150] rather than a dilution or transfer thereof vis-à-vis the UN. Sovereignty as control was thus re-framed as "responsibility in both internal functions and external duties".[151]

141 At 28.
142 Thakur, R 2016, 'The responsibility to protect', *International Affairs*, vol. 92, no. 2, p. 415, 421.
143 At 418.
144 Indeed, Article 2(A) of the R2P Core Principles state that one of the foundations thereof lie in 'obligations inherent in the concept of sovereignty'.
145 Report of the International Commission on Intervention and State Sovereignty (International Development Research Centre, December 2001) at [2.18].
146 At 7, para 1.35.
147 Thakur, n 2, at 330.
148 At 331.
149 Thakur, n 142, at 415.
150 Thakur, n 142, at 415.
151 'Report of the International Commission on Intervention and State Sovereignty', n 140, at 13, 2.14.

R2P thus realizes (at least in principle) Hugo Grotius's *fiduciary* conception of state sovereignty and the law of nations, which "was based on the assumption that the rules governing the organisation and behaviour of states exist ultimately for the benefit of the actual subjects of the rights and duties concerned, individual human beings",[152] meaning that "other states could use force to prevent a tyrannical ruler [from] mistreating his people".[153] Similarly, Vattel maintained that a sovereign's "right is derived from duty" and that when a sovereign does injury to any one of his subjects, he acts without real authority.[154]

Although R2P is limited to protection against genocide, war crimes, ethnic cleansing and crimes against humanity, the International Commission on Intervention and State Sovereignty report, in discussing the fundamental components of human security, cautions against the traditional, narrow perception of security – that is, national security. Rather, the report calls for a broader view that would encourage governments to "guard [their citizens] against the omnipresent enemies of good health . . . from chronic insecurities of . . . environmental hazard" and thereby secure citizens against threats to life, health, livelihood, personal safety and human dignity.[155] In this light, commentators have considered whether R2P should or could be extended to situations where environmental pressures (for example, resource shortages) and/or emergencies present human security concerns. Evans counsels against this, noting that its extension would become about "protecting everybody from everything and will end up protecting nobody from anything".[156] Such an outcome would undermine the "[w]hole point" of R2P, which was "to ensure new language [was] capable of generating effective, consensual response to extreme, conscious-shocking cases in a way that 'right to intervene' language simply cannot".[157] The application and effectiveness of the relatively new R2P framework are emergent at best and thus fragile. Whilst some states (particularly those in the Global South) remain suspicious of its possible abuse, it is understandable that its framers caution against extending it beyond its narrow parameters.

152 Stahn, C 2007, 'Responsibility to protect: political rhetoric or emerging legal norm?', *American Journal of International Law*, vol. 101, p. 99, 111 (citing Grotius, H 1609, *De Mare Liberum*, RD Magoffin (trans, 1916) ch. V, in Criddle, EJ 2014, 'A sacred trust of civilization', in AS Gold & PB Miller (eds), *Philosophical foundations of fiduciary law*, Oxford University Press, p. 404, 14.

153 Criddle, see n 152.

154 Criddle, see n 152.

155 "Report of the International Commission on Intervention and State Sovereignty", n 140, at [2.22].

156 Evans, G 2009, 'The responsibility to protect in environmental emergencies', *American Society of International Law*, vol. 103, p. 27, 29.

157 Evans, 'The responsibility to protect in environmental emergencies'.

That has not prevented the consideration of the possible framing of environmental problems as threats to territorial sovereignty within the discourse of ecological security, for "it does not require any great stretch of the imagination to classify an environmental emergency or imminent environmental disaster with international ramifications . . . [a]s a threat to peace and security".[158] As Litfin notes, "countries can also be 'invaded' by foreign pollutants or even by the depletion of a crucial resource".[159] Similarly, Eckersley has argued:

> Direct and major incursions of pollution or hazardous substances into the territory of neighbouring states are analogous to an "armed attack" with chemical, biological, or nuclear weapons; they enter or threaten to enter the territory of the victim state without its consent and with equally grave consequences.[160]

Seen in this light, Eckersley suggests, the right of states to use force in self- or "ecological" defence (including the use of pre-emptive measures when a serious threat or attack is imminent and likely to be overwhelming) may be understood as representing an appropriate response to a wrongful intervention in the territorial integrity or political independence of the defending state, pursuant to Article 51 of the UN Charter.[161] By interpreting "territorial integrity" as inclusive of ecological integrity and "political independence" as the political autonomy of states to determine their own levels of environmental quality without having them undermined by the wilful or reckless actions of another state, it is possible to "overcome the limitations in the current state remedies available under the customary law principle relating to transboundary environmental harm", which "has been interpreted not to permit unilateral pre-emptive measures or even injunctive relief . . . to head off serious environmental damage".[162] Eckersley sums up her case for ecological intervention this way:

> [I]f it is accepted that the right of sovereign states to control *people* should be subject to certain minimal moral strictures, then why should not the right of sovereign states to control their *territories* be likewise subject to minimal moral strictures?[163]

158 Eckersley, R 2007, 'Ecological intervention: prospects and limits', *Ethics & International Affairs*, vol. 21, no. 3, p. 293, 299.
159 Litfin, n 8, at 12.
160 Eckersley, n 158, at 299.
161 Eckersley, n 158, at 299.
162 At 300.
163 At 309. Emphasis added.

But there is, understandably, a general degree of "unease about the wisdom of securitising ecological problems in this way", which "may serve to legitimate militarisation of state responses to environmental threats".[164] Deudney distinguishes between military (humanitarian) threats and environmental threats, noting that the former are "usually discrete, specific, and deliberate involving a zero sum game and an 'us-and-them' mentality"[165] whilst "environmental threats are usually diffuse, transboundary, unintended, operate over longer time scales, and implicate a wide range of actors, and resolution usually carries common benefits".[166] They should thus be addressed via different processes and agents. To this end, "[M]any environmental scholars see very little advantage, and considerable dangers, in 'securitising; our understanding of ecological problems in order to elevate them to the status of 'high politics'".[167] There is, nevertheless, the possibility that

> [I]f the actions of a particular government threaten the environmental integrity of its own or other states, or impair the life-support capability of the earth, such actions, if found to be crimes perpetrated against the environment, may also be crimes against humanity.[168]

A question mark remains, however, around the prospects of introducing an international crime of ecocide, which would not be measured by reference to human well-being or, indeed, in terms of threats to international peace and security.[169] It is, in fact, perplexing that in international law, we have *erga omnes* obligations covering acts of aggression, genocide and basic human rights, yet no hard law obligation for humanity to protect the environment from degradation.[170] Considered in light of other *jus cogens* – mandatory, non-derogable international norms based on that which is so inherently

164 At 225.
165 Deudney, D 1999, 'Environmental security: a critique', in D Deudney & RA Matthew (eds), *Contested grounds: security and conflict in the new environmental polities*, State University of New York Press, Albany, cited in Eckersley, n 153, at 225.
166 Deudney, 'Environmental security'.
167 At 295.
168 Evans, n 156, at 420.
169 In June 2021, the Independent Expert Panel for the Legal Definition of Ecocide convened by the Stop Ecocide Foundation drafted a definition of ecocide with the intention that it be included in the Rome Statute to enable prosecution of the most egregious offences against the environment. Their draft law defines ecocide as "unlawful or wanton acts committed with knowledge that there is a substantial likelihood of severe and widespread or long-term damage to the environment being caused by those acts." See Stop Ecocide Foundation (June 2021), *Independent expert panel for the legal definition of ecocide, commentary and core text* (https://ecocidelaw.com/independent-expert-drafting-panel/).
170 Bosselmann, K 2015a, *Earth governance: trusteeship of the global commons*, Edward Elgar Publisher, Cheltenham, p. 153.

immoral – "surely destruction of the environment, the basis of all life and hence human existence, should be among them?"[171] Arguably, the environment is even *more* fundamental than human rights as it represents the natural conditions of all life including, human beings.[172] Stone has suggested that "certain acts can be denominated as 'ecocidal' acts and should be likened to genocide in the international community".[173] The challenge, according to Stone, is to make eco-laws as evocative as human rights. With increasing and widespread evidence of ecological collapse and the realization that humanity is facing a civilizational, and, indeed, *existential* crisis, this challenge is no longer insurmountable. Current trends towards global self-destruction are so obvious that the turnaround seems only logical[174] – indeed, imperative!

Nevertheless, for the most part, R2P's relevance to global environmental protection is best seen as normative evidence and (at the least, limited) acceptance of sovereignty as comprising both domestic and international responsibility. However, these responsibilities continue to be cast within the frame of nation-states and human security. The imperative to think beyond the construct of the state and to situate responsibilities within the Earth system as a whole instead is explored next.

Many human rights depend on a healthy environment for their full realization,[175] and there is evidence of an emerging duty to ensure a minimum standard of environmental quality in this regard, particularly in reliance on regional and constitutional human rights protections. Due to definitional uncertainty and judicial deference, the entrenchment of standalone or substantive environmental rights has struggled for justiciability and has thus done little to inform the nature and scope of a state duty to protect the environment. Its intermingling with (and dilution by) references to sustainable development further suggest that the enjoyment of a quality environment does not, in and of itself, have value (even if only measured) in human terms.

In any case, the adoption of a human rights–based approach to such a duty necessarily frames it in reductionist, anthropocentric terms; the environment is thereby simply the backdrop against which human life should be enjoyed and human objectives pursued, separate and "other". Determined on a case-by-case basis, the environmental rights (and attendant duty) approach will be too slow and jurisdictionally limited (and possibly inconsistent) to confront global ecological challenges in the urgent and cooperative spirit

171 At 167.

172 Bosselmann, n 136, at 173 (emphasis added).

173 Bosselmann, n 170, citing Stone, CD 1993, *The Gnat is older than man: global environment and human agenda*, Princeton University Press, Princeton, NJ, p. 38, 167.

174 Bosselmann, n 10, at 6.

175 See generally Raikas, TT 2020, 'The Amazon is on fire: states' responsibility to protect the Amazon environment from a human rights perspective', Master's thesis in International Law and Human Rights, Abo Akademi University.

and with the effort required. Some of these deficiencies may, however, be addressed through the emerging rights of nature and Earth systems discourse, which I consider next.

4. Widening the Frame of Human Rights

a) *Overcoming Anthropocentrism*

Constitutional protection vis-à-vis the environment has been framed predominantly by reference to human rights. However, drawing on the work of writers such as Leopold, Stone and Berry, in 2008, Ecuador became the first nation to provide explicit constitutional recognition of the rights of nature. Accordingly, Chapter 7 variously provides that Mother Nature "is entitled to full respect, existence, and the maintenance and regeneration of its vital cycles, structure, functions, and evolutionary processes" (Article 71); nature is entitled to restoration (Article 72); the state will apply precautionary and restrictive measures to activities that could lead to species extinction, destruction of ecosystems or the permanent alteration of natural cycles (Article 73); but also, people "are entitled to benefit from the environment and natural resources that allow them to live well", and the "production, delivery, use and development of" environmental services are regulated by the State (Article 74). Although Bolivia's constitution recognizes the importance of protecting nature, the "Laws of Mother Earth" are set out in two separate statutes: one that establishes the rights of Mother Earth and the other a framework for their operationalization.[176]

A parallel approach, spurred by indigenous communities, has been the process of attributing legal personhood to nature. In 2014, a deed of settlement granted legal personhood to New Zealand's Whanganui River, and the Te Urewera Act 2014 aims to "establish and preserve in perpetuity a legal identify and protected status for Te Urewera for its intrinsic worth, its distinctive natural and cultural values, the integrity of those values, and for its national importance". Legal personhood is also now enjoyed by other rivers, including the Atrato River in Colombia, the Klamath River in the United States and the Muteshekau Shipu (Magpie River) in Canada.[177]

These constitutional and legislative protections of the rights of nature best reflect an ecocentric ethic that recognizes nature's intrinsic value, "wholly

176 For a full summary of existing rights of nature law, see the United Nations, 'Harmony with nature', *Rights of Nature Law and Policy Webpage* (http://www.harmonywithnatureun.org).

177 Townsend, J, Bunten, A, Lorns, C & Borrows, L 2021, 'Rights for nature: how granting a river 'personhood' could help protect it', *The Conversation*, viewed 3 June 2021, (https://theconversation.com/rights-for-nature-how-granting-a-river-personhood-could-help-protect-it-157117).

independent of its instrumental value to humanity".[178] In reviewing the effectiveness of the rights of nature movement, Calzadilla and Kotzé conclude that it has

> significant potential (especially symbolically, but also otherwise) to frame political, legislative and academic debates on ways to confront the persistent anthropocentrism of law that legitimises and perpetuates the neoliberal development model the world over. Clearly, however, law also has its limitations and we need to remain realistic about its potential to achieve the desired type of behavioural transformation and to effectively counter deeply vested corporate-driven neo-liberal and political economic interests. It is further evident that it remains immensely difficult to implement rights of nature in practice and to balance them with development priorities, especially in a developing country context such as Bolivia where poverty is rife and ecologically destructive extractivism is often the easiest and most lucrative way to fill state coffers, regardless of what the constitution and the law say.[179]

Thus we can observe that the effect of an ecocentric ethic and the granting of rights to nature will take time to overturn, or at least constrain, the economic growth paradigm. To an extent, such rights force nature

> to compete against other rights holders (humans) in a contest of moral norms. And, devoid . . . a radical shift in ethics, we already know which rights holders have the acute advantage in a flawed legal arena.[180]

Nevertheless, indigenous laws and cultural relationships with nature, which "share an understanding that humans are an integral part of the natural world" and "emphasise respect for all beings and responsibilities to care for lands and waters"[181] can provide exemplars of how an ecocentric ethic can work in practice.

There is evidence that the wider UN system has also "accommodated, at least to some degree, innovative international discussion in this area [rights of nature], initiating a 'Harmony with Nature' intergovernmental

178 Calzadilla, PV & Kotzé, LJ 2018, 'Living in harmony with nature? A critical appraisal of the rights of mother Earth in Bolivia', *Transnational Environmental Law*, vol. 7, no. 3, p. 397.

179 Calzadilla & Kotzé, 'Living in harmony with nature?'

180 Bosselmann, n 170, at 120.

181 See Townsend and others, n 177. See also Geddert, JS 2021, 'Indigenous sovereignty and the (enlarged) responsibility to protect', *The American Review of Canadian Studies*, vol. 51, p. 251.

negotiating process and inaugurating International Mother Earth Day".[182] UN Resolution 63/278 noted that this had been done in recognition of the "interdependence that exists among human beings, other living species and the planet we all inhabit"[183] and the aim of the General Assembly "in adopting its nine resolutions on Harmony with Nature, has been to define [a] newly found relationship based on a non-anthropocentric relationship with Nature".[184]

The IUCN World Declaration on the Environmental Rule of Law has since described as "emerging substantive principles for promoting and achieving environmental justice" the obligation of each state, public or private entity and individual "to care for and promote the well-being of nature, regardless of its worth to humans, and to place limits on its use and exploitation"; the inherent right of Nature "to exist, thrive, and evolve"; the right of each human and other living being to the conservation, protection and restoration of the health and integrity of ecosystems; and the right of current and future generations to "a safe, clean, healthy, and sustainable environment".[185] Their realization, evidently, remains a work in progress!

b) Overcoming the "Othering" of Nature

As the rights of nature discourse evolves, we can (hopefully) expect a recalibration of "our understanding of who we are in regard to nature"[186] and that we "cannot harm nature without directly or indirectly harming ourselves".[187] But, undertaken on a river-by-river/nation-by-nation *ad hoc* basis, progress will be uneven and unequal to the need for a globally coordinated approach. And, paradoxically, insofar as rights of nature operate in parallel with, and as a counter to, human rights, might the effect be to continue an approach that separates humans from (and objectifies) nature? Is Vatter correct that a

> key obstacle to developing a more ecological conception of law is tension between the ecocentric belief in the interconnectedness of all life on earth and the prevalent tendency of human legal traditions to link rights and

182 Morrow, K 2014, 'Peoples' sustainability treaties at Rio+20: giving voice to the other', in M Maloney & P Burdon (eds), *Wild law: In practice*, Routledge Taylor and Francis Group, London, p. 47.

183 United Nations 2009, 'International Mother Earth Day', Resolution 63/278, at [1].

184 United Nations, 'Harmony with nature', Programme (http://www.harmonywithnatureun.org).

185 IUCN World Declaration on the Environmental Rule of Law (2016), Principles 1–3.

186 Townsend, n 137, at 38.

187 Townsend, n 137, at 38.

duties to conceptions of personhood that may be inapplicable to other living beings?[188]

Does the dehumanizing and extension of the legal personhood artifice to non-human life obscure, or indeed deny, its "inherent or intrinsic value"?[189]

Vatter argues that "[t]he real problem is that human systems and networks are constituted as self-protecting (autopoietic) constructions that seek to control the alterity found in their environment".[190] To counter this, Vatter proposes a "biopolitical discourse" to "give access to a non-immunitary source of law" which "is not reduced to a system or network that projects personification in order to cope with alterity, but is the reality of shared or common life that is presupposed by any and every immunitary prosthesis".[191] To realize this, he advocates a reconstructed form of trust, informed by the principle of solidarity, which "allows one to avoid the over-arching familial metaphor of some members of the association being the 'carers' for other members who are deemed to be lacking in one respect or another".[192] Vatter's trust is informed by a biopolitical recovery of Franciscan highest poverty,[193] whereby the community of life, subject to considerations of equity, can use but neither own nor consume the global commons: "[W]hat is to be used without being owned by the community of life on earth becomes, in such trusts, the property of trustees held for the present and future use of a third person which is a group personality of beings living on earth".[194]

Vatter's reference to group personality based on the community of life calls for a more holistic paradigm that extinguishes the human/nature dichotomy. An Earth systems paradigm, within which the "earth is an adaptive and multifaceted system comprising human-social and ecological elements"[195] could be the answer.

188 Vatter, M 2019, 'Nature's law or law's law? Community of life, legal personhood, and trusts?', in M de Leeuw & SV Wichlen (eds), *Personhood in the age of biolegality*, Palgrave Macmillan, Switzerland, p. 2. See also Laitos, J 2021, *Rethinking environmental law why environmental laws should conform to the laws of nature*, Edward Elgar Publishing, Cheltenham.
189 At 5.
190 At 6.
191 At 6.
192 At 12.
193 At 14.
194 At 17.
195 Kotzé, LJ & Kim, RE 2019, 'Earth system law: the juridical dimensions of Earth system governance', *Earth System Governance Journal*, vol. 1, p. 100003, 5.

c) *A Duty to Protect the Earth System?*

> So, is there a legal obligation of states to protect the global environment and integrity of the Earth's ecosystem after all? The short answer is no. The current system of international law does not require the sovereign state to protect the natural environment within or beyond national boundaries. It only expects states to consider – but not necessarily avoid – disastrous environmental consequences of their actions. There is huge discretion involved here, a degree of moral responsibility, but no legal obligations whatsoever.[196]

The Stockholm Conference in 1972 was the first time

> that environmental concerns became a prominent matter of international concern and a new responsibility of the United Nations . . . [giving] rise to a normative statement of global principles, a new UN organisation (UNEP), and program of action and an Environment Fund to facilitate implementation.[197]

Since then, hundreds of bilateral and multilateral environmental treaties have been concluded, including those dealing with genuinely global problems, like ozone depletion, climate change and the decline of global biodiversity.[198] There have also been resolutions, decisions in various international courts and tribunals (though there is no international environmental court) and soft law instruments such as declarations following environmental conferences, which together

> put into place goals for reducing environmental harm and establish specific practices toward the achievement of such goals and focus both on transboundary harm and domestic practices that cumulatively degrade global commons areas or the overall infrastructure that supports life on earth.[199]

In addition, "[T]he international acceptance of principles such as the precautionary principle and [that] of common but differentiated responsibilities gives expression to stronger moral norms of environmental protection and environmental justice".[200]

196 Bosselmann, K 2021, 'Environmental trusteeship and state sovereignty: can they be reconciled?', in E. Webster & L. Mai (eds), *Transnational environmental law in the anthropocene: reflections on the role of law in times of planetary change*, Routledge, New York, p. 4.
197 Eckersley, n 32, at 212.
198 At 213.
199 Wapner, n 48, at 282.
200 Eckersley, n 32, at 229.

Authors seem divided on the extent to which the international environmental regulation operates to constrain the behaviour of states in pursuit of agreed environmental goals.[201] International environmental law is perhaps best described as "still an exercise in persuasion rather than concrete limitation".[202] In any case, there is little argument that its effectiveness has been insufficient to reverse the global ecological crisis.

As Kotzé notes, "[T]he success of global environmental law and governance effort seems to be disproportionately small when compared to its growth".[203] There are various reasons for this, one of which is that there is no obligation on a state to agree to be bound by the terms of international agreements; state sovereignty ensures that this is a voluntary right of consent. Efforts to ensure widespread uptake of treaty obligations ensures that nations will "almost inevitably reach consensus on only the lowest common denominator standards",[204] terms are vague and difficult to implement, do not create justiciable rights and, in the absence of robust monitoring and enforcement mechanisms or a dedicated judicial body, compliance is uneven at best.

But what Gumplova describes as "the most salient failure of the international regime of international [environmental] protection"[205] is that

> [T]here is no legally and politically relevant conception of global or ecological system(s) overlying and complementing the deeply embedded division of the Earth into sovereign territories. Not only has international environmental law failed to provide a systematic and elaborate descriptive and prescriptive conception of vital planetary ecosystems (here, the ozone layer, climate system, ocean ecosystem, and tropical rainforests would

201 See here Gumplova, n 20, at 108. See also Schofer, E & Hironaka, A 2005, 'The effects of world society on environmental protection outcomes', *Social Forces*, vol. 84, no. 1, p. 25, who observe evidence of more diffuse influences within the field of global environmentalism. Whilst the authors accept that, for example, "environmental impact assessment laws are often quite ineffectual by themselves. . . . They create procedural opportunities for pro-environmental groups to intervene via the court system. Likewise, treaties, laws and other formal commitments increase the leverage of social movement groups and international environmental organisations that can point out embarrassing failures and hypocrisies. This may lead to tighter coupling of policies and predictability of outcomes over time" (at 27). Similarly, they contend that "[a]ccompanying organizational expansion, the ideas and cultural understandings of the global environment have become increasingly dominant and elaborated. Environmental protection has become a taken-for-granted and highly legitimated discourse. Scientifically-legitimated environmental ideals have profound impacts in some cases literally reshaping economic value and/or shifting collective goals away from pure economic expansion and toward greater environmental protection" (at 29).

202 Bosselmann, n 170, at 73.

203 Kotzé, n 116, at 201.

204 Tarlock, AD 1992, 'The role of non-governmental organizations in the development of international environmental law', *Chicago-Kent Law Review*, vol. 68, no. 1, p. 23.

205 Gumplova, n 20, at 109.

> be the most obvious examples); it has not . . . adopted any consistent framework or jurisdiction for domains that are outside of state boundaries (the atmosphere, polar regions, high seas). The common heritage of humankind regime . . . remains a regime of resource use and exploitation with relatively vague implications. An alternative approach, for example that of "ecological stewardship" (Chapin et al., 2009), which might better respond to the idea of responsible and sustainable use and conservation of the environment, has not yet made it into philosophical and legal debates.

Contrary to the latter contention, it should be noted that references to Earth stewardship and care for the integrity of ecological systems can be found in many passages of the 1987 Brundtland Report, the 1992 Rio Declaration, and no fewer than 25 international agreements, from the 1982 World Charter for Nature right through to the 2015 Paris Climate Agreement.[206] Indeed, the repeated and consistent references to ecological integrity amount to an emerging fundamental goal or *grundnorm* of international environmental law.[207]

Whilst it can be argued that ecological stewardship and trusteeship approaches have more currency in philosophical and legal debates than Gumplova suggests, the contention that both the state sovereignty frame and global governance regime around which it is based neglect an Earth system approach *in practice* is unquestionably correct. Treaties and agreements have addressed global environmental concerns on a reactive, sectoral basis, which has failed to recognize the "functional interdependency of all Earth system elements",[208] resulting in what can described as "the tragedy of ecological fragmentation".[209] This has resulted in problem shifting[210] and the pursuit of incremental – and insufficient – change[211] disconnected from the magnitude

206 Bosselmann, K 2017, 'The next step: earth trusteeship', presentation at the seventh interactive dialogue of the general assembly on harmony with nature, UN Headquarters, New York, 21 April, p. 2.

207 Bosselmann, n 170, at 250.

208 Kotzé & Kim, n 195, at 5. Interestingly, Kim and Mackey note that the evolution of international environmental law, including the treaty system, does exhibit increasing adaptive capacity but lacks "a single, legally binding superior norm, a clearly agreed common goal to which each of the MEAs must contribute to – for example to maintain global ecological integrity as defined by the nine planetary boundaries". See Kim, RE & Mackey, B 2013, 'International environmental law as a complex adaptative system', *International Environmental Agreements: Politics, Law and Economics*, vol. 14, no. 1, p. 5, 17.

209 Bosselmann, n 196, at 108.

210 See here Kim, RE & Bosselmann, K 2015, 'Operationalising sustainable development: ecological integrity as a *Grundnorm* in international law', *Review of European, Comparative and International Environmental Law*, vol. 24, no. 2, p. 194, 298. The authors discuss MEA's "neglect for cross-sectoral interactions" which "comes with a high risk of transfer of harm or hazards from one area or medium to another".

211 Kotzé & Kim, n 195, at 4.

of the Anthropocene's regulatory challenges.[212] Kotzé describes this result as "an 'Anthropocene gap', which signifies the inability of social regulatory human systems and their scientific domains to contend with and respond to a complex Earth system".[213]

Further, in the absence of ambitiously binding norms and the prevalence of anthropocentric concerns, "the function of environmental law has been to promote a short-termist, utilitarian, and neoliberal growth agenda by protecting environmental resources for the socio-economic (and therefore unsustainable) development of some privileged humans of the present generation".[214] International environmental law's segmented regulatory model has served to externalize the environment as something that can be "managed" by "ingenuous human masters",[215] perpetuating the "crisis of human hierarchy"[216] whilst ignoring the interdependencies and complexities that characterize the Earth system.[217]

Earth system law seeks to overcome these deficiencies. Firstly, Earth system law shifts the focus of regulation to the planetary scale "to more fully accommodate and respond to complex and dynamic Earth system processes, irreversible impacts of interacting stresses, multiple scales of organisation, and the various actors and their agendas that influence Earth system change".[218] If the Earth is viewed as a single adaptive ecological system, "environmental effects cannot be confined to the states in which they occur, but inevitably have impacts on the globally integrated Earth system and the global commons".[219] Secondly, recognition of this waterbed effect requires regulatory "coherence across different and often sectoral institutions at all levels of

212 Kotzé & Kim, n 195, at 4.

213 At 6.

214 Adelman, S 2018, 'The sustainable development goals, anthropocentrism and neoliberalism', in D French & LJ Kotzé (eds), *Sustainable development global goals: law, theory and implementation*, Edward Elgar, Cheltenham, cited in Kotzé & Kim, n 195, at 5.

215 Kotzé, LJ 2019, 'The anthropocene, Earth system vulnerability and social-ecological injustice in an age of human-rights', *Journal of Human Rights and the Environment*, vol. 10, no. 1, pp. 62–85, 76. Kim and Mackey further note that traditional top-down command-and-control approaches are of limited effectiveness as ecosystem responses to human impacts are non-linear, uncertain and unpredictable. Adaptive governance that better aligns with the complex dynamics of the Earth's ecological systems is necessary. See Kim and Mackey, n 208, at 6.

216 Kotzé, see n 215, at 64.

217 At 84.

218 Biermann, F, Betsill, MM, Gupta, J, Kanie, N, Lebel, L, Liverman, D, Schroeder, H, Siebenhüner, B & Zondervan, R 2010, 'Earth system governance: a research framework', *International Environmental Agreements: Politics, Law and Economics*, vol. 10, pp. 277–298, cited in Kim, RE & Kotzé, LJ 2021, 'Planetary boundaries at the intersection of the Earth system law, science and governance: a state-of-the-art review', *Review of European, Comparative and International Environmental Law*, vol. 30, no. 1, p. 3, 6.

219 Bosselmann, n 10, at 5.

governance".[220] A single, legally binding, superior planetary integrity norm could help provide "all international regimes and organisations a shared purpose to which their specific objectives must collectively contribute".[221] This norm would recognize that "humans have become dominant geological agents that must be restrained by setting limits that would keep us within a safe operating space",[222] but also that humans are part of, dependent on and entirely vulnerable to ecological integrity, and the ultimate goal must be to enable "desirable futures for *all* Earth system components and processes, including human and more-than-human entities".[223]

d) *From Rights to Responsibilities*

In exploring whether there is a duty under international law to protect the global environment, some common impediments emerge: Neoliberal interpretations of state sovereignty favour development rights in pursuit of economic growth above (and at the expense of) environmental protection; the focus is predominantly on "rights" over "responsibilities", both in respect of the exercise of state sovereignty and individual freedoms; the pursuit of human rights has assumed that their exercise should be unrestrained and has served to frame the environment as incidental to (though increasingly critical to and evidently inseparable from) their full realization, and where environmental protection has been attempted, its sectoral approach has ignored the wider planetary context within which it should be situated.

The disaggregated framework of sovereign states and its current approach to protecting the global environment are difficult to reconcile with the "Earth's wholeness and complexity".[224] How, then, might the role and legitimacy of the sovereign state be reframed in pursuit of planetary integrity and an Earth systems imperative? Is an Earth trusteeship model the answer? And how can the prevailing anthropocentric, neoliberal paradigm be unravelled and rights be recharged as responsibilities? This calls for a radical counter-narrative underpinned by a universal, planetary integrity supra-norm, which will be explored in Part III.

220 Kim & Kotzé, n 195, at 9.
221 At 10.
222 At 12.
223 At 12.
224 Bosselmann, K 2016, 'Shifting the legal paradigm: earth-centred law and governance', in P Magalhaes & W Steffen (eds), *The safe operating space treaty: a new approach to managing our use of the earth system*, Cambridge Scholars, Cambridge, p. 65.

Part III

Incorporating Earth Trusteeship

Chapter 8

Sovereignty and Trusteeship

1. Introduction

The purpose of this chapter is to explore various aspects trusteeship relationships between states and citizens. One focus is on Benvenisti's theory of a state as a trustee of humanity (which includes persons inside and outside a state's borders). In this regard, Benvenisti's trusteeship theory (at 3) is closely linked to the Responsibility to Protect (at 5) in which the principle of "sovereignty as responsibility" emerges at the forefront. This chapter will also discuss the public trust doctrine (at 4), in which the state is perceived as the trustee for common natural resources. There are some limitations to the public trust doctrine as its scope differs from jurisdiction to jurisdiction. What is therefore required is a more uniform approach to global governance, such as the state acting as a trustee for the environment or even the prospect of Earth trusteeship. (Due to matters pertaining to time and resources, the two latter aspects are not fully discussed in this section.) In conclusion, the chapter highlights the importance of trusteeship and the shift in the "sovereignty tide". States now have to accept sovereignty sooner or later as a responsibility to the environment and the planet.

2. Fiduciary Duties of the State

Few governments could argue that they do not owe a fiduciary duty to their constituents.[1] Yet the fiduciary conception of state authority can be traced back to the writings of Plato and Aristotle, who each referred to public officials as "guardians" charged with promoting the public good.[2] Today, the preliminary question as to whether or not the state can be considered a

1 Bosselmann, K 2019a, 'The atmosphere as a global commons', in J Jaria-Monzano & S Borrás (eds), *Research handbook on global climate constitutionalism*, Edward Elgar Publishing Ltd, Gloucestershire, p. 75, 84.

2 Criddle, EJ & Fox-Decent, E 2009, 'A fiduciary theory of Jus Cogens', *Yale Journal of International Law*, vol. 34, p. 331, 13.

DOI: 10.4324/9781032674049-12

fiduciary is still subject to a widespread discussion by contemporary legal theorists and political scholars. Before probing further into this debate and to put matters into some perspective, it is worthwhile to first describe the contours of a fiduciary. A fiduciary refers to someone who has undertaken to act for or on behalf of another in a particular matter in circumstances which give rise to a relationship of trust and confidence.[3] The key phrase of "trust and confidence" was duly captured in the words of Millett J in the English case of *Bristol v Mothew*, in which the learned judge said, "[T]he distinguishing obligation of a fiduciary is the obligation of loyalty".[4] Fiduciary duties have therefore been applied to solicitor-client, trustee-beneficiary, director-company and even parent-child relationships.[5] Therefore, the first step in determining whether the fiduciary analogy captures a state-citizen relationship is to ask, "Does a state act on behalf of its citizens?" The simple answer to this is yes. On a general level, we accept that political leaders – whether they be heads of state, presidents, prime ministers or foreign emissaries accredited to the United Nations – all represent the face of the nation and their citizens. This is the core idea of a modern, democratic state: namely, that it acts through the people, by the people and for the people.[6] This idea is consistent with, for example, the Virginia Declaration of Rights (1776), which stated that "all power is vested in, and consequently derived from, the people; that magistrates are their trustees and servants and at all times amenable to them".[7] This must be juxtaposed with James Madison's note in the Federalist Papers: "The federal and State governments are in fact but different agents and trustees of the people . . . [because] the ultimate authority . . . resides in the people alone".[8] Locke also added to this debate by saying that legislative power is "only a fiduciary power to act for certain ends" and that "there remains still in the people a supreme power to remove or alter the legislative, when they find the legislative act contrary to the trust reposed in them".[9] This idea of "popular sovereignty" has found its way into international law. Article 21(3) of the Universal Declaration of Human Rights states: "[T]he will of the people shall be the basis of the authority of

3 *Bristol v Mothew* [1996] 4 All ER 698 at 711.
4 At 711–712.
5 Lui, H 2014, 'A fiduciary perspective on the state's duty to protect the environment', *Auckland University Law Review*, vol. 20, p. 101, 106.
6 Bosselmann, K 2015a, *Earth governance: trusteeship of the global commons*, Edward Elgar Publisher, Cheltenham, p. 82.
7 The Virginia Declaration of Rights 1776 (United States), s 2. See also Benvenisti, E 2015, 'The paradoxes of sovereigns as trustees of humanity: concluding remarks', *Theoretical Inquiries in Law*, vol. 16, no. 2, p. 535, 545.
8 Benvenisti, E 2013, 'Sovereigns as trustees of humanity: on the accountability of states to foreign stakeholders', *American Journal of International Law*, vol. 107, p. 295, 305.
9 Bosselmann, n 6, at 82.

government".[10] This concept of popular sovereignty – that is, the state being created by and subject to the will of the people – is derived from a nascent theory which specifies that the government holds in trust sovereignty, which inheres in the people.[11] The 17th century writings of Richard Overton and William Walwyn, two parliamentary pamphleteers, also address this trusteeship model between the state and the people. As the pamphleteers recorded:[12]

> We (the people) are your principals, and you (the Parliament) our agents . . . if you or any other should assume or exercise any power that is not derived from our trust and choice thereunto, that power is no less than usurpation and an oppression.

Based on this agency relationship, a fiduciary power should not be abused, and, as a result, *ultra vires* actions on the part of a state cannot bind the principals.[13]

This brings us to the second step. Assuming that a "trust/confidence" relationship does exist, why do citizens place all their trust in governments? The answer to this question has its roots in the social contract theory of consent. In order for society to function peacefully, citizens enter into a social contract, thereby transferring their autonomy and prerogatives to the state.[14] By so doing, citizens accept state power as legitimate because the state is seen as an entity that will protect their interests.[15] This is in line with a state's fiduciary duty, which is to act in the best interests of all citizens within its sphere of influence.[16] The next question which arises is what are the citizens' "best interests"?

The American revolutionaries swore that "the Creator" endowed all individuals with certain rights that could not be taken away, including "life, liberty and the pursuit of happiness".[17] These rights were inalienable and perceived to be fundamental interests of the people and the priority of any legitimate government.[18] In other words, these rights served the "best interests" of the citizen and were guaranteed by the state to be protected. In acknowledgment of this, historian Yuval Harari argues that the legitimacy

10 *Universal Declaration of Human Rights* GA Res 217A (1948), art 21(3).
11 Purdy, J & Fielding, K 2007, 'Sovereigns, trustees, guardians: private-law concepts and the limits of legitimate state power', *Law and Contemporary Problems*, vol. 70, p. 165, 173.
12 At 173.
13 Lui, n 5, at 109. See also Purdy & Fielding, n 11, at 165.
14 At 102.
15 At 108.
16 At 109.
17 Kuhner, TK 2020, *Trump, corruption and the revolution to come*, Stanford University Press, Stanford, 59.
18 Kuhner, *Trump, corruption and the revolution to come.*

of the modern state is based on its promise to keep the public sphere free of political violence.[19] According to this argument, over the last few centuries states (especially Western states) have gradually established their legitimacy on the explicit promise to tolerate no political violence within their borders.[20] This, in effect, means that citizens place their trust in the state to keep them safe (e.g. from terrorism), and, in exchange for this, the state is under a duty to be loyal to its promise. This scenario actually presents itself as being a win-win situation because no citizen wishes to live in fear, and no state desires its citizens to feel as if the social order is about to collapse.[21] The role of government is also seen as a "conscientious trustee of the citizens' resources".[22] Following this line of reasoning, in theory, the government ought to be a trustee of all our common assets: namely, all creations of nature that we inherit jointly and freely.[23]

Another point of view is that the state's legitimacy to govern is based on its ability to serve the common interest – or what Aristotle may have perhaps referred to as the "common good".[24] Vattel picked up where Aristotle left off when he stated that "sovereign authority" is "established only for the common good of all citizens".[25] It is the collective understanding of the common good which must trump the state's understanding and its widely held views on a particular matter.[26] But what exactly is the common good, and what does it include?[27] Locke's definition of the "common good" was what arose from there being surplus produce that could be sold in the marketplace.[28] This definition was observed as being a quantifiable one (as opposed to a moral construct), which nowadays would reflect the Gross Domestic Product – a poor measure of any society's real quality of life.[29] The Lockean definition of "common good" may not be free from complications as its focus is on economic indicators, and there are many other enabling factors to consider, such as Gross National Happiness (GNH), as adopted by Bhutan. Some of the indices being represented in the GNH include their citizens' psychological well-being, health, education and the country's ecological diversity

19 Noah Harari, Y 2019, *21 Lessons for the 21st century*, Vintage, London, p. 193.
20 Noah Harari, *21 Lessons for the 21st century*.
21 At 195.
22 Bosselmann, n 6, at 83.
23 Barnes, P, Rowe, J & Bollier, D 2004, *The state of the commons 2003/04: a report to owners*, Tomales Bay Institute, p. 3, 29.
24 Bosselmann, n 6, at 83.
25 Criddle & Fox-Decent, n 2, at 1.
26 Dyzenhaus, D 2015, 'Kelsen, Heller and Schmitt: paradigms of sovereignty thought', *Theoretical Inquiries in Law*, vol. 16, no. 2, p. 337, 364.
27 Bosselmann, n 6, at 83.
28 Bosselmann, n 6, at 83.
29 Bosselmann, n 6, at 83.

and resilience.[30] Some scholars have even extended the argument to claim that states have ecological aspects to their fiduciary duty – an aspect which is often neglected for wrong reasons.[31] That being said, and at the very least, the legitimacy of the state rests on its ability to care for the well-being of its citizens.[32] It is the "well-being" of the citizens, also construed as their "best interests", which is considered the priority of all states.

In the real world, where there are many varying and competing interests, every single decision of the state may not always be in the best interest of each citizen. Citizens, even after voting, will accept that their elected representatives might sometimes make decisions which they do not agree with.[33] This is because citizens, while they choose who they elect, do not have actual control over the state's exercise of power.[34] This is the reason scholars (such as Lui) critique the consent theory: the relationship between the state and the citizen is not always consensual.[35] Since citizens have surrendered many of their legal and political rights to the state, all they can hope for is that the government will exercise its powers in their best interests.[36] So if states are not 100% guaranteed to act in our best interests, then why do we continually place our trust in them? Heller, a German legal scholar, attempted to justify this question when he found that the state is the organization equipped to make final and effective decisions on any matter that requires a resolution for the maintenance of social cooperation between all inhabitants of the territory.[37]

Kant's theory of the Doctrine of Right has also been applied by certain scholars to justify the application of fiduciary duties.[38] Here, Kant focuses on two types of rights – acquired rights and innate rights.[39] Under the first form of rights, the rights-holder (in our scenario, the citizen) agrees to acquire a set of rights while the other party (the state) acquires corresponding duties.[40] For Kant, these duties are said to be acquired because the rights-holder has the moral capacity to delegate decision-making powers to someone entrusted

30 A Compass Towards a Just and Harmonious Society – 2015 GNH Survey Report (Centre for Bhutan Studies, 5 July 2016), 212, (www.grossnationalhappiness.com), pp. 5–6.
31 Bosselmann, n 6, at 84.
32 At 80–81.
33 Lui, n 5, at 108.
34 At 107.
35 At 107.
36 At 107.
37 Dyzenhaus, n 26, at 349.
38 These scholars include Evan Fox-Decent and Himmy Lui. See Lui, n 5, at 106.
39 Kant, I 1996 [1797], *The metaphysics of morals*, MJ Gregor (ed), Cambridge University Press, Cambridge, pp. 29–30 as cited in Lui, n 5, at 106.
40 Kant, *The metaphysics of morals*. See also Denis, L (ed) 2010, *Kant's metaphysics of morals: a critical guide*, Cambridge Text in the History of Philosophie, Cambridge University Press, Cambridge, pp. 79–80.

to care for his or her interests.[41] This must be compared to an innate right which "belongs to everyone by nature, independently of any act that would establish a right".[42] According to Kant every person has only one innate right – namely, freedom – or, to put it into context, the right to as much freedom as can coexist with everyone else's freedom.[43] Kant adduces four rights which fall under the category of the innate right and which are implicit in our modern day understanding of human rights.[44] One of these rights permits a person to act in any manner towards others so long as that person does not curtail their rights.[45] Applying this principle, a person who was granted power (e.g. a state) to wield over another cannot use that power for his or her own benefit, as that would involve exercising a freedom which is inconsistent with a beneficiary's (e.g. citizen's) freedom.[46] In other words, under fiduciary theory, a state cannot use its conferred powers to adopt laws which would deny beneficiaries of their equal rights and freedoms.[47] So for example, states cannot support slavery or arbitrary discrimination without forfeiting their claim to exercise sovereignty on behalf of the people under their authority.[48] As Criddle and Fox-Decent acknowledge, when states fail to accord their subjects equal freedom under the law, they contravene the basic fiduciary principle that furnishes the theoretical framework for state sovereignty.[49] The theory, which Criddle and Fox-Decent defend, is that the state and its institutions are fiduciaries of the people subject to state power, and therefore, a state's claim to sovereignty, properly understood, relies on its fulfilment of a multifaceted and overarching fiduciary obligation to respect the agency and dignity of the people subject to state power.[50] To summarize, the fiduciary theory of a state places limits on state sovereignty, thereby thwarting any conception of its absolute quality.

The next issue to discuss is that of vulnerability. Criddle and Fox-Decent argue that the state-citizen relationship is distinctively fiduciary because it shares constitutive features common to all fiduciary relationships: namely, trust, discretionary power and vulnerability.[51] These three general characteristics outlined would have originated from the dictum of Wilson J in his

41 Kant, n 39, at 47.
42 At 30.
43 Lui, n 5, at 106.
44 Denis, see n 40, at 87.
45 At 89.
46 Lui, n 5, at 106–107.
47 Criddle and Fox-Decent, see n 2, at 369. Also see Purdy and Fielding, n 11, at 174. The authors wrote: "[N]o state can receive the power to act against its people's interests and freedoms".
48 Criddle and Fox-Decent, n 2, at 369.
49 Criddle and Fox-Decent, n 2, at 369.
50 At 347.
51 At 4.

judgment (dissenting) in the Canadian Supreme Court case of *Frame v Smith*.[52] This section has already described the "trust/confidence" feature when citizens entrust their rights to elected members of the government, expecting that such members will, in return, use their powers in the citizens' best interests.[53] A fiduciary duty therefore exists by virtue of the state's immense discretionary power to affect citizens' interests (for better or for worse).[54] The beneficiaries (citizens) then become particularly vulnerable because they are now at the mercy of the fiduciary (state) holding the discretionary power.[55] A fiduciary duty requires those with power over more vulnerable parties not to abuse that power.[56] Therefore, when a state breaches its fiduciary duty, its legitimacy is eroded.[57] For Lui, it is this "power imbalance" between the state and the citizen, built on mutual trust and understanding, which creates a fiduciary relationship.[58]

3. State as a Trustee of Humanity

In the preceding section, we sought to define a fiduciary and to justify why the fiduciary analogy can be extended to a state-citizen relationship. In that section, emphasis was placed on the domestic dimension, in which citizens are within the sphere of the state's control. This section now seeks to test whether an understanding of "sovereignty" entails responsibilities and obligations of states not only to their own citizens but also to others who are directly or indirectly influenced by their acts and omissions.[59] Since the fiduciary theory is posited on the premise that a state must protect its citizens' interests, the default position has been that sovereigns are unlikely to commit voluntarily to taking strangers' concerns and global welfare seriously into account.[60] The issue as to whether the concept of sovereignty can be reconciled with obligations to others and the reasons for such reconciliation have been carefully studied by Eyal Benvenisti, a leading scholar on this topic.[61]

Benvenisti champions the idea of sovereignty as a trusteeship for humanity and that the principal-agent model should be viewed as extending beyond the state.[62] As "agents of humanity", sovereigns are obligated to take

52 *Frame v Smith* [1987] 2 SCR 99 at 60].
53 Lui, n 5, at 107.
54 At 108.
55 *Frame v Smith*, n 52, at [60].
56 Lui, n 5, at 109.
57 At 108.
58 At 105.
59 Benvenisti, n 7, at 536.
60 Benvenisti, n 8, at 296.
61 Benvenesti, n 7, at 536.
62 Dyzenhaus, n 26, at 337 and 359. See also Benvenisti, n 8, at 306.

other-regarding considerations seriously into account, even in the absence of specific treaty obligations.[63] For Benvenisti, sovereignty as a concept ought not to be condemned but rather celebrated so long as it incorporates responsibility towards the rest of humanity.[64] Benvenisti admits that the reinterpretation of sovereignty in a manner which requires states to assume certain underlying obligations towards strangers beyond national boundaries is utopian.[65] He goes further, however, by admitting that such a reconceptualization of sovereignty is morally required.[66] Benvenisti presents three theoretical approaches[67] supporting the interpretation of contemporary sovereignty as a trusteeship that entails other-regarding obligations.[68] These approaches are all interrelated because they examine sovereignty along the broad spectrum of a global order which serves not only as a source of power and rights but also as a source of obligations.[69] These obligations require the sovereign to exercise its authority in ways that take into account the right of all individuals to equality and democracy and, while so doing, to bear in mind the promotion of the global welfare.[70]

Benvenisti bases his theory on John Stuart Mill's implicit recognition of the equal moral worth of all human beings and the fact that, under international law, the entire system of state sovereignty is subject to the duty to respect human rights.[71] The latter point is clearly demonstrated after considering the mandate of the Office of the High Commissioner for Human Rights (OHCHR) and the UN Human Rights Council (HRC), which provides that all states have an obligation to promote and protect all human rights.[72] To paraphrase Max Huber, as the global legal order has its foundation in human rights, sovereigns should therefore be viewed as organs and even trustees of this global system.[73] As trustees, states are collectively required to protect everyone's human rights.[74] Consequently, there is a long line of scholarship which perceives the state as "a unit at the service of the human beings for

63 Benvenisti, n 8, at 300.
64 At 301.
65 At 297. See also Dyzenhaus, n 26, at 338–339.
66 Benvenisti, n 8, at 297.
67 These three theoretical approaches presented by Benvenisti are (1) sovereignty as the vehicle for the exercise of self-determination, (2) justification of government authority as an agent of human society and (3) justification of exclusive ownership over portions of the Earth.
68 Benvenisti, n 8, at 301.
69 Benvenisti, n 8, at 301.
70 Benvenisti, n 8, at 301.
71 At 307.
72 *High Commissioner for the Promotion and Protection of all Human Rights* A/RES/48/141 (1994), preamble. See also Human Rights Council GA Res 60/251 (2006), preamble.
73 Benvenisti, n 8, at 308.
74 At 307.

whom it is responsible", "a social function of the global community of peoples" and even "a branch of humanity".[75] As Benvenisti asserts:[76]

> [T]he wide recognition of the equal moral worth of all human beings, require the recognition of a fundamental legal obligation upon sovereigns to note the interests of others when making policy choices that directly affect them.

Benvenisti carefully takes stock of the fact that the policies of one government may affect foreign stakeholders residing in near or even faraway states on a regular basis.[77] Perhaps one example in support of his assertion is a carbon-intensive greenhouse gas policy of an industrialized country that has inimical transnational effects on small island developing states (SIDS). Following Benvenisti's reasoning, foreign citizens who are negatively affected by such a policy are unable to meaningfully participate, by a vote or otherwise, on matters that have a direct impact on them.[78]

One type of other-regarding obligation that Benvenisti considers is the treatment of individuals who seek refuge in foreign countries.[79] Benvenisti reasons that each sovereign must assume more robust positive obligations towards outsiders who can benefit from its exercise of power – for example, foreigners who are subject to persecution by their own governments.[80] Such an obligation is evident today with the current political stalemate in Afghanistan, where calls have been made for the United States to rescue fleeing Afghans.[81] On the point of refugees (which will be explored in further detail in the next section), Benvenisti explores the work of Criddle, who, in turn, focuses on the writings of Grotius. Grotius proposed that states intervene as temporary legal "guardians" of foreign nationals abroad who have suffered intolerable cruelties at the hands of their own state.[82] Post-Grotius, Vattel was credited with saying: "[N]o nation can, without good reasons, refuse even a perpetual residence to a man driven from his country".[83] Kant interprets this obligation as a right of hospitality: that is, the right of a stranger not to be treated in a hostile manner by another upon his arrival on the

75 At 308.
76 At 317.
77 At 298 and 304.
78 At 304.
79 At 326.
80 At 311.
81 'Biden defiant as chaotic scenes unfold at airport', *The New Zealand Herald* (Auckland, 18 August 2021), pp. 17–19.
82 Criddle, EJ, 'Three Grotian theories of humanitarian intervention' as cited in Benvenisti, E 2015, 'The paradoxes of sovereigns as trustees of humanity: concluding remarks', *Theoretical Inquiries in Law*, vol. 16, p. 537.
83 Benvenisti, n 8, at 307.

other's territory.[84] Kant bases his claim on the size, shape and surface of the planet where "all human beings have a claim", and "no one has more of a right to be at a given place on earth than anyone else".[85]

The tenor of Benvenisti's argument is that it is morally required that we reconceive sovereignty where states are understood to have obligations to strangers beyond their borders.[86] Anne Peters's writings may lend some support to Benvenisti's argument when she expressed that "sovereignty is normatively derived from humanity", and, as a result, "humanity is the A and Ω of sovereignty".[87] If we accept this argument, then we simultaneously have to accept the hypothesis that the state-subject fiduciary relation is not limited to the state's interactions with its own nationals but also includes foreign citizens.[88]

a) Ensuring Minimum Obligations

Benvenisti's proposition leads to further inquiries. The first inquiry or threshold question by Benvenisti is whether the concept of sovereignty can be reconciled with obligations to others.[89] Benvenisti's response to this question hinges on set examples in international legal practice of sovereign states being made answerable to obligations to others, including non-nationals, outside their borders.[90] As previously mentioned, one rigorous other-regarding obligation identified by Benvenisti is the treatment of refugees.[91] States have assumed some obligations concerning refugees and are also obliged under human rights treaties[92] to protect foreigners who may be subject to maltreatment by foreign governments.[93] On this point, Benvenisti argues that despite the lack of facilities and resources at a global level, there should be certain limitations on the sovereign's right to exclude.[94] One such limitation would be an obligation not to deny entry to migrants and refugees without taking into account the asylum seekers' individual concerns and without at least providing justification for their exclusion.[95]

84 Kant, I 2006, *Toward perpetual peace and other writings on politics, peace and history*, P Kleingeld (ed), Yale University Press, New Haven, p. 82.
85 Kant 2006, *Toward perpetual peace and other writings on politics, peace and history.*
86 Dyzenhaus, n 26, at 338.
87 Peters, A 2009, 'Humanity as the A and Ω of sovereignty', *European Journal of International Law*, vol. 20, no. 3, p. 513, 514, 531.
88 Criddle & Fox-Decent, n 2, at 370.
89 Benvenisti, n 7, at 536. See also Dyzenhaus, n 26, at 339.
90 Dyzenhaus, n 26, at 339.
91 Benvenisti, n 7, at 326.
92 United Nations Convention Relating to the Status of Refugees, Treaty Series Vol. 189, 137 (opened for signature 28 July 1951, entered into force 22 April 1954), art 3 and art 4.
93 Benvenisti, n 7, at 326.
94 At 311.
95 At 311.

Another question which can be raised is whether a state as a trustee of humanity can also take environmental or planetary concerns into account. In other words, to what extent does a state, as a trustee of humanity, have responsibilities to "others": for example, climate refugees, affected by existential threats caused by the environment or climate change? An answer to this question remains unclear. According to Benvenisti, the extension of the right to refuge to individuals who have lost their homes and livelihoods as a result of severe climatic changes is still a widely debated issue.[96]

Benvenisti remains very clear in his position that the wide recognition of the equal moral worth of all human beings requires the recognition of a fundamental legal obligation upon sovereigns to note the interests of others when making policy choices that directly affect them.[97] But does taking the interests of strangers into account necessarily mean that sovereigns have an obligation to sacrifice the interests of their own citizens? To this question, Benvenisti agrees with the proverb "Charity begins at home" and that the state's duty to itself is still good law.[98] Benvenisti does not suggest that under the trustee concept, all sovereigns are obliged to treat the interests of all foreigners as being on par to those of their own citizens.[99] However, he recognizes that there must be some form of treatment to others even if it does not demand an "elaborate balancing act between national and foreign interests".[100] All it means is that if a state had the opportunity to weigh others' interests but did not, then the burden is now on that particular state to account for that omission.[101] This procedure is familiar to courts and tribunals as it is akin to an administrative or public law action to review a decision of a state entity[102] (although Benvenisti carefully notes that his theory does not imply that a sovereign's discretion should be subject to review by third parties).[103]

The next natural question is how much weight sovereign states should give to the interests of others.[104] Benvenisti's response is that there should be a minimum obligation on the acting state to explain to those affected why it disregarded them.[105] This minimum obligation implies that whenever sovereigns are considering the adoption and pursuit of policies that potentially affect

96 At 326.
97 At 317.
98 At 300.
99 At 313.
100 At 317–318.
101 At 318.
102 At 318.
103 At 314.
104 At 318. See also Frost, C & Pullen, RK 2022, 'In the eyes of all mankind: interests and independence in Vattelian statehood', *Journal of International Political Theory*, vol. 18, p. 294.
105 Frost & Pullen, 'In the eyes of all mankind'.

foreign stakeholders or, more generally, global welfare, they must give due respect to foreign and global interests.[106] Benvenisti uses the restricted Pareto outcome to prove his argument. The result of a restricted Pareto outcome is that "one benefits and the other sustains no loss" with no compensation.[107] So, for example, a coastal state must allow access to a landlocked neighbour if such access entails no harm to itself.[108] In this scenario, the coastal state suffers no loss, there is no cost involved and the landlocked neighbour benefits from traversing the coastal state's waters. The application of a restricted Pareto outcome is reflected in the ICJ's *Corfu Channel* judgment, which provided that an international custom existed in which states had a right of innocent passage through straits used for international navigation between two parts of the high seas without the previous authorization of a coastal state.[109] This right was eventually recognized under the UN Convention of the Law of the Sea.[110] Grotius, in his work *Mare Liberum*, also invoked the restricted Pareto criterion and referred to it as "the law of human society".[111]

After examining the *Corfu Channel* case and subsequent ICJ judgments, Benvenisti maintains that these decisions acknowledge that sovereignty may not be used to violate the restricted Pareto criterion.[112] Drawing on this, Benvenisti claims that international tribunals have shown an appetite for developing and imposing other-regarding obligations on states.[113] Benvenisti therefore views the trustee sovereignty concept as supporting the restricted Pareto criterion as a minimal obligation.[114] Benvenisti therefore claims that "sovereigns should be regarded as trustees of humanity and therefore subjected to at least some minimal normative and procedural other-regarding obligations".[115]

b) Reconciling Sovereignty and Trusteeship

The line of scholarly work presented here may suggest that a sovereign as a "trustee of humanity" places some constraints and is incompatible with the concept of traditional sovereignty. As trustees of humanity, national decision-makers have an obligation to take into account the interests of others

106 At 314.
107 At 320.
108 At 320.
109 At 322.
110 United Nations Convention on the Law of the Sea (10 December 1982) 1833 U.N.T.S 397, art 125.
111 Grotius, H 1916, *Mare Liberum [the freedom of the seas]*, R Van Deman Magoffin (trans), Oxford University Press, Oxford as cited by Benvenisti, n 8, at 321.
112 Benvenisti, n 8, at 322–324.
113 At 330.
114 At 321.
115 At 332.

when devising their policies.[116] Although sovereigns are entitled to prioritize their citizens' needs, they must weigh the interests of other stakeholders and consider internalizing them into their balancing calculus.[117] A sovereign can no longer act capriciously. There are therefore limitations to sovereignty if one takes into account the sovereign's relation to foreigners who are not subject to its authority.[118]

Georg Jellinek, a German philosopher, viewed the will of the state as subject to a "logically inherent limitation".[119] Jellinek reasoned that a state's internally based purpose was to "engage in relations with other states in an ever more interdependent international community".[120]

In 1955, Kelsen also presented a vision of sovereignty that derives its authority not just from the human beings forming the state but from the whole of humanity.[121] Kelsen wrote:[122]

> By demonstrating that absolute sovereignty is not and cannot be an essential quality of the state existing side by side with other states, it removes one of the most stubborn prejudices which prevent political and legal science from recognizing the possibility of an international legal order constituting an international community of which the state is a member, just as corporations are members of the state.

Today, modern-day scholars are coming to grips with this presumably new normal of sovereignty. Like Benvenisti, who asserts, "[T]here is nothing new in conceiving the sovereign as inherently limited".[123] Dyzenhaus also wrote:[124]

> In liberal democracies sovereignty in the sense of national sovereignty is often perceived as being under threat, or at least "in transition," as power devolves from nation states to international bodies.

Dyzenhaus goes on to acknowledge that some scholars have already concluded that we are living in some post-sovereign order or, more likely,

116 At 314.
117 At 314.
118 Benvenisti, n 7, at 542.
119 Benvenisti, n 7, at 542.
120 Benvenisti, n 7, at 542.
121 At 540.
122 Kelsen, H 1955, 'Foundations of democracy', *Ethics*, vol. 66, no. 1, p. 1, 34 as cited by Benvenisti, n 7, at 540.
123 Benvenisti, n 7, at 542.
124 Dyzenhaus, n 26, at 338.

disorder.[125] It is therefore arguable that the era of Westphalian sovereignty of individual states has been replaced by a kind of constitutional pluralism in which all states are bound together in a federal structure in which there is no sovereign or overarching state.[126]

Even if one holds firm to the position that trusteeship, including a "trustee of humanity", will form part of a post-sovereign order, this does not necessarily mean that sovereignty under a trusteeship arrangement will be constrained. Benevenisti argues that the vision of trusteeship does not downgrade state governments but, to the contrary, it assigns to them immensely important tasks that are manifested in states' basic obligations towards the rest of humanity.[127] Benvenisti even drew parallels between trusteeship and John Donne's ode: "no man is an island":[128]

> [I]t would be wrong to imply that taking other-regarding interests into account is necessarily harmful to one's goal of maintaining a relative edge. To the contrary: cooperation may be beneficial to all without modifying the comparative balance; through cooperation, the enlarged pie could be allocated in proportion to states' relative power positions. More importantly, with increased interdependency, as demands for resources grow and supplies dwindle, more and more states may not be able to afford the luxury of ensuring the relative edge through unilateral action.

Seen from this perspective, being a trustee of humanity does not diminish state sovereignty but rather reinforces it.

Even if we assume that sovereignty can be reconciled with inherent obligations towards others, several scholarly contributions have expressed some concerns about such an approach.[129] Vattel was said to have invoked the concept of humanity to justify colonialism.[130] In a similar vein, Carl Schmitt argued that liberals like to fight their battles in the name of universal ideals associated with the idea of humanity.[131] Schmitt added that this idea of humanity[132]

> is an especially useful ideological instrument of imperialist expansion, and in its ethical-humanitarian form it is a specific vehicle of economic

125 At 338 and 359.
126 At 338.
127 Benvenisti, n 8, at 308.
128 At 327–328.
129 Benvenisti, n 7, at 543.
130 At 543–544. See also Benvenisti, n 8, at 183.
131 Dyzenhaus, n 26, at 357.
132 Schmitt, C 2007, *The concept of the political*, The University of Chicago Press, Chicago, 54 as cited in Dyzenhaus, n 26, at 357.

> imperialism. Here one is reminded of a somewhat modified expression of Proudhon's: whoever invokes humanity wants to cheat.

Schmitt thought that use of "humanity" was a "highly political" use of a "non-political term" because war was waged in the name of humanity.[133]

Fitzmaurice, writing in the same journal as Benvenisti and Dyzenhaus, opined that the idea of trustees of humanity has a long historical genealogy since it has been closely bound with European expansion and empire.[134] The English conquest, for example, was justified as a venture undertaken for the benefit of the Native Americans.[135] Fitzmaurice went on to examine the Berlin Conference and its constituent document, The General Act of the Berlin Conference (The General Act). The principal aim of the Berlin Conference was to take the interests of non-European peoples into account.[136] The General Act, signed by diplomats on 26 February 1885, expressly illustrated this when it declared in its preamble that the aim of the conference was to discover "the means of furthering the moral and material well-being of the native populations (of Africa)".[137] Article 6 of The General Act stipulated:[138]

> All the Powers exercising sovereign rights or influence in the aforesaid territories bind themselves to watch over the preservation of the native tribes, and to care for the improvement of the conditions of their moral and material well-being.

History reveals that the Berlin Conference did not fulfil its original promise of improving the "moral and material well-being" of the African people. Rather, the conference marked the process for what became commonly known as the Scramble for Africa and the climax of European competition for territory on the continent.[139] Years later, in 1919, the League of Nations used trusteeship – in the form of a "sacred trust of civilisation" – to justify a new form of colonialism.[140]

133 Dyzenhaus, n 26, at 357.
134 Fitzmaurice, A 2015, 'Sovereign trusteeship and empire', *Theoretical Inquiries in Law*, vol. 16, no. 2, p. 447, 463.
135 Fitzmaurice, 'Sovereign trusteeship and empire'.
136 Fitzmaurice, 'Sovereign trusteeship and empire'.
137 Fitzmaurice, 'Sovereign trusteeship and empire'.
138 The General Act of the Berlin Conference on West Africa (signed 26 February 1885), Article 6.
139 Elizabeth Heath "Berlin Conference of 1884–1885" (2010) Oxford reference, *Encyclopaedia of Africa*, (www.oxfordreference.com).
140 League of Nations, *Covenant of the league of nations*, 28 April 1919, Article 22. See also Benvenisti, n 7, at 544.

All these arguments point to a sophisticated suspicion of "whoever invokes humanity wants to cheat".[141] This led Martti Koskenniemi, a Finnish international lawyer, to question how a particular tradition (international law) can speak in the name of humanity.[142]

Citing Criddle, Dyzenhaus realizes that examples such as these place a serious challenge to Benvenisti and others who wish to resurrect the idea of sovereignty as trusteeship for humanity.[143] Dyzenhaus therefore suggests that the idea of trusteeship for humanity is "too laden with bad history to make it worth resurrecting".[144] Benvenisti admits that the term trusteeship carries with it "historic baggage".[145] However the motivation for him using this term (beyond its application in private law) begins when it enters into the realm of domestic public law.[146] According to Benvenisti: "Interestingly, the concept of trusteeship as the basic concept of administrative law has garnered renewed attention in recent years from domestic administrative and constitutional law scholars".[147]

c) Three Paradigms of Sovereignty

After evaluating three paradigms of sovereignty (namely, Kelsen, Heller and Schmitt), Dyzenhaus opines, inter alia, that Heller's paradigm might be helpful to Benvenisti's "trustee of humanity".[148] According to Dyzenhaus' paradox of sovereignty, "[I]f the sovereign is the highest authority, and hence not answerable to any other authority, how can the sovereign be subject to law?"[149] Heller wishes to maintain this paradox due to his treatment of the *Rechtsstaat* (i.e. the rule of law).[150] For Heller, the sovereign is free of positive law in the sense that the sovereign has the legal means to change the law.[151] The sovereign, however, is never free of the fundamental principles of law.[152] The fundamental principles of law, according to Heller, can be categorized as logical and ethical principles.[153] Logical principles are "constitutive principles of the pure legal form", and under this heading, Heller offers

141 Koskenniemi, M 2005, 'International law in Europe: between tradition and renewal', *The European Journal of International Law*, vol. 16, no. 1, p. 113, 120.
142 At 115.
143 Criddle, n 82, at 359.
144 Dyzenhaus, n 26, at 359.
145 Benvenisti, n 7, at 544.
146 Benvenisti, n 7, at 544.
147 At 546.
148 Dyzenhaus, n 26, at 338.
149 At 343. See also Benvenisti, n 7, at 536.
150 Dyzenhaus, n 26, at 354.
151 Dyzenhaus, n 26, at 354.
152 Dyzenhaus, n 26, at 354.
153 At 352.

the example of equality before the law.[154] In order to recognize this fundamental principle of equality before the law, one must first give some content to the idea of equality.[155] To formulate this content, one must positivize an understanding of substantive ethical fundamental principles of law.[156] For instance, the substantive *Rechtsstaat* is derived from these ethical fundamental principles.[157] As a result, Heller opines that states are inherently bound by the concept of the rule of law.[158]

Dyzenhaus suggests that Heller's paradigm of sovereignty may be compatible with the aims of Benvenisiti's argument since it represents "something like a principle of humanity".[159] This principle, however, is not about what justifies a state in intervening either in the lives of individuals beyond its borders or in the internal affairs of other states.[160] Rather, Heller recognizes that there are obligations that attend on any exercise of sovereign power that affects important individual interests.[161] In other words, a sovereign, when exercising its power, is cognisant of the fact that its actions can encroach upon critical individual interests, such as equality before the law (a fundamental principle to which the sovereign is bound). Heller's paradigm of sovereignty therefore entails that individuals who are subject to the acts of sovereign power are placed in a normative relationship with the sovereign. This relationship imposes an onus on the sovereign to be attentive to the interest of individuals.[162] This is what justifies the sovereign's exercise of power over its subjects.[163]

Dyzenhaus makes it clear that Heller's theory did not claim that sovereigns should be subject to other-regarding obligations.[164] For Dyzenhaus, the sovereign's obligations under Heller's paradigm are political and particular.[165] The obligations are political in that they are not informed by some abstract moral idea such as humanity. And they are particular since the obligation is not to humanity as such, but rather an obligation of a particular sovereign to particular individuals.[166] In the end, what is noteworthy is that Heller returned to the paradox of sovereignty in order to evaluate its implication for the individual citizen.[167]

154 At 352–353.
155 At 352.
156 At 352–353.
157 At 353.
158 Benvenisti, n 7, at 541–542.
159 Dyzenhaus, n 26, at 360–361.
160 At 361.
161 At 361.
162 At 362.
163 At 362.
164 At 362.
165 At 362.
166 At 362.
167 At 363.

Apart from Heller, Dyzenhaus also compares Benvenisti's theory with that of Kelsen. Benvenisti's line of thinking also appeared to be consistent with that of Kelsen, who opposed the classical idea that each state is sovereign in that it is not subject to an externally imposed law.[168] For Kelsen, the concept of sovereignty would be supressed if states were to conceive of each other as equal actors within an international legal system.[169] Dyzenhaus therefore asserts that Kelsen's views also provide a useful perspective on the idea of sovereignty as a trusteeship for humanity, thereby justifying Benvenisti's theory.[170]

Dyzenhaus also examined Schmitt, who he notes was a "critique of liberalism".[171] As it was important for Schmitt to preserve the idea of a sovereign as absolute, he denied that there were other-regarding obligations in international law.[172] As previously mentioned, Schmitt saw the term "humanity" as a "highly political" use of a "non-political term".[173] For a Schmittean, there is also a historical case that in international law, the idea of trusteeship was to serve the economic interests of the imperial powers.[174]

4. Trusteeship Theory and State Sovereignty

a) *Classic Trusteeship Theory*

The theory of trusteeship and its application to state sovereignty has been at the centre of jurisprudential and philosophical debates for centuries. The fully developed trusteeship theory of constitutional government was exemplified in Locke's *Second Treatise of Government*.[175] Revisiting Locke, he bases his trusteeship theory on the reserved power of popular sovereignty over constitutive legislative power.[176] Under Locke's theory, there is one supreme power and that was the "Legislative" (Parliament). Although the Legislative possess the fiduciary power to act for certain ends, there remains in the people a power to remove or alter the Legislative if it acts contrary to the trust reposed on it.[177] In his trusteeship theory, Locke was invoking the theory of resistance: people could rise in arms if their rights or interests were violated.[178]

168 At 341.
169 At 341.
170 At 342.
171 At 357.
172 At 357.
173 At 357.
174 At 358.
175 Purdy & Fielding, n 11, at 171.
176 At 178.
177 Locke, J 1689, *Two treatises of government*, 271 as cited in Purdy, J & Fielding, K 2007, 'Sovereigns, trustees, guardians: private-law concepts and the limits of legitimate state power', *Law and Contemporary Problems*, vol. 70, p. 165, 178–179.
178 Purdy & Fielding, n 11, at 175 and 179.

Locke's use of the concept of a trust on governments has been described as deliberate and consistent.[179] For Locke, a trustee has a fiduciary obligation to comply with the terms of the trust and to pursue the ends it is established to advance.[180] Once the conditions of the trust are violated, sovereignty reverts to the settlor of the trust: namely, the political community.[181] Purdy and Fielding suggest that Locke was interested in the trust concept not as a private law simile for the express terms of a constitutional grant of power but rather as a conceptual key to the nature and inherent limits of sovereign power.[182] Locke, therefore, was said to have perfected the idea of sovereignty as a public species of a private law arrangement.[183]

Locke formulated his constitutional trusteeship theory in response to his predecessor Robert Filmer, who claimed that the trusteeship conception of constitutionalism was theoretically incoherent and dangerously unworkable in practice.[184] One argument that Filmer put forth was that it was impossible to make a trusteeship theory of sovereignty operational because no individual or entity had the right to accuse the government (in Filmer's case, the king) of transgressing the law, thereby triggering the people's power of reprimand, revision or resistance.[185] Although Locke articulated the 17th century's most refined trusteeship theory, it is not entirely clear that he addressed Filmer's issue of standing: namely, who is entitled to judge that the government violated the trust and no longer pursued the common good?[186]

The application of a trusteeship theory on sovereignty was also manifested under colonial rule. The Dominican jurist Francisco de Vitoria was said to have first raised the possibility of a trust relationship between an imperial sovereign and a colonial people.[187] Vitoria, while examining Spanish imperial claims on the Americans, referred to the natural right of dominium, or ownership of one's actions and liberties.[188] Vitoria regarded "political dominium", or sovereignty, as a product of natural right and reason which is secular and unrelated to Christianity.[189] Since sovereignty was a secular matter, Vitoria reasoned that Native Americans enjoyed the power to rule themselves without being subjected to Spanish sovereign claims based on their "pagan" or allegedly "sinful nature".[190]

179 At 178.
180 At 179.
181 At 179.
182 At 179.
183 At 180.
184 At 175 and 177.
185 At 176–177.
186 At 177 and 180.
187 At 183.
188 At 183.
189 At 183.
190 At 183.

Although Vitoria generally defended the interests of Native Americans against Spanish conquest, he presented another argument to justify Spanish rule. He argued that natives were essentially children incapable of self-government and, as a result, were susceptible to a civilizing European trusteeship.[191] Since the natives, like children, possessed actual dominium (sovereignty), but not the ability to exercise it on their own behalf, they would have to surrender the management of their dominium to others who were more fully mature.[192] Those mature others (Spanish conquistadors) would become the trustees and would treat the natives' dominium as a trust corpus, which they would return in full upon their entrance into adulthood.[193] By introducing such an argument, Vitoria paved the way for a theory of colonial sovereignty founded on the idea that colonial rulers govern as provisional trustee sovereigns.[194] This is an idea that eventually flowered, centuries later, in the League of Nations' Mandate System.[195]

Vitoria's trusteeship theory can be compared to that of Edmund Burke, a British Parliamentarian, who articulated a special category of "derivate trusts" under a constitutional and colonial trusteeship theory.[196] Burke, a conservative critic of the British government in India, regarded all political power as having the form of a trust and believed the East India Company enjoyed a derivative trust granted by Parliament.[197] During his speech at the House of Commons during the debate of Mr Fox's East India Bill, Burke stated:[198]

> Every species of political dominion . . . [is] in the strictest sense a trust; and it is of the very essence of every trust to be rendered accountable, and even totally to cease, when it substantially varies from the purposes for which alone it could have a lawful existence.

With a similar sympathy as Vitoria – but this time extended to Indians subject to British rule – Burke argued that the East India Company had breached the trust-like authority that Parliament had given it over colonial India.[199] As a consequence of this breach of fiduciary obligation, Burke argued that the governing powers that had been entrusted to the East India Company be

191 Criddle & Fox-Decent, n 2, at 15.
192 Purdy & Fielding, n 11, at 184.
193 Purdy & Fielding, n 11, at 184.
194 Purdy & Fielding, n 11, at 184.
195 At 185.
196 At 185–186.
197 At 185.
198 Whelan, FG 1996, *Edmund Burke and India: Political morality and empire*, University of Pittsburgh Press, Pittsburgh, p. 24. For full debate, see www.quod.lib.umich.edu.
199 Criddle & Fox-Decent, n 2, at 15.

reverted to the Parliament (not to India as the beneficiaries of the trust).[200] According to Burke, the original trust relationship that Parliament held to the Indian government implied "a duty on us (Parliament) to interfere . . . wherever power and authority originating from ourselves are perverted from their purposes and become instruments of wrong and violence".[201] Burke added:[202]

> I ground myself therefore on this principle – that if the abuse is proved, the contract is broken; and we re-enter into all our rights; that is, into the exercise of all our duties. Our own authority is indeed as much a trust originally, as the Company's authority is a trust derivatively; and it is the use we make of the resumed power that must justify or condemn us in the resumption of it.

To summarize, Vitoria's colonial trust was justified on the account that the natives belonged to a juridical category of persons (namely, children)[203] who were incapable at that time of exercising their sovereignty. Burke, on the other hand, proposed a bold marriage of constitutional and colonial aspects into his trusteeship theory.[204] By so doing, Burke's view was something more analogous to the Lockean right of resistance, except this time, the focus was on Parliament reining in its power against the East India Company.[205]

b) *The Mandate System and the Theory of Sovereignty*

The mandate system created by the Covenant of the League of Nations ("the Covenant") is a critical international instrument as it highlights how sovereign states, post–World War I, perceived themselves as "trustees for humanity". The ICJ confirmed this in the *International Status of South-West Africa* case, when it opined that the mandate system was created in the interest of inhabitants of the territory and of humanity in general.[206] In effect, the mandate system was designed to hold in a "sacred trust of civilization" the sovereignty of less-developed nations while guiding them along the road to "civilization" and self-determination.[207] Notwithstanding their formal fidu-

200 Criddle & Fox-Decent, n 2, at 15.

201 Burke, E 1973, *Reflections on the revolutions in France and on the proceedings on certain societies in London*, Anchor Books, London, pp. 291–292 as cited in Purdy & Fielding, n 11, at 186.

202 Purdy & Fielding, n 11, at 186–187. For full debate, see www.quod.lib.umich.edu.

203 At 184.

204 At 185.

205 At 186.

206 International Status of South-West Africa (Advisory Opinion) [1950] ICJ Rep 128 at 132.

207 Purdy & Fielding, n 11, at 190–191.

ciary structure, the mandate and trusteeship systems have been described as devices that perpetuated Western domination and neo-colonialism in the 20th century.[208]

During the interwar period, the mandate system entrenched the colonial trusteeship ideas championed by Vitoria and Burke.[209] Scholarly opinions have claimed that the mandate system was the first coordinated attempt by international institutions to give legal force to a trusteeship theory of sovereignty.[210] Such a claim is premised under Article 22 of the Covenant, where three private law concepts recur: mandate, trust and tutelage.[211]

The challenge with incorporating private law terminology into the theory of sovereign power in international law is that it was difficult to assume where sovereignty would lie. The words "mandate", "trust" and "tutelage" all formed part of the description of the mandate system, and each had a different meaning in private law.[212] A difficulty arose with interpretation because private law terms in international treaties are presumed to express the meaning attributed to them by public international law, and at the time the Covenant was written, there was scant evidence that any of these terms had fixed meanings in international law.[213] Paul Hymans, a former president of the League of Nations, anticipated such difficulties when he wrote, "I shall not enter into a controversy – though it would certainly be very interesting – as to where sovereignty in mandated territories resides".[214]

As the mandate system was susceptible to several competing interpretations,[215] there were several possibilities where sovereignty would lie. For example, sovereignty could exist in (1) the mandated territories, 2) in the mandatories (states) that governed them, (3) in the principal and Allied powers to whom Germany and Turkey formally ceded the territories, (4) in the League of Nations or (5) in some combination of these options.[216] From these options, some authors prefer the fourth argument – that the concept of "mandate" implied that the League of Nations held sovereignty over the mandates and that the mandatories exercised their authority "on behalf of the League".[217] In other words, the word "mandate" implied the "ultimate

208 Criddle, EJ 2014, 'A sacred trust of civilization', in AS Gold & PB Miller (eds), *Philosophical foundations of fiduciary law*, Oxford University Press, Oxford, p. 404, 410.
209 Criddle & Fox-Decent, n 2, at 15.
210 Purdy & Fielding, n 11, at 189.
211 At 194.
212 At 192.
213 At 192.
214 Hymans, P 1920, *Responsibilities of the league arising out of article 22* as cited in Purdy & Fielding, n 11, at 192.
215 Purdy & Fielding, n 11, at 192.
216 Purdy & Fielding, n 11, at 192.
217 At 195.

sovereignty" of the League.[218] However, there are some limitations to this argument, especially when one turns to examine the meaning of the word "mandate".

(1) The Mandate

The concept of the mandate is closely related to that of agency.[219] Jan Smuts, the South African prime minister and proposer of the mandate system, was noted as having introduced the word "mandate" in the conference and used "agent" and "mandatory" interchangeably.[220] To make the matter even more complicated, a "mandate" had specialized meanings under Roman law and Anglo/Saxon traditions.

In Roman law, a mandate was a gratuitous execution by one person (*mandatarius* or agent) of a commission given by another (*mandans* or principal).[221] Mandates could be limited or general in time and scope, and the agent could not exceed the scope of the mandate.[222] Although there is an assumption that the mandate is gratuitous, the agent would be repaid for reasonable expenses incurred during the execution of the mandate and would sometimes even receive an honorarium.[223] The concept of a mandate in civil law – at the time when the League of Nations was born – was, in effect, similar to the Roman law (with a few permitted exceptions).[224] This must be contrasted with the Anglo-Saxon juridical world, where "mandate" had a more specialized meaning and referred to "personal property upon which some special act is to be performed and to which the principal retains title".[225]

If the League of Nations was born out of the Roman/civil law conceptions, then the mandates did not necessarily involve property, nor did they imply that the principal owned the property involved.[226] Therefore, under the Roman/civil law tradition, one could not infer that, by using the word "mandate", the League of Nations held sovereignty (or "property rights") over the mandated territories.[227] This was the position held by Germany in the years following the Versailles Conference.[228]

218 At 195.
219 Wright, Q 1930, *Mandates under the League of Nations*, University of Chicago Press, Chicago, p. 377 as cited in Purdy & Fielding, n 11, at 195.
220 Wright, *Mandates under the League of Nations*.
221 Purdy & Fielding, n 11, at 195.
222 Purdy & Fielding, n 11, at 195.
223 Purdy & Fielding, n 11, at 195.
224 Purdy & Fielding, n 11, at 195.
225 Purdy & Fielding, n 11, at 195.
226 At 196.
227 At 196.
228 At 196.

Purdy and Fielding contended that the only indispensable conclusion is that the League was a principal and the mandatory an agent. The mandatories were therefore bound to adhere to the contours of their commissions.[229] As a result, some scholars have accepted that the League was constituted for the purposes of peace and security and not governance, thereby debunking the idea that the League was the repository of ultimate sovereignty.[230] Despite these arguments, some authors still attempt to present the mandate system as a "shared or divided sovereignty" in which sovereign power was parcelled out between the League and the mandatories or the League and the mandated territories.[231]

Ultimately, for Purdy and Fielding, the mandate concept is insufficient to define the "ownership" of sovereignty since its powers and legal relationship (among the League of Nations, the mandatory and the mandate) are limited and set by the Article 22 notion of a "sacred trust of civilization".[232]

(2) The Sacred Trust of Civilization

The "sacred trust of civilization" phraseology, found in Article 22 of the Covenant, reinforces the fiduciary aspects of the mandate system.[233] But what does this "sacred trust of civilization" mean? Does in generate any specific legal rights or obligations under the Covenant? Before any attempt is made to answer these questions, it is important to note that the trust arrangement is more prominently and widely applied in Anglo-American common law traditions than its Roman/civil law counterparts.[234] For this reason, the literature emanating from Anglo-Saxon writers, who were familiar with the workings and mechanisms of private law trusts, was heavily promoted.[235]

In a trust arrangement, one party (the trustee) undertakes a property right for the benefit of another party (beneficiary).[236] A trust differs from a mandate in that it implies the ownership of the corpus, or an object or property owned – in this case, "sovereignty".[237] A trust therefore implies dual ownership: a legal ownership vested in the trustee (the power to use and dispose of the corpus) and an equitable ownership vested in the beneficiary (who has an enforceable right to benefit from the trustee's use).[238]

229 At 196.
230 At 196.
231 At 196.
232 At 196.
233 At 197.
234 At 197.
235 At 197.
236 At 197.
237 At 197.
238 At 197.

If the trust concept, as advocated by Anglo-American writers, were to be strictly applied as a key structure to the mandate system, it would locate sovereignty in the mandatories as trustees of the corpus.[239] By further analogy, the beneficiaries of the trust would be the mandated territories.[240]

The Permanent Mandate Commission (PMC), which was constituted to advise the Council on all matters relating to the observance of the mandates,[241] vigorously opposed any interpretation of Article 22 that gave sovereignty directly to the mandatories.[242] Instead, the PMC opted for an interpretation that was based on the spirit of Article 22 – one which viewed the mandatory as "a government exercising authority".[243] As a corollary to this, the Supreme Courts of South Africa and Palestine agreed that although the mandatories possessed plenary powers, they were not sovereigns.[244] For these reasons, Purdy and Fielding wrote, "[N]owhere describes the mandatory powers as sovereign bodies vis-à-vis the mandate territories".[245]

Another argument that some commentators have suggested was that the League was a trustee. The reason behind this suggestion was the phrase immediately following "a sacred trust of civilization" under Article 22, which is "and that securities for the performance of this trust should be embodied in this Covenant".[246] However, to conclude that the League was a trustee would mean giving up on the independent system of accountability that the Council had to oversee the mandatory powers under Article 22.[247]

As the "trust" is considered a domestic private law concept, the ICJ sought to determine the extent, if any, of the obligation derived under a "sacred trust of civilization" in international law. This point is pertinent because under the statute of the ICJ, the Court's function is to decide disputes submitted to it in accordance with international law.[248] In his separate opinion in *International Status of South-West Africa*, Sir Arnold McNair wrote:[249]

> To what extent is it useful or necessary to examine what may at first sight appear to be relevant analogies in private law systems and draw help and inspiration from them? International law has recruited and continues to recruit many of its rules and institutions from private systems of law.

239 At 197.
240 At 197.
241 The Covenant of the League of Nations, n 140, art 22.
242 Purdy & Fielding, n 11, at 197.
243 Purdy & Fielding, n 11, at 197.
244 Wright, n 219, at 326–327.
245 Purdy & Fielding, n 11, at 197.
246 At 198.
247 At 198.
248 Statute of the International Court of Justice, art 38(1).
249 International Status of South-West Africa (Advisory Opinion), n 206, at 148.

In determining the status of the trust, the Court considered whether it could apply private law systems as a category of "general principles of law recognised by civilized nations".[250] On this, McNair opined that international law does not borrow private law systems "lock, stock and barrel" and that it would be difficult to reconcile private law processes within the application of general principles of law.[251] International tribunals should therefore consider rules and institutions of private law as an indication of policy and principles rather than importing such rules and institutions in a wholehearted manner.[252] McNair went on to express that any English lawyer preparing legal instruments required to give effect to the policy of Article 22 would be influenced by the trust of English and American law and would even realize the need of adaptation to suit the purposes of the new international institution.[253]

As a result, McNair held that "no technical significance can be attached to the words 'sacred trust of civilization'".[254] More than a decade later, the ICJ made similar remarks in the *South West Africa* judgment. There, the ICJ ruled that a sacred trust must be or become something more than a moral or humanitarian ideal.[255] The Court added that for the sacred trust to generate legal rights and obligations, it must be given juridical expression and clothed in legal form. (The Court admitted that one such legal form could be the UN trusteeship system, which was established after the mandate system.)[256]

One can even compare the ICJ decisions with national courts and their treatment of the trust concept. In the English case of *Tito v Waddell,* the Court noted that "there is no magic in the word 'trust'" since in various circumstances it may represent many things.[257] The Court then made a distinction between a "true trust", which is a conventional trust that is enforceable by the courts of equity, and a "trust in the higher sense", which expresses the discharge of duties under the direction of the Crown. The Court in *Tito v Waddell* went on to conclude that a "trust in the higher sense" was not enforceable.[258]

Ultimately, the question of who "owned" sovereignty under the League's "sacred trust of civilization" is a point which remains unclear for some scholars.[259]

250 International Status of South-West Africa (Advisory Opinion), n 206, at 148.
251 International Status of South-West Africa (Advisory Opinion), n 206, at 148.
252 International Status of South-West Africa (Advisory Opinion), n 206, at 148.
253 International Status of South-West Africa (Advisory Opinion), n 206, at 148.
254 International Status of South-West Africa (Advisory Opinion), n 206, at 148.
255 *South West Africa* (Second Phase, Judgment) [1966] ICJ Rep 6 at 34.
256 *South West Africa* (Second Phase, Judgment) [1966] ICJ Rep 6 at 34.
257 *Tito v Waddell and others* N 2 (1977) Ch. 106 at 215. See also Purdy & Fielding, n 11, at 200–201.
258 Tito v Waddell and others, n 257, at 215.
259 Purdy & Fielding, n 11, at 198.

(3) *Tutelage*

Unlike the "mandate" and the "trust", the tutelage (*tutelle* in French) had a technical use in both the civil and common law systems in the early 20th century.[260] According to the Covenant, the tutelage was seen as the "best method of giving practical effect" to the principle of the sacred trust of civilization.[261]

The object of the tutelage system was the protection of minors.[262] Tutelage has been compared to a guardian relationship in which the parent looks after a child's well-being. Like a parent, the "tutor" directs the ward's (a child or minor) actions towards appropriate development and eventual adulthood and independence.[263] Under the Covenant, the "advanced nations", by reason of their resources, experience and geographical position, were deemed to be the most suitable to exercise this tutelage over the territories which were unable to "stand by themselves under the strenuous conditions of the modern world".[264] Tutelage therefore implies definitive duties owed by the mandatory to the mandate in preparing it for the national version of statehood.[265] The concept also implies that the mandatory has a fiduciary duty to act in the interest of the mandate and may be held accountable for failure to do so.[266]

This concept of tutelage, which was popular among French academics and politicians, suggests by analogy that sovereignty lies in the mandated territories, even though it was exercised by the mandatories or the League of Nations.[267] Some contemporary writings on the mandate system described the tutelage as separating sovereignty between the mandatory and the mandated territory.[268] As one writer put it:[269]

> The sovereignty of the territories submitted to mandate resides in the peoples of those territories. The exercise of the attributes of sovereignty is provisionally confided to a power acting in the capacity of tutor to these minor peoples.

This reasoning implies that the mandatory would have nearly absolute control over the ward.[270] However, by recognizing that sovereignty is provisionally

260 Wright, see n 219, at 377 as cited in Purdy & Fielding, n 11, at 198.
261 League of Nations, *Covenant of the league of nations* (1919), art 22.
262 Purdy & Fielding, n 11, at 198.
263 Purdy & Fielding, n 11, at 198.
264 Purdy & Fielding, n 11, at 198.
265 At 199.
266 At 199.
267 At 198.
268 At 199.
269 Wright, n 219, at 199.
270 Purdy & Fielding, n 11, at 199.

vested in the mandatory implies a point of termination of the mandate when sovereignty will be fully reverted to the inhabitants of the mandated territories once they have achieved the capacity to exercise it.[271]

In applying the trusteeship concept to the theory of tutelage, the mandatory powers would "legally" hold sovereignty on behalf of the mandate population until the latter achieved the preconditions of sovereignty.[272] To put it another way: Until they "graduated" to statehood, mandated territories would retain equitable sovereignty while the mandatories held legal sovereignty.[273]

The mandate system was unique in that it created a melange of three private law arrangements, flexibly adapted to fit a new approach to sovereignty (although it was noted that this approach was never robustly enforced).[274] It has been argued that the tutelage – as well as the alternative concepts of the "mandate" and the "trust" – is more useful as an analogy than as proof of the exact locus of sovereignty under the mandate system.[275] Ultimately, what remains as some form of guidance are the interpretations of national and international tribunals as well as scholarly writings on the subject.

5. The Public Trust Doctrine

The earliest origins of the public trust doctrine can be traced back to Roman law and to a famous maxim in the *Corpus Iuris Civilis* of Emperor Justinian I (533 AD).[276] This law was motivated by the earlier writings of Aelius Marcianus (circa 220 AD), who wrote, "So surely by the law of nature, the atmosphere, watercourses, the sea and hence the seashores are common to all".[277] The origins of the public trust doctrine are ancient or, as one scholar put it, as "old as humanity".[278] However it took centuries for the public trust doctrine to develop in theory in modern-day jurisdictions such as the United States, where the doctrine became well known as a result of the scholarly writings of Joseph Sax.

271 Purdy & Fielding, n 11, at 199.
272 Purdy & Fielding, n 11, at 199.
273 Purdy & Fielding, n 11, at 199.
274 At 200.
275 At 199–200.
276 Sand, PH 2014, 'The rise of public trusteeship in international environmental law', *Environmental Policy and Law*, vol. 44, no. 1, p. 210.
277 Sand, 'The rise of public trusteeship in international environmental law'.
278 Wood, MC, Leonard, S, Bartz, D & Peart, N 2013, 'Securing planetary life sources for future generations: legal actions deriving from the ancient sovereign trust obligation', in MB Gerrard & GE Wannier (eds), *Threatened island nations: legal implications of rising seas and a changing climate*, Cambridge University Press, New York, p. 535.

a) Public Trust of Natural Resources

The public trust doctrine, as developed in the United States, can be defined as "an ancient Roman law doctrine which provides that states must hold certain natural resources, particularly submerged lands under tidal and navigable waters, in trust for the use and benefit of the public and future generations".[279] The United States Supreme Court referred to the doctrine "public trust" for the first time in 1842 in *Martin v Waddell's Lessee*.[280] The scope and parameters of the theory were laid down half a century later in *Illinois Central Railroad Co v Illinois*.[281] By 1896, the public trust doctrine had become firmly entrenched in American jurisprudence with the advent of the case *Geer v Connecticut*.[282] The decision of *Geer v Connecticut* was unique because it was the first time the Supreme Court extended the public trust doctrine to include wildlife. Prior to that, the doctrine's application was limited to navigable waters and underlying beds.[283] Courts subsequently applied the public trust doctrine to those limited common spaces until 1970, when Joseph Sax suggested that the courts use the public trust doctrine to compel the government to apply fiduciary duties not only to submerged lands and navigable waters but also to other natural resources on public lands.[284]

Following the years of Sax's publication, the public trust doctrine has evolved for purposes that include ecological preservation.[285] In the United States, some state courts (such as California, Hawaii, New York and Louisiana) have applied the public trust doctrine outside submerged lands, including groundwater, lakes, wetlands, parkland, the dry sand area of beaches and archaeological remains.[286] Regrettably, the Court in *Juliana v United States* missed the opportunity of recognizing the atmosphere as falling within the scope of the public trust doctrine as it decided not to decisively rule on the issue.[287] The cause of these discrepancies is the fact that the public trust doctrine in the United States falls under state rather than federal jurisdiction.[288]

279 Roy, S 2020, 'The potential of the trusteeship theory for Canadian public law and environmental governance', in K Anker, PD Burdon, G Garver, M Maloney & C Sbert (eds), *From environmental to ecological law*, Routledge, Oxfordshire, p. 150.

280 *Martin v Waddell's Lessee* 41 US 367 (1842) at 411. See also Roy, n 279, at 150.

281 *Illinois Central Railroad Co v Illinois* 146 US 387 (1892) at 452.

282 *Geer v Connecticut* 161 US 519 (1896) 519 at 529. See also Wood, et al., n 278, at 536.

283 Roy, n 279, at 150.

284 Roy, n 279, at 150.

285 Blumm, MC & Moses, AP 2017, 'The public trust as an antimonopoly doctrine', *Boston College Environmental Affairs Law Review*, vol. 44, no. 1, p. 1, 25–26 as cited in Roy, n 279, at 150.

286 Roy, n 279, at 150.

287 *Juliana v United States* 217 F Supp 3d 1224 (D Or 2016) at 1255. See also Roy, n 279, at 150.

288 See, for example, the Pennsylvanian Constitution 1874 (as amended in 1967), which states at art 1(27): "Pennsylvanian's public natural resources are the common property of all people, including generations to come".

As a result, the doctrine has evolved in different ways within state jurisdictions.[289] As Sand explains:[290]

> Within the United States, interpretation of the public trust doctrine differs from one of the component states to another and has also been codified in the legislative and constitutional provisions of individual states.

The lack of uniformity of application at the state level may result in one of the limitations of the public trust doctrine in the United States. According to Roy: "Despite these developments (of the public trust doctrine), for most states, the doctrine remains limited to the protection of use and access to navigable waters, submerged lands and fishing".[291] To this Wood adds, "[T]he scope of states' jurisdiction on natural resources is still limited by the high-water mark in many places".[292]

b) Application in Common Law Countries

Outside the United States, the public trust doctrine has taken root, in case law and legislation, in other common law countries. Although there are many examples, this section will focus on four countries – India, Kenya, South Africa and Uganda.[293]

The public trust doctrine has had its most persistent and profound effect in India, where the Indian Supreme Court fully embraced the doctrine over a substantial period of time.[294] In fact, academics Blumm and Gutherie have asserted that the public trust doctrine is now much more fundamental to Indian jurisprudence than it is in the United States.[295]

In India, the public trust doctrine originated in the 1997 landmark decision of *Mehta v Kamal Nath*.[296] In arriving at its decision, the Supreme Court noted that the English common law, which is part of the Indian legal system, includes the public trust doctrine as part of its jurisprudence.[297] In an elaborated opinion, the Court examined a line of American public trust cases (including *Illinois Central Railroad Co v Illinois*) and the literature of

289 Roy, n 279, at 150.
290 Sand, n 276, at 210.
291 Roy, n 279, at 151.
292 Wood, MC 2013, *Nature's trust: environmental law for a new ecological age*, Cambridge University Press, New York, p. 147.
293 For further examples, see Blumm, MC & Gutherie, RD 2012, 'Internationalizing the public trust doctrine: natural law and constitutional and statutory approaches to fulfilling the Saxion vision', *UC Davis Law Review*, vol. 45, p. 741, 760.
294 Blumm & Gutherie, 'Internationalizing the public trust doctrine'.
295 Blumm & Gutherie, 'Internationalizing the public trust doctrine'.
296 *Mehta v Kamal Nath* (1997) 1 SCC 388.
297 At 25 (as found on Supreme Court's website: www. main.sci.gov.in).

Professor Sax. The Court found that the public trust doctrine has ecological purposes, and, for that reason, it should be expanded to include all ecosystems operating within the country.[298] The Court stated:[299]

> The State is the trustee of all natural resources which are by nature meant for public use and enjoyment. [The] public at large is the beneficiary of the sea-shore, running waters, airs, forests and ecologically fragile lands. The State as a trustee is under a legal duty to protect the natural resources. These resources meant for public use cannot be converted into private ownership.

The Supreme Court then held that the public trust doctrine is a part of the "law of the land" of India.[300]

Three years later, the Supreme Court invoked the public trust doctrine in *MI Builders Private Ltd v Shyam Sahu*.[301] This case involved a decision permitting the appellants to construct an underground shopping complex at the Jhandewala Park. The Court followed its previous decision in *Mehta v Kamal Nath* and confirmed that the public trust doctrine is part of the law of the land. Interestingly, the Court went further than in *Mehta v Kamal Nath* and also based its decision on a constitutional provision: namely, Article 21 (the right to life).[302] In its judgment, the Court ruled that the public trust doctrine "has grown from article 21 of the Constitution".[303] As a result, the Court accepted that the residents were deprived of their quality of life and the ability to maintain the ecology of the area.[304] The Supreme Court's decision of *MI Builders Private Ltd v Shyam Sahu* solidifies that the public trust doctrine is a fundamental part of India's jurisprudence due to its inherited English common law tradition as well as the constitutional right to life provision.[305]

The public trust doctrine has also made its way into case law, the constitution and legislation in countries in Africa, such as Kenya, South Africa and Uganda. In Kenya, the High Court defined the public trust as a fiduciary duty of the state:[306]

> The essence of the public trust is that the state, as trustee, is under a fiduciary duty to deal with the trust property, being the common natural resources, in a manner that is in the interests of the general public.

298 At 25 (as found on Supreme Court's website: www. main.sci.gov.in).
299 At 25 (as found on Supreme Court's website: www. main.sci.gov.in).
300 At 17.
301 *MI Builders Private Ltd v Shyam Sahu* [1999] INSC 228.
302 Constitution of the Republic of India 1949.
303 *MI Builders Private Ltd v Shyam Sahu*, n 301, at 40.
304 At 5 and 50.
305 Blumm & Gutherie, n 293, at 762.
306 *Waweru v Republic* HC Nairobi Misc civ appli 118 of 2004, 2 March 2006 at 31.

The Court further found that land resources, forests, wetlands and waterways were examples of these "common natural resources" that the state managed under a public trust.[307]

Section 24 of South Africa's Constitution falls under the Bill of Rights chapter and speaks to the right of everyone to an environment that is not harmful to their health or well-being.[308] South Africa's National Environment Management Act (NEMA) was enacted to give effect to Section 24 of the Constitution.[309] Section 2(4)(o) of NEMA provides that:[310]

> The environment is held in public trust for the people, the beneficial use of environmental resources must serve the public interest and the environment must be protected as the people's common heritage.

The trust principle is further refined by Section 3 of the National Environmental Management Biodiversity Act (NEMBA)[311] under the heading of "State's trusteeship of biological diversity".[312] This section states:

> In fulfilling the rights contained in section 24 of the Constitution, the state through its organs that implement legislation applicable to biodiversity, must (a) manage, conserve and sustain South Africa's biodiversity and its components and genetic resources, and (b) implement this Act to achieve the progressive realisation of those rights.

Blackmore, a South Africa academic, argues that these provisions suggest that the government, through all its organs of state, has a proactive duty to act as a trustee of the environment, the country's biodiversity and its genetic resources.[313] To put it simply, the state is the trustee of all natural resources, which are, by nature, meant for public use and enjoyment.[314]

One of the critiques of the public trust doctrine relates to the evaluation of property rights.[315] Authors defending the liberal theories of property argue that the doctrine is incompatible with private property rights as it can

307 At 41.
308 Constitution of the Republic of South Africa 1996, s 24(a).
309 *Fuel Retailers Association of Southern Africa v Director-General Environmental Management* CCT 67/06, 7 June 2007 at [59]. See also *HTF Developers (Pty) Ltd v Minister of Environmental Affairs and Tourism* (2006) ZAGPHC 132 at [15].
310 National Environmental Management Act 1998 (South Africa), s 2(4)(o).
311 National Environmental Management Biodiversity Act 2004 (South Africa), s 3.
312 Blackmore, AC 2018, 'The rediscovery of the trusteeship doctrine in South African environmental law and its significance in conserving biodiversity in South Africa', PhD thesis, University of Tilburg.
313 Blackmore, 'The rediscovery of the trusteeship doctrine in South African'.
314 Blackmore, 'The rediscovery of the trusteeship doctrine in South African'.
315 Roy, n 279, at 151.

limit these in favour of public property rights.[316] On the other side of the argument, green property theorists believe that the classical liberal property theory is outdated, and they criticize the fact that the public trust doctrine is deeply rooted in the notion of private property.[317] How this argument develops is illustrated by cases arising out of Uganda and South Africa.

The Constitution of Uganda declares that the central or local government shall hold in trust "natural lakes, rivers, wetlands, forest reserves, game reserves, national parks and any land to be reserved for ecological and touristic purposes for the common good of all citizens".[318] The local High Court in *Advocates Coalition for Development and Environment v Attorney General*[319] examined and applied this particular article of the constitution. There, the Court made the distinction between *jus publicum* (the public right to use and enjoy trust land) and *jus privutum* (the private property right that may exist in the use and possession of trust land).[320] The Court, in applying the public trust doctrine, held that the state may convey the *jus privutum* to private owners, but its interest is subservient to the *jus publicum*, which is the state's inalienable interest that it continues to hold in trust land or water.[321] Similarly, in *HTF Developers (Pty) Ltd v Minister of Environmental Affairs and Tourism*, the High Court of South Africa held that "owners of land no longer enjoy the absolute real rights known to earlier generations".[322] The Court added that an owner may not use his or her land in a way that may prejudice the community because the owner, to a degree, holds the land in trust for future generations.[323] The jurisprudence originating from Uganda and South Africa therefore tend to favour the argument of the green property theorists.

On further examination, one could draw a connection between the public trust (the green property theorist argument) and the German constitutional law concept of social restrictions on property rights (*Sozialpflichtigkeit*).[324] This concept of social restrictions or "social obligation" can be compared to the decisions alluded to in the courts of Uganda and South Africa. In Rudolf Dolzer's IUCN study on *Property and Environment: The Social Obligation Inherent in Ownership*, he discussed how the West German legal order

316 At 152.
317 At 152.
318 Constitution of Uganda 1995, art 237(2)(b).
319 *Advocates Coalition for Development and Environment v Attorney General* HC No. 0100 of 2004, 13 July 2005.
320 At 13–14.
321 At 14.
322 *HTF Developers (Pty) Ltd v Minister of Environmental Affairs and Tourism* [2006] ZAGPHC 132 at [19].
323 *HTF Developers (Pty) Ltd v Minister of Environmental Affairs and Tourism* [2006] ZAGPHC 132 at [19].
324 Sand, n 276, at 211.

determined limitations on private property ownership to meet legitimate public interests.[325] According to the study, "[O]wnership does not furnish absolute power over the owned object", and since property is limited in certain ways, its use "must be accommodated within the general social and legal order".[326] The social obligation is therefore invoked in limited cases in which specific uses of property conflict with the public interest.[327] For these reasons, environmental law tends to require a limitation of private property rights.[328]

c) General Validity

The public trust doctrine is not without any limitations or flaws. As seen in the United States, one of the limitations of the doctrine is that there is a lack of uniform application at the federal level. Even on a global level, what constitutes the corpus of the public trust differs from country to country. So whilst Roy defines the public trust doctrine as "a type of trusteeship in action", she envisages the trusteeship theory, suggested by Wood's nature's trust and by the trusteeship of global commons, as possessing a broader application.[329] A global governance model is necessary to manage the environment because environmental issues know no boundaries, and ecosystems are diffuse and interconnected, regardless of states' sovereignty.[330] As a result, this global problem cannot be solved at the state level, but rather must be solved at the international level.[331] Potentially, at least, states act as environmental trustees to protect resources on their sovereign land and also cooperate to protect the Earth's commons.[332]

Notwithstanding these limitations, there is a school of thought that affirms that the public trust doctrine has served as an antimonopoly doctrine since it has protected against states' attempts to create private monopolies over natural resources.[333] Roy argues, as a counter-argument, that although the public trust doctrine has been effective in reversing the monopoly of states, the rate of ecosystem degradation and species extinction proves that environmental law and the public trust doctrine are unsuccessful.[334]

325 Dolzer, R 1976, *Property and environment: the social obligation inherent in ownership – A study of the German constitutional setting*, International Union for Conservation of Nature and Natural Resources, IUCN Environmental Policy and Law Paper No. 12, p. 14.
326 At 13.
327 At 58.
328 At 58.
329 Roy, n 279, at 149–150.
330 Bosselmann, n 6, at 154.
331 Roy, n 279, at 154.
332 At 155.
333 Blumm & Moses, n 285, at 152.
334 Roy, n 279, at 152.

Unlike the conventional Anglo-Saxon trust, the public trust belongs to the field of public law (including constitutional law and administrative law) and should not be confused with classical legal analogues in the field of private property law.[335] In a like manner, the public trust ought not to be confused with the corresponding contractual institutions found in continental Europe: for example, the *fiduziarische Treuhand* or "fiduciary trust" found in Germany.[336]

Also similar to the public trust is the French public/administrative law concept of *domaine public*.[337] This concept invests the state with custodianship (*droit de garde*) rather than ownership over natural resources, such as the seashore.[338] Apart from these similarities, contemporary civil law systems do not have a direct equivalent to a trust in either private or public law.[339] Sand argues that this result tends to lead to trusteeship being mistranslated or discarded as "inappropriate private law analogies" by lawyers trained in the civil law tradition.[340] If one were to follow this line of argument, then civil law jurisdictions may be more hesitant than their common law counterparts to incorporate elements of trusteeship into the sovereignty matrix. So, while Sand notes that there may some growing transnational convergence surrounding the doctrine, there is not sufficient evidence of it being recognized as a general principle of law.[341]

6. The Responsibility to Protect

The doctrine of the responsibility to protect (R2P) permits humanitarian intervention by states to prevent human rights abuses in another state when the latter's government is unwilling or unable to act. The scope of R2P focuses on the protection of human beings from traditional harms, the "big four" human rights abuses being genocide, war crimes, crimes against humanity and ethnic cleansing.[342] The central theme of R2P is that world actors should protect and assist the vulnerable citizens if their governments cannot or will not uphold their responsibilities to protect them.[343]

As previously mentioned, the idea of a state basing its legitimacy on the protection of the human rights of their citizens is not remote. Such a

335 Sand, n 276, at 210.
336 At 210–211.
337 At 211.
338 At 211.
339 At 211.
340 At 211.
341 At 211.
342 Botrel, M 2019, 'The suitability of the "responsibility to protect" to address the ecological crisis', LLM (Hons) dissertation, University of Auckland, p. 8.
343 At 13.

responsibility has existed since at least the Westphalian era, when Pufendorf was recorded as saying, "Let the people's welfare be the supreme law".[344] Centuries later, states still violate Pufendorf's "supreme law", thereby triggering the international appeal for foreign intervention. The result of this appeal is now shaped in the doctrine of R2P.

R2P originated from a plea made by UN Secretary-General Kofi Annan at the 54th General Assembly in 1999, on the brink of the 20th century.[345] In his report, Annan stressed the need for humanitarian intervention to halt gross and systematic human rights violations such as those witnessed in, for example, Rwanda and Kosovo.[346] To achieve this objective, Annan spoke about the UN having to adapt to a world with "new actors, new responsibilities and new possibilities for peace and progress".[347] The following year, Canada responded to Annan's challenge by announcing the establishment of the International Commission on Intervention and State Sovereignty (ICISS). The ICISS Report, issued in December 2001, sets out the framework of R2P.[348] For instance, the report acknowledges that where a population is suffering harm as a result of internal war, insurgency, repression or state failure, then the principle of non-intervention by states yields to the international responsibility to protect.[349] It was only until October 2005, with the adoption of the World Summit Outcome by the General Assembly, that world leaders formally embraced the "responsibility to protect" populations from genocide, war crimes, ethnic cleansing and crimes against humanity.[350]

It is noteworthy that the ICISS Report stipulates that once a state is granted membership to the UN, the international community welcomes that state as a responsible member of the community of nations. From that moment of admission, there is a re-characterization of sovereignty: from "sovereignty as control" to "sovereignty as responsibility" in both internal functions and external duties.[351] The ICISS Report further maintained that state sovereignty implies a dual responsibility: (1) to respect the sovereignty of other states (the external responsibility) and (2) to respect the dignity and basic rights of all persons within the state (the internal responsibility).[352] This modern

344 Criddle & Fox-Decent, n 2, at 10.

345 Annan, K 1999, *UN Secretary-General "annual report to general assembly"*, United Nations, New York, 20 September 1999. For full speech see: (www.un.org).

346 Annan, *UN Secretary-General.*

347 Annan, *UN Secretary-General.*

348 Report of the International Commission on Intervention and State Sovereignty (International Development Research Centre, December 2001).

349 At xi.

350 *2005 World Summit Outcome* GA Res 60/1 (2005), [138] and [139].

351 Report of the International Commission on Intervention and State Sovereignty, n 348, at [2.14].

352 At [1.35].

understanding of sovereignty is embraced under UN practice and international human rights law and is central to the development of the core theme of R2P.[353] In other words, the doctrine of R2P acts in tandem with the principle of sovereignty as responsibility.

The further work of Francis Deng on "sovereignty as responsibility" is also pertinent and should not go unnoticed. Deng, a former special adviser to the UN Secretary-General for the prevention of genocide, opined that it was the Canadian-sponsored ICISS Report that brought into the mainstream the principle of "sovereignty as responsibility".[354] But what exactly does "sovereignty as responsibility" entail? For Deng, if a state fails to discharge its responsibility for the welfare of its citizens – due to their lack of political will or capacity – then the concerned international community, acting collectively or through coalitions, is obliged to intervene to provide the necessary assistance.[355] Therefore, the role of the international community to render protection and assistance to those in need and to hold governments accountable in the discharge of their national responsibilities is the very essence of "sovereignty as responsibility".[356] As Sadako Ogata, a former Japanese UN high commissioner for refugees, once explained, the principle of "sovereignty as responsibility" is "the most powerful idea that emerged in the international arena in the last decade".[357] For these reasons, "sovereignty" cannot be disassociated from "responsibility" as it is sovereignty that holds a state government accountable to its domestic constituency as well as to the international community.[358]

The next issue, which is open to scholarly debate, is whether R2P is a binding principle in international law. In response to this, the ICISS Report was quick to propose that R2P was an emerging concept. As the Report stated: "What has been gradually emerging is a parallel transition from a culture of sovereign impunity to a culture of national and international accountability".[359] Whilst in 2001, the ICISS Report acknowledged that there was not yet a sufficiently strong basis to claim R2P as a new principle of customary international law, there was growing state practice and Security Council precedent to suggest an emerging guiding principle termed "responsibility to protect".[360] This notion of an emerging principle in favour of military intervention for the protection of human beings was supported by

353 At [1.36].
354 Deng, F 2010, 'From "sovereignty as responsibility" to the "responsibility to protect"', *Global Responsibility to Protect*, vol. 2, p. 353, 368.
355 At 354–355.
356 At 354.
357 At 369.
358 Botrel, n 342, at 6.
359 Report of the International Commission on Intervention and State Sovereignty, n 348, at [2.18].
360 At [2.24].

a number of sources, including fundamental natural law principles, human rights provisions of the UN Charter, the UDHR, the Geneva Conventions and the Statute of the International Criminal Court.[361]

In 2004 the High-level Panel on Threats, Challenges and Change, which was convened by Secretary-General Kofi Annan, issued a report on collective security entitled "A More Secure World: Our Shared Responsibility".[362] In its report, the High-level Panel stated:[363]

> We endorse *the emerging norm* that there is a collective international responsibility to protect, exercisable by the Security Council authorizing military intervention as a last resort, in the event of genocide and other large scale killing, ethnic cleansing or serious violations of international humanitarian law which sovereign Governments have proved powerless or unwilling to prevent.

In March 2005, months before UN member states endorsed the doctrine of R2P, Kofi Annan agreed with the approaches taken by ICISS and the High-level Panel on Threats, Challenges and Change that described R2P as "an emerging norm".[364] Therefore, up to 2005, it is arguable that the UN considered R2P as an emerging principle of international law. Despite this, recent scholarly opinion on this subject differs from this suggestion. Benvenisti, for instance, observed that although concepts such as "sovereignty as responsibility" and "responsibility to protect" have been recognized by states, most states strongly resist the expansion of such responsibilities.[365] Criddle, however, offers a middle ground when he cautions that the international community's responsibility to protect human rights is best understood as a moral ideal rather than a legally binding obligation.[366] Criddle comes to this conclusion based on scholarly findings that there is a conspicuous lack of support for R2P in state practice.[367] These views must be contrasted with that of Parmar, who argues that sovereignty in the form of a responsibility (which extends to the R2P doctrine) has gained the status of an international legal norm.[368]

As it stands, whether R2P could be considered a legally binding obligation in international law is still a grey area and open to debate. At the very least, as Criddle suggests, the mere fact that a state would consider intervening in another state – whether by the insistence of the latter state or not – to protect

361 At [2.26].

362 Follow-up to the outcome of the *Millennium Summit* UN Doc A/59/565 (2 December 2004).

363 At [203] (emphasis added).

364 *Report of the Secretary General*, 59th Session of the UN General Assembly, UN Doc A/59/2005 (21 March 2005) at [135].

365 Benvenisti, n 8, at 297.

366 Criddle, n 208, at 417.

367 Criddle, n 208, at 417.

368 Parmar, SS 2019, *Sovereignty and trans-boundary environmental issues: a search for co-existence*, Dharmsahastra National Law University, February 2019, p. 8.

that state's citizens from acts of genocide or other crimes against humanity raises the question of a moral responsibility. For this reason, Bosselmann stated, "[N]ow is the time to advance the concept of state sovereignty as a concept of rights and responsibilities".[369]

One argument put forward is that the moral foundation that underscores the notion of responsibility stems from the concept of the common concern of humankind.[370] The R2P therefore can be interpreted as a trusteeship duty given to sovereign states to protect global human rights – which include the human rights of their citizens as well as foreigners.[371] In these circumstances, there is a nexus between the common concern of humanity and R2P,[372] which, in turn, buttresses Benvenisti's theory of a state as a trustee of humanity.

a) R2P and Natural Catastrophes

With the adoption of the World Summit Outcome in October 2005, it is evident that states have accepted, in principle, a responsibility to protect populations from genocide, war crimes, ethnic cleansing and crimes against humanity. Whether the doctrine of R2P has obtained the status of customary international law is still yet to be proven. If we contend that states, at the very least, accept that R2P as a doctrine exists as a moral construct, then the next central issue is whether we can use the language of R2P to create a system of protection in situations of natural and environmental catastrophes or, even further, for the protection of the Earth's ecological integrity.[373] One argument in favour of this idea was advanced by Axworthy and Rock, two initiators of the ICISS, who wrote about an "unbundled R2P".[374] The rationale behind this argument is that even though R2P is solely intended to deal with situations of mass atrocities, when R2P is "unbundled", it becomes clear that its foundational principles can be applied to other problems that engage humanity as a whole.[375] This rationale makes sense when it is juxtaposed with the text of the ICISS Report which recommended that a "conscience-shocking" situation such as an "overwhelming natural or environmental catastrophes, where the state concerned is either unwilling or unable to cope, or call for assistance, and significant loss of life is occurring or threatened" should be one possible ground for foreign intervention.[376] One flaw with this reasoning is that, although the ICISS's recommendation included "natural or

369 Bosselmann, n 6, at 54.
370 Botrel, n 342, at 7.
371 At 8.
372 At 8.
373 At 3.
374 Axworthy, L & Rock, A 2009, 'R2P: a new and unfinished agenda', *Global Responsibility to Protect*, vol. 1, pp. 54, 64–65.
375 At 64.
376 Report of the International Commission on Intervention and State Sovereignty, n 348, at [4.20].

environmental catastrophes", this proposal was not accepted by states when the General Assembly adopted the World Summit Outcome in 2005.[377] This provides clear evidence that at that time, there was no consensus among states to broaden the scope of R2P to include intervention in times of natural or environmental catastrophes.

In 2007, the statement made by UN Secretary-General Ban Ki-moon could have been interpreted as a turning point of the doctrine:[378]

> In 2005, world leaders embraced the responsibility to protect populations from genocide, war crimes, ethnic cleansing and crimes against humanity. We must continue to dedicate our energies to the challenge of implementation. Furthermore, too many people are still denied the right to live in dignity, displaced in their attempts to escape the violence of natural and man-made catastrophes. Those violations undermine the foundations of the security and development throughout the world.

Subsequent to the secretary-general's statement, there was an attempt to invoke the R2P in the circumstances of a natural disaster involving the devastating passage of Typhoon Nargis in Myanmar in May 2008.[379] In the aftermaths of the typhoon, the government refused to open the borders to permit the delivery of international aid for those directly impacted by the natural disaster. France argued that this was a case that justified coercive intervention, under the "responsibility to protect" principle and proposed that the Security Council pass a resolution that authorized the delivery of aid on the Burmese government.[380] Such a proposal was resisted by China and Russia, which considered it to be an intervention in Myanmar's internal affairs.[381] On this point, Gareth Evans, one of the original architects of the doctrine, argued that R2P as it was originally conceived is about protecting vulnerable populations from genocide, war crimes, ethnic cleansing and crimes against humanity.[382] In other words, the scope of R2P must adhere to the four corners of the language of the 2005 General Assembly resolution.

What was interesting, however, was that Evans counter-argued that even if natural disasters are not per se "responsibility to protect" situations, they can be made subject to the principle if mass atrocity crimes are involved.[383] So,

377 *2005 World Summit Outcome* GA Res 60/1 (2005), [138] and [139].

378 Report of the Secretary-General on the Work of the Organisation Supplement No. 1 A/62/1 (31 August 2007).

379 Botrel, n 342, at 9.

380 Evans, G 2009, 'The responsibility to protect in environmental emergencies', *American Society of International Law*, vol. 103, p. 27, 29–31.

381 Evans, G 2008, 'Facing up to our responsibilities', *The Guardian*, online edn, London, 12 May.

382 Evans, 'Facing up to our responsibilities'.

383 Evans, n 381, at 30–31.

for instance, if the Burmese government's inaction or resistance to external aid exposed thousands of persons to suffering and the real risk of death, then it was possible to argue that such an omission amounted to a crime against humanity.[384] The point to be made is that outside the "big four" human rights abuses, expanding the scope of R2P to other matters (such as natural and environmental catastrophes) appears to be dubious in practice. To expand the R2P doctrine to address environmental crises has been described as being a "slippery slope" and even "far-fetched".[385] As Benvenisti points out:[386]

> Although the concepts of "sovereignty as responsibility" and "responsibility to protect" have been recognized by states, most states strongly resist the expansion of such responsibilities even to cases of natural disasters.

b) Greater Platform of R2P

Currently, it appears that the expansion of R2P outside the confines of the traditional "big four" human rights abuses remains uncertain and requires political will. Notwithstanding this, convincing arguments can be advanced in the future to alter the status quo, thereby shaping a more robust R2P. The ICISS Report makes it clear that the substance of the responsibility to protect is the provision of "life-supporting protection and assistance to populations at risk".[387] If this is the case, can R2P be relied on to protect populations directly affected by climate-induced catastrophes such as severe flooding in Western Europe or wildfires in Australia? What about rising sea levels that can ultimately devastate homes and agricultural lands in the Pacific Islands? Similarly, could R2P be invoked to protect persons fleeing from their drought-stricken home regions, where the presiding state is hamstrung from acting? If R2P is "unbundled" and its foundational principles examined, it should apply to problems such as these because they "engage humanity as a whole".[388] As Axworthy and Rock claim:[389]

> There is perhaps no phenomenon more pertinent to the lessons of R2P than the global challenge of climate change, arguably the most serious threat to international peace and security at present.

384 At 30.
385 Botrel, n 342, at 2 and 3.
386 Benvenisti, n 8, at 297.
387 Report of the International Commission on Intervention and State Sovereignty, n 348, at [2.32].
388 Axworthy & Rock, n 374, at 64. See also Khardori, A 2021, 'What does the state owe to its people? Toward a "responsibility to develop"', *Brigham Young University Law Review*, vol. 46, p. 1027.
389 At 64–65.

It must be recalled that R2P is intertwined with the principle of "sovereignty as responsibility", and the purpose of R2P is not to weaken global responsibility but rather to expand the available tools necessary towards effective global protection.[390] The environmental crisis (which includes climate-induced catastrophes) is no less a global issue than the "big four" human rights abuses and should therefore be accounted for in a state-driven R2P architecture. If for some reason this cannot be achieved, then the R2P framework would effectively dilute the principle of "sovereignty as responsibility" – a principle in which the R2P doctrine is primarily substantiated. A state cannot be regarded as a trustee of the well-being of humanity[391] under R2P if it has no responsibility for environmental concerns which affect humanity itself. The supremacy of Pufendorf's "people's welfare" undeniably depends on a healthy environment. Any attempt, therefore, to limit the scope of R2P and to ignore environmental crises in the R2P equation will make a mockery of the principle of "sovereignty as responsibility". For these reasons, it is unreasonable to argue that "sovereignty as a responsibility" applies exclusively to the protection of global human rights and not to environmental crises. Just as it is for human rights, there must be some accountability by our leaders for actions taken which harm the well-being of the Earth.

For "sovereignty as responsibility" to be fully understood and implemented in this 21st century, it must include in its package a "responsibility to protect" in times of environmental crises and, if I dare say, circumstances which lead to ecological destruction. We live on planet Earth, and it is only natural, as its host, that we have a responsibility to preserve and protect its ecological integrity.[392] Our responsibility to protect the Earth should be an emerging concept based on fundamental natural law principles.[393] If we admit this planetary responsibility, then the next hurdle to overcome is whether we should exercise such a responsibility through a greater platform borrowed from the R2P doctrine.[394]

In her writings, Eckersley explored the idea of humanitarian or ecological intervention for "crimes against nature". She posed this question: "If the international community condemns genocide, might it one day be ready to condemn ecocide?"[395] Eckersley reasoned that ecological intervention could be a worthwhile exercise since there are some ecological problems that do constitute environmental emergencies in the sense that they are

390 Botrel, n 342, at 13.

391 At 21.

392 At 13.

393 Report of the International Commission on Intervention and State Sovereignty, n 348, at [2.26].

394 Botrel, n 342, at 13.

395 Eckersley, R 2004, *The green state: rethinking democracy and sovereignty*, The MIT Press, Cambridge, p. 293.

grave and imminent and require a military or paramilitary response (e.g. the Chernobyl nuclear explosion).[396] Eckersley, however, admits that there are some limitations pertaining to ecological intervention. One limitation is that it might provide a licence for powerful states to act as "global green action heroes" to further their own environmental values and priorities that may not be widely shared.[397] Secondly, and quite ironically, military intervention can often result in civilian casualties and further environmental damage.[398] So while a case for eco-humanitarian intervention to prevent ecocide or crimes against nature still appears "particularly shaky" on the question of political legitimacy, the moral case should not be whimsically dismissed.[399]

States must now strive towards a higher threshold of responsibility, where the common concern for humanity acknowledges a larger community that includes the non-human world. Indeed, by paying recognition to this non-human world, we would be also catering for the well-being of humanity. As Judge Weeramantry in the International Court of Justice, in his separate opinion in the *Gabčíkovo-Nagymaros* case, noted:[400]

> We have entered an era of international law in which international law subserves not only the interests of individual States but looks beyond them and their parochial concerns to the greater interests of humanity and planetary welfare.

In this new era, it is possible to defend the idea that this "greater platform" of responsibility, which goes beyond the traditional R2P mandate, can be envisaged as states acting as environmental trustees or as trustees for the Earth. The words of Ngcobo J are pertinent on this point: "The present generation holds the earth in trust for the next generation. This trusteeship position carries with it the responsibility to look after the environment".[401]

396 At 295.
397 At 312.
398 At 312.
399 At 312.
400 *Gabčíkovo-Nagymaros Project (Hungary v Slovakia)* [1997] ICJ Rep 7 at 118.
401 *Fuel Retailers Association of Southern Africa v Director-General Environmental Management*, n 309, at [102].

Chapter 9

The State as Earth Trustee

> [Y]ou may be thinking that there's a disturbing gap between the comprehensive principle of Earth trusteeship and the harsh realities of economics, finance and nation-states. But . . . [s]ometimes an ideal is closer to reality than we may think.[1]

1. States as Fiduciaries of Humanity

Criddle and Fox-Decent have separately and jointly articulated a fiduciary model of sovereignty informed by the way in which international law "regulates the distribution and exercise of sovereign powers"[2] in recognition of the fiduciary relationship between a state and its people and its constitutive features of "trust, discretionary power, and vulnerability".[3] Notwithstanding "the intellectual disowning of the colonial era, so much a source of retrospective and continuing shame,"[4] Criddle explains that this is when the fiduciary structure of international law originated:

> History suggests that the fiduciary structure of international law developed through colonial confrontations between imperial powers and first nations. By framing colonial governance as a fiduciary relationship, Vitoria and his followers laid the foundation for an international legal order in which all states would be viewed as fiduciaries charged with a duty to respect, protect, and fulfil human rights for their own nationals and others subject to their care.[5]

1 Bosselmann, K 2017, 'The next step: earth trusteeship', presentation at the seventh interactive dialogue of the general assembly on harmony with nature, UN Headquarters, New York, 21 April, p. 2.
2 Criddle, EJ & Fox-Decent, E 2009, 'A fiduciary theory of Jus Cogens', *Yale Journal of International Law*, vol. 34, p. 331, 13, 4.
3 Criddle & Fox-Decent, 'A fiduciary theory of Jus Cogens'.
4 Purdy, J & Fielding, K 2007, 'Sovereigns, trustees, guardians: private-law concepts and the limits of legitimate state power', *Law and Contemporary Problems*, vol. 70, p. 165, 166.
5 Criddle, EJ 2014, 'A sacred trust of civilization', in AS Gold & PB Miller (eds), *Philosophical foundations of fiduciary law*, Oxford University Press, Oxford, p. 404, 24.

DOI: 10.4324/9781032674049-13

Fox-Decent applies this fiduciary theory to set out how and why sovereign states owe a domestic and cosmopolitan duty (to national and extra-territorial citizens respectively) to "respect the right of the world's inhabitants to a healthy environment".[6] First, he sets out how the fiduciary relationship between state and citizen arises:

> [T]he state's legislative, judicial, and executive branches all assume discretionary powers that are institutional, purposive, and other-regarding. Private parties are not legally entitled to exercise the state's powers and thus are particularly vulnerable to public authority, despite their ability within democracies to participate in democratic processes. The state's monopolization of public powers over its people can be understood therefore as a fiduciary relationship mediated by legality – rather than a relationship of domination or instrumentalization – only if a principle of legality prevents public institutions from exploiting their position to set unilaterally the terms of interaction with their people. The fiduciary principle is a principle of legality that does just this: it authorizes the state to exercise public powers for and on behalf of its people, but subject to strict legal norms that safeguard subjects' inherent dignity as free and equal co-beneficiaries of state action.[7]

To realize this duty, the state must

> adopt and enforce laws protecting persons from private domination and instrumentalization, such as may arise when non-state actors unjustifiably degrade the environment. Human rights are constitutive of state sovereignty on this account because they supply a normative framework within which the state can establish a secure order of equal freedom, an order marked by the absence of private or public domination and instrumentalization. In this sense, all public powers are constrained and constituted by the state's fiduciary duty to respect, protect, and fulfil human rights.[8]

Respect for, and the protection and fulfilment of, human rights thus become "a function of the fiduciary obligations that accompany [states'] exercise of sovereignty – even if they have yet to ratify relevant human rights conventions",[9] and consequently, the measure of sovereign legitimacy or criteria "for testing the validity of state action. . . . [I]f the action falls below the

6 Fox-Decent, E 2012, 'From fiduciary states to joint trusteeship of the atmosphere: the right to a healthy environment through a fiduciary prism', in K Coguill, C Samford & T Smith (eds), *Fiduciary duty and the atmospheric trust*, Ashgate Publishing, Farnham, p. 253, 255.

7 At 260.

8 At 260–261.

9 At 263.

standard set by the right. . . . Then the impugned act is not a sovereign act that can benefit from the doctrine of sovereign immunity".[10]

Fox-Decent's fiduciary framework therefore assumes an anthropocentric human rights rationale within which to derive a duty to protect the global environment. First, he asserts that although "the conventional view of human rights is hard pressed to accommodate the right to a healthy environment", the right "can readily be seen to satisfy [the fiduciary theory's] substantive qualifying criteria of integrity, formal moral equality, and solicitude".[11] That is, it (1) has as its object "the good of the people rather than the good of the state's institutions or officials,[12] (2) regards all persons "as equal co-beneficiaries",[13] and (3) reflects "proper solicitude toward the legitimate interests of a state's subjects"[14] – in short, the well-being of every current and future citizen is advanced through the protection of a healthy environment.

Having established that the right to environment qualifies as a human right (under the fiduciary theory at least), Fox-Decent suggests that "every state owes a cosmopolitan duty to extra-territorial noncitizens . . . correlative to those persons' right to a healthy environment".[15] That is because "public authorities owe relevant duties to *anyone affected*[16] by their possession or exercise of public power, regardless of where the person happens to be and regardless of their civil or political status".[17] And since

> every inhabitant of earth is subject to every state's possession and exercise of its environmental power . . . every state's environmental power is constrained by a duty to exercise that power in a manner consistent with the cosmopolitan right of every person to a healthy environment.[18]

Applying this logic to the example of greenhouse gas emissions, Fox-Decent is able to neatly articulate "a cosmopolitan *erga omnes* obligation to respect the right of the world's inhabitants to a healthy environment"[19] since "the possession and exercise of sovereign powers over the emission of greenhouse gases engages the interest in a healthy environment held by every person in the world".[20] The "cosmopolitan reach of the fiduciary theory" implies

10 At 266.
11 At 266.
12 At 261.
13 At 261.
14 At 261.
15 At 255.
16 Further described by Fox-Decent as "anyone, anywhere, whose legally cognisable interests are implicated by the possession or exercise of sovereign power", at 255.
17 At 270.
18 At 270.
19 At 255.
20 At 255.

"a commitment to the idea that states are essentially joint trustees of the earth's atmosphere"[21] in respect of which the Earth's inhabitants are beneficiaries. In this way, Fox-Decent is able to delineate "a legal framework from within which to ground every state's duty to respect the right to a healthy environment";[22] "they have a *legal* duty to do so because the joint trust or fiducial relationship is a legal relationship".[23]

Writing together, Criddle and Fox-Decent have further refined this fiduciary model, describing it as a " 'relational theory' in the sense that it conceptualizes state sovereignty under international law as arising from, and being defined and constrained by, features of the distinctive juridical relationship that international law constitutes between states and their people"[24] and which "although analogous to trusteeship – are not fully captured in the law of trust".[25] They note that "[c]ontemporary international law entrusts states with authority to exercise sovereign powers, but only in the name and for the benefit of the people subject to those powers (including, in some cases, foreign nationals)".[26] This, they note, "is the criterion of legitimacy that flows from the fiduciary theory".[27] To this end, "a state's claim to exercise sovereign authority is derived from, and wholly dependent upon, the satisfaction of its relational duties to the people subject to its legal powers".[28] In this way, Criddle and Fox-Decent demonstrate that "a state's sovereign *authority to rule* and its *duty to serve the people* entrusted to its care are *mutually dependent* features of the fiduciary constitution of sovereignty under international law".[29] Accordingly, "the fiduciary model of state sovereignty operates as an emerging 'constitution' for international society by providing a legal framework for evaluating claims to sovereign authority".[30]

The fiduciary relationship between a state and its people arises because (1) "[c]itizens, by virtue of living in a state, surrender many of their legal and political rights to the state";[31] (2) as a result, "[a]ll agents and instrumentalities of the state . . . are vested by law with discretionary power to make, interpret, or enforce laws on behalf of their people";[32] (3) that is because "international law confers these [discretionary public] powers on legally

21 At 272–285.
22 At 285.
23 At 285.
24 Criddle & Fox-Decent, n 2, at 3.
25 At 2.
26 At 3.
27 At 3.
28 At 3.
29 At 4 (emphasis added).
30 At 18.
31 Lui, H 2014, 'A fiduciary perspective on the state's duty to protect the environment', *Auckland University Law Review*, vol. 20, p. 101, 107.
32 Criddle & Fox-Decent, n 2, at 25.

designated institutions – typically states – to be exercised through their constitutive agencies and instrumentalities";[33] and (4) these

> [p]ublic powers are other-regarding and purpose-laden in that they are to be exercised for the benefit of a state's people, and relate to the construction of a legal order that makes equal freedom possible, but which the state's people, in their separate and individual capacities, cannot provide.[34]

And it is the purpose of international law and international institutions, Criddle and Fox-Decent contend, to hold states accountable for the fulfilment of their fiduciary obligations upon which their claims to sovereign authority rely.[35] This is particularly so where the exercise of domestic sovereignty "would create justice-sensitive spillover effects affecting extraterritorial non-nationals".[36]

In cases "that affect humanity generally, [i.e.] the regulation of carbon emissions, the "people" subject to the local state's sovereign power is humanity at large",[37] and the "fiduciary model reconceives sovereignty in a manner that makes its territorial dimension consistent with the universal entitlement of every member of humanity to have his or her physical existence not treated as a wrong".[38] That is because "a fiduciary duty prohibits undue interference with another's freedom [regardless of where they happen to live, so] distinguishing between a state's protection of its own citizens and another state's citizens is unjustified if a state's actions will affect both".[39] As Lui puts it, "[T]he state owes a duty to act in the best interests of all citizens within its sphere of influence".[40]

Criddle and Fox-Decent's "fiduciaries of humanity" model is attractive insofar as it (1) properly resituates sovereignty primarily as responsibility and (2) overcomes the artificiality of territorial boundaries with respect to the environment by expanding the beneficiary pool according to an "affectedness" measure, thereby enfranchising humanity at large. Lui further explains that the "affectedness" measure of the fiduciary duty operates to safeguard the interests of future generations:

> A fiduciary duty requires the fiduciary to be able to affect the beneficiary's interests, with that beneficiary being peculiarly vulnerable to the fiduciary's power. Because the present generation can irreparably damage environmental conditions for future generations, the present generation meets

33 At 26.
34 At 26.
35 At 29.
36 At 267.
37 At 268.
38 At 267.
39 Lui, n 31, at 109.
40 Lui, n 31, at 109.

> the requirement for discretionary power over a beneficiary. Future generations are peculiarly vulnerable because they cannot ensure that the present generation will exercise its power in their best interests.[41]

When a state's fiduciary duty is informed by the need to ensure intergenerational equity, the state must adopt a longer decision-making horizon underpinned by long-term ecological concerns, rather than quantifiable short-term economic and social interests. In this way, states can be seen as joint fiduciaries owing cosmopolitan duties to protect the ecological integrity of the Earth.

Whilst the "fiduciaries of humanity" model helpfully reframes state sovereignty, legitimacy and, indeed, accountability, as responsibility to the global citizenry by reason of international law, human rights and the principle of "affectedness", the duty to protect the global environment remains a reconciliation of state, non-state and future citizens' interests, within which nature's interests do not feature, and the environment is of instrumental value insofar as its protection underpins the full realization of certain human rights. Humans remain "the measure and benchmark for anything that matters on Earth",[42] with the result likely to be "weak sustainability"[43] at best. The conception of Earth trusteeship seeks to overcome these anthropocentric shortcomings of the fiduciary model, which is explored next.

2. Trusteeship of the Earth

> Earth trusteeship is the institutionalisation of the duty of states to protect the integrity of Earth's ecological systems.[44]

Grotius is attributed with articulating the origins of the trusteeship theory of constitutional government whereby sovereignty is a social construction based on the voluntary coordination and aggregation of powers of individual persons already inherent in individuals.[45] Writing during the English Revolution, Overton further maintained that

> self-sovereignty contains inherent restrictions, and that these persist as limits on the power of any legitimate ruler. The trust or agency relationship environed in this account thus includes constraints on the trustee's power that are not derived from the intent of the settlor or the terms of the trust,

41 At 113.

42 Bosselmann, K 2020a, 'The role of trusteeship in earth governance', in L Westra & K Bosselmann (eds), *Ecological integrity in science and law*, Springer, Cham, p. 241.

43 At 245.

44 Bosselmann, n 1, at 292.

45 Purdy & Fielding, n 4, at 171.

> but are instead mandatory, defining this type of trust – that is, defining political sovereignty. Those constraints comprise a duty to promote the well-being of the population and a prohibition on violating its liberties.[46]

Drawing on property law concepts, Locke subsequently referred to "sovereignty" as the property conditionally transferred to the state to be used for the benefit of the settler, and a legitimate legislature acts pursuant to its trust, and reserved power (or a reversionary right)[47] remains with the beneficiaries when the trustee acts contrary to the trust reposed in them:[48]

> Sovereignty, then, is conceived . . . as an inherently conditioned property claim that, upon violation of its conditions, dissolves in forfeiture so that sovereignty reverts to the political community built, in turn, out of self-sovereignty, the "Property" each person has in herself.[49]

By conceptualizing the state-citizen relationship as a trust, the state (trustee) necessarily assumes fiduciary obligations to act in the best interests of its citizens (beneficiaries). Trusts imply:

> a sort of dual ownership, legal in the trustee, who enjoys the power to use and dispose of the corpus, and equitable in the beneficiary, who has an enforceable right to benefit from the use of her property. The limits of the powers the trustee may exercise by virtue of her legal ownership correspond to the beneficiary's rights of equitable ownership.[50]

In this case, the corpus of the trust – the natural environment – is considered to be the common property of the citizens, and the state must thus manage it in their best interests.[51]

In doing so, the state must act loyally (it must not benefit from the position it holds unless explicitly authorized), perform personally, invest the trust assets, act impartially, account and provide information. As Roy notes:

> If governments were to apply these duties, it . . . could force a government to take positive actions towards the environment, not only conservation

46 At 174.
47 At 180.
48 Locke, J 1988, 'Two treaties of government', in P Laslett (ed), *Cambridge texts in the history of political thought*, Cambridge University Press, Cambridge, Section 11.1.7 at 271.
49 Locke, 'Two treaties of government'.
50 At 194.
51 Roy, S 2020, 'The potential of the trusteeship theory for Canadian public law and environmental governance', in K Anker, PD Burdon, G Garver, M Maloney & C Sbert (eds), *From environmental to ecological law*, Routledge, Oxfordshire, p. 147, 487.

ones, as the government would have the duty to make nature thrive (that is, to "invest the trust assets").[52]

Wood draws "upon ancient trust concepts originating in property law"[53] to describe her vision of Nature's Trust:

> Long ago, the Supreme Court said that government, as the only enduring institution with control over human actions, is a trustee of Nature's resources. What does this mean? You can imagine all of the resources essential to our human welfare and survival – including waters, wildlife, and air – as being packaged together in a legal endowment which I call Nature's Trust. Our imperilled atmosphere is one of the assets in that trust. Government holds this great natural trust for all generations of citizens – past, present and future. . . . Protecting our natural trust is more consequential than anything else government does.[54]

By portraying "Nature as a trust rather than an ill-defined commons",[55] Wood submits that "we vest citizens with expectations of enduring property rights to a defined, bounded asset".[56] This is significant because:

> Any loss of the trust becomes manifest. This frame resonates with and motivates the public because it taps into concepts that are familiar and important. . . . Most people have heard of a trust. . . . Children get angry when they think of our generation spending down a trust that they are entitled to take in the same abundance we have enjoyed".[57]

Wood further argues that "by defining Nature in familiar property terms . . . you are fitting Nature into the system of property rights".[58] To this end, "[t]he Nature's Trust frame is not anti-property rights. To the contrary, it affirms our collective property rights in assets that support humanity".[59] This would not deny private property rights, but their exercise would be subject

52 At 490–491.

53 Wood, MC, Leonard, S, Bartz, D & Peart, N 2013, 'Securing planetary life sources for future generations: legal actions deriving from the ancient sovereign trust obligation', in MB Gerrard & GE Wannier (eds), *Threatened island nations: legal implications of rising seas and a changing climate*, Cambridge University Press, New York, p. 531, 594.

54 At 595.

55 At 599.

56 At 599.

57 At 599.

58 At 601.

59 At 601.

to communal constraints and better conceived of as stewardship rights to protect for the benefit of all.[60]

Globally, Wood suggests that nation-states would all stand as sovereign Earth trustees and considered co-tenants of a planetary trust.[61] By appealing to notions of common ownership and co-tenancy, Wood further notes that property law helps make clear that there is a duty not to degrade or waste common assets[62] and to defend against injury.[63] Accordingly, where there is environmental damage, the state must ensure its restoration.[64]

Benvenisti similarly conceives of the state within the trust frame, describing states as "trustees of humanity" or "global trustees", with duties toward citizens within and beyond their borders. Global resources "are humanity's resources and sovereigns only have management rights in them as the trustees of humanity".[65] This, he argues, is not inconsistent with the rights of states to self-determination under international law, which he clarifies is "the right to be free from other nations, but not the right to be free from the obligation toward the collective.[66]

Like Wood, Benvenisti references property law in setting out how dominion entails responsibility, quoting Cohen to this end:

> [T]he large property owner is viewed, as he ought to be, as a wielder of power over the lives of his fellow citizens; the law should not hesitate to develop a doctrine as to his positive duties in the public interest.[67]

This, Benvenisti suggests, can be extrapolated to the global context:

> [T]he powers that sovereigns exercise, both in their management of their "own" internal resources and when they make rival claims on transboundary and public resources, yield a direct and indirect impact on others. The increasing global pressures on the available resources and the emerging recognition of moral obligations that inhibit the exercise of exclusion challenge the idea of exclusive ownership and give rise to the demand that sovereigns manage the resources under their

60 Bosselmann, K 2017, 'Governing the global commons, the "planetary boundaries approach"', *Policy Quarterly*, vol. 13, no. 1, pp. 38–39.
61 Roy, n 51, at 497.
62 Wood, et al., n 53, at 602.
63 At 595.
64 At 595.
65 Benvenisti, E 2013, 'Sovereigns as trustees of humanity: on the accountability of states to foreign stakeholders', *American Journal of International Law*, vol. 107, p. 295, 13.
66 At 7.
67 Cohen, MR 1927, 'Property and sovereignty', *Cornell Law Review*, vol. 13, p. 8, 13, in Benvenisti, n 65, at 7.

> control efficiently and sustainably, taking into account global welfare considerations.[68]

"Affectedness" (not voting rights) thereby shapes the constituency to which states owe their fiduciary duties and to whom they should be accountable.[69]

Like Criddle and Fox-Decent's fiduciary theory, Benvenisti's trusteeship theory is ultimately a "human-rights theory",[70] albeit explained in terms of "joint ownership",[71] which "imposes strict limits on states with respect to acts that affect the human rights of individuals, no matter how they are defined".[72] This, he says, "requires sovereigns to take into account global welfare considerations in all of their activities – even those related to the management of purely domestic resources".[73] Benvenisti paraphrases Huber to explain:

> [I]nfused by the precedence of human rights and humanity's ownership, sovereigns can and should be viewed as organs of a global system that allocates competences and responsibilities for promoting the rights of all human beings and also their interest in sustainable utilisation of global resources. As trustees of this global system – to use another paraphrasing of Huber – the competency of contemporary sovereigns to manage public affairs within their respective jurisdictions brings with it a corollary duty to account for external interests and, often, even to balance internal against external interests as well.[74]

This theory captures Vattel's contentions that "[t]he Earth belongs to mankind in general"[75] for the purpose of "common habitation",[76] and "one state owes to another state whatever it owes to itself"[77] and Kant's assertion that "all men are originally in common possession of the land of the entire earth",[78] and all its inhabitants must "tolerate one another as neighbours" based on equal entitlement to the surface of the earth.[79]

68 Benvenisti, n 65, at 11.
69 At 13.
70 At 14.
71 At 14.
72 At 14.
73 At 14.
74 At 14.
75 De Vattel, E 1853, *The law of nations or the principles of natural law*, based on the 1797 edn, Republished by T & JW Johnson Law Booksellers, Philadelphia, 1853 at Book I, Chapter 18, § 208.
76 Vattel, *The law of nations or the principles of natural law*.
77 At § 3.
78 Kant, I 1996 [1797], *The metaphysics of morals*, MJ Gregor (ed), Cambridge University Press, Cambridge.
79 Kant, I 2006, *Toward perpetual peace and other writings on politics, peace and history*, P Kleingeld (ed), Yale University Press, New Haven, 2006.

Accordingly, Benvenisti maintains that "[b]ecause sovereigns are trustees of humanity, they must use the resources available to them in a way that does not harm, and even contributes, to global welfare".[80] "Harm" is defined expansively: not "by the damage caused to a neighbouring state or to specific foreign individuals, but by the diminution of the resources available or potentially available to humanity".[81] This, he notes, does not preclude a state from prioritizing its citizens' needs. Indeed, he envisions a "graduated set of responsibilities that distinguish between affected stakeholders"[82] and is clear that

> sovereigns are not expected to give foreigners the same access to their resources and their democratic processes, as this would undermine the opportunities of communities to promote their own unique preferences and destroy their incentives to invest in promoting their communal goods.[83]

This necessitates a balanced approach. So whilst a state cannot be oblivious to the needs of non-citizens,[84] equally "[a] system that imposes other-regarding obligations on sovereigns must not compromise the rights and interests of these sovereigns and their citizens".[85]

Like the fiduciary theory, Benvenisti's trusteeship model recasts sovereignty as a bundle of duties, which, with regard to environmental protection, are sometimes (according to the principle of "affectedness") other regarding. However, like the fiduciary theory, Benvenisti's trusteeship model is underpinned by human rights and is thus, necessarily, anthropocentric, distracting "from the feeling of duty to value nature *for itself*".[86] In both models, the natural world is seemingly reduced to its instrumental value to humanity, and the human/nature dichotomy persists. By contrast, a theory of Earth governance can be based on the idea of stewardship sovereignty, which, as Tarlock observes, "involves imposing duties of wise resource use across nations and generations as well as the extension of moral standing to non-humans".[87] The Earth trusteeship model aims to revive "the ecological components of what it means to be sovereign and to govern"[88] based around

80 Benvenisti, n 65, at 17.
81 At 18.
82 At 21.
83 At 21.
84 At 18.
85 At 21.
86 Bosselmann, K 2015a, *Earth governance: trusteeship of the global commons*, Edward Elgar Publisher, Cheltenham, 2015, p. 120.
87 A Dan Tarlock Law of Water Rights and Resources (Environmental Law Series) (Clark Boardman Callaghan, 1988), at 26.
88 Bosselmann, n 86, at 111.

the common heritage of life – that is, the state is a trustee of "all life on earth, and humanity is the steward".[89] Caring for the Earth becomes central to the state's mandate to govern.

The Earth trusteeship model, like Wood's Nature Trust, is predicated on the legal concept of the trust in common law: "[T]he trustee has full legal responsibility and usually a large degree of discretion to affect the best interests of the beneficiary or beneficiaries, subject to a fiduciary duty to them, and a duty to act in good faith".[90] Trust law establishes that, by reason of the fiduciary relationship that arises through the beneficiaries' vulnerability to the exercise of entrusted power,[91] the trustee must exercise their discretionary power in good faith and for the benefit of the beneficiaries, take into account proper considerations, be rational and exercise their discretion with a duty of care and without delegation or conflict of interest and not for their own personal benefit.[92] It is not difficult to see how the proper exercise of these duties by the state vis-à-vis the community of life would combat the overreach of corporatism and spread of privatization. Indeed, they would require it, and the beneficiaries – the community of life – would be entitled to compel the state to this effect and seek injunctive relief and/or compensation for any failure by the state to do so.[93]

The concept of trusteeship under international law is not novel, but it does suffer "the unfortunate spectre of paternalism due to its early links to empire and its use as a tool in the European civilising mission".[94] Its abuse during the era of imperialism perversely led to the territorially defensive, self-interested guarding of state sovereignty that calls for its reincarnation. Nevertheless, the United Nations Trusteeship Council, although now inactive, continues to exist as an organ of the United Nations. This is relevant because "we need a legal entity responsible for protecting the global commons that is inherited from past generations, [and] is presently being created, on behalf of current and future generations".[95] It is therefore necessary to emphasize that:

> Despite its somewhat controversial history in international relations, the problems and failure of trusteeship (in global politics) ought not to detract

89 At 109.
90 At 136.
91 The fiduciary relationship also reflects what Lui describes as the reality of modern democracy, which he says is "founded on the fiction that citizens have full power to give and withdraw consent as they see fit. In reality, citizens only exercise their right to vote within a constitutional framework". Lui, n 31, at 102. Thus, whilst citizens may have a say in who governs them, they do not actively consent to state decision-making. This necessitates that the state, entrusted with the power to govern, must do so in the best interests of the citizenry.
92 Bosselmann, n 86, at 142.
93 At 145.
94 At 145.
95 At 152.

from its utility as a mechanism for global commons governance. The problems that have been experienced do not stem from an inherently flawed concept, but rather from flawed application.[96]

Accordingly, the United Nations Trusteeship Council could be revived to oversee trusteeship of the global commons, which are "held in trust and 'owned' by all".[97]

Under this model, nature is given standing through the broad definition of beneficiaries as "the community of life", which necessitates an intergenerational, inter-species, Earth-centred ethic of care.[98] The role of the state would be redefined so as to reflect "the irrefutable reality that maintaining a healthy environment is essential to ensuring ongoing human prosperity, and, as representatives of the governed, states are tasked with this responsibility".[99] This necessitates opening up state's governance mandate "to include other types of wealth and value – ecological, social, democratic, moral – values that need to be fully recognised and actively protected by those who purport to govern on behalf of the people".[100] To do so requires states to recognize the empirical flaw of (un)sustainable development and its "false assumption that limitless growth is possible",[101] which has been the prevailing paradigm within which environmental protection is accommodated, but only insofar as it enables or does not unduly compromise economic development. Such "weak" sustainability is a result of the neoliberal economic capture of our democratic institutions[102] and a failure of the state to exercise the trusteeship role that is "inherent in their mandate to govern".[103]

To the extent that governments are environmental trustees at present, their primary duty, as they perceive it, is not to preserve the land itself but the income streams it generates.[104] To this end, "[w]e need to address and scrutinise the role states play as our putative 'representatives' since states' 'sovereign interests' are supposed to be the interests of those governed",[105] which, in turn, calls into question the state's legitimacy to govern.

It is time for our political institutions to shed their exclusively economically imagined mandate and adopt an ethic of care for the commons. This includes recognizing that they are responsible for maintaining the health of the

96 At 147.
97 At 152.
98 At 152.
99 At 156.
100 Bosselmann, n 86, at 156.
101 Bosselmann, n 42, at 4.
102 Bosselmann, n 86, at 161.
103 At 157.
104 At 168.
105 At 156.

environment, and this can only be achieved through sustainability. The prosperity that governments are designated to affect is a much larger concept than material well-being and involves maintaining the common ecological basis of the economy. Only the state is in a position to make and enforce rules based on fundamental principles, and only the state has the power to govern.[106]

3. The Democratic Context

Eckersley notes that the liberal capitalist state is neither representative of, nor responsive to, all interests, but needs "to be sensitive to the public sphere to maintain legitimacy".[107] Indeed, the state gains its legitimacy exclusively from the people who created it.[108] However, we may have democracy in a technical sense (and many countries do not), but we have lost sight of the duties that the state owes those it governs. At the most basic level, the state's legitimacy to govern depends on its ability to serve the common interest of its citizens.[109]

This ability has been deeply compromised by neoliberal economic hegemony. The role of government is to act as the counterweight to the hijacking of our democratic institutions (and their ability to manage the domestic and global commons) by neoliberal economics, but government is dominated by those same corporations[110] that have privatized and commercialized, enclosed and diminished the common wealth.[111] The way to combat this is to call into question the legitimacy of the state. The legitimacy of the state as a legal institution rests on its ability to care for its citizens. To this end, the state has fiduciary obligations and fundamentally acts, in fact, as a trustee for its citizens and their cultural and natural commons. In order to strengthen its legitimacy, the sovereign state of the 21st century must act as a legal trustee for the natural environment. This trusteeship function cannot end at national boundaries but exists beyond boundaries to include the global commons and, ultimately, the Earth as a whole.[112]

To the extent that the state fails to fulfil its fiduciary obligations to act by, through and for its citizens, the state can be held to account.[113] Much of

106 At 178.
107 Eckersley, R 2004, *The green state: rethinking democracy and sovereignty*, The MIT Press, Cambridge, p. 36.
108 Bosselmann, K 2019, 'Large-scale acquisitions of the commons: the need for Earth governance', in L Westra, K Bosselmann & V Zambrano (eds), *Ecological integrity and land uses: sovereignty, governance, displacements and land grabs*, Nova Science Publishers, p. 9.
109 At 10.
110 Bosselmann, K 2020, 'Environmental trusteeship and state sovereignty: can they be reconciled?', *Transnational Legal Theory*, vol. 11, p. 15.
111 Bosselmann, 'Environmental trusteeship and state sovereignty'.
112 Bosselmann, n 1, at 294.
113 Bosselmann, n 1, at 294.

contemporary decision-making is arguably the result of "illegitimate power because it is no longer accountable to citizens according to the ideals of liberal democracy".[114]

The answer, Eckersley contends, "lies in deepening democratic accountability and responsiveness of states to their citizens' environmental concerns while also extending democratic accountability to the environmental concerns of transnational civil society, intergovernmental organizations and the society of states in general".[115] Eckersley seeks "to enlarge the spatial and temporal boundaries of the moral community"[116] by qualifying, supplementing and/or compensating for the shortcomings of citizenship (pursuant to which the communitarian principle of belongingness or membership restricts democratic rights and entitlements to those who are members of the tribe, regardless of affectedness[117]) with the cosmopolitan principle of "affectedness" (which asserts that persons should not be bound by norms that potentially affect them if they haven't given them their free and informed consent).[118]

Eckersley's ecological democracy[119] further extends the ideal of potential affectedness to "all those potentially affected, regardless of social class, geographic location, nationality, generation or species"[120] and sets out how they should have some meaningful opportunity to participate or otherwise be represented in the making of risk-generating policies or decisions.[121] In this way, Eckersley's affectedness measure is broader than Habermas's ideal communication community since it expands the community of affectedness to include those lacking communicative competence.[122] As a result, an ecologically democratic state is "less exclusionary and more public spirited"[123] and its power thus more accountable and, hence, more legitimate.

But the merits of Eckersley's "ecological democracy" "ought to be judged not simply in terms of their procedures but also in terms of the ultimate values they seek to serve and uphold".[124] And to this end, the legitimacy of state decision-making should be measured in relation to its accountability to the *demos* as well as "the validity or truth of the values incorporated into

114 Eckersley, n 107, at 93.
115 At 15.
116 At 190.
117 At 173.
118 At 173.
119 Eckersley, R 2020, 'Ecological democracy and the rise and decline of liberal democracy', *Environmental Politics*, vol. 29, p. 214.
120 Eckersley, n 107, at 112.
121 At 171.
122 At 112.
123 At 93.
124 At 138.

substantive law".[125] The latter gives rise to the "more fundamental question of the moral justification of the existence of sovereign political authority and of the rights, duties, and demands that belong to it".[126] In this vein, Eckersley writes:

> The environmental demands as to what the state ought to be doing (or not doing) in public policy presuppose a more fundamental normative theory of the proper character and role of the nation-state vis-à-vis its own society and territory, the society of states, global civil society, and the global environment. Such a normative theory of the state would need to provide an account of the basis of state legitimacy by developing the regulative ideals that confer authority on, and provide the basis of acceptance of, decisions made in the name of the state. In the past, legitimacy was acquired by the provision of military and domestic security and the regulation and enforcement of contracts. Nowadays that legitimacy is primarily acquired by appeal to democracy, typically representative democracy of the liberal democratic variety.[127]

This is where a *grundnorm* could serve a legitimation imperative "by mounting a discursive challenge to the growth imperative through articulating a more appealing version of the lifeworld than what is experienced in consumer capitalist societies".[128] To this end,

> [The] integrity of the Earth community . . . [could] act as a bedrock standard or measure for the legal equality of a purported law. Thus, laws that contravene the standard of ecological integrity are considered defective and do not bind a population in conscience. Put otherwise, purported laws that undermine the health and future flourishing of the Earth community are not binding and citizens are justified in engaging in non-violent acts of civil disobedience to amend or repeal the law.[129]

125 Hermann, DHJ 1983, 'Max Weber and the concept of legitimacy in contemporary jurisprudence', *DePaul Law Review*, vol. 3, no. 1, p. 29. This is contrary to Weber's measure of legitimacy, which is essentially the acceptance thereof, evidenced by compliance, and the derivation of rights and duties "in a formally rational manner" and which comprise abstract legal principles without reference to external norms, ethics or moral philosophies – that is, evaluative standards.

126 Gumplova, P 2014, 'Restraining permanent sovereignty over natural resources', *Enrahonar Quaderns de Filosofia*, vol. 53, p. 93, 103.

127 Eckersley, n 107, at 1.

128 At 7.

129 Burdon, PD 2014, 'Earth jurisprudence and the project of Earth democracy', in P Burdon & M Maloney (eds), *Wild law: In practice*, 1st edn, Routledge, London, p. 25.

One caution or caveat may be warranted in relation to the biopolitics that may (already be) play(ing) out around a planetary integrity or Earth-care norm. As De Lucia writes:

> In order to accommodate the need to transform the operations of law from a modality of exploitation to one of care, sovereign power thus morphs into biopower, and more specifically biopolitics. Biopolitics offers in this respect an answer, as it shifts the focus of power, changes it modalities of interventions, and rearticulates its legitimacy on the idea of taking responsibility for the Earth, for nature.[130]

However, a closer analysis of the exercise of sovereign biopower suggests that its "protective mode of caring" is evidenced through not just the protection but also the regularization and optimization of nature *for* nature and as a set of processes central to human well-being.[131] To this end, we see the qualification, appraisal, measurement and taxonomical categorization of the community of life. By way of example, the Global Biodiversity Census assesses and monitors, identifies and categorizes and, in the end, enables the commodification of nature: "[N]onhumans are ultimately regulated and rationalised in matrices of knowledge and science, through which they are readied as productive resources of capitalism and mined as repositories of genetic information".[132] Knowledge and power coalesce into regulatory frameworks and govern through technical norms and scientific regimes in "a seamless matrix of care and control that effectively rests on a biopolitical sovereignty".[133]

The inherent problem is that biopolitics

> remains inevitable underpinned by an epistemology of mastery and often needs to be operationalised by sovereign command. Sovereignty in fact, while diminished/dormant in a legal framework that focuses on the biopolitical notions of conservation and sustainability rather than on exploitation, stands ready to be re-activated when a forceful intervention is needed to discipline recalcitrant nature.[134]

As a result, a biopolitical reorientation of law "engulfs nature in its entirety under its framework of control, where protection and subjugation, vulnerability and productivity, life and death are constantly entangled in a reciprocal

130 De Lucia, V 2020, 'Rethinking the encounter between law and nature in the anthropocene: from biopolitical sovereignty to wonder', *Law and Critique*, vol. 31, p. 329, 335.
131 At 335–336.
132 At 336.
133 At 336.
134 At 336.

and inevitable relation of indistinguishability".[135] Consequently, De Lucia argues that the emergence of the idea of the Earth as vulnerable and in need of protection is transforming, not displacing, the project of human control of the Earth.[136] "Law must be used strategically to destabilise the dominant paradigm and reform it into something that recognizes our responsibility towards the oceans and the biosphere".[137]

4. Responsibility for Human Rights and the Earth

Seventy-five years ago, in 1948, the United Nations General Assembly adopted the Universal Declaration of Human Rights. The UDHR defined "inherent dignity" and "equal and inalienable rights of all members of the human family" as the foundation for a just and peaceful future. It also stated, in Article 29 (1), that "everybody has duties to the community in which alone the free will and development of his personality is possible" in recognition of the fact that human rights cannot flourish without corresponding duties. Since then, a profusion of global declarations and documents have expressed the importance of individual and collective duties as a prerequisite for the well-being of humans and the natural environment. In today's interconnected world, individual well-being depends on the well-being of human and non-human beings alike. The communities that we as individuals belong to are simultaneously local, national, regional and global and, above all, not confined to human communities. Our human destiny depends on the recognition that we are all part of the "community of life" or "Earth community".

The first global declaration to recognize this ecological truth was the Earth Charter. Adopted in the Peace Palace, The Hague, in 2000, the Earth Charter expressed what the 1987 report of the World Commission on Environment and Development (the "Brundtland Report") had called for: namely, a new international charter that recognizes Earth as our common home and destiny. The Earth Charter, translated into over 40 languages and endorsed by over 7,000 organizations (including UNESCO and IUCN), describes a global ethic shared by all cultures and religions beyond their specific characteristics. With its 16 main principles under four themes – Respect and Care for the Community of Life; Ecological Integrity; Social and Economic Justice; and

135 At 329.

136 At 331. To resolve this internal contradiction, De Lucia imagines a different trajectory for law through an aesthetics of wonder, premised on relational diversity and a centre-less relational modality within which there is no privileged subject or true law as such, but a better, more natural way of knowing good law. How this would be operationalized pursuant to De Lucia's "relational dispositionalism" remains obscure and beyond the scope of this chapter, but for further discussion, see De Lucia, n 130, at 340–341.

137 At 335.

Democracy, Nonviolence and Peace – the Earth Charter describes the ethical framework for a just, peaceful and sustainable future.

What this ethical framework means with respect to human rights and responsibilities is the subject of the Hague Principles. The drafting process that eventually led to the adoption of the Hague Principles on the occasion of the 70th anniversary of the UDHR (10 December 2018) built on the UDHR and other human rights declarations and equally on the Earth Charter. Further, 17 declarations of human responsibilities and rights of nature were considered,[138] in addition to over 25 international environmental agreements expressing concern for the integrity of the Earth's ecological system. The combined assessment of international human rights law (including the rights of indigenous peoples) and international environmental law (including rights of nature) allowed for a broader, all-inclusive perspective on human rights and responsibilities with respect to each other and the Earth as a whole. To define humanity's role in the Anthropocene, we need a new universal declaration of human rights and responsibilities. The essentials of such a declaration are expressed in three concise principles, known as the Hague Principles.

Part I ("Background") of the adopted document explains the urgency and feasibility of the Hague Principles and calls upon

> the United Nations, and the international community of states, not only to reaffirm their responsibilities for human rights, but also to recognise their responsibilities to the Earth community and the Earth system, and to adopt Earth trusteeship as an active and all-encompassing way forward.

The Earth system, while relatively new in its scientific conceptualization and importance, is well known in international environmental law. There is, in fact, a central theme that has underpinned international environmental law since the first agreements on sustainable development, climate change and biological diversity in 1992.

The health and integrity of the Earth's ecosystem is a pre-condition for all life forms, including human life. This has been acknowledged in more than 25 international environmental agreements, including the 1992 Rio Declaration on Environment and Development, Agenda 21, the Earth Charter and the 2012 Rio+20 outcome document *The Future We Want*, right through to the 2015 Paris Agreement on Climate Change and the 2022 Montreal outcome document. Principle 7 of the 1992 Rio Declaration, for example, requires states to "co-operate in a spirit of global partnership to conserve, protect and restore health and integrity of the Earth's ecosystem". The problem is that this central concern has not yet shaped design and operations of global governance. International environmental agreements cover climate,

138 Listed in the Annex of the Hague Principles.

oceans, biodiversity and many other areas of the global environment, but they do so in a fragmented and uncoordinated manner. As a result, the interrelations between the atmosphere (climate), the hydrosphere (oceans, freshwater systems), the lithosphere (soils) and the biosphere (biodiversity) have been neglected, causing ever-increasing threats to the integrity of the Earth ecosystem. In the same vein, global governance remains fragmented and inadequate.

Earth system science, political theory and jurisprudence have made the case for an evidence-based transformation of global governance.[139] Conceptually, Earth governance[140] requires a shift from thinking about the environment from a state-centred perspective to an Earth-centred perspective. This involves the creation of Earth trusteeship mechanisms at local, national and global levels.

Following the framework of the Earth Charter, the Hague Principles conceive rights and responsibilities as embedded in the Earth community. The Hague Principles define responsibilities for (1) the Earth, (2) the community of life and (3) human rights. They are designed around the need for trusteeship responsibilities that people and their political institutions have for the protection of human rights and the Earth system. In this regard, both citizens and states have responsibilities as trustees of the Earth.[141] Trusteeship – whether public, private or "hybrid" – implies a legal mandate to govern, however, bound by the duty to benefit those who cannot speak and act for themselves (in contrast to the self-interest implicit in private or corporate ownership and the national interest served by sovereign states). Earth trusteeship would apply this concept to global governance ensuring care for the Earth system, or Earth community, for the benefit of future generations.

Following the adoption of the Hague Principles in 2018 was a period of exchanges in various fora and of further studies.

Among the documents to guide education, academia and activism is the Declaration on Education for Earth Trusteeship, which was adopted in 2020 by the laureates of the Right Livelihood Award:[142]

> It is vitally important to alert all Earth citizens to their responsibilities as trustees for current and future generations of life on our planet home.

139 Rockström, J, et al., 'Redefining the global commons in the anthropocene', *Proceedings of the National Academy of Sciences* (forthcoming 2023) (https://www.pnas.org/).

140 Bosselmann, n 86.

141 van Willenswaard, H 2022, 'Concept note: expert roundtable in support of our common agenda', High Level Advisory Board on Effective Multilateralism (HLAB) (https://highleveladvisoryboard.org/resources/).

142 School for Wellbeing 2020, 'Declaration for education on earth trusteeship' (February 2020) (https://schoolforwellbeing.org/c35).

> Education for Earth Citizenship is necessary for all people of all cultures and religions, across all generations. This aspect tends to be neglected in educational curricula throughout the world.

Trusteeship implies protection and care of the commons, the environment, conservation of the rights and interests of future generations, protection of our cultural heritage, the protection of human rights and dignity worldwide.

An inter-generational, inter-disciplinary and cross-cultural approach needs to be inspired with the thought that every individual can make some contribution to this cause, through Right Livelihood: ethical living to achieve Earth Democracy.

False ideas of ownership of natural resources as opposed to the Principles of Earth Trusteeship; individual rights as opposed to community rights, social duties, and trusteeship of the commons; present profit at the cost of future damage – all these tend to dominate modern society.

It is vitally important to take educational measures on Earth Trusteeship, including strengthening and spreading learning centres, widely organized through the support of Right Livelihood Laureates and others. We can correct the negative trends and make a lasting, transformative contribution worldwide to develop a shared global Right Livelihood consciousness through Principles of Earth Trusteeship leading to the preservation of our humanity and our planet.

5. Earth Trusteeship as a Global Concern

At the level of the United Nations, the process towards the Summit of the Future in September 2024 offered new opportunities. A report of the High-Level Advisory Board on Effective Multilateralism (HLAB) noted: "The triple planetary crisis is accelerating and intensifying". It then summarized its various recommendations by stating: "Our responsibilities to current and future generations can only be met if we act in trusteeship for the planet".[143] How these trusteeship responsibilities can be defined and incorporated into the United Nations system and its member states will dominate the debate for years to come.

Some practical steps have been articulated in recommendations to the HLAB and the United Nations:[144]

> The High-Level Advisory Board on Effective Multilateralism (HLAB) has a unique opportunity to further develop *Our Common Agenda*'s idea of a

143 High-Level Advisory Board on Effective Multilateralism (HLAB), *A breakthrough for people and planet: effective and inclusive global governance for today and the future*, United Nations University, New York, p. 23.

144 Bosselmann, K 2022, *Recommendations to the high-level advisory board on effective multilateralism concerning the environment as a global public good* (https://highleveladvisoryboard.org/download/integrating-earth-into-global-governance/).

> repurposed Trusteeship Council,[145] especially in the light of some resistance from a number of Member States. Under international law, there is at present no legally binding duty of States to protect the global environment, i.e. the integrity of the Earth's ecosystem. This makes it necessary, and indeed urgent, to investigate the merits of trusteeship responsibilities that Member States may have towards future generations and the Earth. A repurposed Trusteeship Council would remain a UN principal organ and focus on intergenerational equity and the global environment. It could adopt a new multilateral governance model – beyond the traditional state-centric framework – to protect and restore the global commons and Earth's ecological integrity beyond the sovereignty and reach of individual states.[146]

The process towards institutional reform of this nature takes commitment and time; however, it is important to start the process and also to explore new multi-sectoral coalitions at international and national levels to take up common trusteeship challenges. Not taking this opportunity now could cause a situation where any efforts towards effective multilateralism and protection of global public goods will be too late.

There are at least three options for further investigating trusteeship governance.

1. One is the process of further implementing Agenda 2030 and achieving its Sustainable Development Goals. From an Earth system perspective, the seventeen SDGs, while all relevant, need foremost to ensure that humanity stays within the limits of planetary boundaries. The economy- and society-related SDGs will not be achieved without ensuring that the environment-related SDGs including Water (6), Climate (13), Life Below Water (14) and Life on Land (15) are realized. These need to be safeguarded, arguably through trusteeship governance, to make any prospect for sustainable development realistic and achievable. The HLAB should highlight the need for this "strong sustainability" approach in its report and ask the High-Level Political Forum (HLPF) for a systematic review of the implementation of Agenda 2030.
2. Another opportunity is the Summit of the Future in September 2024, where the merits of repurposing the Trusteeship Council – and/or an Earth Trusteeship Dialogue programme in conjunction with the appointment of

145 See also Global Governance Innovation Network 2022, *Road to 2023: our common agenda and the pact for the future*, p. 46; Desai, B 2022, 'The repurposed trusteeship council for the future', *Environmental Policy and Law*, vol. 52, p. 223.

146 Bosselmann, K 2017, 'The next step: earth trusteeship', address to the United Nations General Assembly, 21 April 2017 (http://files.harmonywithnatureun.org/uploads/upload96.pdf).

a special civil society envoy – could be discussed, including its mandate, governance structure and possible amendments to the UN Charter (Preamble and Chapter XIII – Trusteeship Council – to include intergenerational equity and future generations). To be successful, the HLAB's report needs to accompany the preparations for the Summit's outcome document "Pact for the Future" and also inform the preparatory ministerial meeting to be held in September 2023.

3. At the Summit, the establishment of a UN special envoy for future generations is likely to be decided on to help ensure that future generations inherit a healthy planet. To have sufficient impact, the envoy needs to be in a position of responsibility and access with a clearly defined mandate and the support of a well-resourced UN Future Generations Office. The terms of reference for both the envoy and the office should include responsibility and the capacity to pursue dialogue on trusteeship, including a repurposed Trusteeship Council.

These three options are not mutually exclusive and should be pursued simultaneously to encourage cross-sectoral discussions within the UN and also in civil society. Critically, the UN needs to open up to citizens and civil society. No recommendations of the HLAB, no matter how ambitious, will be realized without multi-sector collaboration involving governments, the corporate sector and civil society as equal consensus building partners.

It will be of great importance to build partnerships between civil society organizations, the UN and individual member states willing to discuss the Hague Principles and their implications for our trusteeship responsibilities with respect to the Earth.

A key element of these partnerships will be to overcome the dichotomy between the "global" and the "local". Global issues are being discussed at the international level, including the United Nations, but equally at national levels. The problem is the paradoxical behaviour of governments. At the global level, they tend to cooperate in a seemingly constructive way. The very existence of international organizations and agreements is proof that cooperation does happen. At the national level, however, states compete with each other, merely paying lip service to the need to implement international agreements. Internal pressures of corporate organizations, fiscal institutions and international competitiveness make it hard, if not impossible, for governments to incorporate international obligations into domestic laws and policies. Short-term economic interests almost inevitably outweigh long-term global goals.

In international law, this dilemma is known as the implementation deficit, but underpinning it is the misconception of sovereignty. States cannot shake off the capitalistic logic of profits at all costs, even at social and environmental costs of suicidal dimensions. States may well want to avoid collective suicide, but they are as yet unable to resist the forces of global markets. These forces have heavily eroded state sovereignty – the same state sovereignty that is needed to resist the dominance of global markets. The paradox of surrendering sovereignty to free trade and market forces on the one hand and, on the other hand, insisting on sovereignty when expected to protect the commons has been described as the "sovereignty paradox".[147]

The way out of the sovereignty paradox is differentiation: more sovereignty where possible, less sovereignty where necessary. In a globalized world, this means protecting citizens and the environment from global economic forces (more sovereignty) and protecting the global commons through international rules controlling financial and economic markets (less sovereignty). The perspective of differentiated sovereignty, also referred to as "responsible" or "smart" sovereignty, inevitably calls for reforming and strengthening global institutions as outlined in this chapter.

The drivers for responsible and smart sovereignty are not states per se, of course, but real people: citizens, activists, advocates and decision-makers. This makes the cooperation between the United Nations, civil society and states so utterly important. The ultimate justification for this cooperation is the need for effective democracy.

In the following, we take a closer look at both the "democracy paradox" and the "sovereignty paradox".

a) The Democracy Paradox

The latter part of the 20th century and the early 21st century have seen a dramatic expansion of democracy as a governing concept.[148] Out of 192 sovereign states, 120 contain democratic political systems and encompass 58% of the world's population.[149] Patrick Deneen describes this global move towards democracy as "the only regime most living humans now deem worthy of serious consideration".[150] Democracy generally defined is "a system of government in which all the people of the state . . . are involved in making decisions about its affairs", typically through elected representatives.[151]

In a nutshell, the core idea behind democracy is that ultimate authority and power remain with the people. It is a powerful philosophy focused on the innate freedom of every person "to be left alone" or to function as they please. The primary role of any democratically elected government is to ensure the protection of this freedom not only for its citizens but also for

147 Zaum, D 2007, *The sovereignty paradox*, Oxford University Press, Oxford, pp. 226–231; Bosselmann, n 86, at 269.

148 Bosselmann, n 86, at 9.

149 Bosselmann, n 86, at 9. See also Archibugi, D 2002, 'Demos and cosmopolis', *New Left Review*, vol. 13, p. 24, 27.

150 Deneen, P 2005, *Democratic faith*, Princeton University Press, Princeton, p. xvi.

151 Oxford Dictionary 2019, *Democracy*, 3rd edn, online edn.

the state itself in relation to other states.[152] Yet the paradox hidden within democracy in the Anthropocene is that, as Eyal Benvenisti describes it:[153]

> In our era of global governance, the freedom to be left alone no longer holds the promise of providing citizens with control over their lives because no Chinese walls will be capable of insulating communities from the outside. States that seek to ensure freedom to their citizens must act proactively by engaging foreign and international governance bodies, and by ensuring opportunities for their citizens to do the same.

Globalization and technology mean we are more interconnected than ever before. Economic activity and trade flow through porous national borders, creating state interdependency. Open trade brings more prosperity for countries but also worsens ecological footprints as we criss-cross the oceans using them as highways to move goods from one side of the world to the other. The democratic vacuum at the global level has invited powerful states to hollow out single-country agendas in the international space,[154] to negatively affect weaker states and to allow large multinational corporations (with private profit agendas) to hijack economic rules.[155]

This development has eroded state autonomy, reducing democracy through privately negotiated trade deals taking place outside the public democratic arena and reducing states' ability to regulate their own affairs. Of particular concern are the flow-on effects that compromise states' internal social and environmental agendas. States see it as their duty to participate in this economic model in order to secure prosperity for its people – if you don't have a seat at the table, your family will go hungry:[156]

> Needs of the market and needs of society are not the same and must be carefully separated. The fact that governments have increasingly neglected this separation, points to a crisis of democracy. Quite obviously, it is not in the interest of the "demos" if governments allow markets to determine the direction, scope and content of public policies. Democratic process "requires that citizens decide all issues that are politically decidable.

152 Bosselmann, K & Jones, K 2016, *Planetary integrity project: creating a safe operating space through law and governance*, New Zealand Centre for Environmental Law, Auckland, p. 26. Democracy was espoused and popularized by John Locke, Jean-Jacques Rousseau and Immanuel Kant.

153 Benvenisti, E 2015, *The future of sovereignty: the nation state in the global governance space*, The Global Trust Working Paper Series 01/2015, Global Trust Research Project at 1, (www.globaltrust.tau.ac.il/publications).

154 Bosselmann, n 110, at 12.

155 At 10, 11, 12, 13, 18, 30, 31, 38 and 45.

156 At 12.

Democracy now requires deeper construction at the global level if our freedoms are to remain, along with the realization that with any freedoms also come duties and responsibilities. The Anthropocene traffics in complex global environmental problems that no single state can address, like climate change, ocean acidity and acid rain, with no respect for national borders.

This changes the playing field of democracy from an activity that happens only within state borders to include governance systems, activities and institutions that are global. Immanuel Kant foresaw this development in which international society is forced to move slowly and in a non-linear fashion towards global democracy.[157] Benvenisti describes this leavening process taking place (and not particularly desired by states) as "engaged sovereignty" – the growing recognition by democratic states of their embeddedness in a global order to which they are accountable. In 1784, Kant put it this way:[158]

> The same sociability which drives man to the creation of a commonwealth causes any single commonwealth to stand in unrestricted freedom in relation to others; consequently, each of them must expect from another precisely the evil which oppress the individuals and forced them to enter into a lawful civic state. The friction among men, the inevitable antagonism, which is a mark of even the largest societies and political bodies, is used by nature as a means to establish a condition of quiet and security.

The process of global democracy is far from complete but is at the root of unlocking solutions to the ecological crisis. The role of the citizen is expanding from the national to the international scale, with citizens all over the world seriously concerned about the environmental crisis and the ineffectiveness of the existing system to address the problems.

To date, the strongest expression of civil society that announces a new ethic to take responsibility for the Earth is found in the Earth Charter.[159] This provides a new framework for global governance and a new "covenant" between humans and nature.[160] Part IV of the Charter sets out four principles for sustainable earth governance, which are:[161]

1. To strengthen democracy at all levels (including transparency, accountability, participation and access to justice)

157 At 11.

158 Kant, I 1963, 'Idea for a universal history from a cosmopolitan point-of-view', in I Kant (ed), *On history*, L Beck (trans), The Bobbs-Merrill Company, Indianapolis at Seventh Thesis.

159 The Earth Charter Initiative 2000, 'The Earth Charter' (https://earthcharter.org/virtual-library2/the-earth-charter-text/).

160 Bosselmann, n 110, at 39–47.

161 The Earth Charter Initiative, n 159. See also Engel, JR 2010, 'The Earth charter as a new covenant for democracy', in K Bosselmann & JR Engel (eds), *The Earth charter: a framework for global governance*, KIT Publishers, Amsterdam, p. 29.

2. To integrate the required capabilities for a sustainable way of living in a process of lifelong learning;
3. To treat all living beings with respect and consideration; and
4. To promote a culture of tolerance, nonviolence, and peace.

The Earth Charter is not sanctioned by sovereign states but by global citizens:[162]

> A multi-layered transnational system of democratic governance based on constitutional principles such as those expressed in the Earth Charter may still involve states, but is not dependent on them. . . . Any democratic system is accountable only to the demos, neither to states nor corporations nor any other legal constructs.

We need to acknowledge that the existing system of governance is not working and, as citizens, explore and demand a dramatically improved system. This calls for re-imagining and creating institutions at the local, regional and global levels that gain legitimacy through the process of global democracy and have the necessary "teeth" to take the required actions. How do we honour the philosophical heart of the idea of democracy by placing decisions back in the hands of the public? How do we ensure people most affected by ecological damage have a democratic voice? Essentially, this involves a shift away from state-centred governance (which currently occurs in an ad-hoc fashion) to an Earth-focused governance, emphasizing the role of the citizen as the source of legitimacy. Re-conceptualizing and reinvigorating state sovereignty are a fundamental part of this process.

b) *The Sovereignty Paradox*

In the current system of law and governance, the Earth is conceptually divided into two distinct areas. The first is that of sovereign states, and the second is the global commons, which consist of everything outside (or not controllable) by states, such as the atmosphere, the oceans, seabed and fisheries (beyond coastal state limits), Antarctica, outer space (including celestial bodies), the geo-stationary orbit and the electromagnetic spectrum.[163] Westphalia sovereignty and international environment law provide that:

- Sovereign states effectively "own" the natural resources and the environment within their borders and may preserve, use or exploit that environment as they see fit and without external interference.

162 Bosselmann, n 108, at 3.
163 At 72.

- With respect to that part of the environment other nation-states "own", the international principle of good neighbourliness (not to cause damage to another state) applies.
- With respect to the global commons, these are not owned by anyone, and access to them is free to all. This results in the "tragedy of the commons",[164] in which a natural resource becomes overused and eventually exhausted because no limits on use are set.

Nature itself has no legal rights or "standing" in the eyes of the law (it has no legal personality); therefore, any overuse, harm or pollution that occurs whether by a state, a corporation or an individual is difficult to rectify through normal legal channels. There is no legal entity to bring an action against, no property right breached and no plaintiff.

A multitude of environmental treaties and soft law documents for discrete parts of the global commons have been developed over the last 40 years through international negotiation amongst states and with the encouragement of the United Nations and civil society. However, sovereign states choose whether to be bound by these treaties or not, and most of them operate with minimal success in terms of protecting the environment. Each treaty operates independently with legal autonomy, which results in problem shifting,[165] exponential complexity of procedures and rules and a growing administrative burden on states. Where there are "gaps" in environmental law that are not covered by a either a treaty regime at the international level or legislation at the national level, the vacuum is filled by default with either sovereign state legal rights or individual property rights, which allows exploitation of the commons without accompanying duties or responsibilities to do so in a sustainable manner.[166]

International environmental law is based on respect for state sovereignty, which is the international mirror of private property rights.[167] However, the paradox within state sovereignty is that an examination of its history uncovers the potential for understanding state sovereignty as a trustee for the preservation and protection of the ecological integrity of the environment. The United Nations has a history of trusteeship concepts that we can draw on, which itself is based on sovereign state trusteeship traditions.[168]

164 Hardin, 'The tragedy of the commons'.

165 Problem shifting occurs when one treaty ignores environmental problems outside its own narrow mandate. For example, the UNFCCC treats carbon capture by the oceans as a carbon sink rather than acknowledging the environmental impact of excess CO_2 on the oceans. See also Kim, R 2013, 'Unravelling the maze of multilateral environmental agreements: a macroscopic analysis of international environmental law and governance in the anthropocene', PhD Thesis, Australian National University, p. 89.

166 Jóhannsdóttir, 'The significance of the default'.

167 Bosselmann, n 110, at 167.

168 At 198–232.

c) *Global Citizenship*

We have already briefly discussed the notion that political power and the legitimacy of a sovereign state flows from representing its people:[169]

> Popular sovereignty denotes that the state's sovereign powers belong to the people, and so those powers are held in trust by their rulers on condition that they be used for the people's benefits. Popular sovereignty thus implies that the state and its institutions are fiduciaries of the people; for the justification rests exclusively on the authority they enjoy governing and serving the people.

The culture of the Anthropocene has birthed a new and more cosmopolitan citizen who is often more mobile, moving and living in different countries for work and connected via technology with others around the world. Even those citizens living in less developed countries share this connectivity and are aware of matters far outside their immediate environment. The idea of "citizenship" is no longer confined to nations. In fact, if we identify only as a citizen of one country, we undermine the very global conditions we need to flourish.[170] If we reframe our thinking of "home" from our immediate country to the Earth itself and envisage that we are a part of the Earth system and the "community of life" relying on a shared healthy biosphere, this brings an awareness of the need for institutions that reflect this reality:[171]

> The difference between humans and nature is not absolute or categorical, but gradual. This aesthetic experience offers the moral insight of a special responsibility for the nature we are essentially part of.

Once we approach our relationship with the environment in this paradigm-fracturing fashion, an interesting question naturally arises. Who actually owns the Earth? Is it us? What happens if the public asserts property rights over the natural environment? What if there is an *insistence* that environmental public goods are owned by all of us? As legal owners, the public could charge for damage to "common property" and provide rewards to those who protect it. Private property rights and state sovereignty would continue to exist, but only up to the place where common property rights begin.[172] This idea to assert global citizen rights to the environment within the legal system

169 Criddle & Fox-Decent, n 2, at 350.

170 Bosselmann, n 108, at 31.

171 At 37.

172 Bosselmann, K 2016, 'Governing the commons: can states be trustees?', in L Westra, J Gray & A D'Aloia (eds), *The common good and ecological integrity*, Routledge, London, 2016, pp. 270–271.

is what Donella Meadows would call a key "leverage point" – a point of power within a complex system where a small shift can produce big changes.[173] Such a change of mindset or paradigm is only possible through a radical shift in our relationship with the Earth, moving away from viewing Earth as just a resource to create economic growth towards seeing it as a birthright to be protected by and for ourselves, for future generations and for all other forms of life.

The driver to any change towards "responsible sovereignty" rests with real people embracing the idea that democratic citizenship operates at local, national and global levels. If we begin to see ourselves as protectors and stewards of the Earth and our sovereign states as trustees of the Earth for the common good on our behalf, this is the *crucial step* that takes us towards a sustainable system of governance.[174] Meadows points out that the striking aspect of living and social systems is their ability to change themselves by creating new paradigms, structures and behaviours:[175]

> In biological systems that power is called evolution. In human society it's called technical advance or social revolution. In systems lingo, it's called self-organisation. . . . [A] system that can evolve, can survive almost any change, by changing itself. . . . [T]he same could be said of human cultures of course, which are the store of behavioural repertoires, accumulated over not billions, but hundreds of thousands of years. They are a stock out of which social evolution can arise.

Paradigms are the source of our systems. From them flow our social agreements about reality, along with system goals, information flows and feedback.[176] Thomas Kuhn wrote the seminal book about paradigm shifts, but in Meadows' words, the way to create such a shift involves the following:[177]

> In a nutshell, you keep pointing at the anomalies and failures in the old paradigms, you keep speaking louder and with assurance from the new one; you insert people with the new paradigms in places of public visibility and power. You don't waste time with reactionaries; rather you work with active change agents and with the vast middle ground of people who are open-minded.

173 Meadows, D 1999, *Leverage points: places to intervene in a system*, The Sustainable Institute, (https://donellameadows.org/wp-content/userfiles/Leverage_Points.pdf).
174 Bosselmann, n 86, at 289.
175 Meadows, n 173, at 15–16.
176 At 18.
177 At 18.

Having thrown down the gauntlet to take charge of human destiny, we need new institutions that reflect and operationalize this.

6. Institutionalizing Earth Trusteeship

The global commons, as they have traditionally been thought of, are areas outside states' jurisdictions. However, a more thorough understanding also includes things that have no state boundaries – like water, the atmosphere and biodiversity. This broader understanding of the commons is the new framework we need, along with "ownership" of the commons by global citizens being perceived not in the sense of "property" that might be sold or commercialized but rather in the sense of communal possession. Ownership is understood here not as ownership in our individual capacity but as the human community, reflecting the idea of the common heritage of life.[178] This principle, properly understood, creates humanity and all other life as the deserving new "subjects" of international law and expands sovereign state responsibility beyond territorial borders. Collective state trusteeship can be described as protecting all areas of the global commons, inside and outside state borders, that are recognized as the common heritage of life.[179]

For many years, the United Nations has considered the question of the duty of states to act as trustees of the global commons.[180] Currently, the state sees its role largely as a facilitator of economic growth[181] and a protector of private property. Governments must function within short-term political cycles. As a result, the system is structured to encourage short-term solutions. However, environmental trusteeship of states need not be seen as standing in opposition to state sovereignty. An insistence that the global commons belong to all, now and into the future, requires an understanding that governance has the common good as its focus. Maintaining a healthy environment is essential for human prosperity. As representatives of the governed,

178 See Bosselmann, n 86, at 75–79, 108–111 and 248 for the common heritage of mankind and the common heritage of life doctrines. See also Taylor, P & Stroud, L 2013, *Common heritage of mankind: a bibliography of legal writing*, Fondation de Malta, Malta and Weiss, EB 2012, 'The coming water crisis: a common concern of humankind', *Transnational Environmental Law*, vol. 1, no. 1, p. 153.

179 The ideas discussed here go further than the common "concern of mankind" principle by arguing that the common heritage of life prevents appropriation of "common goods" for individual interests. See Bosselmann, n 86, at 248.

180 Bosselmann, n 86, at 233–244.

181 A recent example of this is at the local government level in New Zealand, where the Ashburton District Council was selling a piece of land in its business estate to an overseas bottled water company with a resource consent to extract up to 45 litres of water per second from the town's aquifers. Local residents campaigned against the sale, but District Mayor Angus McKay "said the Council had the public's best interests at heart, as the sale of the site would go towards rates remissions". See Murphy, S 2016, 'Council to sell rights to bottled water company', *Radio New Zealand*, viewed 4 April 2016, (www.radionz.co.nz).

states can ensure their people's ecological, social and democratic well-being. Attention shifts from a negotiated consensus settling for the lowest common denominator amongst states (and leaving the commons unprotected) towards a focus on trusteeship governance of the earth as the best approach to foster non-competitive cooperation towards managing the commons.

The public trust doctrine is a simple mechanism that can support the idea that the global commons should be held in trust as assets to serve the public good.[182] The responsibility of sovereign states would be to protect these assets from harm and ensure their use for the public and future generations. Nationally, a government would act as environmental trustee, and internationally, states would act jointly as trustees of the global commons.[183] The idea of global trusts has already been promoted by Mary Wood, Peter Sand and Peter Barnes, among others.[184] We have examples in the United Nations of global institutions that have a trustee mandate. These include the (historical) UN Trusteeship Council, which oversaw the transition of territories from colonialization to independence; the World Health Organization (WHO) holding governance powers with respect to public health; and the World Trade Organization (WTO) in relation to trade matters.[185]

a) A World Environment Organization (WEO)

- A legal entity or trustee, such as a world environmental organization (WEO), would be required to be responsible for the protection of the beneficiaries: present and future generations and the community of life. The trustee would exercise discretion and the administration of the trust corpus (the biosphere) in the beneficiaries' interest. As the corpus is common to all, the commons are insulated from individual claims by companies, governments or specific individuals.[186]
- Current generations would be the donors or settlers (as well as the beneficiaries) of the trust.
- Beneficiaries would consist of humans and other life, which currently have no existing legal personality. In other words, the beneficiaries are *the community of life*. This gives nature standing, which is an important new aspect of any proposed trusteeship regime and reduces the likelihood of

182 Sand, PH 2014, 'The rise of public trusteeship in international environmental law', *Environmental Policy and Law*, vol. 44, p. 210. See also Sax, JL 1970, 'The public trust doctrine in natural resource law: effective judicial intervention', *Michigan Law Review*, vol. 68, p. 471; Redgwell, C 2000, *Intergenerational trusts and environmental protection*, Manchester University Press, Manchester; Coghill, K, Smith, T & Samford, C (eds) 2014, *Fiduciary duty and the atmospheric trust*, Ashgate Publishing, Farnham.

183 Bosselmann, n 86, at 271.

184 At 267–280.

185 Bosselmann, n 110, at 199–232.

186 At 152.

environmental governance simply being about preventing the worst harm and slowing exploitation, as has happened so far. Such a trust concept approaches the trusteeship obligations from the perspective of first restoring and then maintaining ecological integrity of the biosphere. This is its focus. Unless a WEO (or similar institution) has equivalent powers to the existing WHO and WTO, failure is a distinct possibility. Likewise, the necessary funding uncontaminated by political pressures is integral to success.[187]

- The exercise of the trustee's discretion would be framed by a number of fundamental obligations or guiding principles, which are:
  - Sustainability.
  - The common heritage of life doctrine: giving nature standing alongside humans.
  - Decisions to be guided by the precautionary principle.
  - Intergenerational equity: ensuring that the planet is passed on to future generations in a condition capable of sustaining life.
  - Intragenerational equity: providing a legal voice to the less powerful in the global community, both human and non-human. This provides the trustees with a significant role in managing the equitable use of the global commons amongst developed and developing nations.[188] Serious thought about voting rights and structure that would allay developing countries' concerns around power ratios would require careful consideration.[189]
  - The ecological integrity of the biosphere, perhaps through recognition of a legal *grundnorm*.

A WEO would have a number of advantages. Political friction between states (caused by domestic interests and competitive economic pressure) would be reduced in the face of a clear trusteeship regime applying equally to all. As long as states compete for natural resources, the negative feedback loop race towards the bottom to use up resources continues.[190] Collective action must be *at least* at the same scale as collective harm.[191]

The world community would benefit from the presence of an authoritative environmental voice in the international arena and a recognised forum for

187 At 264. The experience of the UNEP has highlighted the problems faced by underfunding.
188 At 153.
189 Biermann, F 2011, 'Reforming global environmental governance: the case for a United Nation's Environmental Organisation (UNEO)', Stakeholder Forum for a Sustainable Future, London, p. 10.
190 Esty, DC & Ivanoa, MH 2001, *Making international environmental efforts work: the case for a global environmental organisation*, Yale Center for Environmental Law and Policy, New Haven, p. 4.
191 At 5.

national officials and other stakeholders to work cooperatively to address global issues.

Currently, Earth system governance is not accountable to any one international institution solely devoted to supporting the biosphere. The existing institutional structure is highly fragmented and spread across many institutions (too many cooks in the kitchen) with little coordination; this results in duplication of effort, funding and personnel and a lack of strategic planning.[192] At the time the UN Charter was implemented in 1945, international security, not the environment, was the prime concern. The term "environment" does not even appear in the UN Charter.[193] It was not until the early 1970s that the UNEP was set up[194] "as a mere programme, without legal personality, without budgets, and, according to its founding instruments, only with a 'small secretariat'".[195] Frank Biermann points out that the UNEP is no match to other specialized international organizations and has had to compete for "time and attention and resources with more than a dozen other UN bodies":[196]

> The existing international environmental institutions, especially UNEP, are hampered by narrow or vague mandates, small budgets, and limited political support. No one organisation has the political authority, vitality, expertise, and profile to serve as the centre of gravity for the international environmental regime and to exert sustained political influence and other global fora.

A WEO would provide high-level expertise and accountability along with a long-term orientation more suited to a global institution than to state governments. Core functions would be decision-making, implementation, monitoring and dispute resolution. Esty and Ivanova point out that sound environmental decision-making hinges on some necessary factors. First, scientific assessment of high-quality information to enable long-term forecasting of environmental trends. Second, the ability to approach problems from multiple perspectives and to draw on a wide range of information sources. Third, the establishment of guidelines and international norms, which, over time, could develop into more formal rules.[197]

192 For example, UNEP, the United Nations Development Programme, the World Meteorological Organization and the OECD all have climate change programmes with little strategic coordination. See Esty and Ivanoa, n 190, at 7.
193 Frank Biermann, n 189, at 8.
194 UNEP was set up in 1973 following the 1972 Stockholm Conference on the Human Environment and is not an intergovernmental institution but a subsidiary body of the General Assembly.
195 Biermann, n 189, at 8.
196 Esty & Ivanova, n 190, at 7–8.
197 At 10–11.

States' authorization of a WEO would lend legitimacy to any enforcement measures. A judicial arm similar to the dispute settlement body of the WTO would encourage the fleshing out and development of the guiding principles suggested earlier. Environmental interests do not currently fit well into the law. Further administrative and judicial remedies are needed.[198] The growing area of international environmental administrative law regarding procedural rights is a possible area of evolution. Trustees of a WEO would include the sovereign states and, importantly, also other parts of civil society.[199] Earth governance then becomes a much broader affair.

A WEO could be created by treaty or by a United Nations General Assembly resolution that would endow it with independent institutional status and the power to resolve disputes. Christopher Stone has proposed the creation of a global commons trust fund,[200] which is able to impose levies on use of the commons, ensuring a dependable flow of money each year.[201] This mechanism would secure funding directly from those most responsible for using the commons:[202]

> Trusteeship says that the duty to protect the environment should not have to be negotiated. Sustainability is the goal – this will never change. Like justice and human rights, sustainability should be a foundational norm of humanity that guides the functions of states rather than be guided by them. Territorial sovereignty over natural resources . . . can only be perceived, therefore, as inherently linked to an obligation to protect the environment. The use of resources is covered by territorial sovereignty only within the parameters of ecological sustainability. This would read as: "the sovereign right of states to exploit their resources pursuant to the principle of sustainability".

b) *Repurposing the United Nations Trusteeship Council (UNTC)*

The UN Trusteeship Council suspended operation in the early 1990s but continues to exist on paper. It was created to encourage respect for human rights and fundamental freedoms by administering the transition to self-determination to colonies and territories occupied under World War I and others which were detached from nations defeated at the end of World

198 Bosselmann, n 86, at 265–267.

199 For example, the IUCN, the World Wildlife Fund, Greenpeace and the World Meteorological Organisation.

200 Stone, CD 1993a, 'Defending the global commons', in P Sands (ed), *Greening international law*, Earthscan, London, p. 34. See also Bosselmann, n 86, at 265.

201 Governments are well aware that institutions can only function with adequate funding. See Bosselmann, n 86, at 264.

202 At 195.

War II.[203] These colonies and territories were then placed under the trusteeship of the UN. However, now that its original decolonization missions concluded 30 years ago,[204] this unused council could be re-purposed.

Article 85 of the UN Charter reads:

1. The functions of the United Nations with regard to trusteeship agreements for all areas not designated as strategic, including the approval of the terms of the trusteeship agreements and of their alteration or amendment, shall be exercised by the General Assembly.
2. The Trusteeship Council, operating under the authority of the General Assembly, shall assist the General Assembly in carrying out these functions.

While this article does not explicitly allude to "the global commons", "the global environment", "the Earth" or anything related to environmental and geological entities, it also does not refer to the physical trust territories to decolonize that existed in 1945. The use of the term "areas" instead of "territories" allows it to broaden itself to an entirely new scope of imagination. It is a field of possibilities that UN Secretary-General António Guterres suggested in his 2021 report "Our Common Agenda" that the UNTC be repurposed to an inter-governmental body for intergenerational issues. He invited states to:

> [C]onsider making the Council available as a multi-stakeholder body to tackle emerging challenges and, especially, to serve as a deliberative forum to act on behalf of succeeding generations. Among other tasks, it could issue advice and guidance with respect to long-term governance of the global commons, delivery of global public goods and managing global public risks.[205]

Guterres's proposal received considerable support and applause. For example, Madeleine Albright, former US secretary of state, and Ibrahim Gambari, former Nigerian foreign minister, expressed:[206]

> [W]e support Guterres's suggestion to repurpose the UN Trusteeship Council. But effectively delivering global public goods and managing

203 Desai, BH 2018, 'On the revival of the United Nations Trusteeship Council with a new mandate for the environment and the global commons', *Environmental Policy and Law*, vol. 48, no. 6, p. 48 at 334.

204 The UNTC suspended its operation after the independence of Palau in 1994. See UN Security Council Resolution S/RES/956 (10 November 1994).

205 UNSG Report 2021, *Our common agenda*, United Nations, New York at chapter 5, para 125.

206 Albright, M & Gambari, I 2021, 'Our common agenda and the road to 2023' (21 October 2021), (www.projectsyndicate.com).

> global public risks will require authorities that go beyond the reconfigured body's proposed "advice and guidance" role.

Indeed, repurposing the UNTC to make it a mere advisory body would not be enough once we approach the complexity and challenges of the Anthropocene. While a revision of the UNTC had the merit of being called for, Guterres seems to overlook the idea of trusteeship originally empowered by the TC which was the basis of its mandate, comprising supervising the functioning of the trust territories and the administering authorities' relationships (or even being one itself).[207] It is now expected from the referred High-level Advisory Board[208] (HLAB) to closely examine the concept of *trusteeship*, and provide, in greater detail, a *trusteeship* role that the UNTC could assume in the future.

The idea of reviving the UNTC was, in fact, long proposed by the global environmental doctrine,[209] some UN member states, and former president of the General Assembly Samir Shihabi, who suggested in 1995 that the UNTC's mandate be broadened to:[210]

> [H]old in trust for humanity its common heritage and its common concerns: the environment; the protection of extraterritorial zones and resources of the sea and the seabed; the climate and the rights of future generations.

The same year, the Commission on Global Governance named the UNTC to perform the role of exercising "overall responsibility acting on behalf of all nations, including the administration of environment treaties related to the commons".[211] But perhaps the most significant proposal of all was that of former Secretary-General Kofi Amman, who stated in 1997 that this council could become:[212]

> [T]he forum through which member states exercise their collective trusteeship for the integrity of the global environment and common areas such as the oceans, atmosphere and outer space.

207 See Article 81 of the UN Charter.

208 United Nations Universities, 'Our common agenda; high-level advisory board on global public goods', (https://unu.edu/projects/our-common-agenda-high-level-advisory-board-on-global-public-goods.html#outline).

209 See for example, Report of the Commission on Global Governance 1995, *Our global neighbourhood*, Oxford University Press, Oxford.

210 Concluding statement of the General Assembly President (1991) A/45/PV.82, at 21, cited in Willson, CL 1996, 'Changing the charter: the United Nations prepares for the twenty-first century', *American Journal of International Law*, vol. 90, p. 122.

211 Commission on Global Governance, n 209, at 216.

212 Report of the Secretary-General, Renewing the United Nations: A Programme for Reform, UN Doc. A/51/950 (1997) at 85.

Prior to the UNTC's entrance into duties in 1946, the Leagues Council was given the task of supervising certain areas in order to assure their advance and development towards independence while safeguarding human rights and freedoms.[213] After surviving the disillusion of years of World War II, it looks like the concept of "sacred trust" – to act on behalf of entities that are not recognized and cannot be heard – underlays the pivotal linchpin of both the mandate system of the League and the UN.[214] Likewise, given a new environmental orientation to the UNTC to act in favour of the global commons and ecological communities which have no legal standing and no representation would embody a similar spirit. However, Annan's 1997 proposal did not get much support at the time.[215] Debai reasons, "[I]nitially, there was too much complexity in understanding the concept of the 'global commons'".[216] Proposing to give a new "sacred trust" to this institution "over issues as ill-defined as 'global commons' was too complex for the concrete delimitations of a political and legal mandate".[217]

The Trusteeship Council was set up as one of the principal organs of the United Nations. A "constitutional" placement within the UN system would be highly beneficial since ecological interests should be placed at the higher level of global governance. An environmental supervisory organ at the UN headquarters would "put into place different pieces of the jigsaw puzzle in order to ensure an effective architecture for the supervision of the global environment and the global commons".[218] Moreover, a coherent and appropriately empowered international institution of trusteeship would provide a credible foundation from which international obligations of a collective nature, such as a clean and safe atmosphere, could be asserted.

Ultimately, a new mandate for the UNTC would require a few – but not an unreachable number of – amendments to the UN charter. Entered into

213 Article 22(1) of the Covenant of the League of Nations.

214 Sherman, H 1951, 'The trusteeship council: its first three years', *Policy Science Quarterly*, vol. 66, no. 2, p. 226. See also Desai, BH 2021, 'A new mandate for the revived UN trusteeship council', in BH Desai (ed), *Our earth matters*, IOS Press, Amsterdam, p. 190 and Desai, BH 2022, 'The repurposed UN trusteeship council for the future', *Environmental Policy and Law*, vol. 52, p. 223.

215 The Task Force on Environment and Human Settlements, established in April 1998, was charged with examining the Secretary General's 1997 report on UN reform and the environment. However, regarding the UNTC, the task force avoided any final recommendations about its possible future use. See The Report of the United Nations Task Force on Environment and Human Settlements to the Secretary-General, annexed in the Report of the Secretary-General: United Nations Reform – Measures and Proposals – Environment and Human Settlements, A/53/463, 6 October 1998, at [20].

216 Desai, n 214, at 193.

217 Biermann, F 2015, *Earth system governance: world politics in the Anthropocene*, MIT Press, Cambridge, p. 105.

218 Desai, n 214, at 191.

force in 1945, since that date, the charter has only formally been amended on three occasions. It was first amended in 1963 to increase the size of the Security Council from 11 to 15 member states and the size of the Economic and Social Council from 18 to 27.[219] A second amendment was introduced in 1965 to correct a textual oversight arising from the first amendment.[220] A final amendment was adopted in 1971 to increase the size of the Economic and Social Council to 54 member states.[221]

The procedures for amending the charter are laid out in Article 108 – and Article 109, although this article has never been used in practice – stating:[222]

> [The charter can be amended] by a vote of two-thirds of the members of the General Assembly and ratified in accordance with their respective constitutional processes by two-thirds of the Members of the United Nations, including all the permanent members of the Security Council.

A great deal of talk and thought has already been given in the past decade to formally amending the charter provisions in relation to the trusteeship system and its respective council. Given the limited amendment history of the charter, such far-reaching changes are difficult to imagine. However, Chapters XII and XIII were drafted at a time when the concept of planetary destruction was not topical and unimaginable, and the UN charter has proven itself to be a living instrument that is flexible enough to adapt to new challenges consistent with its spirit.[223] A challenging obstacle remains, as Desai depicts, that:[224]

> [S]tates have generally been unwilling to establish powerful institutions, and have sought to stifle institutions that fail to meet the self-designated policy goals. As primary subjects of international law, states continue to be the final arbiters of the strength and authority of international environmental institutions.

Many states would perceive those changes as threatening the principle of sovereign equality (Article 1 of the UN charter). However, state sovereignty would not necessarily have to be infringed; as Redgwell argues, a renewed

219 G.A. Res. 1991 A and B (XVIII), 17 December 1963.
220 G.A. Res. 2101 (XX), 20 December 1965.
221 G.A. Res. 2847 (XXIV), 20 December 1971.
222 Article 108 of the UN Charter.
223 See Kofi Annan's 1999 report to the General Assembly, stating that "the UN Charter is a living document, whose high principles still define the aspirations of peoples everywhere for lives of peace, dignity and development". The United Nations 1999, 'Secretary-General presents his annual report to the General Assembly' (20 September 1999) Press Release SG/SM/7136 GA/9596 (https://www.un.org/press/en/1999/19990920.sgsm7136.html).
224 Desai, BH 2014, 'Revitalising international environmental institutions', in BH Desai (ed), *International environmental governance*, Brill, Leiden, p. 218.

UNTC's purview would mainly be restricted to those matters that are "the common concern of mankind", but she does not see any reason why "the Council should not exercise oversight of the state of the environment located within as well as beyond states",[225] although acknowledging that "considerable political will would be necessary for states to accord an oversight function to an external body concerned with matters located within the sovereignty of states".[226] She then explains that, theoretically, sovereign rights cannot be infringed by collective trusteeship:[227]

> Trust arrangements do not challenge sovereignty directly, for one of the advantages of trusteeship arrangements is the absence of sovereignty in the exercise of trusteeship functions – there is no transfer of sovereignty to the trust authority. This is a reflection of the separation of legal and beneficial interest fundamental to the trust law concept.

Suppose the majority of states were to consider the dormant trusteeship system as a vital institution to enforce the protection of our vulnerable planet in the interests of present and future generations as well as for the sake of the Earth itself; then, in that case, it is possible that evidence of state practice along these lines could be used to directly challenge the related charter provisions. Therefore, in view of this possibility, the case for a revival of the UNTC needs to amend several provisions of Chapter XII of the UN Charter, including Article 76, in relation to the objectives of the trusteeship system; Chapter XIII, including Article 86, relating to the composition of the Council; and Articles 87 and 88, regarding its functions and powers.

The current basic objectives of the UN trusteeship system are laid down in Article 76 of the UN charter and comprise:

a. to further international peace and security;
b. to promote the political, economic, social, and educational advancement of the inhabitants of the trust territories, and their progressive development towards self-government or independence as may be appropriate to the particular circumstances of each territory and its peoples and the freely expressed wishes of the peoples concerned, and as may be provided by the terms of each trusteeship agreement;
c. to encourage respect for human rights and for fundamental freedoms for all without distinction as to race, sex, language, or religion, and

225 Redgwell, C 2005, 'Reforming the UN Trusteeship Council', in B Chambers & JF Green (eds), *Reforming international environmental governance: From institutional limits to innovative reforms*, United Nations University Press, p. 178.
226 Redgwell, 'Reforming the UN Trusteeship Council'.
227 At 179.

to encourage recognition of the interdependence of the peoples of the world; and

d. to ensure equal treatment in social, economic, and commercial matters for all Members of the United Nations and their nationals, and also equal treatment for the latter in the administration of justice, without prejudice to the attainment of the foregoing objectives and subject to the provisions of Article 80.

Two possibilities are out for discussion: Whether the inclusion of the protection of the global environment and the global commons can be read within one (or more) of the original four basic objectives of the UN trusteeship system as cited here or whether is it more suitable to rely on the amendment of Article 76.

The first option was once unofficially proposed, under Article 76 (b), to the UNTC by a petition from the Women's International League for Peace and Freedom asking for the Antarctica and Arctica regions to be placed under its tutelage in order to prevent utilization for military purposes and to secure development to the fill scientific and economic value.[228] However, the UNTC refrained from answering, and the large majority of the international legal doctrine presumed that the original objectives of the UN trusteeship system did not apply to the polar regions.[229]

Redgwell seems to suggest the writing of new objectives that would suit an environmental orientation given to a revived UN trusteeship system, which she formulates as follows:[230]

Article 76: The basic objectives of the environmental trusteeship system shall be:

(a) to recognise the integral and interdependent nature of the Earth and the necessity for states to cooperate in a spirit of global partnership with key sectors of societies and peoples to conserve, protect and restore the health and integrity of the Earth's ecosystem;

(b) to safeguard the global environment for present and future generations; and

(c) to ensure that international agreements protect and promote the integrity of the global environmental and developmental system and contribute to the achievement of sustainable development.

228 Petition from the Women's International League for Peace and Freedom, Geneva, Switzerland. UN DOC. T/PET/General 15 (4 October 1947).

229 Hanessian, J 1960, 'The Antarctic Treaty 1959', *The International and Comparative Law Quarterly*, vol. 9, no. 3, p. 436.

230 Redgwell, n 225, at 193.

With respect to Article 86, the current organization of this Council consists of the 15 members of the Security Council and members elected by the UNGA for a three-year term.[231] The elected members of the Trusteeship Council were to act as a balancing factor to ensure an equal number of UN member states that were administering trusts were represented. In order to possess legitimate standing, such a revived institution would need to be widely democratic, representative and participatory.[232] It means that, in addition to member states, a revived UNTC must also gather among its members civil society, NGOs and indigenous community representants. Desai further asserts that "no member of the revived TC would be assigned any special role or conferred with any veto or special or privileged voting rights".[233]

Broad governance arrangements would enable humanity to work together towards the transformative aspect of Earth governance. For this, a global democratic appeal to select the qualified individuals who would represent this wide spectrum of members, considering regional balance and geographic representativeness.[234] These representatives should be politically independent and of high eminence and moral integrity to be seen as both legitimate and an authoritative voice for environmental issues. The question is then raised about how the composition of these eminently qualified people would be reached. One solution is to select individuals from a pool of the best qualified individuals representing a wide spectrum of civil society, including indigenous peoples, NGOs and persons with environmental, ethical and scientific expertise.[235] The actual nomination could occur through the UN General Assembly.

Redgwell's proposed amendment is as follows:[236]

> **Article 86**: (1) The Trusteeship Council shall consist of the following members:
>
> (a) Fifteen members elected by the General Assembly, based on equitable geographic representation of the five regional groups.
> (b) Election shall be for a three-year term. Outgoing members may be re-elected for one consecutive term. Members of the Council shall be nominated by members of the United Nations and shall serve in their

231 Article 86 of the UN Charter. See also Desai, BH 2016, 'On the revival of the United Nations Trusteeship council with a new mandate for the environment and the global commons', *Yearbook of International Environmental Law*, vol. 27, no. 1, p. 9.

232 Bosselmann, see n 86, at 262.

233 Desai, n 214, at 195.

234 Bosselmann, n 86, at 262. See also the composition of the Earth Commission, (www.earthcommission.org).

235 Bosselmann, n 83, at 263.

236 Redgwell, n 225, at 194.

personal capacity. Members shall have recognized competence relating to the environment and in related fields, such as the scientific, technical, socio-economic or legal fields.

(2) Provision shall be made for observer status for non-governmental organizations representing the interests of international civil society in the protection of the global environment and in the promotion of sustainable development. Provision shall also be made for observer status for representatives of UN agencies and specialized programmes with competence in the environment and related fields.

With respect to Articles 87 and 88, Desai proposes a suitable formulation of a possible new mandate for the UNTC:[237]

Article 87: The General Assembly and, under its authority, the Trusteeship Council, in carrying out their functions, may:

a. examine progress in reversing global environmental deterioration in consultation with the UN Environment or (its future upgrade into a UN specialized agency) United Nations Environment Protection Organization (UNEPO; or known by any other nomenclature);
b. consider reports submitted by the UN Environment or UNEPO as well as relevant multilateral environmental agreements (preferably climate change, biological diversity, desertification, which have universal membership and were crystallized through the UNGA mandated law-making processes) duly sanctioned by their respective Conferences of Parties on the basis of relationship agreements with the Trusteeship Council;[238]
c. review the status of each of the designated global commons keeping in view the overall interest of all the inhabitants of the planet earth, in consultation with decision-making organs of their respective regulatory regimes through relationship agreements and provide a mandate for further law-making processes as deemed most appropriate;
d. adopt appropriate decisions and other actions, as deemed proper, from time to time, consistent with the respective international agreements, arrangements and mechanisms.

Article 88: The Trusteeship Council shall prepare the form and modalities for submission of periodic reports by each of the regulatory regime of

237 Desai, n 214, at 195.

238 Redgwell suggests that in addition to institutions and states, Article 87(b) should "introduce a petition mechanism for, or on behalf of, both present and future generations". See Redgwell, n 225, at 196.

multilateral environment agreement as well as the global commons areas placed under its supervision. The decision-making organs of the respective regimes shall provide an annual report to the Trusteeship Council and, through it, to the General Assembly.

7. Implementing Earth Trusteeship

So far, we have been discussing Earth trusteeship at the global level, but the idea of trusteeship and acting as Earth trustees or guardians of the environment is one that needs to permeate all levels of society to be effective. In New Zealand, a first experiment of "rights for nature" can be found in a deed of settlement signed between the Whanganui River's Iwi (the local indigenous people) and the New Zealand Government: The Te Awa Tupua (Whanganui River Claims Settlement) Act 2017. The deed of settlement recognizes the river itself as a "legal person" with standing before the courts.[239] Two human trustees have been appointed, one by the Crown, the other by Iwi; they are known as "the face of the river".[240] A list of the river's intrinsic values is also recorded in the bill including that (1) the river is a source of "spiritual and physical sustenance", (2) the river is "an indivisible entity" and (3) the local Iwi have "an inalienable connection to the river".[241]

239 The Te Awa Tupua (Whanganui River Claims Settlement) Act 2017, ss 3 and 14. The Whanganui River is New Zealand's longest navigable river and is of special spiritual significance to New Zealand's indigenous people. This claim brought by local Iwi has been one of the longest and most fiercely contested in New Zealand history, dating back to the late 19th century. In a report in 1999, the Waitangi Tribunal found that the Crown had taken control and possession of the river in breach of the Treaty of Waitangi and the Crown's obligations.

240 Jones, K 2015, 'Legal personality for the Whanganui River', LLM Thesis, University of Auckland.

241 This promising example of stewardship of a particular part of nature at the local and national level was hard fought for and the result of unwavering pressure on the New Zealand government by the local Iwi, combined with early unlawful colonial activity recognized by the New Zealand Courts along with a blending of Māori and Western cultural ideas and concepts during the negotiation process. See also Barraclough, T 2013, 'How far can the Te Awa Tupua (Whanganui River) proposal be said to reflect the rights of nature in New Zealand?', LLB (Hons) dissertation, University of Otago; Harris, RC 2015, 'The changing face of co-governance in New Zealand', LLM thesis, University of Canterbury; Douglas, J 2009, 'Affording New Zealand rivers legal personality: a new vehicle for achieving Māori aspirations in co-management?', LLM thesis, University of Otago; Hardcastle, L 2014, 'Turbulent times: speculations about how the Whanganui river's position as a legal entity will be implemented and how it may erode the New Zealand landscape', *February Māori Law Review*, p. 6.

Christopher Stone has observed that human societies seem to evolve through certain stages of development, and the law itself participates in this process:[242]

> Throughout legal history, each successive extension of rights to some new entity has been, theretofore, a bit unthinkable. We are inclined to suppose the rightlessness of right less "things" to be a decree of Nature, not a legal convention acting in support of some status quo. . . . The fact is, that each time there is a movement to confer rights onto some new "entity", the proposal is bound to sound odd or frightening or laughable. This is partly because until the right-less thing receives its rights, we cannot see it as anything but a thing for the use of "us" – those who are holding rights at the time.

Perhaps the way forward is *more* sovereignty through environmental trusteeship and, at the same time, *less* sovereignty in the sense of states preparing to be bound by their trusteeship obligations through a WEO. Its functions, carefully constituted, could level the playing field between the politically strong and weak states and between the world marketplace and the environment, opening up a space for the creation of an emerging sustainable world system. Esty and Ivanova note that "An extraordinary mix of political idealism and pragmatism is required to strengthen the international environmental regime".[243] The ideas expressed in this chapter of trusteeship and cooperation are viewed by many as utopian, yet, given the reality and seriousness of the issues, which threaten security and existence, we must demand that the political paradigm of environmental governance be transformed.[244]

Re-imagining state sovereignty to accept limits to jurisdiction and to act as trustees for humanity under international standards of strong environmental institutions is the start of reclaiming and sustaining the commons we are so rapidly losing.[245]

The current system of law, governance and institutions is inadequate for the task of keeping human impacts within planetary boundaries. It has been too focused on economic and social systems, neglecting the wider ecological context in which it operates. As a result, we are faced with the continuous deterioration of global ecological systems, such as the atmosphere, the oceans and biodiversity, but also of human systems, such as public health,

242 Stone, CD 2010, *Should trees have standing? And other essays on law, morals and the environment*, 3rd edn, Oxford University Press, Oxford, pp. 2–3.
243 Esty & Ivanoa, n 190, at 18.
244 Bosselmann, n 86, at 263.
245 At 270.

the economy and financial markets. To reverse this trend, we need to recognize that ecological and human systems are intertwined, and they can only function if their integrity is not compromised.

Since its launch in December 2018, the Earth Trusteeship Initiative has been, and continues to be, a vital platform to provide measurable guidance for multilevel governance that reflects solid science (such as planetary boundaries) and preserves planetary integrity.[246] Partnered with the Planetary Integrity Project,[247] they both have the principle of "ecological integrity" at the heart of their missions. The overall thesis is that any form of governance responding to planetary boundaries must aim to preserve planetary integrity at the levels of local communities, nation-states, and regional and global organizations, in order to sustain the integrity of social as well as economic systems.

To appreciate this, we must first understand why existing arrangements are ineffective and insufficient. Fundamentally, there is a mismatch between global systems and the different interests of diverse states. In such a context, the sum of national interests is not always sufficient to meet systemic requirements.

To help meet systemic requirements, "gap reports" could show how single global systems – for example, climate, social security or finance stability – suffer from too narrowly defined, fragmented or contradictive policies and strategies. These gap reports would also show how global perspectives and responsibilities can be integrated into the process of international and national decision-making.

The Earth Trusteeship Initiative will engage in the debate on responding to the challenges of the Anthropocene through:

- The dissemination and publication of reports, including a comprehensive report to the United Nations;
- The participation in United Nations conferences and other key meetings involving states and civil society;
- The establishment of an Earth Governance Commission to comment on international policies and practices (including the 2030 Agenda and the Sustainable Development Goals); and
- Mock trials, workshops and other means of promoting more efficient forms of governance aiming for system integrity.

246 Earth Trusteeship (https://www.earthtrusteeship.world). See further Sobion, J & van Willenswaard, H (eds) 2023, *Reflections on earth trusteeship: mother Earth and a new 21st-century governance paradigm*, INI Books, Nonthaburi.

247 The PIP is an initiative gathering academics, researchers, civil society groups, social scientists, economist and lawyers. See Bosselmann & Jones, n 152.

This book has:

1. *Introduced* the challenges that the design of law and governance is facing in light of the "safe operating space" for humanity that the scientific concept of planetary boundaries is suggesting.
2. *Examined* deficiencies in existing law and governance and selected national jurisdictions to meet the challenge.
3. *Explored* the jurisprudential context of systemic integrity in terms of its effectiveness to guide legal and institutional arrangements.
4. *Developed* ecological integrity as an overarching objective of international environmental law that can be simultaneously identified as a fundamental legal norm to guide domestic laws and constitutions.
5. *Analyzed* the notions of Earth system and "world system"[248] as concepts describing Earth as a complex, interconnected, finite ecological-social-psychological-economic system. This approach can be used to further identify segments or sub-systems, such as financial systems, economic systems, social systems, political systems and socio-psychological systems – that is, systems whose integrity *ultimately* depends on the preservation of the integrity of ecological systems.
6. *Contrasted* integrity with collapse following systems theory and historical anthropological research to demonstrate the fundamental and normative importance of the concept of systemic integrity.
7. *Applied* the concept of integrity to socio-ecological systems including natural (physical) systems and human (social, economic) systems.
8. *Shown* the fundamental importance of ecological integrity for the long-term sustainability of both natural (physical) and human (social) systems.
9. *Demonstrated* how protecting and restoring the integrity of ecological and human systems requires an approach of stewardship and trusteeship. Trusteeship functions can, and should, be exercised by political institutions at all levels (including states).
10. *Recommended* possible institutions of trusteeship at the international level (World Environment Organization, UN Earth Trusteeship Council) and the national level (state as trustee, "smart" sovereignty).

The common and most noble course for everyone concerned with humanity's future should be to try living within a safe operating space defined by planetary boundaries and, in this way, act as an Earth trustee. Only if we are committed to trying can we be successful.

248 Meadows, n 173.

Conclusion

> The world has changed. Our institutions not. We cannot effectively address problems as they are if institutions do not reflect the world as it is. Instead of solving problems, they risk becoming part of the problem.[1]

The gap between the Earth system (Chapters 2–4) and the world system (5–7) can be likened to the difference between reality and fantasy. The reality of a complex Earth system requires coherent governance of social-ecological systems at the global, regional and local levels. The world system of sovereign nations lacks such coherence, favouring the national over the global, competition over cooperation and short-term interests over long-term objectives. Hoping for more coherence remains a fantasy as long as the human sphere is perceived as separate from the dynamics of the Earth system's four spheres.

As the book's chapters have shown, our institutions are not ready for Earth system governance. We have entered the Anthropocene, know that planetary boundaries have been overstepped and can see the Earth system disintegrating. Yet, by not reacting to these changed realities, governments are moving into fantasyland.

The Earth does not need humans and probably functions better without us. But we need the Earth and can no longer take its life-supporting capacities for granted. Over the last 50 years, it has become overwhelmingly clear that the Westphalian system of sovereign states is ill equipped. Can it be advanced to ensure the preservation and restoration of the Earth system's integrity?

Sadly, the answer to this question may be negative. Quite possibly a case of too little, too late. Prevailing economic and corporate interests have consistently prevented governments from transformative action. And while there may be political willingness to improve the 17th-century Westphalian system

1 UN Secretary-General Antonio Guterres' address to the UN General Assembly, 19 September 2023, (https://www.un.org/sg/en/content/sg/speeches/2023-09-19/secretary-generals-address-the-general-assembly).

DOI: 10.4324/9781032674049-14

to meet the challenges of the 21st century, it has not been strong enough. Ideas themselves won't change anything without sufficient political support. However, the opposite is also true: without new ideas, no positive change will happen.

Earth trusteeship has the well-being of the Earth, our common home, at its core. It seems logical, therefore, to look to the United Nations to remind and lead us towards trusteeship governance of the Earth. Yet, realistically, the United Nations cannot be expected to take leadership. Its dependence on member states occupied with defending and advancing their sovereign independence prevents that. The driver for change can only be citizens themselves, the members of civil society. After all, the people in society created the concept of state sovereignty in the first place. The call for Earth trusteeship has to come from civil society.[2] And while the United Nations has, in principle, acknowledged the need for institutional change to protect people and the planet, only a collaborative effort of civil society, the UN and at least some member states can generate enough momentum to make it happen.

At the centre of this pursuit lies the institution of democracy. Understood as government of the people, by the people and for the people, democracy must capture people in their connectedness with nature. It is as simple as that. No pursuit of people's will and well-being can be successful without awareness of its ecological dimensions. Democracy as we know it has only ever been concerned with the social dimensions of people's will and well-being.

To remedy the flaws of ecological ignorance, a number of issues need to be addressed, and all have to do with growing ecological awareness. This process started 50 years ago but was severely hampered and set back by economic globalism. Yet the process has never stopped and arguably reached various currents within society, including its educational and political institutions. And while existing power structures may still be unaffected by the currents of ecological awareness, the close human-nature nexus shaped all cultures, including Western culture, until the beginnings of the industrial age.[3] The need for fully recognizing this has also been part of the postmodernist discourse and is foundational to posthumanism[4] and transhumanism.[5] This is likely to bear fruit the more obvious the failure of the dominant economic, social and political forces becomes. The challenge for our age, the Anthropocene, is to understand the utterly unsustainable nature of human development if pursued in opposition to, or isolation from, ecological processes.

2 See Sobion, J & van Willenswaard, H (eds) 2023, *Reflections on earth trusteeship: mother Earth and a new 21st-century governance paradigm*, INI Books, Nonthaburi.

3 Bosselmann, K 1995, *When two worlds collide: society and ecology*, RSVP Publishing, Auckland, pp. 27–50.

4 Wolfe, C 2010, *What is posthumanism?*, University of Minnesota Press.

5 Ferrando, F 2019, *Philosophical posthumanism*, Bloomsbury Academic, Bloomsbury.

The good news is that the reality of planetary interconnectedness, the Earth system, can only be ignored to a point.

This point may have been reached now. We live in a disastrous situation where climate change, extreme weather, fires, draughts, floods, disrupted supply chains, rising living costs and poverty are felt all over the world and, critically, recognized in their context of the planetary ecological *and* global economic systems. Yet most public attention and money is invested in a dysfunctional economic system that created the disastrous situation in the first place.[6] Most governments' response to the triple planetary crisis reveals not just short-sightedness, but dangerous one-sidedness. Governments can clearly see that their modest environmental agenda of energy efficiency and climate measures is insufficient, but they are blind to addressing the root causes.

This one-sidedness may be embedded in the very concept of liberal democracy and, hence, irreversible. On closer inspection, though, it is economic liberalism that poses an existential threat, not liberal democracy per se.[7] This harbours the prospect for liberal democracy to reject economic liberalism, embrace ecological realism and, in this way, (re-)gain control,[8] although it will not be championed by governments. Political parties and governments are foremost a reflection of dominant socio-economic structures. If, however, their constituents change, they will follow suit. These constituents are ultimately the citizens of a country or community. It is all important how individuals see themselves. Purely as citizens of a nation or also as citizens of the globe? We as individual citizens need to perceive ourselves as both national and global – or ecological – citizens.

Ecological citizenship poses a new relationship between humans and the natural world that stresses non-reciprocal obligations and responsibilities.[9] The adoption of an ethical standpoint that embraces ecocentrism involves a shift in social and political thought to a new concept of rights of responsibilities.[10]

Implicit in much of the discussion on ecological citizenship is the need for a vibrant and active civil society. The concern for active engagement of civil society in designing and practicing trusteeship for the Earth is mirrored more generally in the discourse of governance for sustainability. Essentially, Earth trusteeship is Earth democracy in practice.

6 Patel, R & Moore, JW 2020, *A history of the world in seven cheap things: a guide to capitalism, nature, and the future of the planet*, Verso, London.

7 Bosselmann, K 2015, *Earth governance*, Edward Elgar Publishing, Cheltenham, pp. 26–30.

8 Bosselmann, *Earth governance*, pp. 30–35.

9 Dobson, A 2003, *Citizenship and the environment*, Oxford University Press, Oxford, chapter 3.

10 Bosselmann, K, 'The Hague principles: responsibilities and rights concerning humans and the earth', in J Sobion & H van Willenswaard (eds), *Reflections on earth trusteeship*, n 2, pp. 115–127.

Earth democracy[11] is not a one-size-fit-all concept for governance. Historically, sustainable forms of governance have existed in a variety of cultural, social and local settings.

The notion of Earth democracy is, however, more conducive to today's global realities in which governance needs to be multilateral and inclusive but also multidimensional: i.e. global and local, ecological and economic, cultural and political, rational and spiritual. These dimensions of Earth democracy are all related, but they can also be differentiated as each reflects a different concern.

Such differentiation includes the following:[12]

Covenantal democracy describes a political system that fundamentally rests on consent and shared norms and responsibilities across generations and all forms of life.

Political democracy provides for public processes and institutions to facilitate active citizens, the rule of law and human rights.

Representative democracy refers to the election of representatives who operate within the appropriate body (e.g. parliament or council).

Participatory democracy happens when members of the public are more directly involved in decision-making.

Cultural democracy promotes cultural diversity and multicultural approaches to governance and decision-making.

Global democracy aims for more effective participation of citizens in existing or future international organizations.

Local democracy enables people to directly participate in decision-making that affects their community.

Ecological democracy promotes decision-making that is reflective of the relationships between human and non-human spheres and their ecological balancing.

Economic democracy ensures participation of all people affected by the economic system and the just production and distribution of material wealth.

Gender democracy strives for gender balance in decision-making and equal access of women to (natural, educational, social etc.) resources.

Spiritual democracy holds that spirit is the source of all life and aims for decision-making that is inspired in this way.

11 Shiva, V 2015, *Earth democracy: justice, sustainability, and peace*, North Atlantic Books; Bosselmann, K 2015, 'Earth democracy: institutionalizing ecological integrity and sustainability', in R Engel, L Westra & K Bosselmann (eds), *Democracy, ecological integrity and international law*, Cambridge Scholars Publishing, Cambridge, 319–330.

12 Klaus Bosselmann, Ron Engel and Prue Taylor, *Governance for Sustainability – Issues, Successes and Challenges* (IUCN Environmental Law and Policy Series Vol. 70, Bonn, 2008).

Each of these dimensions of democracy can be further classified in terms of its functions. Some are normative, others institutional in character. We can, for example, identify attributes such as covenantal, cultural, ecological, gender or spiritual as normative categories and the attributes political, representative, participatory, global and local as institutional categories. Within institutional categories, a further distinction could be made between methods (political, representative, participatory) and levels (global, supranational, national, regional, local, corporate).

All these dimensions and functions of democracy should be understood as being captured by the notion "Earth democracy". They may not all be present to the same degree in actual practices of Earth democracy, but they should inform and guide it as much as possible. Earth democracy is based on socio-ecological values or ecological wisdom for short. As a framework for governing people and the planet, Earth democracy calls for reframing the sovereign state to include Earth trusteeship.

Bibliography

A. Cases

1 *Canada*

Frame v Smith [1987] 2 SCR 99.

2 *England and Wales*

Bristol v Mothew [1996] 4 All ER 698.

Tito v Waddell (1977) Ch. 106.

3 *India*

MI Builders Private Ltd v Shyam Sahu [1999] INSC 228.

Mehta v Kamal Nath (1997) 1 SCC 388.

4 *International*

Certain Activities carried out by Nicaragua in the Border Area (Costa Rica v Nicaragua) and Construction of a Road in Costa Rica along the San Juan River cases (Judgment) [2015] ICJ Rep 665.

Pulp Mills on the River Uruguay (Argentina v Uruguay) (Judgment) [2010] ICJ Rep 14.

The MOX Plant Case (Ireland v United Kingdom) (Provisional Measures) [2001] ITLOS Reports 95.

Southern Bluefin Tuna Cases (New Zealand v Japan) (Australia v Japan) (Request for provisional measures) (ITLOS Case No. 3 and 4) [1999] ITLOS Reports 280.

Gabčíkovo-Nagymaros Project (Hungary v Slovakia) [1997] ICJ Rep 7.

Legality of Threat or Use of Nuclear Weapons (Advisory Opinion) [1996] ICJ Rep 226.

Request for an Examination of the Situation in Accordance with Paragraph 63 of the Court's Judgment of 20 December 1974 in the Nuclear Tests Case (New Zealand v. France) [1995] ICJ Rep 288.

Barcelona Traction Case (Belgium v Spain) [1970] ICJ Rep 3.

South West Africa (Second Phase, Judgment) [1966] ICJ Rep 6.

Affaire du Lac Lanoux (Espagne v France) (1957) 12 UN Reports of International Arbitral Awards 281.

International Status of South-West Africa (Advisory Opinion) [1950] ICJ Rep 128.

The Corfu Channel Case (Merits) [1949] ICJ Rep 4.

Trail Smelter Arbitration (United States v Canada) (1941) 3 U.N. Rep. International Arbitration Awards 1905.

5 *Kenya*

Waweru v Republic HC Nairobi Misc civ appli 118 of 2004, 2 March 2006.

6 *Netherlands*

State of the Netherlands v. Urgenda Foundation, ECLI:NL:HR:2019:2007, Judgment (Sup. Ct. Neth. 20 December 2019).

7 New Zealand

Trio Holdings Ltd v Marlborough District Council [1997] NZRMA 97.

North Shore City Council v Auckland Regional Council [1997] NZRMA 59.

NZ Rail Ltd v Marlborough District Council [1994] NZRMA 70.

8 *Regional*

Krytatos v Greece, No. 41666/98, ECHR 2003 VI.

9 *South Africa*

Fuel Retailers Association of Southern Africa v Director-General Environmental Management [2007] CCT 67/06.

HTF Developers (Pty) Ltd v Minister of Environmental Affairs and Tourism [2006] ZAGPHC 132.

10 *Uganda*

Advocates Coalition for Development and Environment v Attorney General HC [2005] No. 0100.

11 *United States of America*

Juliana v United States 217 F Supp 3d 1224 (2016).

Geer v Connecticut 161 US 519 (1896).

Illinois Central Railroad Co v Illinois 146 US 387 (1892).

Martin v Waddell's Lessee 41 US 367 (1842).

B. Legislation

1 *Bhutan*

Constitution of the Kingdom of Bhutan 2008.

2 *Columbia*

Constitution of Columbia 1991.

3 *India*

Constitution of the Republic of India 1949.

4 *Kenya*

Constitution of Kenya 2010.

5 *New Zealand*

Climate Change Response (Zero Carbon) Amendment Act 2019.

Te Awa Tupua (Whanganui River Settlement) Act 2017.
Te Urewera Act 2014.
New Zealand's Crown Minerals Act 1991.
New Zealand's Resource Management Act 1991.
Natural and Built Environment Act 2023.

6 *Portugal*
Constitution of Portugal 1976.

7 *South Africa*
National Environmental Management Biodiversity Act 2004.
National Environmental Management Act 1998.
Constitution of the Republic of South Africa 1996.

8 *Uganda*
Constitution of Uganda 1995.

9 *United States*
Texas Water Code 2015.
The Pennsylvanian Constitution 1874.
The Virginia Declaration of Rights 1776.

C. Treaties, Charters, Protocols and Declarations

Aarhus Convention on Access to Information, Public Participation in Decision-Making and Access to Justice in Environmental Matters, 2161 UNTS 447 (adopted 25 June 1998, entered into force 30 October 2001).

Charter of the United Nations, 1 UNTS XVI (adopted 24 October 1945).

Conference of the Parties, *The Paris Agreement*, U.N. Doc. FCCC/CP/2015/L.9/Rev/1 (adopted 12 December 2015, entered into force 4 November 2016).

Convention on the Conservation and Management of High Seas Fishery Resources in the South Pacific Ocean (signed in Auckland, 14 November 2009, entered into force 24 August 2012).

Convention on the Conservation of Antarctic Marine Living Resources, 1329 UNTS 48 (signed 20 May 1980, entered into force 7 April 1982).

Convention on Wetlands of International Importance especially as Waterfowl Habitat T.I.A.S., 996 U.N.T.S. 245 ('Ramsar Convention') (signed 2 February 1971, entered into force 21 December 1971).

Declaration of the United Nations Conference on the Human Environment ('Stockholm Declaration') UN Doc. A/Conf.48/14/Rev. 1 (16 May 1972).

Framework Agreement for the Conservation of the Living Marine Resources of the High Seas of the South Pacific ('Galapagos Agreement') (signed 14 August 2000, not yet in force).

The General Act of the Berlin Conference on West Africa, C 4361 1885 (adopted 26 February 1885).

Great Lakes Water Quality Agreement, United States-Canada, 1978, 30 U.S.T. 1383, T.A.I.S. No. 9257 (signed 22 November 1978, entered into force 22 November 1978).

The Hague Declaration on the Environment, 28 I.L.M. 1308 (11 March 1989).

The Hague Principles for a Universal Declaration on Responsibilities for Human Rights and Earth Trusteeship (10 December 2018).

International Covenant on Civil and Political Rights, A/RES/2200 A (XXI) (adopted 16 December 1966, entered into force 23 March 1976).

International Covenant on Economic, Social and Cultural Rights, A/RES/2200 A (XXI) (adopted 16 December 1966).

IUCN World Declaration on the Environmental Rule of Law (IUCN, Rio de Janeiro, April 2016).

League of Nations, Covenant of the League of Nations, 225 Parry 195; 1 Hudson 1; 112 BFSP 13; 13 AJIL Supp. 128 (1919).

Montevideo Convention on the Rights and Duties of States, 165 LNTS 19 (opened for signature 26 December 1933, entered into force 26 December 1934).

Organisation for Security and Co-Operation in Europe, Final Act of the Conference on Security and Co-Operation in Europe ('Helsinki Accord') (1 August 1975).

Organisation of African Unity, African Charter on Human and Peoples' Rights ('Banjul Charter') CAB/LEG/67/3 rev. 5, 21 I.L.M. 58 (adopted 27 June 1981, entered into force 21 October 1986).

Organisation of American States, Additional Protocol to the American Convention on Human Rights in the Area of Economic, Social and Cultural Rights ('Protocol of San Salvador') (16 November 1999).

Statute of the International Court of Justice, 3 Bevans 1179, 59 Stat 1031, TS 993, 39 AJIL Supp 215 (26 June 1945, entered into force 24 October 1945).

Treaty on Principles Governing the Activities of States in the Exploitation and Use of Outer Space, including the Moon and Other Celestial Bodies, A/RES/2222 (XXI) (signed 19 December 1966, entered into force 10 October 1967).

United Nations Convention on Biological Diversity, 1760 UNTS 79 (signed 5 June 1992, entered into force 29 December 1993).

United Nations Convention on the Law of the Sea 1833 UNTS 3 (adopted 10 December 1982, entered into force 16 November 1994).

United Nations Convention on the Rights of the Child, A/RES/44/25 (signed 20 November 1989, entered into force 1990).

United Nations Convention Relating to the Status of Refugees, Treaty Series Vol. 189, 137 (opened for signature 28 July 1951, entered into force 22 April 1954).

United Nations Framework Convention on Climate Change, 1771 UNTS 107 (adopted 9 May 1992, entered into force 21 March 1994).

Universal Declaration of Human Rights, A/RES/217 A (III) (adopted 10 December 1948).

Vienna Convention for the Protection of the Ozone Layer 26 I.L.M. 1516 (signed 22 March 1985, entered into force 22 September 1988).

D. Books and Chapters in Books

Alexy, R 2002, *The argument from injustice: a reply to legal positivism*, SL Paulson and BL Paulson (trans), Clarendon Press, Oxford.

Amirante, D & Bagni, S (eds) 2022, *Environmental constitutionalism in the Anthropocene*, 1st edn, Routledge, London.

Arias-Maldonado, M 2016, 'Nature and the Anthropocene: the sense of an ending?', in P Pattberg & F Zelli (eds), *Environmental politics and governance in the Anthropocene: institutions and legitimacy in a complex world*, 1st edn, Routledge, London.

Aristotle 2000, *Politics*, B Jowett (trans), Infomotions, Inc.

Arrighi, G 2010, *The long twentieth century: money, power and the origins of our times*, Verso, New York.

Bahro, R 1994, *Avoiding social and ecological disaster: the politics of world transformation*, Gateway, Bath.

Bartelson, J 2014, *Sovereignty as symbolic form*, Routledge, Oxon.

Bennett, HL 2019, *African kings and black slaves*, University of Pennsylvania Press, Philadelphia.

Bentham, J 2007, *An introduction to the principles of morals and legislation*, Dover Publications, New York.

Berry, C, Ryan-Collins, J & Greenham, T 2015, *Financial system resilience index: building a strong financial system*, New Economics Foundation, London.

Beyerlin, U 2007, 'Different types of norms in international environmental law: policies, principles and rules', in D Bodansky, J Brunnée & E Hey (eds), *The Oxford handbook of international environmental law*, Oxford University Press, Oxford.

Biermann, F 2007, 'Reforming global environmental governance: the case for a United Nation's Environmental Organisation (UNEO)', in L Sward & E Perry (eds), *Global environmental governance: perspectives on the current debate*, Center for UN Reform Education, New York.

Biermann, F 2015, *Earth system governance: world politics in the Anthropocene*, MIT Press, Cambridge.

Bindreiter, U 2002, *Why Grundnorm? A treatise on the implications of Kelsen's doctrine*, Kluwer Law International, The Hague.

Birnie, P, Boyle, A & Redgwell, C 2009, *International law and the environment*, 3rd edn, Oxford University Press, Oxford.

Bonanno, A 2004, *The legitimation crisis of neoliberalism: the state, will-formation, and resistance*, Palgrave Macmillan, New York.

Bosselmann, K 1995, *When two worlds collide*, RSVP Publishing, Auckland.

Bosselmann, K 2010, 'Outlook: the Earth charter – a model constitution for the world?', in K Bosselmann & R Engel (eds), *The Earth charter: a framework for global governance*, Kit Publishers, Amsterdam.

Bosselmann, K 2013a, 'A legal framework for sustainable development', in K Bosselmann, D Grinlinton & P Taylor (eds), *Environmental law for a sustainable society*, 2nd edn, New Zealand Centre for Environmental Law Monograph Series, Vol. 1, Auckland.

Bosselmann, K 2013b, 'Sustainable development and international environmental law', in S Alam, MdJH Bhuiyan, TMR Chowdhury & EJ Techera (eds), *Routledge handbook for international environmental law*, Routledge, London.

Bosselmann, K 2015a, *Earth governance: trusteeship of the global commons*, Edward Elgar Publisher, Cheltenham.

Bosselmann, K 2015b, 'Mind the gap: state governance and ecological integrity', in L Westra, J Gray & V Karageorgou (eds), *Ecological systems integrity: governance, law and human rights*, Routledge, London.

Bosselmann, K 2016, 'Shifting the legal paradigm: earth-centred law and governance', in P Magalhaes & W Steffen (eds), *The safe operating space treaty: a new approach to managing our use of the earth system*, Cambridge Scholars, Cambridge.

Bosselmann, K 2017, *The principle of sustainability: transforming law and governance*, 2nd edn, Routledge, Abingdon.

Bosselmann, K 2019a, 'The atmosphere as a global commons', in J Jaria-Monzano & S Borrás (eds), *Research handbook on global climate constitutionalism*, Edward Elgar Publishing Ltd, Gloucestershire.

Bosselmann, K 2019b, 'Large-scale acquisitions of the commons: the need for Earth governance', in L Westra, K Bosselmann & V Zambrano (eds), *Ecological integrity and land uses: sovereignty, governance, displacements and land grabs*, Nova Science Publishers.

Bosselmann, K 2019c, 'Towards a world constitutional order', in PD Burdon, K Bosselmann & K Engel (eds), *The crisis in global ethics and the future of global governance: fulfilling the promise of the Earth charter*, Edward Elgar Publishing Limited, Gloucestershire.

Bosselmann, K 2020a, 'The role of trusteeship in earth governance', in L Westra & K Bosselmann (eds), *Ecological integrity in science and law*, Springer, Cham.

Bosselmann, K 2020b, 'Sustainable development law', in KN Scott, J Lindley, E Techera & A Telesetsky (eds), *Routledge handbook of international environmental law*, 2nd edn, Routledge, London.

Bosselmann, K 2022, 'A normative approach to environmental governance: sustainability at the apex of environmental law', in D Fisher (ed), *Research handbook on fundamental concepts of environmental law*, 2nd edn, Edward Elgar Publisher, Cheltenham, pp. 23–44.

Bosselmann, K, Engel, R & Taylor, P 2008, *Governance for sustainability: Issues, successes and challenges*, IUCN Environmental Law and Policy Series, Vol. 70, Bonn.

Bosselmann, K & Taylor, P 2019, 'Promoting global ethics: The Earth trusteeship initiative', in PD Burdon, K Bosselmann & K Engel (eds), *The crisis in global ethics and the future of global governance: fulfilling the promise of the Earth charter*, Edward Elgar Publishing Limited, Gloucestershire.

Boucher, D & Kelly, P 1994, 'The social contract and its critics: an overview', in D Boucher & P Kelly (eds), *The social contract from Hobbes to Rawls*, Routledge, New York.

Bowers, C 1997, *The culture of denial*, State University of New York Press, New York.

Boyd, DR 2012, *The environmental rights revolution: a global study of constitutions, human rights, and the environment*, UBC Press, Vancouver.

Braungart, M & McDonough, W 2009, *Cradle to cradle: re-making the way we make things*, Vintage Books, London.

Brickman, P & Campbell, D 1971, 'Hedonic relativism and planning the good society', in MH Appley (ed), *Adaptation-level theory*, Academic Press, New York.

Brown, L, Gardner, G & Halweil, B 2000, *Beyond Malthus: nineteen dimensions of the population challenge*, Earthscan, London.

Brownlie, I 2012, *Principles of public international law*, 7th edn, Oxford University Press, Oxford.

Bugge, HC & Voigt, C (eds) 2000, *Sustainable development in international and national law*, Europa Law Publishing, Groningen.

Burdon, PD 2014, 'Earth jurisprudence and the project of Earth democracy', in P Burdon & M Maloney (eds), *Wild law: In practice*, 1st edn, Routledge, London.

Burdon, PD 2023, 'Ecological integrity', in *The Anthropocene: new trajectories in law*, 1st edn, Routledge, London.

Burke, E 1973, *Reflections on the revolutions in France and on the proceedings on certain societies in London*, Anchor Books, London.

Byrd, S & Hruscha, J 2010, *Kant's doctrine of right*, Cambridge University Press, Cambridge.

Capra, F & Luisi, PL 2014, *The systems view of life: a unifying vision*, Cambridge University Press, Cambridge.

Capra, F & Mattei, U 2015, *The ecology of law: toward a legal system in tune with nature and community*, Berrett-Koehler Publisher, Oakland.

Car, CL & Seidler, MJ 1994, *Political writings of Samuel Pufendorf*, Oxford University Press, New York.

Carson, R 1962, *Silent spring*, Houghton Mifflin, Boston.

Clark, N 2011, *Inhuman nature: sociable life on a dynamic planet*, Sage, London.

Coghill, K, Smith, T & Samford, C (eds) 2014, *Fiduciary duty and the atmospheric trust*, Ashgate Publishing, Farnham.

Costanza, R, Graumlich, LJ & Steffen, W 2007, 'Integrated global models', in R Costanza, LJ Graumlich & W Steffen (eds), *Sustainability or collapse? An integrated history and future of people on Earth*, The MIT Press with Dahlem University Press, Cambridge.

Costanza, R, Kubiszewski, I, Anderson, S & Sutton, P 2020, 'The future value of ecosystem services: global scenarios and national implications', in KN Ninan (ed), *Environmental assessments: scenarios, modelling, and policy*, Edward Elgar, Cheltenham.

Crawford, J 2012, *Brownlie's principles of public international law*, 8th edn, Oxford University Press, Oxford.

Criddle, EJ 2014, 'A sacred trust of civilization', in AS Gold & PB Miller (eds), *Philosophical foundations of fiduciary law*, Oxford University Press, Oxford.

Criddle, EJ & Fox-Decent, E 2016, *Fiduciaries of humanity: how international law constitutes authority*, Oxford University Press, New York.

De Vattel, E 1853, *The law of nations or the principles of natural law*, based on the 1797 edn, Republished by T & JW Johnson Law Booksellers, Philadelphia.

Deneen, P 2005, *Democratic faith*, Princeton University Press, Princeton.

Denis, L (ed) 2010, *Kant's metaphysics of morals: a critical guide*, Cambridge University Press, Cambridge.

Desai, BH 2014, 'Revitalising international environmental institutions', in BH Desai (ed), *International environmental governance*. Series International Environmental Law, Vol. 10, Brill, Leiden.

Desai, BH 2021, 'A new mandate for the revived UN trusteeship council', in BH Desai (ed), *Our earth matters*, IOS Press, Amsterdam.

Deudney, D 1999, 'Environmental security: a critique', in D Deudney & RA Matthew (eds), *Contested grounds: security and conflict in the new environmental polities*, State University of New York Press, Albany.

Diamond, J 2011, *Collapse: how societies choose to fail or succeed*, 2nd edn, Penguin Group, New York.

Dobson, A 2003, *Citizenship and the environment*, Oxford University Press, Oxford.

Dolzer, R 1976, *Property and environment: the social obligation inherent in ownership – A study of the German constitutional setting*, International Union for Conservation of Nature and Natural Resources, IUCN Environmental Policy and Law Paper No. 12.

Eason, T, Flournoy, AC, Cabezas, H & Gonzalez, MA 2014, 'Incorporating resilience and innovation into law and policy', in AS Garmestani & CR Allen (eds), *Social-ecological resilience and the law*, Columbia University Press, New York.

Eckersley, R 2004, *The green state: rethinking democracy and sovereignty*, The MIT Press, Cambridge.

Elksins, Z, Ginsburg, T & Melton, J 2009, *The endurance of national institutions*, Cambridge University Press, Cambridge.

Emerson, RW 1887, *Emerson's complete works*, vol. XI, Houghton, Mifflin & Co, Boston.

Emmett, R & Nye, D 2017, *The environmental humanities: a critical introduction*, MIT Press, New York.

Engel, JR 2010 'The Earth charter as a new covenant for democracy', in K Bosselmann & JR Engel (eds), *The Earth charter: a framework for global governance*, KIT Publishers, Amsterdam.

Esty, DC & Ivanoa, MH 2001, *Making international environmental efforts work: the case for a global environmental organisation*, Yale Center for Environmental Law and Policy, New Haven.

Ferrando, F 2019, *Philosophical posthumanism*, Bloomsbury Academic, Bloomsbury.

Finnis, J 2011, *Natural law and natural rights*, 2nd edn, Oxford University Press, Oxford.
Fisher, D 2013, *Legal reasoning in environmental law: a study of structure, form and language*, Edward Elgar, Cheltenham.
Fitzmaurice, A 2014, *Sovereignty, property and empire, 1500–2000*, Cambridge University Press, Cambridge.
Forrester, J 1961, *Industrial dynamics*, The MIT Press, Cambridge.
Fox-Decent, E 2012, 'From fiduciary states to joint trusteeship of the atmosphere: the right to a healthy environment through a fiduciary prism', in K Coguill, C Samford & T Smith (eds), *Fiduciary duty and the atmospheric trust*, Ashgate Publishing, Farnham.
Fowler, MR & Bunck, JM 1995, *Law, power, and the sovereign state: the evolution and application of the concept of sovereignty*, Pennsylvania State University, University Park.
Franks, N & Bourke, AFG 1995, *Social evolution in ants*, Princeton University Press, Princeton.
Freud, S 2003, *Psychopathology of everyday life*, Dover, New York.
Fullerton, J 2015, *Regenerative capitalism: how universal principles and patterns will shape our new economy*, Capital Institute, Greenwich.
Galaz, V 2014, *Global environmental governance, technology and politics: the Anthropocene gap*, Edward Elgar, Cheltenham.
Garmestani, AS & Allen, CR (eds) 2014, *Social-ecological resilience and the law*, Columbia University Press, New York.
Garver, G 2020, *Ecological law and the planetary crisis: A legal guide for harmony on Earth*, 1st edn, Routledge, London.
Grant, WE 1997, *Ecology and natural resource management, systems analysis and simulation*, John Wiley and Sons, Toronto.
Greenham, T, Cox, E & Ryan-Collins, J 2013, *Mapping economic resilience*, Friends Provident Foundation, York.
Grinlinton, D 2015, 'Defining the nature and boundaries of environmental law', in P Salmon & D Grinlinton (eds), *Environmental law in New Zealand*, Thomson Reuters, Wellington.
Grinlinton, D & Taylor, P (eds) 2011, *Property rights and sustainability: The evolution of property rights to meet ecological challenges*, Martinus Nijhoff, Amsterdam.
Grober, U 2012, *Sustainability: a cultural history*, Green Books, Devon.
Grotius, H 1916, *Mare Liberum [the freedom of the seas]*, R Van Deman Magoffin (trans), Oxford University Press, Oxford.
Gwiazdon, KA 2019, 'From stardust to sacred sands: protecting life on Earth through a human story of ethics, care and the cosmos', in PD Burdon, K Bosselmann & K Engel (eds), *The crisis in global ethics and the future of global governance: fulfilling the promise of the Earth charter*, Edward Elgar Publishing Limited, Gloucestershire.
Hickey, W 2020, *The sovereignty game: neo-colonialism and the Westphalian system*, Springer Nature, Singapore.
Higgins, K 2015, *Economic growth and sustainability: systems thinking for a complex world*, Elsevier Academic Press, San Diego.
Hobson, JM 2000, *The state and international relations*, Cambridge University Press, Cambridge.
Horkheimer, M & Adorno, T 2002, *Dialectic of the enlightenment*, Stanford University Press, Stanford.
Jackson, R 2007, *Sovereignty: evolution of an idea*, Polity Press, Cambridge.
Kamieniecki, S & Granzeier, MS 1998, 'Eco-cultural security and indigenous self-determination: moving toward a new conception of sovereignty', in KT Litfin (ed), *The greening of sovereignty in world politics*, MIT Press, Massachusetts.

Kant, I 1963, 'Idea for a universal history from a cosmopolitan point-of-view', in I Kant (ed), *On history*, L Beck (trans), The Bobbs-Merrill Company, Indianapolis.

Kant, I 1991, 'On the common saying: "This may be true in theory: but it does not apply in practice"', in HS Reiss (ed), *Kant: political writings*, HB Nisbet (trans), 2nd edn, Cambridge University Press, Cambridge.

Kant, I 1993, *Grounding for the metaphysics of morals*, J Ellington (trans), 3rd edn, Hackett Publishing, Indianapolis.

Kant, I 1996 [1797], *The metaphysics of morals*, MJ Gregor (ed), Cambridge University Press, Cambridge.

Kant, I 2006, *Toward perpetual peace and other writings on politics, peace and history*, P Kleingeld (ed), Yale University Press, New Haven.

Kelsen, H 1945, *General theory of law and state*, Harvard University Press, Cambridge.

Kelsen, H 1967, *Pure theory of law*, M Knight (trans), 2nd edn, UCLA Press, Berkeley.

Kiss, A & Shelton, D 1971, *International environmental law*, 2nd edn, Transnational, New York.

Kissinger, H 2014, *World order*, Penguin Press, New York.

Krasner, SD 1999, *Sovereignty: organized hypocrisy*, Princeton University Press, New Jersey.

Kuhn, T 1977, *The essential tension: selected studies in scientific tradition and change*, University of Chicago Press, Chicago.

Kuhn, T 2012, *The structure of scientific revolutions: fiftieth anniversary edition*, 4th edn, University of Chicago Press, Chicago.

Kuhner, TK 2020, *Trump, corruption and the revolution to come*, Stanford University Press, Stanford.

Laitos, J 2021, *Rethinking environmental law why environmental laws should conform to the laws of nature*, Edward Elgar Publishing, Cheltenham.

Lanni, S 2023, 'Nature as grundnorm', in *Greening the civil codes: comparative private law and environmental protection*, 1st edn, Routledge, London.

Leiser, D & Azar, OH 2008, 'Behavioral economics and decision making: applying insights from psychology to understand how people make economic decisions', *Journal of Economic Psychology*, vol. 29, p. 613.

Leopold, A 1986, *A sand county almanac (outdoor essays and reflections)*, 7th edn, Ballantine Books, New York.

Leopold, A 1991, 'The ecological conscience', in SL Flader & JB Callicott (eds), *The river of the mother of god and other essays by Aldo Leopold*, University of Wisconsin Press, Wisconsin.

Levy, MA, Keohane, RO & Haas, P 1993, 'Improving the effectiveness of international environmental institutions', in MA Levy, RO Keohane & P Haas (eds), *Institutions for the Earth: sources of effective international protection*, Massachusetts Institute of Technology, Cambridge.

Litfin, KT (ed) 1998, *The greening of sovereignty in world politics*, MIT Press, Massachusetts.

Locke, J 1988, 'Two treaties of government', in P Laslett (ed), *Cambridge texts in the history of political thought*, Cambridge University Press, Cambridge.

Lüdert, J 2023, *Non-state actors at the United Nations: Contesting sovereignty*, Routledge, London.

Luhmann, N 2012, *Theory of society*, R Barrett (trans), vol. I, Stanford University Press, California.

Lupin Townsend, D 2020, *Human dignity and the adjudication of environmental rights*, EE Elgar, Cheltenham.

Marquardt, B 2003, *Umwelt und recht in mitteleuropa: von den grossen rodungen des hochmittelalters bis ins 21. Jahrhundert*, Zürich, Schulthiess.

Martinson, C 2011, *The crash course: the unsustainable future of our economy, energy and environment*, John Wiley and Sons, New Jersey.
Marx, K 1967, *Das Kapital: critique of political economy*, F Engels & E Untermann (eds), vol. III, Aristeus Books, St. Frederick.
Matthews, D 2021, *Earthbound: the aesthetics of sovereignty*, Edinburgh University Press, Edinburgh.
Maturana, H & Varela, F 1973, *Autopoiesis and cognition: The realization of the living*, D. Reidel Publishing Company, Dordrecht.
McIntosh, SCR 2002, *Caribbean constitutional reform: rethinking the west Indian polity*, The Caribbean Law Publishing Company, Kingston.
Meadows, DL 2007, 'Evaluating past forecasts: reflections on one critique of the limits to growth', in R Costanza, LJ Graumlich & W Steffen (eds), *Sustainability or collapse? An integrated history and future of people on Earth*, The MIT Press with Dahlem University Press, Cambridge.
Meadows, DL 2008, *Thinking in systems: a primer*, Chelsea Green Publishing, Vermont.
Meadows, DL, Meadows, DH, Randers, J & Behrens, WW 1972, *The limits to growth*, Universe Books, New York.
Mogilner, C, Whillans, A & Norton, M 2018, 'Time, money and subjective well-being', in E Diener, S Oishi & L Tay (eds), *Handbook of well-being: noba scholar handbook series: subjective well-being*, DEF Publishers, Salt Lake City.
Montini, M & Volpe, F 2016 'The need for a new regulatory approach for the promotion of ecological sustainability', in L Westra, J Gray & A D'Aloia (eds), *The common good and ecological integrity*, Routledge, London.
Montini, M & Volpe, F 2019, 'The need for an "integral ecology" in connection with the UN sustainable development goals', in F Pasquale (ed), *Care for the world: laudato Si' and catholic social thought in an era of climate crisis*, Cambridge University Press, Cambridge.
Moore, J & Patel, R 2017, *The history of the world in seven cheap things: a guide to capitalism, nature, and the future of the planet*, University of California Press, Oakland.
Morrow, K 2014, 'Peoples' sustainability treaties at Rio+20: giving voice to the other', in M Maloney & P Burdon (eds), *Wild law: In practice*, Routledge Taylor and Francis Group, London.
Newton, I 1995, *Principia mathematica*, A Motte (trans), Prometheus Books, Amhurst.
Noah Harari, Y 2019, *21 Lessons for the 21st century*, Vintage, London.
Orange, C 2013, *The story of a treaty*, Bridget Williams Books Ltd, Wellington.
Ostrom, E 1990, *Governing the commons: the evolution of institutions for collective action*, Cambridge University Press, Cambridge.
Parrotta, JA & Trosper, RL (eds) 2012, *Traditional forest related knowledge*, Springer, New York.
Patel, R & Moore, JW 2020, *A history of the world in seven cheap things: a guide to capitalism, nature, and the future of the planet*, Verso, London.
Percival, RV & Alevizatos, DC 1997, *Law and the environment: a multidisciplinary reader*, Temple University Press, Philadelphia.
Philippopoulos-Mihalopoulos, A 2011, 'Towards a critical environmental law', in A Philippopoulos-Mihalopoulos (ed), *Law and ecology: new environmental foundations*, Routledge, London.
Piketty, T 2013, *Capital in the twenty-first century*, A Goldhammer (trans), Brilliance Audio, Grand Haven.

Plumwood, V 2002, *Environmental culture: the ecological crisis of reason*, Routledge, London.

Redgwell, C 2000, *Intergenerational trusts and environmental protection*, Manchester University Press, Manchester.

Redgwell, C 2005, 'Reforming the United Nations trusteeship council', in WB Chambers & JF Green (eds), *Reforming international environmental governance: from institutional limits to innovative reforms*, United Nations University Press, Tokyo.

Rosen, BA 2016, 'Potted review of economic theory: the complex evolving system', in J-P Close (ed), *AIREAS sustainocracy for a healthy city: the invisible made visible*, Springer International, New York.

Ross, WD 2011, *The Nicomachean ethics of Aristotle*, Pacific Publishing, Seattle.

Roy, S 2020, 'The potential of the trusteeship theory for Canadian public law and environmental governance', in K Anker, PD Burdon, G Garver, M Maloney & C Sbert (eds), *From environmental to ecological law*, Routledge, Oxfordshire.

Sands, P 1995, *Principles of international environmental law*, 1st edn, Manchester University Press, Manchester.

Sands, P 2003, *Principles of international environmental law*, 2nd edn, Cambridge University Press, Cambridge.

Schmitt, C 2007, *The concept of the political*, The University of Chicago Press, Chicago.

Shelton, D 2007, 'Environmental rights in the state constitutions of the United States', in I Larmuseau (ed), *Constitutional rights to an ecologically balanced environment*, Gent, Belgium, V.V.O.R.

Smith, M 2011, *Against ecological sovereignty: ethics, biopolitics, and saving the natural world*, University of Minnesota Press, Chicago.

Sobion, J & van Willenswaard, H (eds) 2023, *Reflections on earth trusteeship: mother Earth and a new 21st-century governance paradigm*, INI Books, Nonthaburi.

Steffen, W, Sanderson, A, Tyson, P, Jäger, J, Matson, P, Moore, B, Oldfield, F, Richardson, K, Schellnhuber, HJ, Turner, BL & Wasson, RJ 2004, 'Global change and the Earth system: a planet under pressure', in *IGBP global change*, 1st edn, Springer, Heidelberg.

Stern, N 2006, *The economics of climate change: the Stern review*, Her Majesty's Treasury, London.

Stone, CD 1993a, 'Defending the global commons', in P Sands (ed), *Greening international law*, Earthscan, London.

Stone, CD 1993b, *The gnat is older than man: global environment and human agenda*, Princeton University Press, Princeton.

Stone, CD 2010, *Should trees have standing? And other essays on law, morals and the environment*, 3rd edn, Oxford University Press, Oxford.

Tainter, JA 1988, *The collapse of complex societies*, Cambridge University Press, Cambridge.

Tainter, JA & Patzek, TW 2012, *Drilling down: the Gulf oil debacle and our energy dilemma*, Copernicus, New York.

Taylor, C 2004, *Modern social imaginaries*, Duke University Press, North Carolina.

Taylor, P & Stroud, L 2013, *Common heritage of mankind: a bibliography of legal writing*, Fondation de Malta, Malta.

Teubner, G 2011, 'A constitutional moment? The logics of "hitting the bottom"', in P Kjaer & G Teubner (eds), *The financial crisis in constitutional perspective: the dark side of functional differentiation*, Hart Publishing, Bloomsbury.

Theys, S 2017, 'Constructivism', in S McGlinchey, C Scheinpflug & R Walters (eds), *International relations theory*, E-International Relations, Bristol.

Troper, M 2016, 'The modern state and the concept of authority', in R Cotterrell & M Del Mar (eds), *Authority in transnational legal theory: theorising across disciplines*, Edward Elgar Publishing, Cheltenham.

Turner, S 2014, 'A global environmental right', in *Routledge explorations in environmental studies*, Routledge, London.

Vatter, M 2019, 'Nature's law or law's law? Community of life, legal personhood, and trusts?', in M de Leeuw & SV Wichlen (eds), *Personhood in the age of biolegality*, Palgrave Macmillan, Switzerland.

Victor, PA & Jackson, T 2015, 'Toward an ecological macroeconomics', in PG Brown & P Timmerman (eds), *Ecological economics for the Anthropocene*, Columbia University Press, New York.

Vinx, L 2007, *Hans Kelsen's pure theory of law: legality and legitimacy*, Oxford University Press, Oxford.

Wackernagel, M & Rees, W 1996, *Our ecological footprint: Reducing human impact on the earth*, New Society Publishers, Gabriola Island.

Wacks, R 2014, *Philosophy of law: a very short introduction*, 2nd edn, Oxford University Press, Oxford.

Walker, N 2013, 'Sovereignty frames and sovereignty claims', in R Rawlings, P Leyland & AL Young (eds), *Sovereignty and the law*, Oxford University Press, Oxford.

Waltz, KN 1986, 'Political structures', in RO Keohane (ed), *Neorealism and its critics*, Columbia University Press, New York.

Wapner, P 1998, 'Reorienting state sovereignty: rights and responsibilities in the environmental age', in KT Litfin (ed), *The greening of sovereignty in world politics*, MIT Press, Massachusetts.

Wendt, A 1999, *Social theory of international politics*, Cambridge University Press, Cambridge.

Westerlund, S 2008, 'Theory of sustainable development, towards or against?', in HC Bugge & C Voigt (eds), *Sustainable development in international and national law*, Europa Law, Groningen, p. 49.

Whelan, FG 1996, *Edmund Burke and India: Political morality and empire*, University of Pittsburgh Press, Pittsburgh.

Wiener, JB 2007, 'Precaution', in D Bodansky, J Brunnée & E Hey (eds), *The Oxford handbook of international environmental law*, Oxford University Press, Oxford.

Wood, MC 2013, *Nature's trust: environmental law for a new ecological age*, Cambridge University Press, New York.

Wood, MC, Leonard, S, Bartz, D & Peart, N 2013, 'Securing planetary life sources for future generations: legal actions deriving from the ancient sovereign trust obligation', in MB Gerrard & GE Wannier (eds), *Threatened island nations: legal implications of rising seas and a changing climate*, Cambridge University Press, New York.

Wright, Q 1930, *Mandates under the league of nations*, University of Chicago Press, Chicago.

E. Journal Articles

Abbott, KW & Snidal, D 2000, 'Hard and soft law in international governance', *International Organisation*, vol. 54, no. 3, p. 421.

Alexy, R 2015, 'Inclusive non-positivism', *Joaçaba*, vol. 16, no. 2, p. 283.

Alves, F, Costa, PM, Novelli, L & Vidal, DG 2023,'The rights of nature and the human right to nature: an overview of the European legal system and challenges for the ecological transition', *Frontiers in Environmental Science*, vol. 11, DOI:10.3389/fenvs.2023.1175143

Archibugi, D 2002, 'Demos and cosmopolis', *New Left Review*, vol. 13, p. 24.
Axworthy, L & Rock, A 2009, 'R2P: a new and unfinished agenda', *Global Responsibility to Protect*, vol. 1, p. 54.
Bamber, JL, Oppenheimer, M, Kopp, RE, Aspinall, WP &Cooke, RM 2019, 'Ice sheet contributions to future sea-level rise from structured expert judgment', *PNAS*, vol. 116, no. 23, pp. 11195–11200.
Bardi, U 2013, 'Mind sized world models', *Sustainability*, vol. 5, no. 3, pp. 896–911.
Barroso, LR 2015, 'Major transformations in contemporary law and the teachings of Robert Alexy', *Panorama of Brazilian Law*, vol. 3, nos. 3–4, p. 107.
Baskini, J 2015, 'Paradigm dressed as epoch: the ideology of the Anthropocene', *Environmental Values*, vol. 24, no. 1, pp. 9–29.
Becker, C, Ewringmann, D, Faber, M, Petersen, T & Zahrnt, A 2015, 'Endangering the natural basis of life is unjust: on the status and future of the sustainability discourse', *Ethics Policy and Environment*, vol. 18, no. 1, p. 60.
Benvenisti, E 2013, 'Sovereigns as trustees of humanity: on the accountability of states to foreign stakeholders', *American Journal of International Law*, vol. 107, p. 295.
Benvenisti, E 2015, 'The paradoxes of sovereigns as trustees of humanity: concluding remarks', *Theoretical Inquiries in Law*, vol. 16, no. 2, p. 535.
Berkes, F & Palmer, T 2015, 'Managing shared resources: collective community action is the best way to close the curtain on the tragedy of the commons', *Alternatives Journal*, vol. 41, no. 1, p. 67.
Biber, E 2017, 'Law in the Anthropocene epoch', *The Georgetown Law Journal*, vol. 106, p. 1.
Biermann, F, Abbott, K, Andresen, S, Bäckstrand, K, Bernstein, S, Betsill, MM, Bulkeley, H, Cashore, B, Clapp, J, Folke, C, Gupta, A, Gupta, J, Haas, PM, Jordan, A, Kanie, N, Kluvánková-Oravská, T, Lebel, L, Liverman, D, Meadowcroft, J, Mitchell, RB, Newell, P, Oberthür, S, Olsson, L, Pattberg, P, Sánchez-Rodríguez, R, Schroeder, H, Underdal, A, Vieira, SC, Vogel, C, Young, OR, Brock, A & Zondervan, R 2012, 'Transforming governance and institutions for global sustainability: key insights from the earth system project', *Current Opinion in Environmental Sustainability*, vol. 4, no. 1, pp. 51–60.
Biermann, F, Betsill, MM, Gupta, J, Kanie, N, Lebel, L, Liverman, D, Schroeder, H, Siebenhüner, B & Zondervan, R 2010, 'Earth system governance: a research framework', *International Environmental Agreements: Politics, Law and Economics*, vol. 10, pp. 277–298.
Biermann, F & Kim, RE 2020, 'The boundaries of the planetary boundary framework: a critical appraisal of approaches to define a 'safe operating space' for humanity', *Annual Review of Environment and Resources*, vol. 45, pp. 497–521.
Blumm, MC & Gutherie, RD 2012, 'Internationalizing the public trust doctrine: natural law and constitutional and statutory approaches to fulfilling the Saxion vision', *UC Davis Law Review*, vol. 45, p. 741.
Blumm, MC & Moses, AP 2017, 'The public trust as an antimonopoly doctrine', *Boston College Environmental Affairs Law Review*, vol. 44, no. 1, p. 1.
Böckernförde, M 2003, 'The operationalization of the precautionary approach in international environmental law treaties: enhancement or façade ten years after Rio', *Zeitschrift Für Ausländisches Öffentliches Recht und Völkerrecht*, vol. 63, p. 313.
Bollard, J 2010, 'The resource management regime and private property rights and interests: is there an untoward tension between the two?', *The New Zealand Journal of Environmental Law*, vol. 14, pp. 1–24.
Bosselmann, K 2001, 'Sustainability and university: compatible agendas?', *Educational Philosophy and Theory*, vol. 33, p. 167.

Bosselmann, K 2015, 'Global environmental constitutionalism: mapping the terrain', *Widener Law Review*, vol. 21, p. 171.
Bosselmann, K 2017, 'Governing the global commons, the "planetary boundaries approach"', *Policy Quarterly*, vol. 13, no. 1, DOI:10.26686/pq.v13i1.4648
Bosselmann, K 2018, 'Losing the forest for the trees: environmental reductionism in the law', *Environmental Laws and Sustainability: Special Issue of Sustainability*, vol. 2, no. 8, p. 2424.
Bosselmann, K 2020a, 'Environmental trusteeship and state sovereignty: can they be reconciled?', *Transnational Legal Theory*, vol. 11, p. 47.
Bosselmann, K 2020b, 'The framework of ecological law', *Environmental Policy and Law*, vol. 50, no. 6, pp. 479–486, at pp. 479–480.
Bosselmann, K & Botrel, M 2020, 'Constitutionalizing international environmental law', *Sciences Po Law Review*, vol. 18, pp. 11–16.
Bradshaw, CJA, Ehrlich, PR, Ehrlich, PR, Beattie, A, Ceballos, G, Crist, E, Diamond, J, Dirzo, R, Ehrlich, AH, Harte, J, Harte, ME, Pyke, GH, Raven, PH, Ripple, WJ, Saltré, F, Turnbull, C, Wackernagel, M & Blumstein, DT 2021, 'Underestimating the challenges of avoiding a ghastly future', *Frontiers Conservation Science*, DOI:10.3389/fcosc.2020.615419
Brandy, C 2015, 'Safeguarding the Earth system as a priority for sustainable development and global ethics: the need for an Earth system SDG', *Journal of Global Ethics*, vol. 11, no. 1, p. 32.
Braudo, Y 2015, 'Introduction: Sovereignty as trusteeship for humanity – Historical antecedents and their impact on international law', *Theoretical Inquiries in Law*, vol. 16, no. 2.
Bridgewater, P, Kim, RE & Bosselmann, K 2015, 'Ecological integrity: a relevant concept for international environmental law in the Anthropocene?', *Yearbook of International Environmental Law*, vol. 25, no. 1, pp. 61–78.
Brondizo, ES, O'Brien, K, Bai, X, Biermann, F, Steffen, W, Berkhout, F, Cudennec, C, Lemos, MC, Wolfe, A, Palma-Oliveira, J & Chen, C-TA 2016, 'Re-conceptualizing the Anthropocene: a call for collaboration', *Global Environmental Change*, vol. 39, pp. 318–327.
Brook, B, Ellis, EC, Perring, MP, Mackay, AW & Blomqvist, L 2013, 'Does the terrestrial biosphere have planetary tipping points?', *Trends in Ecology & Evolution*, vol. 28, no. 7, p. 396.
Calzadilla, PV & Kotzé, LJ 2018, 'Living in harmony with nature? A critical appraisal of the rights of mother Earth in Bolivia', *Transnational Environmental Law*, vol. 7, no. 3, pp. 1–28.
Clark, N 2017, 'Geosocial formations and the Anthropocene', *Theory, Culture and Society, Special Issue*, vol. 34, nos. 2–3, pp. 3–23.
Cohen, MR 1927, 'Property and sovereignty', *Cornell Law Review*, vol. 13, p. 8.
Collins, LM 2019, 'Environmental resistance in the Anthropocene', *Oñati Socio-legal Series, Forthcoming – Governing the Political: Law and the Politics of Resistance*, DOI:10.35295/osls.iisl/0000-0000-0000-1048
Conca, K 1994, 'Rethinking the ecology-sovereignty debate', *Millennium Journal of International Studies*, vol. 23, no. 3, p. 701.
Costanza, R, de Groot, R, Sutton, P, van der Ploeg, S, Anderson, SJ, Kubiszewski, I, Farber, S & Turner, RK 2013, 'Changes in the global value of ecosystem services', *Global Environmental Change*, vol. 26, p. 152.
Costanza, R, Fioramonti, L & Kubiszewski, I 2016, 'The UN sustainable development goals and the dynamics of well-being', *Frontiers in Ecology and the Environment*, vol. 14, no. 2, p. 59.

Criddle, EJ 2015, 'Three Grotian theories of humanitarian intervention', *Theoretical Inquiries in Law*, vol. 16, p. 473.
Criddle, EJ & Fox-Decent, E 2009, 'A fiduciary theory of Jus Cogens', *Yale Journal of International Law*, vol. 34, p. 331.
Crowe, J 2016, 'Natural law theories', *Philosophy Compass*, vol. 11, no. 2, p. 91.
Daly, E 2012, 'Constitutional protection for environmental rights: the benefits of environmental process', *International Journal of Peace Studies*, vol. 17, no. 2, pp. 71–80.
De Lucia, V 2020, 'Rethinking the encounter between law and nature in the anthropocene: from biopolitical sovereignty to wonder', *Law and Critique*, vol. 31, pp. 329–349.
Demiray, MR 2015, 'Natural law theory, legal positivism and the normativity of law', *The European Legacy*, vol. 20, no. 8, p. 807.
Demsetz, H 1967, 'Toward a theory of property rights', *American Economic Review*, vol. 51, no. 2, p. 347.
Deng, F 2010, 'From "sovereignty as responsibility" to the "responsibility to protect"', *Global Responsibility to Protect*, vol. 2, p. 353.
Dernbach, JC & Cheever, F 2015, 'Sustainable development and its discontents', *Transnational Environmental Law*, vol. 4, no. 2, p. 247.
Desai, BH 2016, 'On the revival of the United Nations Trusteeship council with a new mandate for the environment and the global commons', *Yearbook of International Environmental Law*, vol. 27, no. 1, pp. 3–27.
Desai, BH 2018, 'On the revival of the United Nations trusteeship council with a new mandate for the environment and the global commons', *Environmental Policy and Law*, vol. 48, no. 6, pp. 333–344.
Desai, BH 2022, 'The repurposed UN trusteeship council for the future', *Environmental Policy and Law*, vol. 52, p. 223.
Dyzenhaus, D 2015, 'Kelsen, Heller and Schmitt: paradigms of sovereignty thought', *Theoretical Inquiries in Law*, vol. 16, no. 2, p. 337.
Eckersley, R 2007, 'Ecological intervention: prospects and limits', *Ethics & International Affairs*, vol. 21, no. 3, p. 293.
Eckersley, R 2020, 'Ecological democracy and the rise and decline of liberal democracy', *Environmental Politics*, vol. 29, pp. 214–234.
Ellis, EC 2011, 'Anthropogenic transformation of the terrestrial biosphere', *Philosophical Transactions of the Royal Society*, vol. 369, p. 1010.
Etty, T, van Zeben, J, Carlarne, C, Duvic-Paoli, L-A, Huber, B & Huggins, A 2022, 'Crossing (conceptual) boundaries of transnational environmental law', *Transnational Environmental Law*, vol. 11, p. 1.
Evans, G 2009, 'The responsibility to protect in environmental emergencies', *American Society of International Law*, vol. 103, p. 27.
Ferreira-Snyman, A 2010, 'Intervention with specific reference to the relationship between the United Nations Security Council and the African Union', *The Comparative and International Law Journal of Southern Africa*, vol. 43, no. 2, pp. 139–172.
Finnis, J 2014, 'What is the philosophy of law?', *American Journal of Jurisprudence*, vol. 59, p. 133.
Fitzmaurice, A 2015, 'Sovereign trusteeship and empire', *Theoretical Inquiries in Law*, vol. 16, no. 2, p. 447.
Fitzmaurice, M 2017, 'Legitimacy of international environmental law. The sovereign states overwhelmed by obligations: responsibility to react to problems beyond national jurisdiction?', *Heidelberg Journal of International Law*, vol. 77, p. 339.

Frost, C & Pullen, RK 2022, 'In the eyes of all mankind: interests and independence in Vattelian statehood', *Journal of International Political Theory*, vol. 18, p. 294.
Fukuda-Parr, S 2016, 'From the millennium development goals to the sustainable development goals: Shifts in purpose, concept, and politics of global goal setting for development', *Gender and Development*, vol. 24, no. 1, p. 43.
Gaines, SE 1997, 'Re-imagining environmental law for the 21st century', *University of Chicago Legal Forum*, vol. 1997, pp. 231–292.
Geddert, JS 2021, 'Indigenous sovereignty and the (enlarged) responsibility to protect', *The American Review of Canadian Studies*, vol. 51, p. 251.
Glazebrook, S 2009, 'Human rights and the environment', *Victoria University of Wellington Law Review*, vol. 40, no. 1, pp. 293–350.
Gumplova, P 2014, 'Restraining permanent sovereignty over natural resources', *Enrahonar Quaderns de Filosofia*, vol. 53, pp. 93–114.
Gumplova, P 2020, 'Sovereignty over natural resources: a normative reinterpretation', *Global Constitutionalism*, vol. 9, no. 1, pp. 7–37.
Hajer, M, Nilsson, M, Raworth, K, Bakker, P, Berkhout, F, De Boer, Y, Rockström, J, Ludwig, K & Kok M 2015, 'Beyond cockpit-ism: four insights to enhance the transformative potential of the sustainable development goals', *Sustainability*, vol. 7, p. 1651.
Hák, T, Janoušková, S & Moldan, B 2016, 'Sustainable development goals: a need for relevant indicators', *Ecological Indicators*, vol. 60, p. 565.
Halsall, F 2012, 'Nikklas Lhumann and the body: irritating social systems', *The New Bioethics*, vol. 18, no. 1, pp. 4–20.
Hanessian, J 1960, 'The Antarctic Treaty 1959', *The International and Comparative Law Quarterly*, vol. 9, no. 3, pp. 436–480.
Hansen, J, Sato, M, Hearty, P, Ruedy, R, Kelley, M, Masson-Delmotte, V, Russell, G, Tselioudis, G, Cao, J, Rignot, E, Velicogna, I, Tormey, B, Donovan, B, Kandiano, E, von Schuckmann, K, Kharecha, P, Legrande, AN, Bauer, M & Lo, K-W 2016, 'Ice melt, sea level rise and super storms: evidence from paleoclimate data, climate modelling, and modern observations that 2°C global warming could be dangerous', *Atmospheric Chemistry and Physics*, vol. 16, p. 3761.
Haraldson, HV 2004, 'Introduction to systems and causal loop diagrams: reports in ecology and environmental engineering', *Lund University*, vol. 1.
Hardcastle, L 2014, 'Turbulent times: speculations about how the Whanganui river's position as a legal entity will be implemented and how it may erode the New Zealand landscape', *February Māori Law Review*.
Hardin, G 1968, 'The tragedy of the commons', *Science*, vol. 162, p. 1243.
Harris, JW 1971, 'When and why does the Grundnorm change?', *Cambridge Law Journal*, vol. 20, no. 1, p. 103.
Hathaway, OA 2008, 'International delegation and state sovereignty', *Law and Contemporary Problems: The Law and Politics of International Delegation*, vol. 71, no. 1, pp. 115–149.
Hermann, DHJ 1983, 'Max Weber and the concept of legitimacy in contemporary jurisprudence', *DePaul Law Review*, vol. 3, no. 1.
Herrington, G 2021, 'Updates to limits to growth: comparing the world3 model with empirical data', *Journal of Industrial Ecology*, vol. 5, no. 3, pp. 614–626.
Hochella, MF, Mogk, DW, Ranville, J, Allen, IC, Luther, GW, Marr, LC, McGrail, BP, Murayama, M, Qafoku, NP, Rosso, KM, Sahai, N, Schroeder, PA, Vikesland, P, Westerhoff, P & Yang, Y 2019, 'Natural, incidental, and engineered nanomaterials and their impacts on the Earth system', *Science*, vol. 363, no. 6434, p. eaau8299.
Horn, C 2016, 'Kant's political philosophy as a theory of non-ideal normativity', *Kant-Studien*, vol. 107, no. 1, p. 89.

Järnberg, L, Quinlan, A & Ryan, P 2021, 'Wayfinder: a resilience guide for navigating towards sustainable futures', *Ecology and Society*, vol. 26, no. 2, p. 39.

Josefsson, H 2012, 'Achieving ecological objectives', *Laws*, vol. 1, p. 39.

Kahan, DM, Jenkins-Smith, H & Braman, D 2011, 'Cultural cognition of scientific consensus', *Journal of Risk Research*, vol. 14, no. 2, p. 147.

Kahneman, D & Deaton, A 2010, 'High income improves evaluation of life but not emotional well-being', *Proceedings of the National Academy of Sciences*, vol. 107, no. 38, p. 16489.

Kelsen, H 1955, 'Foundations of democracy', *Ethics*, vol. 66, no. 1, p. 1.

Khardori, A 2021, 'What does the state owe to its people? Toward a "responsibility to develop"', *Brigham Young University Law Review*, vol. 46, p. 1027.

Kim, RE & Bosselmann, K 2013, 'International environmental law in the Anthropocene: towards a purposive system of multilateral environmental agreements', *Transnational Environmental Law*, vol. 2, p. 285.

Kim, RE & Bosselmann, K 2015, 'Operationalising sustainable development: ecological integrity as a *Grundnorm* in international law', *Review of European, Comparative and International Environmental Law*, vol. 24, no. 2, p. 194.

Kim, RE & Kotzé, LJ 2021, 'Planetary boundaries at the intersection of the Earth system law, science and governance: a state-of-the-art review', *Review of European, Comparative and International Environmental Law*, vol. 30, no. 1, pp. 3–15.

Kim, RE & Mackey, B 2013, 'International environmental law as a complex adaptative system', *International Environmental Agreements: Politics, Law and Economics*, vol. 14, no. 1, pp. 5–28.

King, N & Jones, A 2021, 'An analysis of the potential for the formation of "nodes of persisting complexity"', *Sustainability*, vol. 13, p. 8161.

Kleingeld, P 2016, 'Kant's moral and political cosmopolitanism', *Philosophy Compass*, vol. 11, no. 1, p. 14.

Koskenniemi, M 2005, 'International law in Europe: between tradition and renewal', *The European Journal of International Law*, vol. 16, no. 1, p. 113.

Koskenniemi, M 2007, 'Constitutionalism as mindset: reflection on Kantian themes about international law and globalization', *Theoretical Inquiries in Law*, vol. 8, p. 9.

Kotzé, LJ 2012, 'Arguing global environmental constitutionalism', *Transnational Environmental Law*, vol. 16, no. 1, pp. 199–233.

Kotzé, LJ 2019, 'The Anthropocene, Earth system vulnerability and social-ecological injustice in an age of human-rights', *Journal of Human Rights and the Environment*, vol. 10, no. 1, pp. 62–68.

Kotzé, LJ & Kim, RE 2019, 'Earth system law: the juridical dimensions of Earth system governance', *Earth System Governance Journal*, vol. 1, p. 100003.

Kotzé, LJ & Kim, RE 2020, 'Exploring the analytical, normative and transformative dimensions of Earth system law', *Environmental Policy and Law*, vol. 50, no. 6, pp. 457–547.

Kotzé, LJ & Kim, RE 2022, 'Towards planetary nexus governance in the Anthropocene: an earth system law perspective', *Global Policy*, vol. 13, p. 86.

Lambert, J, Hall, CAS, Balogh, S, Gupta, A & Arnold, M 2014, 'Energy, EROI and quality of life', *Energy Policy*, vol. 64, p. 153.

Langford, M 2016 'Lost in translation? The politics of the sustainable development goals', *Ethics and International Affairs*, vol. 30, no. 2, p. 167.

Lazarus, R 2005, 'Human nature, the laws of nature, and the nature of environmental law', *Virginia Environmental Law Journal*, vol. 24, p. 231.

Leach, M 2023, 'Seeking systems in Earth system law: boundaries, identity and purpose in emergent field', *Earth System Governance*, vol. 15, p. 100162.

Leach, M, Reyers, B, Bai, X, Brondizio, ES, Cook, C, Díaz, S, Espindola, G, Scobie, M, Stafford-Smith, M & Subramanian, SM 2018, 'Equity and sustainability in the anthropocene: a social-ecological systems perspective on their intertwined futures', *Global Sustainability*, vol. 1, pp. 1–13.

Li, Z, Farmanesh, R, Kirikkaleli, D & Itani, R 2021, 'A comparative analysis of COVID-19 and the global financial crisis: evidence from US economy', *Economic Research*, vol. 35, pp. 2427–2441.

Lin, J, Shen, Y, Li, X & Hasnaoui, A 2021, 'BRICS carbon neutrality target: measuring the impact of electricity production from renewable energy sources and globalization', *Journal of Environmental Management*, vol. 298, p. 113460.

Little, G 2016, 'Developing environmental law scholarship: going beyond the legal space', *Legal Studies*, vol. 36, p. 48.

Lui, H 2014, 'A fiduciary perspective on the state's duty to protect the environment', *Auckland University Law Review*, vol. 20, p. 101.

Magallanes, CJI 2015, 'Forward: new thinking on sustainability', *New Zealand Journal of Public and International Law*, vol. 13, no. 1, p. 1.

Martin, R 2023, 'The river as a separate legal person: implications for sustainability law and governance', *Environmental and Planning Law Journal*, vol. 39, p. 166.

Matthews, D 2021, 'Reframing sovereignty for the Anthropocene', *Transnational Legal Theory*, vol. 12, no. 1, p. 44.

Miller, G 1956, 'The magic number seven, plus or minus two: some limits on our capacity for processing information', *Psychological Review*, vol. 63, no. 2, p. 81.

Montini, M & Volpe, F 2015, 'Sustainable development goals: much ado about nothing?', *Environmental Liability: Law, Policy and Practice*, vol. 4, p. 141.

Moore, J 2011, 'Ecology, capital, and the nature of our times: accumulation and crisis in the capitalist world-ecology', *American Sociological Review*, vol. 42, no. 1, p. 108.

Muys, B 2013, 'Sustainable development within planetary boundaries: a functional revision of the definition based on the thermodynamics of complex socio-ecological systems', *Challenges in Sustainability*, vol. 1, no. 1, p. 41.

Mysicka, S 2015, 'Environmental justice and the Rawlsian social contract theory', *Filosofie Dnes*, vol. 1, no. 7, p. 39.

Narain, V & Vij, S 2016, 'Where have all the commons gone?', *Geoforum*, vol. 68, p. 21.

Nate, S, Bilan, Y, Cherevatskyi, D, Kharlamova, G, Lyakh, O & Wosiak, A 2021, 'The impact of energy consumption on the three pillar of sustainable development', *Energies*, vol. 14, p. 1372.

Nordblad J 2021, 'On the difference between anthropocene and climate change temporalities', *Critical Inquiry*, vol. 47, p. 328.

Onwe, S & Nwogbaba, D 2015, 'Conceptual issues and theoretical analysis of sovereignty', *Research on Humanities and Social Sciences*, vol. 5, no. 3.

Parmar, SS 2017, 'Understanding the concept of 'sovereignty', *International Journal of Law*, vol. 3, no. 1, p. 31.

Pata, UK 2021, 'Linking renewable energy, globalization, agriculture, CO_2 emissions and ecological footprint in BRIC countries: a sustainable perspective', *Renewable Energy*, vol. 173, pp. 197–208.

Pearle, A 2015, 'The tragedy of the vital commons', *Environmental Law*, vol. 45, no. 4, p. 1021.

Pelenc, J & Ballet, J 2015, 'Strong sustainability, critical natural capital and the capability approach', *Ecological Economics*, vol. 112, p. 36.

Pelizzon, A & Ricketts, A 2015, 'Beyond anthropocentrism and back again: from ontological to normative anthropocentrism', *American Journal of Neuroradiology*, vol. 18, no. 2, p. 105.

Persson, L, Almroth, BMC, Collins, CD, Cornell, S, de Wit, CA, Diamond, ML, Fantke, P, Hassellöv, M, MacLeod, M, Ryberg, MW, Jørgensen, PS, Villarrubia-Gómez, P, Wang, Z & Hauschild, MZ 2022, 'Outside the safe operating space of the planetary boundary for novel entities', *Environmental Science & Technology*, vol. 56, pp. 1510–1521.

Peters, A 2009, 'Humanity as the A and Ω of sovereignty', *European Journal of International Law*, vol. 20, no. 3, p. 513.

Prosser, D, Nagel, J, Howlin, S, Marbán, PR, Day, DD & Erwin, RM 2018, 'Effects of local shoreline and subestuary watershed condition on waterbird community integrity: influences of geospatial scale and season in the Chesapeake Bay', *Estuaries and Coasts*, vol. 41, pp. 207–222.

Purdy, J & Fielding, K 2007, 'Sovereigns, trustees, guardians: private-law concepts and the limits of legitimate state power', *Law and Contemporary Problems*, vol. 70, p. 165.

Rees, W 2023, 'The human eco-predicament: overshoot and the population conundrum', *Vienna Yearbook of Population Research*, vol. 19, p. 1.

Riley, P 1973, 'On Kant as the most adequate of the social contract theorists', *Political Theory*, vol. 1, no. 4, p. 450.

Rockström, J, Gupta, J, Lenton, TM, Qin, D, Lade, SJ, Abrams, JF, Jacobson, L, Rocha, JC, Zimm, C, Bai, X, Bala, G, Bringezu, S, Broadgate, W, Bunn, SE, DeClerck, F, Ebi, KL, Gong, P, Gordon, C, Kanie, N, Liverman, DM, Nakicenovic, N, Obura, D, Ramanathan, V, Verburg, PH, van Vuuren, DP & Winkelmann, R 2021, 'Identifying a safe and just corridor for people and the planet', *Earth's Future*, vol. 9, no. 4, DOI:10.1029/2020EF001866

Rockström, J, Kotzé, LJ, Milutinović, S, Biermann, F, Brovkin, V, Donges, JF, Ebbesson, J, French, D, Gupta, J, Kim, RE, Lenton, TM, Lenzi, D, Nakicenovic, N, Neumann, B, Schuppert, F, Bosselmann, K, Winkelmann, RC, Folke, CW, Lucht, WmD, Schlosberg, DP, Schlosser, DW, Steffen, W & Richardson, K 2024, 'Planetary commons for the anthropocene', *Proceedings of the National Academy of Sciences* (PNAS), DOI:10.1073/pnas.2301531121

Rockström, J, Polasky, S, Rockström, J, Galaz, V, Westley, F, Lamont, M, Scheffer, M, Österblom, H, Carpenter, SR, Chapin, FS, III, Seto, KC, Weber, EU, Crona, BI, Daily, GC, Dasgupta, P, Gaffney, O, Gordon, LJ, Hoff, H, Levin, SA, Lubchenco, J, Steffen, W & Walker, BH 2021, 'Our future in the Anthropocene biosphere', *Ambio*, vol. 50, pp. 834–869.

Rockström, J, Steffen, W, Noone, K, Persson, Å, Chapin, FS, III, Lambin, E, Lenton, TM, Scheffer, M, Folke, C, Schellnhuber, H, Nykvist, B, De Wit, CA, Hughes, T, van der Leeuw, S, Rodhe, H, Sörlin, S, Snyder, PK, Costanza, R, Svedin, U, Falkenmark, M, Karlberg, L, Corell, RW, Fabry, VJ, Hansen, J, Walker, B, Liverman, D, Richardson, K, Crutzen, P & Foley, J 2009, 'Planetary boundaries: exploring the safe operating space for humanity', *Ecology and Society*, vol. 14, no. 2, p. 32.

Rose, DB, van Dooren, T, Chrulew, M, Cooke, S, Kearnes, M & O'Gorman, E 2012, 'Thinking through the environment: unsettling the humanities', *Environmental Humanities*, vol. 1, p. 1.

Sand, PH 2014, 'The rise of public trusteeship in international environmental law', *Environmental Policy and Law*, vol. 44, no. 1, p. 210.

Saunders, FP 2015, 'Planetary boundaries: at the threshold . . . again: sustainable development ideas and politics', *Environment, Development and Sustainability*, vol. 17, p. 823.

Sax, JL 1970, 'The public trust doctrine in natural resource law: effective judicial intervention', *Michigan Law Review*, vol. 68, p. 471.

Schluter, M, Tavoni, A & Levin, S 2016, 'Robustness of norm-driven cooperation in the commons', *Proceedings of the Royal Society B: biological Sciences*, vol. 283, no. 1822, p. 283.
Schofer, E & Hironaka, A 2005, 'The effects of world society on environmental protection outcomes', *Social Forces*, vol. 84, no. 1, p. 25.
Schrijver, NJ & Desai, BH 2021, 'State sovereignty in the planetary management of natural resources', *Environmental Policy and Law*, vol. 51, p. 13.
Seitzinger, SP, Gaffney, O, Brasseur, G, Broadgate, W, Ciais, P, Claussen, M, Erisman, JW, Kiefer, T, Lancelot, C, Monks, PS, Smyty, K, Syvitski, J & Uematsu, M 2016, 'International geosphere: biosphere programme and Earth system science: three decades of co-evolution', *Anthropocene*, vol. 12, p. 3.
Sherman, H 1951, 'The trusteeship council: its first three years', *Policy Science Quarterly*, vol. 66, no. 2, pp. 167–179.
Simons, D & Chabris, C 1999, 'Gorillas in our midst: sustained inattential blindness for dynamic events', *Perception*, vol. 28, no. 9, p. 1059.
Stahn, C 2007, 'Responsibility to protect: political rhetoric or emerging legal norm?', *American Journal of International Law*, vol. 101, p. 99.
Steffen, W, Broadgate, W, Deutsch, L, Gaffney, O & Ludwig, C 2015, 'The trajectory of the Anthropocene: the great acceleration', *The Anthropocene Review*, vol. 2, no. 1, p. 81.
Steffen, W, Crutzen, PJ & McNeil, JR 2007, 'The Anthropocene: are humans now overwhelming the great forces of nature?', *Ambio*, vol. 36, p. 614.
Steffen, W & Morgan, J 2021, 'From the Paris agreement to the anthropocene and planetary boundaries framework: an interview with Will Steffen', *Globalizations*, vol. 18, no. 7, pp. 1298–1310.
Steffen, W, Richardson, K, Rockstrom, J, Cornell, SE, Fetzer, I, Bennett, EM, Biggs, R, Carpenter, SR, de Vries, W, de Wit, CA, Folke, C, Gerten, D, Heinke, J, Mace, GM, Persson, LM, Ramanathan, V, Reyers, B & Sorlin, S 2015, 'Planetary boundaries: guiding human development on a changing planet', *Science*, vol. 347, no. 6223, p. 736.
Stiglitz, JE 2010, 'Lessons from the global financial crisis of 2008', *Seoul Journal of Economics*, vol. 23, no. 3, pp. 321–339.
Stone, A 1985, 'The place of law in the Marxian structure-superstructure archetype', *Law & Society Review*, vol. 19, no. 1, p. 39.
Strong, M 1973, 'One year after Stockholm', *Foreign Affairs Magazine*, vol. 51, no. 4, p. 690.
Strumsky, D, Lobo, J & Tainter, J 2010, 'Complexity and the productivity of innovation', *Systems Research and Behavioral Science Journal*, vol. 27, p. 496.
Tainter, J 2000, 'Problem solving: complexity, history and sustainability', *Population and Environment*, vol. 22, no. 1, p. 3.
Tarlock, AD 1992, 'The role of non-governmental organizations in the development of international environmental law', *Chicago-Kent Law Review*, vol. 68, no. 1, p. 61.
Thakur, R 2002, 'Intervention, sovereignty and the responsibility to protect: experiences from ICISS', *Security Dialogue*, vol. 33, no. 3, pp. 323–340.
Thakur, R 2016, 'The responsibility to protect', *International Affairs*, vol. 92, no. 2, pp. 415–434, at p. 421.
Tomuschat, C 1993, 'Obligations arising for states without or against their will', *Collected Courses of the Hague Academy of International Law*, vol. 241, p. 195.
Tribe, LH 1974, 'Ways not to think about plastic trees: new foundations for environmental law', *Yale Law Journal*, vol. 83, no. 7, p. 1315.

Trubek, DM 1972, 'Max Weber on law and the rise of capitalism', *Wisconsin Law Review*, vol. 1, no. 1, p. 720.
Weißbach, D, Ruprecht, G, Huke, A, Czerski, K, Gottlieb, S, Hussein, A & Physik, A 2013, 'Energy intensities, EROIs and energy payback times of electricity generating power plants', *Energy*, vol. 52, p. 210.
Weiss, EB 2012, 'The coming water crisis: a common concern of humankind', *Transnational Environmental Law*, vol. 1, no. 1, p. 153.
Weiss, LK 2018, 'Environmental constitutionalism: aspiration or transformation?', *International Journal of Constitutional Law*, vol. 16, no. 3, pp. 836–870.
Wilkinson, RG & Pickett, KE 2009, 'Income inequality and social dysfunction', *Annual Review of Sociology*, vol. 35, p. 493.
Williams, G 2013, 'Special contribution: interview with Immanuel Wallerstein – retrospective on the origins of world systems analysis', *American Sociological Association*, vol. 19, no. 2, p. 202.
Williams, M, Zalasiewicz, J, Barnosky, AD & Ellis, EC 2015, 'The Anthropocene biosphere', *The Anthropocene Review*, vol. 2, no. 3, pp. 196–219.
Willson, CL 1996, 'Changing the charter: the United Nations prepares for the twenty-first century', *American Journal of International Law*, vol. 90, p. 117.
Wilson, I & Henning, PM 2015, 'A call to action for the systems sciences community', *Journal of the International Society for the System Sciences*, vol. 1, no. 1.
Wolfe, C 2010, *What is posthumanism?* University of Minnesota Press, Chicago.
Wood, H 1985, 'The United Nations world charter for nature: the developing nations' initiative to establish protections for the environment', *Ecology Law Quarterly*, vol. 12, no. 4, p. 977.
Wright, T, Roque, N, Boot, W & Stothart, C 2018, 'Attention capture, processing speed, and inattential blindness', *Acta Psychology (Amsterdam)*, vol. 190, p. 72.
Zucca, L 2015, 'A genealogy of state sovereignty', *Theoretical Inquiries in Law*, vol. 16, p. 399.

F. Resolutions

United Nations General Assembly A/Conf.151/26 Agenda 21: Programme of Action for Sustainable Development (14 June 1992).
United Nations General Assembly A/RES/37/7 World Charter for Nature (28 October 1982).
United Nations General Assembly A/RES/48/141 High Commissioner for the Promotion and Protection of All Human Rights (1994).
United Nations General Assembly Resolution 1803 (XVII) Permanent Sovereignty Over Natural Resources (14 December 1962).
United Nations General Assembly Resolution 1991 A and B (XVIII) (17 December 1963).
United Nations General Assembly Resolution 2101 (XX) (20 December 1965).
United Nations General Assembly Resolution 2847 (XXIV) (20 December 1971).
United Nations General Assembly Resolution 45/94 The Need to Ensure a Healthy Environment for the Well-Being of Individuals (14 December 1990).
United Nations General Assembly Resolution 60/251 Human Rights Council (2006).
United Nations General Assembly Resolution 66/288 The Future We Want: Our Common Vision (2012).
United Nations General Assembly Resolution 70/1 Transforming Our World: The 2030 Agenda for Sustainable Development (2015).
United Nations Resolution 63/278 International Mother Earth Day (2009).
United Nations Security Council Resolution S/RES/956 (10 November 1994).

World Commission on Environment and Development, Brundtland Report ('Our Common Future') UNGA A/42/427 (4 August 1987).

G. Government Materials and Policy Documents.

Ardern, J 2018, *Prime Minister of New Zealand 'New Zealand National Statement to United Nations General Assembly'*, UN General Assembly, New York, 28 September.

European Council 2000, Directive 2000/60/EC of the European Parliament and of the Council Establishing a Framework for Community Action in the Field of Water Policy (200) OJ L327, 22 December.

H. Reports

Barnes, P, Rowe, J & Bollier, D 2004, *The state of the commons 2003/04: a report to owners*, Tomales Bay Institute.

Bosselmann, K & Jones, K 2016, *Planetary integrity project: creating a safe operating space through law and governance*, New Zealand Centre for Environmental Law, Auckland.

BP 2021, *Statistical review of world energy*, 70th edn.

Chancel, L, Piketty, T, Saez, E & Zucman, G 2022, *World inequality report 2022*, World Inequality Lab.

Dabla-Norris, E, Kochhar, K, Suphaphiphat, N, Ricka, F & Tsounta, E 2015, *Causes and consequences of income inequality: a global perspective*, International Monetary Fund Strategy, Policy and Review Department, Washington, DC.

De Schutter, O 2020, *Report on the 'just transition' in the economy recovery: eradicating poverty within planetary boundaries*, Presented to the UNGA A/75/181/REV.1, 9 October.

Faulk, L, Kim, M, Derrick-Mills, T, Boris, ET, Tomasko, L, Hakizimana, N, Chen, T, Kim, M & Nath, L 2021, *Nonprofit trends and impacts 2021: national findings on donation trends from 2015 through 2020, diversity and representation, and first-year impacts of the COVID-19 pandemic*, Research Report, Urban Institute, October.

Hauser, OP, Hendriks, A, Rand, DG & Nowak, MA 2016, *Think global, act local: preserving the global commons, scientific reports*, 6 November.

Hoornweg, D & Bhada Tata, P 2012, *What a waste: a global review of solid waste management*, The World Bank's Urban Development and Local Government Unit of Sustainable Development Network, Washington, DC.

Intergovernmental Panel on Climate Change, Masson-Delmotte, V, Zhai, P, Pirani, S, Connors, C, Péan, S, Berger, N, Caud, Y, Chen, L, et al. (eds) 2021, 'Climate change 2021: the physical science basis', in *Contribution of working group I to the sixth assessment report of the intergovernmental panel on climate change*, Cambridge University Press, Cambridge.

Intergovernmental Panel on Climate Change, Stocker, TF, et al. (eds) 2013, 'Climate change 2013: the physical science basis', in *Contribution of working group I to the fifth assessment report of the intergovernmental panel on climate change*, Cambridge University Press, Cambridge.

International Commission on Intervention and State Sovereignty 2001, *Report of the international commission on intervention and state sovereignty*, International Development Research Centre, December.

International Council for Science 2010, *Earth system science for global sustainability: the grand challenges*, International Council for Science, Paris.

International Development Research Centre 2001, *Report of the international commission on intervention and state sovereignty*, December 2001.

International Energy Agency 2016, *Energy and air pollution: world energy outlook special report*, International Energy Agency, Paris.

International Labor Organisation 2022, *World employment and social outlook 2022*, Geneva.

International Law Commission 2001, *Report of the international law commission to the general assembly on its fifty-third session*, vol. II, no. 2, YILC 146.

International Union for the Conservation of Nature 2015, *The draft international covenant on environment and development*, 5th edn, IUCN, Gland.

Jackson, T & Webster, R 2016, *Limits revisited, a review of the limits to growth debate*, All-Party Parliamentary Group on Limits to Growth, April.

Kaza, S, Yao, L, Bhada-Tata, P & Van Woerden, F 2018, *What a waste 2.0: a global snapshot of solid waste management to 2050*, Urban Development, World Bank, Washington, DC.

Knox, JH 2018, *United Nations human rights special procedures: framework principles on human rights and the environment 2018 – the main human rights obligations relating to the enjoyment of a safe, clean, healthy and sustainable environment*, Final Report, UN Doc. A/HRC/37/59.

Leach, M, Raworth, K & Rockström, J 2013, *Between social and planetary boundaries: navigating pathways in the safe and just space for humanity' in world social science report 2013: changing global environments*, UNESCO and OECD Publishing, Paris.

Millennium Ecosystem 2005, *Assessment ecosystems and human well-being: synthesis*, Island Press, Washington, DC.

Ngā Iwi o Taranaki & The Crown 2017, *Record of understanding for Mount Taranaki, Pouākai and the Kaitake ranges*, 20 December.

Office of the High Commissioner for Human Rights 2002, *Meeting of experts on human rights and the environment*, 2002 Experts' Report.

Raworth, K 2012, *A safe and just space for humanity: can we live within the doughnut?* Oxfam International, 13 February.

Report of the Commission on Global Governance 1995, *Our global neighbourhood*, Oxford University Press, Oxford.

Rockström, J, Sachs, JD, Öhman, MC & Schmidt-Traub, G 2013, *Sustainable development and planetary boundaries: a background report submitted to the high-level panel of eminent persons on the post-2015 development agenda*, Sustainable Development Solutions Network, May.

Rose, G 2011, *Gaps in the implementation of environmental law at the national, regional and global level*, United Nations Environment Programme, Kuala Lumpur.

Sustainable Aotearoa New Zealand 2009, *Strong sustainability for New Zealand: principles and scenarios*, Nakedize Publishing, Auckland.

United Nations Department of Economic and Social Affairs 2019, *Population division world population prospects 2019: highlights ST/ESA/SER.A/423*, United Nations, New York.

United Nations Department of Economic and Social Affairs 2020a, *Population division, world fertility and family planning 2020: highlights ST/ESA/SER.A/440*, United Nations, New York.

United Nations Department of Economic and Social Affairs 2020b, *World economic situations and prospects 2020*, United Nations, New York.

United Nations Environment Programme 2005, *Register of international treaties and other agreements in the field of the environment*, UNEP/Environmental Law/2005/3, 30 December.

United Nations Environment Programme 2021, *Making peace with nature: a scientific blueprint to tackle the climate, biodiversity and pollution emergencies*, UNEP, Nairobi.
United Nations General Assembly 1992, *Report of the United Nations conference on environment and development*, UN Doc A/Conf 151/26/Vol I, 12 August.
United Nations General Assembly 1997, *Report of the secretary-general, renewing the United Nations: a programme for reform*, UN Doc. A/51/950.
United Nations General Assembly 1998, *Report of the secretary-general, United Nations reform: measures and proposals – environment and human settlements*, A/53/463, 6 October.
United Nations General Assembly 2007, *Report of the secretary-general on the work of the organisation*, Supplement No. 1 A/62/1, 31 August 2007.
United Nations General Assembly 2018, *Report of the Secretary-General on the gaps in international environmental law and environment-related instruments: towards a global pact for the environment* A/73/419, 30 November.
United Nations General Assembly 2021, *Report of the secretary-general, our common agenda*, United Nations, New York.
United Nations Stockholm+50 Official Report A/CONF.238/9, 1 August 2022.
Working group on the Anthropocene 2020, *Newsletter of the anthropocene working group*, Report of Activities 2020, vol. 10, Subcommission on Quaternary Stratigraphy, December.
The World Bank Group and International Bank for Reconstruction and Development 2022, *Getting down on Earth: are satellites reliable for measuring air pollutants that cause mortality in low-and middle-income countries?* International Development in Focus.
World Conservation Union 1991, *United Nations environment programme and world wide fund for nature 'caring for the Earth: a strategy for sustainable living'*, October.

I. Conference Proceedings and Presentations.

Bosselmann, K 2017, 'The next step: earth trusteeship', presentation at the seventh interactive dialogue of the general assembly on harmony with nature, UN Headquarters, New York, 21 April.
European Court of Human Rights Judge Tim Eicke 2021, 'Human rights and climate change: what role for the European Court of Human Rights', presentation at the Inaugural Annual Human Rights Lecture, Department of Law, Goldsmiths University, 2 March.
Gerlak, AK, Burch, S, Gupta, A, Inoue, C, Kalfagianni, A, Persson, A, Ishii, A, Patterson, J, Pickering, J, Scobie, M, Van der Heijden, J, Vervoort, J, Adler, C, Bloomfield, M, Djalante, R, Dryzek, J, Galaz, V, Gordon, C, Harmon, R, Jinnah, S, Kim, RE, Olsson, L, Van Leeuwen, J, Ramasar, V, Wapner, P & Zondervan, R 2018, *Earth system governance: science and implementation plan of the Earth System Governance Project*, UNU-IAS Reports, Earth System Governance.
Guterres, A 2020, 'The state of the planet', conference presentation, Columbia University, 2 December.
Robinson, NA 2018, 'Environmental law: is an obligation Erga Omnes emerging?', conference presentation at the panel discussion at the United Nations, 4 June 2018, 1 pm–2.45 pm, Conference Room 12.
Wilson, I & Henning, PB 2015, 'A call to action for the systems science community', proceedings of the 59th annual meeting of the International Society for the Systems Sciences, vol. I, Berlin, Germany, 2–7 August.

J. Internet Resources

'A compass towards a just and harmonious society: 2015 GNH survey report', *Centre for Bhutan Studies*, viewed 5 July 2016, (www.grossnationalhappiness.com).

ABC News 2020, *US President Donald Trump says UN 'must hold China accountable' for COVID-19*, viewed 23 September 2020, (www.abc.net.au).

Albright, M & Gambari, I 2021, *Our common agenda and the road to 2023*, viewed 21 October 2021, (www.projectsyndicate.com).

Ali, Y 2015, 'Who owns outer space?', *BBC News*, viewed 25 September 2015, (www.bbc.com).

Alliance of Small Island States, (www.aosis.org).

Arcanjo, M 2019, *Has climate change rendered the concept of sovereignty obsolete?*, A Climate Institute Publication, viewed 17 January 2019, (http://climate.org/).

Arvin, J 2021, 'More than 20 Republican-led states sue Biden for cancelling the Keystone XL pipeline', *Vox*, viewed 18 March 2021, (www.vox).

BBC News 2020, *UN General Assembly: Us-China tensions flare over coronavirus*, viewed 22 September 2020, (www.bbc.com).

BBC News 2021, *Biden signs 'existential' executive orders on climate and the environment*, viewed 27 January 2021, (www.bbc.com).

Biermann, F & Bernstein, S 2012, 'How Rio+20 can herald a constitutional moment', *The Guardian*, viewed 15 March 2012, (www.theguardian.com).

Blokhin, A 2020, 'The 5 countries that produce the most carbon dioxide (CO_2)', *Investopedia*, viewed 27 October 2020, (www.investopedia.com).

Boskin, M 2020, 'How does the COVID recession compare?', *Project Syndicate*, (https://www.weforum.org).

Bosselmann, K 2019, 'Can kaitiakitanga save the planet?', *Newsroom*, viewed 20 December 2019, (www.newsroom.com).

Cambridge Dictionary, *Sovereignty*, online edn, (www.dictionary.cambridge.org).

Cooper, C 2015, 'Six economists who predicted the global financial crisis', *In The Black*, viewed 7 July 2015, (www.intheblack.com).

Earth Charter Initiative 2000, *The Earth charter*, (https://earthcharter.org/).

Earth Commission, (www.earthcommission.org).

Earth Trusteeship 2018, *The Hague principles for a universal declaration on responsibilities for human rights and earth trusteeship*, viewed as 10 December 2018, (www.earthtrusteeship.world).

Future Earth 2019, *Future Earth announces intent to launch Earth Commission*, viewed 31 January 2019, (https://futureearth.org).

Future Earth: Research for Global Sustainability, (www.futureearth.org).

Global Carbon Atlas, *World map fossil fuels emissions in 2020*, (http://www.globalcarbonatlas.org/en/CO2-emissions).

The Global Commons Alliance, *A plan for the planet*, (https://globalcommonsalliance.org/).

Global Footprint Network, *Has humanity's ecological footprint reached its peak?*, viewed 9 April 2018, (https://www.footprintnetwork.org).

Ha, T-H 2016, 'John Donne's solemn 400-year-old poem against isolationism is resonating today', *Quartz*, viewed 25 June 2016, (www.qz.com).

Habib, B 2015, *Climate change and the re-imagination of state sovereignty*, viewed 8 November 2015, (https://www.e-ir.info).

Hagens, N 2015, *Turning 21 in the anthropocene: an invitation to participate in the future*, viewed 27 April 2015, (www.youtube.com).

Heath, E 2010, *Berlin conference of 1884–1885*, Oxford Reference, Encyclopaedia of Africa, (www.oxfordreference.com).

History, *The Reformation*, (www.history.com).

Horsley, JP 2020, 'Let's end the COVID-19 blame game: reconsidering China's role in the pandemic', *Brookings*, viewed 19 August 2020, (www.brookings.edu).

(https://www.iucn.org/sites/default/files/content/documents/2018/environmental_law_is_an_obligation_erga_omnes_emerging_interamcthradvisoryopinion-june2018.pdf).

International Center for Nonprofit Law, India (last updated on 11 February 2022), (https://www.icnl.org).

International Center for Nonprofit Law, Russia (last updated on 31 November 2021), (https://www.icnl.org).

The International Integrated Reporting Council, (www.integratedreporting.org).

Jenkins, M 2009, *Hobbes, socialism and human nature*, viewed 22 January 2009, Independent Labour Publications, (https://www.independentlabour.org.uk).

Keane, S 2013, 'Financial instability mini-documentary', *New Economic Thinking, YouTube*, viewed 15 April 2013, (www.youtube.com).

Krueger, AO 2020, *Can poor countries avoid a vaccine bidding war?* viewed 7 January 2020, (www.gavi.org).

Lee, M & Borden, A 2017, *The energy in a barrel of oil, let the sun work: sustainable living in a petroleum world*, viewed 17 June 2017, (https://letthesunwork.com/).

MacroTrends 2020, *Crude oil prices: 70 year historical chart*, viewed 7 February 2020, (www.macrotrends.net).

Manifesto, O 2016, *From environmental law to ecological law: a call for re-framing law and governance*, Ecological Law and Governance Association, viewed June 2016, (https://elgaworld.org/oslo-manifesto).

McDonald, C 2015, 'How many earths do we need?', *BBC News*, viewed 16 June 2015, (www.bbc.com).

Meadows, D 1999, *Leverage points: places to intervene in a system*, The Sustainable Institute, (https://donellameadows.org).

Murphy, S 2016, 'Council to sell rights to bottled water company', *Radio New Zealand*, viewed 4 April 2016, (www.radionz.co.nz).

Revkin, A 2011, *Confronting the Anthropocene: a new era*, viewed 2 September 2011, (www.youtube.com).

Rockström, J 2015, 'Bounding the planetary future: why we need a great transition', *Great Transition Initiative*, viewed April 2015, (https://greattransition.org).

The Royal Family, *The role of the monarchy*, (www.royal.uk).

Schuman, M 2014, 'A global financial guru who predicted the crisis of 2008 says more turmoil may be coming', *Time Magazine*, viewed 11 August 2014, (www.time.com).

Senge, P 2014, *Introduction to systems thinking*, viewed 5 August 2014, (www.youtube.com).

Stiglitz, J & Rashid, H 2016, 'What's holding back the world economy?', *The Guardian*, viewed 8 February 2016, (www.theguardian.com).

Stiglitz, J, Tett, G, Tuckett, D, Kinsella, S, Kay, J, Weinstein, D, Keen, S & Bezemer, D 2012, *Financial instability mini-documentary*, viewed 15 April 2012, (www.youtube.com).

Subcommission on Quaternary Stratigraphy *Working group on the anthropocene: results of binding vote by AWG*, viewed 21 May 2019, (http://quaternary.stratigraphy.org/working-groups/anthropocene/).

Szalavitz, M 2012, 'Is human nature fundamentally selfish or altruistic?', *Time Magazine*, viewed 8 October 2012, (https://healthland.time.com).

Townsend, J, Bunten, A, Lorns, C & Borrows, L 2021, 'Rights for nature: how granting a river 'personhood' could help protect it', *The Conversation*, viewed 3 June 2021, (https://theconversation.com).

The UK in a Changing Europe, *What is sovereignty*, (www.ukandeu.uk).
UN Environment Programme 2022, *UNEP@50: success over the years*, (https://www.unep.org/news-and-stories/series/unep50-success-over-years#:~:text=For%20the%20past%20half%2Dcentury,from%20going%20extinct%20and%20more).
UN News, *UN welcomes South Sudan as 193rd member state*, viewed 14 July 2011, (www.un.org).
UNFCC, *Paris agreement: status of ratification*, (www.unfccc.int).
United Nations, *Harmony with nature*, (http://www.harmonywithnatureun.org).
United Nations Universities, *Our common agenda; high-level advisory board on global public goods*, (www.unu.edu.com).
Wijsman, K, 'State sovereignty in a time of global environmental problems: a move towards dynamism?', *Academia*, (www.academia.edu).
The World Bank, *What a waste 2.0: a global snapshot to solid waste management to 2050, trends in solid waste management*, (https://datatopics.worldbank.org).
The World Health Organization, *Air pollution data portal*, (www.who.int).

K. Other Resources

Annan, K 1999, *UN Secretary-General 'annual report to general assembly'*, United Nations, Press Release SG/SM/7136 GA/959620, viewed 20 September 1999, (www.un.org/).
Arcanjo, M 2019, *Has climate change rendered the concept of sovereignty obsolete?*, A Climate Institute Publication, January.
Barraclough, T 2013, 'How far can the Te Awa Tupua (Whanganui River) proposal be said to reflect the rights of nature in New Zealand?', LLB (Hons) dissertation, University of Otago.
Benvenisti, E 2015, *The future of sovereignty: the nation state in the global governance space*, The Global Trust Working Paper Series 01/2015, Global Trust Research Project.
Blackmore, AC 2018, 'The rediscovery of the trusteeship doctrine in South African environmental law and its significance in conserving biodiversity in South Africa', PhD thesis, University of Tilburg.
Botrel, M 2019, 'The suitability of the "responsibility to protect" to address the ecological crisis', LLM (Hons) dissertation, University of Auckland.
Carlarne, C 2015, *Delinking international environmental law and climate change*, Ohio State Public Law Working Paper No. 286, Ohio State University, 22 January.
DiMento, JF 2015, *Protection of our Earth:a half century of environmental law*, Legal Studies Research Paper Series No 94, University of California School of Law.
Douglas, J 2009, 'Affording New Zealand rivers legal personality: a new vehicle for achieving Māori aspirations in co-management?', LLM thesis, University of Otago.
Dziedzic, S 2021, 'New Zealand tops Lowy Institute list as country with best response to coronavirus, Australia sits eighth', *ABC News*, 28 January.
Evans, G 2008, 'Facing up to our responsibilities', *The Guardian*, online edn, London, 12 May.
Gabel, J 2021, 'NSW travel bubble paused', *The New Zealand Herald*, Auckland, 23 June.
Gordon, RJ 2012, *Is US economic growth over? Faltering innovation confronts the six headwinds*, National Bureau of Economic Research Working Paper Series No. 18315, Cambridge, MA, August 2012.
Harris, RC 2015, 'The changing face of co-governance in New Zealand', LLM thesis, University of Canterbury.

International Geosphere-Biosphere Programme 2011, 'Governance experts warn UN overhaul required to govern Earth system', Press Release, 23 November.

Jóhannsdóttir, A 2009, 'The significance of the default, a study in environmental law methodology with emphasis on ecological sustainability and international biodiversity law', Doctor of Law jur dr, Uppsala University.

Jones, K 2015, 'Planetary boundaries and the evolution of global environmental law', LLM thesis, University of Auckland.

Josefsson, H 2015, 'Good ecological status: advancing the ecology of law', Doctor of laws dissertation, University of Uppsala.

Kim, R 2013, 'Unravelling the maze of multilateral environmental agreements: a macroscopic analysis of international environmental law and governance in the Anthropocene', PhD thesis, Australian National University.

Kim, RE, Bosselmann, K & Mauerhofer, V 2020, *Planetary boundaries and post-2015 sustainable development goals: safeguarding ecological integrity as a priority goal and a Grundnorm of international law*, Working Paper 2020, WWF UK, the Planetary Boundaries Initiative on the Sustainability Development Goals.

Kirkwood, CW 2013, *System dynamics methods: a quick introduction*, Arizona State University: Systems Dynamics, 12 January.

Kissinger, HA 2020, 'The coronavirus pandemic will forever alter the world order', *The Wall Street Journal*, online edn, New York, 3 April.

Lewis, A 1977, 'Dignified and efficient', *New York Times*, online edn, archives, New York, 9 June.

Nijs, L 2016–2017, 'Sovereignty in international environmental law: an outdated principle? The case of stratospheric aerosol injections and distributive justice', Master's thesis law and technology, Tilburg University.

Palmer, G 2013, *Protecting New Zealand's environment: an analysis of the government's proposed freshwater management and resource management act 1991 reforms*, Victoria University of Wellington Legal Research Paper Series Palmer Paper No. 44, New Zealand Fish and Game.

Parmar, SS 2019, *Sovereignty and trans-boundary environmental issues: a search for co-existence*, Dharmsahastra National Law University, February 2019.

Raikas, TT 2020, 'The Amazon is on fire: states' responsibility to protect the Amazon environment from a human rights perspective', Master's thesis in International Law and Human Rights, Abo Akademi University.

Rayfuse, R 2011, 'Life after land', *New York Times*, online edn, New York, 18 July.

Turner, G 2014, *Is global collapse imminent? An updated comparison of the limits to growth with historical data*, MSSI Research Paper No. 4, Melbourne Sustainable Society Institute, University of Melbourne.

Walls, J 2020, 'Gates's plea to Arden on vaccine', *The New Zealand Herald*, Auckland, 4 November.

Weekes, J 2021, 'Mutating virus prompts alert call', *The New Zealand Herald*, Auckland, 2 February.

Index

FSC
www.fsc.org
MIX
Papier | Fördert gute Waldnutzung
FSC® C083411

Kolibri 360 GmbH
Ferdinand-Jühlke-Straße 7
99095 Erfurt, Deutschland
produktsicherheit@kolibri360.de